Beyond Description

Beyond Description explores the history and architecture of Singapore. It argues that neither history nor architecture can be fruitfully examined without reference to the other. For this reason, aspects of urban life will always be beyond description, yet these aspects are what most call for analysis. On this premise, the book examines Singapore's built environment by assessing how its past as a colonial port relates to its present as a global hub and how these inform its possible futures. The chapters complicate existing assumptions about global urbanism, post-colonialism and architectural theory from a dedicated interdisciplinary perspective.

The book begins with a wide-ranging and analytical introduction to the key concerns that arise when approaching history and space. It fully explores what it means for an object of knowledge, like a major global city, to be beyond description. The chapters with varying emphases but with consistent reference to Singapore, address issues of space, conditions of historicity, narrative, cultural memory, ecology and the archive. The book aims to establish how these apparently disparate concerns emerge as an urban environment of conflicting stimuli.

By bringing together different disciplines under shared concerns, *Beyond Description* expands the terrain where textuality and architecture meet. Contributors include experts in literary and cultural criticism, critical theory, cultural anthropology, history, sociology, economics, architecture and philosophy, as well as architects and urban planners, whose intellectual commitments are interdisciplinary. Therefore, by taking the complex ramifications of the theoretical concerns posited by what is beyond description in urban processes, this collection represents a significant challenge to the current state of urban studies.

Ryan Bishop is Associate Professor of English and American Studies at the National University of Singapore. **John Phillips** is Associate Professor of English at the National University of Singapore. **Wei-Wei Yeo** is Assistant Professor of English at the National University of Singapore.

THE ARCHI*TEXT* SERIES

Edited by Thomas A. Markus and Anthony D. King

Architectural discourse has traditionally represented buildings as art objects or technical objects. Yet buildings are also social objects in that they are invested with social meaning and shape social relations. Recognizing these assumptions, the Archi*text* series aims to bring together recent debates in social and cultural theory and the study and practice of architecture and urban design. Critical, comparative, and interdisciplinary, the books in the series will, by theorizing architecture, bring the space of the built environment centrally into the social sciences and humanities, as well as bringing the theoretical insights of the latter into the discourses of architecture and urban design. Particular attention will be paid to issues of gender, race, sexuality, and the body, to questions of identity and place, to the cultural politics of representation and language, and to the global and postcolonial contexts in which these are addressed.

Already published:

Framing Places
Mediating power in built form
Kim Dovey

Gender Space Architecture
An interdisciplinary introduction
Edited by Jane Rendell, Barbara Penner and Iain Borden

Behind the Postcolonial
Architecture, urban space and political cultures in Indonesia
Abidin Kusno

The Architecture of Oppression
The SS, forced labor and the Nazi monumental building economy
Paul Jaskot

Words between the Spaces
Building and language
Thomas A. Markus and Deborah Cameron

Embodied Utopias
Gender, social change and the modern metropolis
Rebeccah Zorach, Lise Sanders and Amy Bingaman

Writing Spaces
Discourses of architecture, urbanism, and the built environment, 1960–2000
C. Greig Crysler

Drifting: Migrancy and Architecture
Edited by Stephen Cairns

Beyond Description
Singapore space historicity
Edited by Ryan Bishop, John Phillips, and Wei-Wei Yeo

Forthcoming titles:

Moderns Abroad
Architecture, cities and Italian imperialism
Mia Fuller

Spaces of Global Cultures
Anthony D. King

Sustaining Design
Interpreting green architecture
Edited by Simon Guy and Graham Farmer

**Edited by Ryan Bishop,
John Phillips, and Wei-Wei Yeo**

Beyond Description

Singapore Space Historicity

Routledge
Taylor & Francis Group

LONDON AND NEW YORK

First published 2004
by Routledge
11 New Fetter Lane, London EC4P 4EE

Simultaneously published in the USA and Canada
by Routledge
29 West 35th Street, New York, NY 10001

Routledge is an imprint of the Taylor & Francis Group

Typeset in Frutiger by Florence Production Ltd, Stoodleigh, Devon
Printed and bound in Great Britain by TJ International Ltd, Padstow,
Cornwall

British Library Cataloguing in Publication Data
A catalogue record for this book is available from the British Library

Library of Congress Cataloging in Publication Data
Beyond description: Singapore space historicity/
   Edited by Ryan Bishop, John Phillips, Wei-Wei Yeo.
       p. cm. – (The Architext series)
   Includes bibliographical references and index.
   1. Architecture–Singapore. 2. City planning–Singapore. 3. Architecture
and history–Singapore. 4. Globalization. I. Title: Singapore space historicity.
II. Bishop, Ryan, 1959–   III. Phillips, John, 1956–   IV. Yeo, Wei-Wei.
V. Series.
NA1530.S55B49 2004
307.1'216'095957–dc22

                                                    2003015888

ISBN 0–415–29981–0 (hbk)
ISBN 0–415–29982–9 (pbk)

Contents

Illustrations

Contributors

Ryan Bishop is Associate Professor of English and American Studies at the National University of Singapore. Among his publications are works on international sex tourism in Thailand, critical theory, rhetoric, urbanism, visual culture, and the history of technology in relation to the university, the military, and aesthetics.

Gregory Clancey is Assistant Professor of History at the National University of Singapore. He is co-editor (with M. Roe Smith) of *Major Problems in the History of American Technology*. His recent research centres on constructions of science and nature in modern Japan.

Carole Faucher is currently Visiting Associate Professor in the Research Institute for Languages and Cultures of Asia and Africa (ICLAA), Tokyo University of Foreign Studies. Her main research interests are anthropology of the emotions, social memory, popular culture, and identity. She is conducting research in Singapore and Indonesia.

Robbie B. H. Goh is Associate Professor of English at the National University of Singapore. He has research interests in nineteenth-century English literature, gothic literature, critical theory, postmodernism, and cultural analysis, and is the author of numerous articles on these and related topics.

Philip Holden is Associate Professor of English at the National University of Singapore. He is the author of several books and articles on colonial and post-colonial literature and culture in major international journals, and is currently commencing a research project on postcolonial autobiography.

William S. W. Lim is an architect based in Singapore whose professional work and academic publications include urban planning, development economics, social justice, and contemporary theory. He is the author of many books and articles on these topics and has lectured widely on them. Currently, he is Adjunct Professor of the Royal Melbourne Institute of Technology (RMIT), Australia, and Guest Professor of Tianjin University, China.

Kwek Mean Luck is Deputy Director, Enterprise Division, in the Ministry of Trade and Industry for the Singapore government.

Aihwa Ong is Professor of Anthropology, and Chair of the Center for Southeast Asian Studies, University of California, Berkeley. Her many publications include work on emerging forms of management, neo-liberal government, transnational regimes, and citizenship in Southeast Asia, China, and the United States. Her most recent book is *Buddha in Hiding: Refugees, Citizenship, and the New America.*

Heinz Paetzold is Professor of Communication Theory and Philosophy of Culture at the University of Applied Sciences in Hamburg, Professor of Philosophy at the University of Kassel, and Director of postgraduate courses on social philosophy at the International University Center of Dubrovnik. His is the author of several books including: *Profile der Ästhetik in der Postmoderne* (1990), *The Discourse of the Postmodern and the Discourse of the Avant-Garde* (1994), *Ernst Cassirer* (1995), and *Symbol, Culture, City* (2000).

John Phillips is Associate Professor of English at the National University of Singapore. He has published widely on continental philosophy, critical theory, visual culture, psychoanalysis, modernism, and aesthetics.

Robert Powell is former Associate Professor in the Faculty of Architecture and Building at the National University of Singapore, where his research interests included Asian cities, urban design, and ecology. He has a long association with the region having worked for thirteen years in Singapore. He is the author of several books on architecture and urban design in Southeast Asia, as well as being the editor of *The Singapore Architect.*

Wong Chong Thai Bobby is Associate Professor of Architecture at the National University of Singapore. His research interests include critical theory and architecture.

Wei-Wei Yeo is Assistant Professor of English at the National University of Singapore, whose research interests include Victorian literature, urban processes, and Dante. She is co-editor of *Postcolonial Urbanism: Southeast Asian Cities and Global Processes* (with Ryan Bishop and John Phillips).

Acknowledgements

We would like to thank the Faculty Research Committee for the Faculty of Arts and Social Sciences (FASS) at the National University of Singapore (NUS), Lily Kong, Dean of the FASS, and John Richardson, Head of the English department at NUS, for their encouragement and financial support. We would also like to acknowledge our colleagues in the departments of English, History, Sociology, Architecture, Geography, and Southeast Asian Studies at NUS who have lent intellectual and emotional encouragement to our work. Further thanks are owed to Mac Daly, Jon Simons, and superior support person Sarah Kerr, at the Postgraduate School for Critical Theory and Cultural Studies, the University of Nottingham. We also wish to thank Helen Ibbotson, our editor at Routledge, for her patience and skills at facilitation. To the series editors Anthony King and Thomas A. Markus we are indebted for their unwavering support and intellectual input into the project. Finally we thank our families for their love, patience, and understanding.

Chapter 1: Beyond Description: Singapore Space Historicity

Ryan Bishop, John Phillips, and Wei-Wei Yeo

BEYOND DESCRIPTION

This volume contains a collection of articles that productively interpret the architectural spaces of Singapore, while addressing issues of space, historicity, architecture, and textuality. The main underlying assumption is as follows: any site of the architectural is always going to be more than its mere material presence. Accordingly, the articles consider the ways in which the architectural comes to have specific meanings, and must thus go beyond descriptions of its empirical forms. The key intersection would be between space and history. However, while intersections like this cannot be located through empirical study, we do not accept that independent existing theories can be simply applied to the spaces we wish to deal with. If our accounts of Singapore are to be produced through analysis and interpretation we must more than ever think hard about the problems and possibilities of interpretation.

The collection does not attempt to put into practice claims for alternative epistemological frames. A number of interesting recent studies do attempt to bring alternative ways of conceptualizing urban space to contemporary non-Western urban sites. Ackbar Abbas, in his *Hong Kong: Culture and the Politics of Disappearance* (1997), makes the following observation about present-day Hong Kong: "the apparently permanent-like buildings and even whole towns – can be temporary, while the temporary-like abode in Hong Kong – could be very permanent" (9).[1] Abbas argues that a phenomenon of this kind (which is as relevant for Singapore as it is for Hong Kong) requires "something more" than the so called "cult of the ephemeral" derived from Louis Aragon's novel *Paris Peasant* and established as a key reference for urban studies by Walter Benjamin. Abbas engages a number of key contemporary theoretical models, those variously of Paul Virilio, Henri Lefebvre, Jean Baudrillard, Jean-Francois Lyotard, and Deleuze and Guattari in order to explain the phenomenon of disappearance and its relations to what he identifies as "the ephemeral, to speed and to abstraction" (8), as it pertains to Hong Kong. This allows him to read and interpret a range of Hong Kong cultural productions (cinema, writing, buildings, photography) through a lens constructed from a variety of contemporary theoretical views and subtly refocused through postcolonialism. While effective on its own terms, and justly admired, Abbas's method changes very little either in terms of academic practice or how we understand environments. Despite the subtlety and critical force of the arguments themselves, which address the conditions of Western thought at their most basic, their application simply repeats the maintenance of the subject of science and the dream of objectivity, which is its counterpart. Furthermore, the strategies Abbas deploys are applied to a range of cultural products that are read for what *they* have to say about the built environment, which allows him to ignore the difficulties of what we would argue is the inevitable mediation that conditions all experience.

Our own claim would be, first, that urban space and architecture are at their deepest level of significance always beyond description and, therefore, beyond any epistemological frame whatever. So our alternative is not another epistemological frame. It is an alternative *to* epistemological frames. Second, it follows that knowledge of urban space can only be accessed by engaging with particular architectures and spaces. Accordingly our focus is Singapore. We believe we have achieved two things in this respect. First, we have been able to access aspects of Singapore that add up to a significant contribution to our knowledge and understanding of the city-state in its historical and global relations. Second, we have been able to establish aspects of Singapore that are significant when compared with often vastly different situations that govern other global cities.

We do not accept that sites like Singapore simply exemplify any theory, however it has been constructed. Nor do we believe that theory can be rigorously separated out from or simply applied to empirical spaces or vice versa. Problems emerge whenever this is attempted. We would argue that both urban theory and urban space are subject to very similar constraints at the level of their conditions of possibility. The problem resides most clearly in the ways that Singapore tends to describe itself. As an exemplar of a certain kind of technological rationality, Singapore produces its self-identifications in ways that often conflict with its actual conditions. The collection, therefore, focuses on the relationships and disjunctions between conditions and descriptions, which all dichotomies between theories and actual spaces repeat.

Singapore has a singular position regionally and globally in relation to these concerns insofar as its history involves extended, strategic engagement with the twin enterprises of postcolonialism and globalization, as well as with colonialism. This history is readable in the city-state's architecture and physical environment. The entire Marina Bay area, in fact, materially realizes this history. This area is both the old British colonial center of the city as well as the present commercial and government center. From the renovated luxury hotel the Fullerton, once a fort overlooking the confluence of the Singapore River and the strategic bay, to a host of other "colonial" buildings, Singapore flaunts its colonial past and postcolonial/global present through the historical maintenance of these buildings' façades. The act of renovation preserves the colonial shell of the building while reworking the buildings from the foundation up to better suit contemporary use, whether as luxury hotel, bank, government building, or restaurant. Readable in the buildings, then, is a continuation, perpetuation, and multiplication of colonial richness into the present global order, while also using the striking juxtaposition of colonial buildings and modernist high-rise buildings to reveal a specific continuum and continuity.

The visually jarring but aesthetically attractive connection of the colonial and modernist architecture is also deployed as a mode of attracting global capital to Singapore, a means of demarcating Singapore as both different from other global capitals and a repetition of them. The difference found in the colonial buildings reveals a history and historicity not always so blatantly displayed, often

Figure 1.1
The Padang and the Singapore
Cricket Club (foreground);
skyscrapers of the central
commercial district
(background)

explicitly overturned or rejected, in other postcolonial cities while also marking it as different from the monotonous homogeneity of modernist skyscrapers that dominate financial centers of other global urban sites. The converted shop houses on Boat Quay, now housing upscale restaurants and bars that serve the employees of the banking high-rises towering above the upgraded yet histori- cally maintained buildings, offer transnational corporations a different kind of physical locale for setting up shop, but one that is not too different. And in the continuation and intensification of global capital speculation running from colo- nialism to the present, Singapore's built environment provides a historicity that tells us a great deal about the various phases of the continuum.

This volume, then, considers how various experiences of Singapore, both from within and from outside, help to complicate assumptions about global urbanism, postcolonialism, and architectural theory while producing challenging new ideas from a variety of disciplines concerned with how space, historicity, architecture, and textuality inform one another. Singapore, then, emerges as an exemplar of postcolonialism and global urbanism – or more broadly historicity, space, and architecture – that allows us to read other global cities in light of it while simultaneously allowing us to read other global cities in substantially different ways.

HISTORICITY

The question of Singapore's historicity emerges forcefully with recognition of the country's singular history of self-wonder and affirmation through constant, though varied, moves of self-description. Such moves are a staple of communi- cation from official quarters such as ministerial speeches and government directives, and they are delivered with a certain rhetoric that is underpinned by a belief in and urgency about the need for agile and incessant transformation. In critical explorations of Singaporean culture and history, frequently linked to the question of national identity, the trend of self-description is similarly prevalent. Critique by description regularly re-visits areas such as postcolonialism, ideologies of national survival and economic success, the influence of global popular culture, and multi-racial sensitivities. Such moves demand analysis. We may assume that any system, ensemble, institution – anything, that is, which brings its elements together under a principle or set of principles – has come about on the basis of certain historical and systemic conditions. And no such ensemble would fail to produce moments when its relationship to those conditions are thematized, dramatized, or otherwise represented.

These moments of self-identification produce *récits*, including myths and fictions, as factual narratives. Such representations can always be compared with the historical and systemic conditions themselves, which are also readable at the level of an ensemble's performance. Take the Singapore Merlion for instance. The Merlion, a logo found on government stationery up to the late 1990s and a subject of address for many Singaporean poets, is a mythical creature – one invented by the Singapore Tourist Promotion Board in 1977. Created to lend mystique to the island's history, the Merlion has become the site of other narratives. Poets from the first generation to the present day have written about the Merlion in earnest eulogies, and more recently, with wit and irony. For many locals it is a symbol of geomantic significance. When the Merlion was recently moved from its former home at the mouth of the Singapore river, where it had become obstructed by Esplanade bridge, to a more prominent position facing Marina Bay and the newly opened Esplanade – Theatres on the Bay arts center, this was widely interpreted as a move to arrest the city-state's economic slow-down and perhaps also to signal a new start as it embarks on a new phase of economic restructuring. The Merlion began as a pragmatic gesture from which separate lines of significance have been drawn. Its symbolism for Singapore is not easy to place, just as the very perpetuation of its aura is perplexing. The example of the Merlion shows that it is imperative for our principle of interpretation to be located in the space, the disjuncture, or gap between the *statement about* and the *performance of* the relation between the ensemble and the conditions of its own existence.

This volume is therefore concerned with excavating the spaces *between* the descriptive frameworks and the complex legacy of Singapore's postcolonial and global urban space. As soon as we begin to talk of *spaces between*, it becomes clear that we are no longer simply addressing space in its empirical, observable sense. Observable space would be measurable. Spaces can be described and evaluated, as Bob Powell does in his article on South Bridge Road,

Figure 1.2
The Merlion – a fanciful blending of fish tail and lion head

when he describes the bridge as "a modest structure by today's engineering standards but perfectly serviceable with high arches and slender suspension columns to support the carriageway." This ability to describe, evaluate, and account for the spaces of the city constitutes a key component of urban analysis. However, the many uses of the term space that we would normally regard as figurative also play an indispensable role. For instance, in analogy with the literal bridge, we talk of bridging the space between buildings and their history, and, as we have just done, the gap between the ensemble and the conditions of its existence. This figurability allows us to speak of all kinds of phenomena, which are not strictly spatial, in spatial terms. Conventionally we would suppose that the *literal* logically precedes the *figurative*, and that these figurative uses are thus derived from the literal. However, the difference between these two ways of talking about space presupposes a way of conceptualizing space that is neither literal nor figurative but which allows our use of both literal and figurative senses.

For instance, the Ancient Greek term *topos* reveals how both the literal and the figurative senses of space emerge from a prior form of conceptualization, what Immanuel Kant calls the transcendental imagination. *Topos* gives us the following familiar terms: topic, topography, and topology. The first addresses a space of thought, while the second denotes how we map spaces. The third bridges the two by allowing a flexible or conceptual mapping, which is neither literal nor figurative. This is why – even when we are describing space – our topic will always be in some sense beyond description.

SPACE

Not only does space have unavoidable conceptual dimensions to it but, taking our argument about beyond description a step further, we can also now say that thought itself seems impossible outside its own architectural constraints. The disciplinary division of the institutions of knowledge demonstrates this concretely. So, on the one hand, the possible coherence of any theoretical reflection on urban space seems seriously threatened. If, as modern philosophy teaches, our perceptions are structured spatially *a priori*, then all attempts to treat urban space objectively must fail. On the other hand, however, if we accept the continuity of structural constraints on both environmental and theoretical boundaries, a number of productive possibilities emerge as the space of theory overlaps in curious and productive ways with urban space, each providing means for considering the other. Neither domain can ever contain the other despite attempts to erect barriers and borders demarcating them. Where this containment does not hold is the *topos* (physical and intellectual) from which the articles in this volume emerge.

Architecture does not simply *enclose* but rather it *produces* space. The question of architectural constraints and enclosures forces the space of thinking to interact with the space of dwelling. In the context of contemporary global urbanism the space of thinking is not separable from the technologies of speed, including information technologies and telecommunications. *Speed* in the current moment firmly places space and architecture within geopolitical concerns, especially when one considers the deeply intertwined development and application of virtual reality modeling for military *and* architectural purposes, as evidenced at MIT and the Media Lab founded there by Nicholas Negroponte. The profound relations that converge in space and time interacting with speed in contemporary urban sites demand closer scrutiny.

As Paul Virilio has discussed, speed affects spatial domains as well as temporal ones, having significant effects on architecture itself. The life span of buildings is increasingly being delimited, with cities such as New York and Paris requiring building contractors to obtain demolition permits *at the same time* as they apply for construction permits. The emphemeralization of commodities essential to contemporary global consumer markets has its analogue in the emphemeralization of labor and buildings. Demands for increased speed and foreshortened building lifespans have profound ramifications for the interactions between architectural practices and theory and urbanization processes. One area that demands further study involves the conceptualization of vertical and horizontal space, and how buildings and sites manifest different types of temporality. Further, these demands fundamentally alter the means by which so called historical districts, historical buildings, and older neighborhoods are understood, defined, and delineated, especially with regard to "use." In Singapore, more often than not, conservation planning seems to begin and end with the question of the economic value or opportunity cost of an area or a building. Technologies of speed in these cases are reproduced and developed as part of a general discourse of efficiency and productivity, such that the technologies responsible for *producing* or *transforming* the situations tend to be described in terms of the *improvements* they bring to them. A characteristic of this discourse is that it submerges positions and facts that might contradict its sense of benign progress. This is, once again, why it is necessary to go beyond the empirical and the merely describable aspects of the urban environment.

Once we focus on aspects that cannot be considered empirically, a relation between the built environment and what we would call the *un-built* emerges. Much as the literal and figurative conceptualizations of space reveal a prior condition that makes them possible, the built environment similarly reveals an inescapable connection with its un-built. The built, of course, designates both the concrete structure and the various manifestations of its conception: plans, models, and blueprints. But for the design to have been possible one must consider the undetermined and thus un-conceptualized possibilities against which a design decision is always made. In this exact sense the un-built corresponds to that notion of space that constitutes the condition of possibility for both literal and figurative conceptions and experiences of it.

The point here is to grasp that the un-built plays an intrinsic and essential role for the built environment. The un-built helps us understand what is beyond description in any urban space. Several dimensions are implied beyond the standard three dimensions normally attributed to built space. It is a matter of thinking through the built not only in terms of the concrete decision that it represents, but also in terms of its occupation of the imagination, at the basic level of the image. For instance, the Eiffel Tower in Paris from the outset operates as a repeatable image that is both independent of its original purpose and liable to all kinds of possible appropriation. In this case the tower becomes the imaginal logo of Paris itself. With the invention of the Merlion in Singapore we witness an attempt to appropriate the *effects* of a process that has become iconic of the global city generally.

More forcefully perhaps the un-built allows a building to operate as the focus for a field of contexts, and thus to re-contextualize its own environment. In this way Singapore's "Esplanade – Theatres on the Bay" re-contextualizes the Marina Bay area as the hub of global culture as well as capital. Furthermore, the un-built has apparently interrelated temporal dimensions: the *past un-built* (demolished, transformed, historicized) allows the new to be built on the old site; and the *future un-built* is figured only as *potential,* as yet to be built. The rhetorical form of the un-built would be the empty lot, which marks the un-built in its past and future dimensions as radically outside the present. This radical *outside* would not actually be discoverable or describable as an experience of the present because it functions simply as a structural condition of possibility.

NARRATIVES OF FOUNDING, REGENERATION, AND LOSS

Within the systems of value that dominate attitudes towards global cities, Singapore, like much of developed Southeast Asia, can appear contradictory. The title alone of Stan Sesser's book, *The Lands of Charm and Cruelty,* hints at the flavour of this phenomenon – a blending of repulsion (cruelty) and seduction (charm). Sesser tries his hardest to hunt down an instance of authoritarian injustice in his article on Singapore ("The Prisoner in the Theme Park") and comes away with a small prize.[2] Never mind that the government of Singapore is, by the standards of most home and foreign policies, neither oppressive nor aggressive, there remains amongst commentators an imperative to find the functional absence of a democratic system somehow inherently deficient. A careful historical analysis of the city-state suggests, on the contrary, that Singapore's application of solutions to urban problems would put most nations' cities to shame *on their own terms*. Singapore, sharing its fate with the rest of Southeast Asia, is constructed as a kind of mythologized other, which as such reflects the most intense structures of global urbanism per se. It is not so much that democracy is missing in Singapore but more that the question of democracy has been made redundant – and this is a problem that urbanism must face: the intensification of urban processes, which once certainly thrived on the positing of democratic ideals, increasingly renders democracy irrelevant.

Singapore has experienced extremes of catastrophe and recovery like any other global city. The end of the Second World War is often taken as a founding moment in a history that is written as a series of founding moments.[3] The Japanese Occupation between 1942 and 1945 marked the beginning of the end for British colonialism. The *Sook Ching*, a brutal screening by the occupying force in search of "anti-Japanese Chinese" which left up to 50,000 dead, provides an emblematic moment for Singaporean nationalism. Furthermore, the state of the city in 1945 was catastrophic (like many other cities also as a direct result of the war). In Singapore the main problems were consequences of disastrous over-crowding. The shacks that littered the outskirts of the town (retrospectively romanticized as Kampongs) housed hundreds of thousands of Malay, Indian, and Chinese squatters. In the center of town the situation was considerably worse. The slums in and around Chinatown and the Marina Bay area would house up to a hundred inhabitants each. These "black holes of Singapore" were shop-houses built in blocks, long narrow compartments of one, two, three, or four storeys often with no windows and no cooking or bathing facilities.

It is therefore clear why this moment should have pride of place in most of Singapore's official archives today. It serves to show the development of Singapore's urban solution in an extremely good light. At the start of the twenty-first century Chinatown is busy, well populated but contained, in conspicuous and apparently permanent renewal, and a favorite spot for tourists. Marina Bay has been the focus for intense redevelopment and contains virtually no permanent dwellings but, with its hotels, shopping cities, theaters, historic buildings, and riverside restaurants and bars, has become Singapore's showpiece – its global face. The remainder of the island has fast become the triumph of the Housing Development Board where 85 percent of the population lives in HDB flats, and ninety percent of those in apartments that they own by virtue of a compulsory savings scheme that is also regarded by urban economists as a triumph.

The first of Singapore's founding moments, more or less erasing what is now understood as the island's "prehistory," is the founding of a British urban settlement in 1819. Stamford Raffles, the Lieutenant-Governor of Bencoolen, had recognized Singapore's potential as a *hub,* thus having more value for the twin interests of naval and commercial superiority than the possession of large territories. The role of urbanism as a facilitator of mobility and mobilization is clearly foregrounded by the establishment of Singapore as a strategically sited access point for trade between the industrial west and the pre-industrial east. Singapore's chief role has been as a hub of global urbanism for over 180 years of its development (Fig. 1.3).

Rapid migration from rural and undeveloped areas of Asia into Singapore during the nineteenth century led to chaotic patterns of urban growth and consequently problems of overcrowding and bad sanitation. The pattern according to which urban problems call for urban solutions became properly evident when Raffles formed a committee in 1828 whose job was to remedy the problems that urban development had caused, thus contributing to what we will shortly refer to as the *surenchère*, simultaneously intensifying and raising the stakes of global urbanism. The history of urbanism in Singapore is the history of such committees, solving the problems of urbanism by imposing solutions that are themselves increasingly functions of a developing urbanism.

The sense of contradiction remains evident. Anthony M. Tung's article on Singapore, in his *Preserving the World's Great Cities*, indicates the extent to which a number of values identified with urban life have been inappropriately divorced from the historicity of urbanism generally. He identifies a contradiction between the values of what he calls "preservation" and those of "economic justice."[4] It is as if his architectural eye (appalled at the pragmatic perversion of the international style in the cheap upgrading of purpose built HDBs) cannot be reconciled with his acknowledgment of Singapore's achievement in solving the catastrophe of its postwar economic condition. As Tung acknowledges, the narrative of loss is not separable from the narrative of regeneration. We shall go on to argue that the problems of global urbanism cannot be easily separated from the solutions. Furthermore, older forms of influence, supposedly relegated to the history or even prehistory of an urban ensemble, can come back into play as spectral forms divorced from their original agency but organizing things nonetheless.

In this sense spectral phenomena invoke aspects of historicity that lie beyond description. The coming back into play of a supposedly dead being results in two contradictory implications. Either the being was not properly dead or it

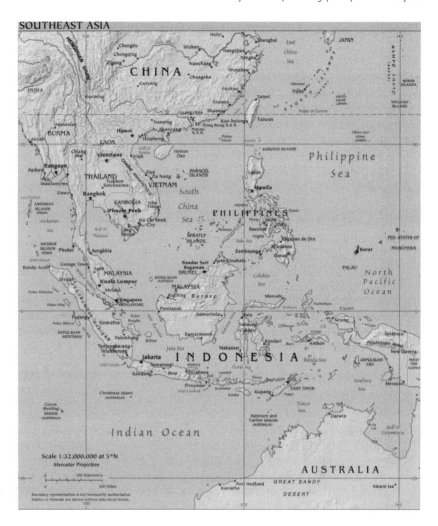

Figure 1.3
Singapore – a hub in Southeast
Asia

was not properly a being, that is, it was never entirely alive. The way to solve this contradiction would be to assume that the process of spectral return is not a transition from one state to another, but rather the uncanny repetition of a condition that could not have been reduced to simple notions of life or existence. In order to study the historicity of Singapore we would need to go beyond the familiar narratives that trace a history from remarkable origins through perceptible progress and by implication to some future prosperous state. But we would not oppose to this the counter narratives of repressed minorities, excluded histories, forgotten events, because such narratives also rely on the structure of narrative that we must rethink. The spectral does not allow the separation of the one from the other (inclusion from exclusion, existence from non-existence, life from death). The grounds of historicity, in other words, can be neither captured in the present nor relegated to the past. It becomes clearer, then, that the spectral operates according to patterns we have already identified as the conditions of possibility for space (in its concrete and figurative senses) and the built environment (in its built and un-built aspects).

A spectral colonialism, for example, haunts Singapore. The specter operates in the name of its earlier incarnation to produce a curious effect whereby an institution such as the justice system has been overtly radically transformed yet maintains a recognizable commonwealth tradition and, thus, covertly a colonial regime. The spectral manifests itself through three main aspects. The first would concern justice and law at an epistemological level – the level of the statement and therefore the sentence. The second manifests the spectral more forcefully at the level of ritual and performance. These include the buildings that compose the houses of justice (the courtrooms, the prisons, the Gallows), the garb that dresses the administrators (the wig, the gown, the scepter, and the gavel), and legal discourse (the jargon and ceremonial speeches). The third, which aims at the deepest level of experience yet functions as an effect of the first two aspects, involves the very spirit of the specter: it is the dimension of belief. It is the belief that the ideal of justice, to which the state would also be accountable, is embodied in the judicial system.

We designate the mode by which the patterns of historicity are perpetuated with the term *surenchère*, which means the intensification of certain formal patterns of operation and a raising of the stakes. There is no term in English that quite captures the combination. Historicity is not a monumental process. Nor is it an interaction between potentially antagonistic multiple particulars. Rather, historicity is what gives rise to the possibility of such interactions but at the cost of potential antagonism. It is the indeterminacy that allows any kind of historical determination to come about. As a consequence, history does indeed emerge as determined and multiple. But historicity also gives rise to conceptions of history that imply regulative or projected ideals, whether holistic or fragmented, that are rendered practically impossible by the perpetual indeterminacy that operates logically prior to the event. A key component of this indeterminacy would be its always yet to be determined future. If the Eiffel Tower becomes, by virtue of the indeterminacy of its image, the logo for Paris, then the Merlion functions as a kind of logo of global urbanism generally. The term *surenchère* designates the kind of process that, without a single cause or aim, produces an illimitable play of forces in interaction and repetition. The implication is that once a process has been set off it gains a momentum independently of its original condition, purpose or cause.

To return to the example of Singapore's Marina Bay area multiple *surenchères* have composed the history of this space. For instance, the renovated luxury hotel, Fullerton, maintains its formal function while undergoing transformations in terms of use. The act of renovation preserves the colonial shell of the building while reworking it from the foundation up to better suit contemporary use, whether as luxury hotel, post office, bank, government building, or restaurant. The Fullerton *surenchère* continues, perpetuates, and multiplies a basic colonial pattern, which is only apparently transformed, in the currency of an increasingly intensified global order. The built (and the rebuilt) environment in this case reveals its plural un-built dimensionality by combining colonial, postcolonial, Cold War, and post-Cold War functions in an increasingly intense way. Each use to which the Fullerton responds would seem to evoke an epoch. As a fort, it functioned as the hub of Britain's imperial aims, serving military and economic ends; as a Post-Office building it helped auger the age of information and contributed to Singapore's participation in the global telecommunications networks central to the roles played by nation states in the Cold War; as a luxury hotel it helps facilitate the circulation of global capital, while valorizing and at the same time archiving its colonial heritage. This convenient separation of epochs in the same building thus in fact exposes the *surenchère* of a series of repetitions, in principle implicating the colonial in the postcolonial and the Cold War in the post-Cold War period. On this reading we must rethink the notion of epoch. As our analysis of spectrality suggests, the colonial does not die nor is the postcolonial born out of it. Rather, the *surenchère* allows patterns and repetitions of patterns to be borne across apparent transitions.

SUSTAINABILITY/ECOLOGY

In our volume on postcolonial urbanism we use the phrase *perpetuating cities* to focus on urbanism as a self-perpetuating pattern of organization subject to increasing intensification.[5] The factors that contribute to, and which are per-petuated by, this intensification compose what is conventionally called global urbanism: national as well as trans-national economic development; accumulation of financial and political power in urban sites; the rapid rise of imported goods and resources into the urban environments; global economies; increasing access to global resources; rapid expansion of technologies including electronic tele-technologies; exploitation of cheap energy supplies; expansion of mass rapid-transport systems; migration and transmigration into and between urban centers; reproduction and multiplication of urban populations. Herbert Girardet, in his analysis of the conditions required to create what he calls "sustainable cities," takes account of these factors in his bleak outline of the current problem: "the growth of modern urban economies usually means two things: increased demands on natural capital and increased discharges of wastes into the local and global environment. Proposals for sustainable development have to be made in this context."[6] Girardet correctly identifies the problem as both conceptual and cultural, that is, urban ways of thinking, whether in urban or rural areas, dominate the globe, such that even those attempts to prevent the urbanization of the world can result in an intensification of it. For instance, when policies are introduced to improve living and sanitation conditions in under-developed rural areas, the kinds of policies introduced tend to add to the cultural migration from rural to urban through the imposition of urban concepts of education and sanitation. The urbanization of the rural is revealed through the improvement and purification of water supplies, village electrification, telecommunications systems, and investment in rural economies. One does not have to dig too deeply beneath the common-sense attractiveness of these processes to find the contradictions. Girardet makes the uncontroversial claim that cities – which were once centers of *civilization* – now appear as both origin and destination in a vast *mobilization*: "cities are the nodes along which mobility emanates: along roads, railway networks, aircraft routes and telephone lines" (11–12). So the problem of our cities has been created by what he calls an urban or urbanized culture: "*Thought* has created the unstable world in which we now live – manifested in mega-technology, mega-cities, global power structures and vast environmental impacts" (71). The trouble with Girardet's analysis is less in his diagnosis and more in his prescription. He claims that:

We now need to develop concepts for *real sustainability* to bring about the reconciliation between cities, their people and nature. These efforts need to:

- Involve the whole person – mind spirit and body
- Place long term stewardship above short term satisfaction
- Ensure justice and fairness informed by civic responsibility
- Encourage diversity within the unity of a given community
- Develop precautionary principles, anticipating the effects of our actions
- Ensure that our use of resources does not diminish the living environment.

It is clear that we need a revolution in problem solving (71).

The bland utopianism of this prescription (perhaps this is intentionally designed to emphasize the bleakness of the situation) which glosses, and glosses over, the most trenchant philosophical problems of the last 2000 years illustrates a failure to see that the prescription is no less an urban solution than any of the damaging processes that Girardet compellingly identifies elsewhere. The idea – suggested in his introductory chapters and returned to here – of a *lost civilization* (the Renaissance city?) is the urban myth par excellence: "Cities [now] are the home of 'amplified man', an unprecedented amalgam of biology and technology, transcending his ancestors" (25). At the mythical level there is little difference between the positions of those who champion and those who are appalled at the specter of the post-human in prosthetic technologies. At the heart of the myth resides "natural man." The dream of completion that governs much of the technological enhancement represented by tele-technologies is no less pervasive in the holism that is supposed to solve the same problem. Our thesis assumes no distinction between the natural and the prosthetically enhanced. Rather, the condition of possibility for prosthetic enhancement constitutes the "human" in its origin, as prosthesis at the origin, hence the unacknowledged but genuine power of electronic amplification.

For this reason we have attempted to address the question of what Girardet calls the *thought* of urbanism more seriously. The dialectic of sanitation and waste, for instance, is inevitably tied in with the unconscious historicity of global processes and we suppose that it cannot be solved (resolved or sublimated) at the level of propositions about it. Brenda Yeoh's study of colonial Singapore reveals a complex and trenchant pattern. She summarizes:

> While the colonial project of sanitizing the city remained vital to the manner in which authorities attempted to structure and control the public environment, it was joined by the equally pressing aims of producing a public landscape which was orderly, disciplined, easily policed, and amenable to the demands of urban development and efficiency. To the vision of a sanitized city was blended the image of a progressive, civilized city.[7]

If this was the case for colonial Singapore then it is no less the case today. Singapore is amongst those few urban sites whose entire existence is manifestly urban so there is manifestly more at stake for Singapore than there may be for other nations. The specter of a colonial Singapore appears wherever these blended demands operate. The excessive waste that urban demands inevitably produce cannot, therefore, be acknowledged. The efficient and sanitized city is overtly the result of attempts to expel, as Yeoh puts it, "filth, darkness, disease, and overcrowding," the conspicuous consequences of modern urbanism in its colonial form (though not uniquely, of course).

Girardet is surely correct in his identification of the disastrous consequences of urbanization, even if his romanticized proposition for revolutionary reform seems hopeless. With the fusing of "ecology" and "urbanization" in the form of "sustainable" cities that operates as one of the dominant intellectual modes of global urbanism, the city as a site of directly or indirectly human-created disaster has become all but elided from most public discourse and memory of urban trajectories. Consequently, the kind of radical intervention offered by Girardet remains an anomaly. The constant hazards caused by urban dwelling go largely unarticulated in the current moment. Primary amongst these is environmental pollution, which, like global capital, knows no boundaries. But the frontiers that divide the urban space from the hinterlands that feed it can be seen as attempts to contain environmental pollution within proscribed boundaries, this despite the fact that virtually all other borders between urban and rural spaces are being eliminated by the hegemony of urbanism. The containment of pollution outside of urban centers that supposedly marks the move from industrial economies to post-industrial ones, however, cannot be guaranteed. Standard interpretations of environmental pollution cohere with the standard discourse of the teleology of urban development insofar as developing cities will be more polluted than developed ones. In fact an important distinction between developing and developed, or industrializing and post-industrial, sites is the adjective found in the phrase "clean technologies," which are the province of the urban, not of the provinces.

But there are at least two distinct types of pollution worth noting in relation to global urbanism: environmental and electromagnetic. The prevalence of one in any given urban site does not necessarily imply the prevalence of the other, nor would it indicate its absence. Singapore, however, as a "Garden City" and a wired "Intelligent Island," has worked hard to maintain their separation and prove the absence of the former makes possible the realization of the latter while simultaneously demarcating the city-state as having moved from industrial to post-industrial status. The two forms of pollution are not isometrically related or mutually exclusive, but they interact in a much more complex and problematic way than is accounted for by current dominant discourses on globalization. The future of urbanism will clearly be worked out in terms of the complex interaction of these two networks, and consequently it will become increasingly difficult to distinguish neatly between terms like culture and environment in the examination of urban sites.

The various technicities of the urban, including its logic and logistics, now work in such a manner that the urban and its influences are no longer neatly distinguishable from ways of understanding the rural. Rural problems, including those of pollution *in* and *from* rural areas and not simply the rural containment of contaminants, now confront urban solutions. And only urban solutions seem to be put forward or listened to with any degree of seriousness. For example, the Indonesian forest fires from Sumatra that regularly plague Singapore's air and air quality index are largely perceived as rural-based and rural-produced pollution problems that create trouble for the urban dwellers of Singapore. But, of course, the pressures that lead to massive forest clearing through the use of fires come from urban demands and urban consumption, from transnational corporations based in global urban centers directing the use and extraction of natural resources found in rural sites. The entire rural world has become the vast, albeit dwindling, hinterland for the *ur*-urban site, selling off its non-renewable commodities at ever shrinking rates in the vain pursuit of participating in the global networks linking urban centers. Girardet calculates that "cities, built on only two per cent of the world's land surface, use 75 percent of the world's resources and discharge similar amounts of waste" (10). The ethics always already operative in ways of conceiving urban futures must take into account the division between rural and urban, its porosity and solidity predicated upon urban technicities and desires. The urban, in other words, divides itself from the rural when and how it wishes to do so while, at the same time, producing that which it divides. Much like the power of modernity itself, the power of urbanism resides in its power to so divide.

The networks themselves that link up and constitute sites of global urbanism are perpetuated and intensified by opto-electronics, tele-technologies, information technologies, and "real time" technologies. It is therefore worth considering the phenomenon of "stereoscopy," the simultaneity of virtual and real environments.[8] Taking Paul Virilio's attempt to cast our contemporary moment as bounded by two global networks, the geopolitical and the electro-magnetic, we observe that many of us spend our day-to-day lives between these two networks. The rapid increase in "real time" tele-technologies, for instance, can be situated as a development within traditions of modern urbanization, which have always had a powerful effect on social experience in its production of urban subjects, and which have explicit connections to Cold War and post-colonial geopolitical concerns. To the familiar technologies of telephony and television, we must now add opto-electronic, electro-acoustic, and even tele-tactile technologies to the list of profoundly influential conditions of contemporary urban life. The role of the independent geopolitical realm is severely weakened in this respect, as the two networks do not correspond in isometric fashion. One cannot understand the electromagnetic realm as having been super-imposed upon geographical space, as if a virtual super-structure had been built upon a real base. The virtual impacts actual conditions of both experience and political economy no less than geopolitical conditions do, leaving us radically divided between two powerful yet relatively heterogeneous worlds.

In urban situations the human being is increasingly caught simultaneously in the "real" space of an increasingly limited environment and real time relations at a distance, to the extent that the human experience of the world and of the world's horizon is becoming, in Virilio's terms, irretrievably polluted.[9] He argues that this pollution by the electromagnetic sphere is every bit as devastating as the more commonly documented forms of ecological pollution. In fact the two types of pollution compound each other for the vast resources required to maintain electromagnetic networks take their toll on the geographic environment just as the networks themselves take their toll on human experience. But we are arguing here a complex interaction between ecological and electromagnetic pollution that often finds form, as we have discussed, in the neat discursive cleaving of the two operative in the clean, post-industrial global urban site and the dirty, industrializing sprawl of developing cities. The power to so distinguish and divide is, yet again, the power of the global urban site, even though it may only appear to have successfully contained the ecological pollution outside its city boundary while allowing in, as much as is technologically possible, the electromagnetic pollution, without acknowledging it *as* pollution.

The electromagnetic sweep of global networks, therefore, tends to manifest as a kind of pollution of the human experience of the world. Concomitantly, the disappearance of frontiers on an electronic level involves a sharpening of frontiers on a geopolitical and economic level. Often this sharpening occurs in direct relation to the extent by which the rural and underdeveloped maintains the urban, especially in relation to the maintenance of electronic global networks (by oil production, silicone production, and hardware manufacturing). The global city can be taken as the clearest manifestation of this worldwide phenomenon, where many of the adjoining regions of cities remain apparently untouched by the most advanced electronic media, other than by exploitation. The borders between the urban and its others are perhaps sharper in Southeast Asia than anywhere else in the globe, as whole populations are exiled to its immediate outside – often within the city itself – but nonetheless inescapably shaped by it, regulated by it, watched over by it in a way neatly encapsulated by the flickering screens that appear with increasing frequency on the outsides of high buildings, sending their silent messages across miles of cityscape.

If we pay attention to the consequences as Virilio lays them out, the situation looks bleak. Electronic techniques have in principle eradicated the horizon of human experience by inserting an absence of duration between individuals at a distance. Relations that occur immediately but on a non-existent electronic plane thus increasingly replace relations of real spatial proximity. Individuals connected to networked telecommunications devices experience no duration where great distances are in fact involved. This is one of the championed and remarkable advantages of electronic cable and satellite media. The consequence, though, is that increasingly less time is spent engaging in real spatial relations, such as the ones between the citizen and the built environment, or that between the citizen and environmental pollution, or the one between one citizen and another that is vastly shaped by a complex historicity. The immaterial realm of electromagnetic networks invariably alters spatial relations and spatial experience in the built environment in ways that reveal a specific historicity of urbanism, but the revelation itself is often oblique, hidden, or rendered quotidian or progressive.

We ought to add to our discussion of the prevalence and rapid escalation of forms of environmental and electromagnetic pollution an acknowledgment of the World Health Organization's (WHO) prediction that by 2020 clinical depression will be in the second place (under heart disease) in the ranking of DALYs (the sum of years of potential life lost due to premature mortality and the years of productive life lost due to disability).[10] Depression is already the fourth leading contributor to the global burden of disease, affecting about 121 million people worldwide. Depression shows up more often in densely populated urban sites. This is not necessarily because it is more prevalent (though that would seem to be the case), but it is certainly more likely to show up as a problem. An escalation in effective medication, of course, has followed, though the WHO declares that there remain at least twenty-five percent of sufferers who have no access to any kind of help.

In light of these escalating problems associated with the expansion of global urbanism (environmental, dromological, and psychological), and the real difficulties that face attempts to find a solution in the notion of *sustainability*, we prefer the notion of *perpetuation*. Perpetuation implies a futural dimension that is indispensable yet, like the conditions we have analyzed as the *surenchère*, the spectral and the un-built, remains beyond all our attempts to capture or to describe it. What perpetuates would thus first of all be that which remains to be determined, the undetermined, of the future – its incalculable aspect. The sense of historicity that we have been gesturing to is evoked here, insofar as the futural trace (always not yet) allows a repetition (we call it the present) of the past. To arrive at any sense of the force of historicity one must resist the temptation to become fascinated by moments or fixated upon paradigmatic or epistemic breaks. A break with the past always implies a repetition of its least flexible forms, so the fixation on the moment or the break would manifest a displaced repetition. To think seriously about what is lost and what remains in the intensification of the processes that we are examining, as the urban site moves through its evident temporal shifts, we must look beyond its physical forms and historical moments.

NOTES

1   Ackbar Abbas, *Hong Kong: Culture and the Politics of Disappearance* (Minneapolis: University of Minnesota Press, 1997).
2   Stan Sesser, *The Lands of Charm and Cruelty: Travels in Southeast Asia* (London: Picador, 1994).
3   As we write, the slogan for National Day 2002 foregrounds yet another founding moment in the making: "Together: a New Singapore" (a slogan borrowed from a Village People song, "Go West," as covered by the Pet Shop Boys auguring a much needed gay utopia during the dark days of the early 1990s and now representing hope for recovery from an analogous economic downturn in Asia).
4   Anthony M. Tung, *Preserving the World's Great Cities: the Destruction and Renewal of the Historic Metropolis* (New York: Three Rivers Press, 2001) 169–189.
5   Ibid.
6   Herbert Girardet, *Creating Sustainable Cities* (Totnes: Green Books, 1999) 22. Further page references in the text.
7   Brenda Yeoh, *Contesting Space: Power Relations and the Urban Built Environment in Colonial Singapore* (Kuala Lumpur: Oxford University Press, 1996) 215.
8   For a detailed discussion of stereoscopy and urban space, see the introduction to *Postcolonial Urbanism: Southeast Asian Cities and Global Processes* (New York and London: Routledge, 2003), ed. by Ryan Bishop, John Phillips, and Wei Wei Yeo.
9   Virilio's *Open Sky* pays particular attention to these concerns.
10 http://www5.who.int/mental_health/main.cfm?p=0000000017.

Chapter 2: Of Trees and the Heartland: Singapore's Narratives[1]

Wei-Wei Yeo

Tree: If humans don't understand, what can trees do?
> Kuo Pao Kun, *The Silly Little Girl and the Funny Old Tree*

Cities held to ransom by their own devils
or collective dream sequences
> Arthur Yap, "Would It have Been"

THE STORY OF A TREE, A CITY, AND A GARDEN

On 23 November 2002 newspapers in Singapore reported the felling of a 150-year-old tree, the last standing specimen of the *Hopea sangal* in Singapore. Changi, the name of the eastern part of the island where the tree was found, is said to have come from the tree's Malay names, "Chengal Pasir" or "Chengal mata kuching". The tree was cut down by a property management company whose officials feared that the tree, already infested with termites and recently struck by lightning, could be a safety hazard to the residents and some of the houses in the area.[2] The felling of the tree caused much upset among conservationists in Singapore; in the Singapore Heritage Society's web discussion group emails flew around, lamenting the loss of the tree and calling for a petition to be sent to the property company and the National Parks Board to demand for the return of the tree trunk. Fuelling unhappiness on the one hand by reporting that the tree had but flowered recently, the papers also provided reassurance that all was not lost, for twenty seeds from the tree were being nurtured by the National Parks Board. The conservationists' distress bore an all-too-familiar strain, rich with nostalgia and a sense of severing with not only the thing but also what it *can* symbolize. The element of possibility is important for it sustains as well as continues to generate the sense of a lost historical landscape as well as what that landscape could have stood for. From the government's viewpoint, the environment does not only make the city-state's "historic" identity evident; it also manifests the city's burgeoning self-projections and future metamorphoses. This dual function of the environment can be inferred from the mission statement of the Heritage Trees Scheme set up by the government's green conservation body, the National Parks Board, on 17 August 2001:

> Majestic mature trees are the natural heritage of Singapore and serve as important green landmarks of our green Tropical Garden City. They help to create a sense of

permanence and identity to the place we live in. Just as our Garden City, it takes decades and in some cases, more than hundred [sic] of years for these trees to mature gracefully in our landscape.[3]

Perhaps symptomatically, the historical significance that is drawn from the tree at Changi does not stem so much from its botanical near-singularity as from the historical relation between its name and location. It is a relation that avails a picture of early Singapore as an island where place names were rooted in the earth. This chapter explores the hold of the relation between landscape and national historic identity over the Singaporean imagination in plays, poems, novels, and films. In these representations Singapore, like the image of an ancient Changi with its forest of *Hopea sangal* trees, appears as an object of longing; the paltry facts of its pre-colonial history bringing forth myth after myth even as the urbanism of its present is pressed for significance.

Singapore is a city-state that has told its tale of origins as a transglobal and multiracial community from one generation to the next. The nation's narrative conveys the historical and contemporary reality of the city's creation and sustenance through the flows and profitable confluences of peoples, capital, and information. And yet in the midst of this teeming "baroque ecology", to use Aihwa Ong's term, the question of Singaporean identity continues to be raised in terms that fail to recognize the city's unique "eco-systems".[4] More precisely, what I am contending is that the association of national identity with roots horticultural and human alike makes little sense in Singapore. Schoolchildren learn from history textbooks that Sir Stamford Raffles founded Singapore in 1819. Little is said about Singapore's history before Raffles and the East India Company arrived, save that it was a small fishing village. Raffles did not have a long term of residence in Singapore; he left in 1823. Nonetheless, his name has become a marker of the city's genealogy. The entrenched or perpetuated association of Raffles with modern Singapore's beginning yields a different perspective of identity, one that suggests the need to think beyond roots when Raffles' interest in botany and the role this played in the shaping of Singapore's natural environment is taken into consideration.

The planning and transformation of Singapore between 1963 and the present into a garden city called upon the resources of the Botanic Gardens. When:

> [b]eautification of Singapore . . . became the order of the day [in 1963 with the first Tree Planting campaign and in 1967 with the "Garden City" campaign] the Gardens' priorities had to shift accordingly. From an essentially research-oriented institution with responsibilities for the entire region, the Gardens' mission was revised to provide a botanical and horticultural service only for Singapore.[5]

Although it was established in 1859, nearly four decades after Raffles' departure, there is a connection between the Botanic Gardens and Raffles that can be traced through the precursors of the Gardens in the earlier half of the nineteenth century. Raffles saw Singapore not only as a profitable port; he also saw it as a place of great botanical economic potential. When he set up base on Fort Canning Hill in 1819, an experimental and botanic garden was laid out at the same time. Raffles planted seedlings of clove and nutmeg he had brought with him from Penang, the two most profitable commercial crops. "The first clove and nutmeg trees planted there created the nucleus for the next thirty-five years of spice production."[6] Native fruit trees ("large durian trees, whose trunks measured as much as 1/83 metres in diameter, lime, pomelo, and langsat trees . . . found growing wild at the bottom of Canning Hill") were chopped down when the area was cleared for settlement.[7] In 1822 Raffles supported Nathanial Wallich, the superintendent of the Botanic Gardens at Calcutta, when the latter proposed to establish "a Botanic and Experimental Garden" in Singapore.[8] Experimentation was geared towards gains in scientific knowledge as well as in monetary terms – the "primeval forests" could be studied and cash crops could be grown in the garden to test the viability of their cultivation on the island. Raffles granted Wallich the land of the existing government garden on Fort Canning Hill and by early January 1823 work had begun in the Garden. The Garden failed to live up to the grand expectations of Wallich and the East India Company; a report on the Garden to the East India Company headquarters in London in 1827 described it as "by no means in good order, and very confused"[9] and in 1829 the Garden was closed. In 1836 the Botanic Gardens was re-opened on a small 2.8 hectare portion of its former grounds but this too closed down by 1846. The present Botanic Gardens was established in 1859 and its layout is very little changed from the original.

The Botanic Gardens is a space that has reflected the governance of Singapore from colonial times to the present.[10] What makes it curious is that it is as open to the possibilities of the future (seen in the cutting-edge horticultural research and the hybridization of orchids, the breeding of new strains of the plant that it houses) as it is publicly recognized as a historic space that dates from the nineteenth century. It was in the gardens that the British under Ridley's supervision began the process of transforming the landscape of Malaya with rubber tree plantations after he successfully nurtured rubber seeds imported from Brazil. New species of trees and plants continue to be introduced into Singapore soil through the gardens. So that while the *Hopea sangal* tree was dated from around the same time the present Botanic Gardens was created, the claim to the island's genealogy through the soil and a historically grounded sense of its identity do not mean the same thing when both are considered side by side. The role played by the Botanic Gardens in the greening of Singapore since 1967 has contributed in part to the extinction of a quarter of the island's native vascular plant species.[11]

RHIZOME NATION

In the notion of the tree giving Changi its name reside organic images: rootedness; origins or an originary landscape. In Singaporean writer Leong Liew Geok's poem "Trees are only Temporary", trees are evoked as emblems of change rather than permanence; transience in the form of the displacement of the natural by the urban delivers a wry critique of the fast pace of change in Singapore: "There is no place for shooting splendours / In the fever of estates and shopping centres."[12] Singapore's transformation in the span of thirty years into a Tropical Garden City of Excellence, a tag from the Urban Redevelopment Authority, has uncounted costs, the poem suggests as it contrasts the image of removed old trees ("Cut to pieces, where have all the rugged gone? / Boles which leave no bloody stump, / But baldness flush to the ground?") with the speedy planting of new trees ("instant trees come / Quick from any nursery.") Ironically, "[t]rees are only temporary / In a flourishing garden city."[13] It is a familiar refrain – the impermanence of not simply buildings but trees too as the distinctive feature of Singaporean landscape. The poem comes from a collection about Singapore as city, *The Ethos Anthology of Urban Poetry* (2000). When the editors went through the submissions to the volume, they found that "[e]erie resonances emerge between the works of poets who at first glance have little to do with each other in terms of age, experience or poetic concerns".[14] The organization of poems in the volume in a sequence of related themes reflects the echoes between poems, showing the persistent resonance of impermanence. Being in a constant process of change seems to be the city's most distinctive imprint for its poets young and old. That there exists a need to inscribe the landscape in words or other forms of art is seen in that the editors' motivation for the volume arose from finding that poetry "was a handle on life, a way to grapple with the issues of growing up in a city that was changing before their eyes, and far too quickly".[15] The need for inscription corresponds to an anxiety about the impermanence of landscape: poetry becomes entrusted with the "mapping" of a "common urban and human landscape".[16] If not borne out of anxiety, the notion that identity can be constructed through writing carries a self-affirmative purpose, testifying to the eventual arrival of the nation at a final destination where she will fully see herself. This is implicit in the majority of individual poetry collections, particularly debut collections, as well as in anthologies of Singaporean poets published by local national agencies. An example of its articulation can be found in the premise for a study of the construction of Singaporean identity in poetry:

> [The] contention here is that beyond the linguistic agenda, state identity can be constructed from the poetry of a nation, and especially from those poems that detail the several journeys undertaken in order to arrive at a destination that is *now* in the unfolding narrative of becoming.[17]

A law of reflection governs the framework of relation between landscape and literature; through it the nation's self-reflection is sought.[18] An order is fixed, connecting environment and representation, making them mutually explanatory sides of one world, but this is an imposed order, flattening the circularity and tidying up the multiplicity of processes, exchanges, as these exist and constitute life and change in landscape. Deleuze and Guattari locate the fallacy of the paradigm: "The book imitates the world, as art imitates nature: by procedures specific to it that accomplish what nature cannot or can no longer do."[19] Thought governed by the binary structure of reflection lags behind nature. The most prevalent way of going about understanding who a person is or what a thing is through beginnings and ends is debunked by Deleuze and Guattari's theory. The metaphor of roots is called into question when the workings of roots in nature are shown to confound their figurative significance in discourse: "in nature, roots are taproots with a more multiple, lateral, and circular system of ramification, rather than a dichotomous one".[20] Deleuze and Guattari's rhizome system is an alternative framework that allows the making of the multiple with its principles of connection, heterogeneity, multiplicity, and asignifying rupture. The rhizome stands in contrast to the root or radicle. It is "a prostrate or subterranean root-like stem emitting roots and usually producing leaves at its apex" (*OED*), "a subterranean stem".[21]

The rhizome appears in the work of Kuo Pao Kun, Singapore's most important theatre practitioner and playwright to date. Kuo deals with questions about identity, history, and place; indeed, two of his plays *The Silly Little Girl and the Funny Old Tree* (1987) and *Descendants of the Eunuch Admiral* (1995) can be studied as explorations of genealogy in rhizomatic terms. Interestingly, Kuo viewed himself as a person without roots. He was a native of Hebei who stayed briefly in Hong Kong before he moved on to Singapore where he attended a Chinese school. After Kuo pursued a drama course in Australia, he returned to Singapore and wrote plays first in Mandarin, then in English too.

In *The Silly Little Girl and the Funny Old Tree* there are two main characters, Tree and Girl. The girl has a special attachment to an old and funny-looking tree in her school's car park. She treats it as her confidante, speaking and singing to it. One day, hearing her sing a familiar old song, the tree tries to sing along. The girl is at first stunned that the tree can speak and sing but soon when she learns that the tree has forgotten the lyrics of the song she forgets her amazement and tries to teach it the song. The tree then tells the girl a story about an island that began with an abandoned tree. A felled tree that was left drying in the sun was carried away by a sudden flood and became submerged in a river, its branches stuck in the riverbed. As it felt its life ebbing away it roused itself with anger and fear to move and make waves, sprouting roots from its branches in the mud and buds on its branches above the water. It flourished into an island, and the story ends with the assurance that generation after generation of trees on that island buried themselves, "turning into ashes and nourishment, feeding those who came after them".[22] In the play the story is told by a tree and its significance has to be considered in the light of the tree's fear that it will soon be cut down. The land where it stands is to be cleared for the building of houses. Eventually the tree is pruned, not felled because of the girl's protest; still, it is incapacitated by the pruning, shorn of its branches and leaves. As if to remind itself of what is possible, the tree tells the story of an older tree's triumph and regeneration, of how it survived the severing from its roots. The miraculous survival of the rootless tree and the other tree's threat of being felled for development bring myth and reality together, painting a picture of how the first compensates for the powerlessness that conditions the second. By the end of the play the girl has attacked the tree out of despair and it is last seen whimpering a song. Yet while both trees are emblems of marginality and displacement, the tree that became an island is a kind of rootstock, its offshoots sprouting roots in the soil of a riverbed. It is as rhizome rather than tree that it continues to exist; and such too is the lot for the trees that came after it, all future generations of rhizome.

In *Descendants of the Eunuch Admiral* Kuo returns to the question of origins through the myth and historical person of Zheng He, the eunuch admiral sent by the Ming emperor to explore the seas from India to Arabia in the fifteenth century. Instead of the rootlessness of a tree, Kuo explores castration, the rootlessness of a man. In Mandarin, the language in which the play was first performed, the penis is also known as the root (*gen*).[23] Zheng He is represented as one for whom all signifiers of root-based identity have been removed: he was castrated at a young age and brought to the palace in Beijing, losing his home, family, ethnicity, and inherited religion of Islam; according to a legend, even his surname Zheng was an invention. Kuo's Zheng is rhizomatic:

Zheng He's vision has a certain lack of place, a fragile sense of belonging to a definite, authentic space, knowing that such a space is always hostile to impurity. His very being is against all totalities, especially any totality averse to qualitative difference.[24]

Singaporean critics have responded to the play as an allegory for multi-racial Singapore's cultural displacement or castration from mother cultures, so that the play's opening monologue by an unnamed speaker who identifies with Zheng He, or "this 600-year-old legend of a molested and incarcerated man",[25] is taken to be the voice of the country's cultural orphans.[26] The speaker calls himself a descendant of the eunuch admiral – a paradoxical lineage but the claim is significant for it demonstrates the rhizomatic condition of the relation, the re-casting of genealogy in terms of rhizome, making roots irrelevant. The speaker's empathy with Zheng He implies not only the sharing of his displacement but also the way in which Zheng He embraces his in-between states of being, "in the limbo between departing and arriving, between being a man and a non-man":

> Nameless, sexless, rootless, homeless
> Everyone's a parent to the orphan
> Every god's a protector to the wanderer
> Every land and sky and water is home
> It's forever *Zaijian, Selamat, Vanakkam*, Farewell.[27]

Zheng He's multi-lingual goodbye calls the Singaporean multi-racial context to mind. In the Singapore context the rhizome provides a new approach to iden-tity, temporality, and space and *Descendants of the Eunuch Admiral* represents this. Identities, intentions, and interiorities of individuals and of communities become lesser priorities next to the processes of transformation and realignment of relations all round. Nostalgia for the never-possessed does not feature in Zheng He's life of "dreaming, hoping, searching, struggling". The lines: "Departing is my arriving / Wandering is my residence"[28] evoke a sense of the rootless self-person that is affirmative rather than despairing of its suspension in the in-between. A rhizomatic space, the

> space of the in-between is the locus for social, cultural, and natural transformations: it is not simply a convenient space for movements and realignments but in fact is the only place – the place around identities, between identities – where becoming, openness to futurity, outstrips the conservational impetus to retain cohesion and unity.[29]

Zheng He embodies this:

> To keep my head
> I must accept losing my tail [. . .]
> Allah knows my bitterness
> Buddha has mercy upon my soul
> Sea Goddess protects my fleet
> Voyages to the West fulfil my life.[30]

MYTH OF A HEARTLAND

In the introduction to *Journeys: Words, Home and Nation: Anthology of Singapore Poetry (1984–1995)* the editors note that place or locale is a predominant theme in Singapore English poetry and that it bridges different generations of poets.

> Typically, this motif is expressed in the form of an abiding attachment to a particular place – Changi Beach in some of Robert Yeo's poems, Dudley de Souza's Kaolin Lane, Desmond Sim's Serangoon Gardens . . . Often too, the attachment to a place is mingled with a sense of its passing: while the older poets tend to dwell on the memory of a place connected with childhood, for the younger poets the sense of place is precisely the sense of its transitions and transmutations.[31]

The international flavour or cosmopolitanism in the work of the younger poets is also noted. What is neglected, and this applies to other existing surveys and critiques of local writing, is the increasing prevalence of images of public housing (Housing Development Board, known by its acronym HDB) estates and flats. The trend is visible not only in the poetry and fiction writing of young poets such as Alfian Sa'at and Daren Shiau, it is also found in the films of local directors Eric Khoo (*12 Storeys* and *Mee Pok Man*), Jasmine Ng and Kelvin Tong (co-directors of *Eating Air*). Locale appears in the work of the earlier poets as reminiscence of particular places in Singapore; from the 1990s onwards the place motif moves away from specified areas to inexact locations in HDB estates – flat, void deck,[32] corridor, town centre.[33] Koh Buck Song's *A Brief History of Toa Payoh and other poems* (1992) features poems about life in Toa Payoh, one of the earliest and also one of the most sprawling HDB estates. The longest piece in Colin Cheong's *Void Decks and Other Empty Places* (1996) is a narrative of twenty poetic vignettes about life in an HDB estate. HDB estates are prominent in the poems of Alfian Sa'at's debut collection *One Fierce Hour* (1998). Estate life is the structuring motif in *Corridor* (1999), Sa'at's first volume of short stories. The same can be said of Eric Khoo's second feature film *12 Storeys* (1997). Khoo's debut feature *Mee Pok Man* (1995) is set partly in a HDB flat. This contemporary fascination with the HDB landscape is also found in the first novels of Daren Shiau – *Heartland* (1999); and Dave Chua – *Gone Case* (1997).

The HDB estates in Eric Khoo's films and in Kelvin Tong's *Eating Air* (2000) were built during the 1960s and 1970s: the early stages of public housing development in Singapore. The preference for older estates over newer estates such as Bishan and Tampines is found not only in representations of HDB life in local films; the same observation can be made of housing estates in Singapore writing. Incidentally, the special status of the older estates was recently endorsed by the setting up of a government-appointed committee to give feedback on HDB conservation issues.[34] In Daren Shiau's novel *Heartland* the old blocks at Ghim Moh are compared to trees:

> Wing had lived there for fifteen years and still felt a warm glow whenever he saw the majesty of the four point blocks piercing the orange dusk sky and the lower blocks, old but graceful, rising proudly from the soil.[35]

The image conveys the buildings' role in a process of identity-formation. The familiarity of HDB flats in the Singapore landscape and their concrete manifestation of Singapore's growth since the beginning of independence to the present day ingrain the image in the public imagination.[36] Conservationists contend, to lose old flats such as the ones found in Tiong Bahru, built by the Singapore Improvement Trust (SIT), the predecessor of the HDB, is to lose a part of national memory. On the other hand, "[r]etaining [such] blocks . . . could well be one way of giving Singaporeans a sense of belonging [. . . since] a part of rootedness comes from visual memories".[37] The title *Heartland* is the idiomatic collective term for HDB estates, and it evokes the community of the majority of the population, creating again a sense of common identity. Shiau expands on the figure in *Heartland*:

> The heart of the heartlands had to be the big, landlocked, densely populated regions of Ang Mo Kio and Toa Payoh, where through its arteries of bus interchanges and hawker centers, the crowds flowed and interacted incessantly. Moving. Buying. Eating. Talking. In the lorongs and the avenues, deceptively similar to outsiders, the river of life meandered, branched, converged, eroding the façade to a worn but radiant sheen.[38]

The majority is made up of neglected minorities, it would seem judging from the filmic, poetic, and fictional narratives mentioned earlier on; another common feature is a recurrent focus on dysfunctional families in estates and heartlanders (residents, mainly Singaporeans, of HDB flats) who are marginalized in one way or another. Adolescence, an in-between phase, is also a key motif. Several of the narratives – *Heartland*, *Gone Case*, *Eating Air*, "Cubicle" and "Umbrella", two of the short stories in *Corridor* – follow the coming of age of main characters. Interestingly they all fail to fit into the mould of conventional success, lacking academic inclination, coming from lower-income and dysfunctional families. From junior college to national service in the army to polytechnic, Wing in *Heartland* is aimless and does not seem to care about anything; *Gone Case* shows twelve-year-old Yong turning thirteen, a year during which his grandmother dies, his parents separate, his best friend Liang leaves school, and his sister becomes a prostitute; Ah Boy in *Eating Air* is a teenager who hangs around arcade centres and rides his motorcycle with his mates. Growing up; the average and yet marginalized Singaporean who is part of the mainstream as well as set apart from it; HDB blocks as the most recognizable image of home – these themes and ways of identification manifest the notion of rootedness in different forms.[39]

The focus on aspects of marginality complements the predilection for old estates as part of the narratives' critique of government policies and the price society pays for economic growth. The displacement of individuals and their rootedness in Singapore, in personal histories, circumstances, and the environment is a contrast that crops up again and again in these narratives. The degree to which the contrast is made varies from work to work, but in general its presence seems to be intended to alert readers and audiences to the gritty and sometimes disturbing reality behind the façade of uniform housing. In Eric Khoo's films there is a raw sense of marginality in the kinds of characters that are portrayed as well as in the director's own self-conscious sense of his art's place in the margins.[40] In a 1991 interview with *Big O*, an "alternative" magazine covering made-in-Singapore music and pop culture, Khoo reveals that from the outset he was self-conscious about where his art should be placed, or rather, of its displacement in the Singaporean mainstream:

> What does have a place in Singapore? Commercialism? I don't know . . . If I went ahead and made a feature film, it will run for two or three days and that's it. No one is going to care. Maybe with the right ingredients, it will work. But not with the stories in my head. It won't with the public here.[41]

And yet in both *Mee Pok Man* and *12 Storeys* Khoo shows characters who are curiously as displaced from Singaporean society as they are impossible to place outside of it. In *Mee Pok Man* necrophilic acts take place in a one-room flat with frames showing a typical HDB landscape. In *12 Storeys* a young man jumps off his block of flats and his ghost follows an obese woman, a resident in the same block, silently around. The films seek to provide an alternative perspective of Singapore, alternative to that found in the official discourse of Singapore's success story. By showcasing failures or misfits of the system, they provide a diametrically opposite view of society. But the focus on displacement belies a belief in the possibility of well being, of being properly grounded in oneself and in society. It suggests that there was a time when people were better rooted, an age before high-rise living distanced the population from the soil.

In representations of HDB living by different writers and filmmakers a common feature recurs: the magnifying of everyday movements, sights, and smells in an estate. In the films a favourite frame consists of blocks of HDB flats with their corridors lit by fluorescent tube-lights in the night. Also popular are scenes of residents going about their everyday business, sitting and chatting in the void decks, or taking the lift and walking down the corridor to their flat. There is a grasping of the local and the Singaporean communal in these scenes; the same can be said of passages found in the novels and poems by Dave Chua, Daren Shiau, and Colin Cheong. In *Gone Case* the protagonist, a twelve-year-old boy Yong, tries to locate the source of a crying voice in his block, bringing the reader with him as he combs through the block, taking note of all the ordinary things going on around him, his sense perceptions penetrating through walls:

> men lighting braziers in the flats, incense in brass braziers hung on thick iron chains dripping white smoke, lights still left from Hari Raya that blink in the evening light, maids bringing down buckets of water to wash their owners' cars, babies in mechanized cots that bounce up and down, construction workers sleeping on the void decks.[42]

In the literature, as in the films, scenes that show the buzz of HDB living are accompanied by scenes that reveal the quiet beauty of the place, most often set in the early morning or in the night. Having spent the whole night in the playground talking to his uncle, Wing, the protagonist in *Heartland*, makes his way home to the flat he shares with his mother:

> By the time he returned, the fluorescent lights were off. People were coming out of their homes in working clothes, slamming and locking their gates.
> For the first time, Wing noticed the rays of grand chrome yellow blushed across the face of his block, the tree and the roads, marking the start of the day. And with the coming of the light, the estate was crowned with a new and simple relevance.[43]

The sense that a communal rhythm is felt through an estate is also evoked in Colin Cheong's poem "Void Decks":

> Across the blocks the neighbours watch
> each other's lights flick on
> to check routines by another's timing
> when all agree that it is morning.[44]

The attention that is paid to the rhythm of life and the blocks of flats themselves in the HDB heartland is curious when the lack of representation of other public spaces that are associated with the masses in Singapore is borne in mind: the area with the highest density of white-collar workers in Singapore, the central commercial district with its towering corporate buildings; the many shopping malls along Orchard Road as well as in HDB town centres. The grasp of the local is less possible in such places where the global orientation of the city state is reflected in the international range of brands that are available in the shops and the number of multi-national corporations who occupy the offices along Shenton Way. In comparison with the old HDB estates, the buildings in the city centre reflect a different side of Singapore – one that is not close to the hearts of local writers and filmmakers it would seem. Perhaps there is a conscious censoring of the central city area because it manifests the global citizenship of Singapore much more powerfully than any sense of the local and the historic. Buildings, like old trees, can be tasked to reflect a nation's identity and history to its people. In a letter to the Forum page of *The Straits Times* (30 September 2002) John Ting K.C., the current president of the Singapore Institute of Architects, draws a comparison between Bilbao and Singapore: "Singapore should have had a number of such iconic buildings [like the Guggenheim Museum of Modern Art in Bilbao], which could become the talk of the world, attract hordes of tourists, revitalize the economy, and build hope in our community." The lack of "iconic buildings" that express Singaporean identity in the city centre has become a hot topic of discussion in recent years, as more and more buildings designed by foreign architects have been built since the late 1980s.[45] I. M. Pei's Raffles City, Philip Johnson's Millenia Walk, Kenzo Tange's UOB Plaza form a list that has seen most recently the addition of James Adam's Parkview Square, a building that some locals have nicknamed Gotham City Hall. The representations of the heartland by Singaporean writers and filmmakers paint a picture of the city-state outside of the city, rejecting its skyline of tall corporate buildings for that of uniform HDB blocks. The divide between city and heartland is made of certain erasures and elisions. Apart from the non-representation of distinctive city buildings, there also seems to be a lack of awareness or a forgetting of the fact that the two main government urban planning bodies in Singapore, the HDB and the URA, have been recruiting architects and planners from overseas since 1992 and 1989 respectively.[46] The expectation that the heartland should look local is seen in that representations of HDB estates are almost all based on flats built in the early stages of the public housing programme and flats that have not been upgraded since then. Upgraded flats "are given façades and other renovations gesturing towards a diverse range of architectural traditions: English Tudor, art deco, mission, classical republicanism and Chinese kitsch . . .".[47] Upgraded flats are almost never present in representations of HDB estates.

The heartland implies by its name that it is the core of Singapore. Geographically the heartland is spread out all over Singapore, but in its representations it is a space that denotes national and local identity beyond coordinates. It is an exclusionary space. Like the old tree in Changi that was felled, it is part of a myth of origins, of a belief that history and landscape that are exclusively Singaporean exist. They are nationalist narratives, taking on "the naiveté of nativity: the pure, true national story that is pure and true because it is native".[48] They are also narratives of how the "native" or the local is a vexed notion – that its presence is located in trees as well as in public housing estates says as much.

NOTES

1   I would like to thank John Phillips, Ryan Bishop, and Chua Beng-Huat for their comments on earlier drafts of this chapter.

2   The National Parks Board has decided to take DTZ-Debenham Tie Leung Property Management to court for flouting the Parks and Trees Act. If convicted, DTZ is liable for a fine of up to $10,000.

3   See http://www.nparks.gov.sg/nat_conv/nat_con-her_tre.shtml. Accessed on 26 November 2002.

4   Aihwa Ong, "Intelligent Island, Baroque Ecology" in this volume.

5   Tinsley, 37.

6   Véronique Sanson, *Gardens and Parks of Singapore* (New York: Oxford University Press, 1992), 17.

7   Ibid., 17. The durian trees are mentioned in R. Hanitsch, ed., "Letters of Nathaniel Wallich Relating to the Establishment of Botanical Gardens in Singapore", *Journal of the Malayan Branch of the Royal Asiatic Society* 42:1 (December 1969), 145–154; J. Bastin, "The Letters of Sir Stamford Raffles to Nathaniel Wallich 1819–1824", *Journal of the Malaysian Branch of the Royal Asiatic Society*, 54 (December 1981), 1–73.

8   Letter dated 2 November 1822. In R. Hanitsch, "Letters of Nathaniel Wallich relating the establishment of the Botanical Gardens in Singapore", *Journal of the Straits Branch, Royal Asiatic Society*, vol 65 (December 1913), 43. Cited in Yueh Siang Chang, *For the Glory of the Empire: The History of the Botanical Gardens in British Malaya* (BA Honours Thesis, National University of Singapore, 1999/2000), 18.

9   Hanitsch, 48. Cited in Chang, 21.

10 See Emma Reisz, "City as Garden: Shared Space in the Urban Botanic Gardens of Singapore and Malaysia, 1786–2000", in *Postcolonial Urbanism* (New York: Routledge, 2003), ed. by Ryan Bishop, John Phillips, and Wei-Wei Yeo, 105–122.

11 Hugh T. W. Tan and T. Morgany, *A Guide to Growing the Native Plants of Singapore* (Singapore: Singapore Science Centre, 2001), 16. 25.6 percent is the exact figure for the extinct native plants. 39.5 percent are now rare, 6.7 percent are considered endangered, and only 10.6 percent are common.

12 Leong Liew Geok, "Trees are only Temporary", in *No Other City: The Ethos Anthology of Urban Poetry* (Singapore: Ethos Books, 2000), ed. by Alvin Pang and Aaron Lee, 60.

13 "Trees are only Temporary", 60.

14 "Introduction", in *No Other City: The Ethos Anthology of Urban Poetry*, 23.

15 Ibid., 22.

16 Ibid., 23.

17 Topo Omoniyi, "Island in Verse: Constructing Identity from Singaporean Poetry", in *Interlogue: Studies in Singaporean Literature* (Singapore: Ethos Books, 1999), vol 2, ed. by Kirpal Singh, 52.

18 See ibid. For an official statement of this notion see the former National Arts Council chairman Tommy Koh's Foreword to *Journeys: Words, Home and Nation: Anthology of Singapore Poetry (1984–1995)* (Singapore: Unipress, 1995), ed. by Edwin Thumboo, Wong Yoon Wah, Ban Kah Choon, Naa Govindasamy, Shaharuddin Maaruf, Robbie

Goh, Petrina Chan, xxiii: "it is literature that gives the most comprehensive expression of both individual and collective life-experience of a people. And of literature, it is poetry that makes a special contribution through its reach, intensity, resonance and ways of seeing, remembering and capturing."

19 Gilles Deleuze and Felix Guattari, *A Thousand Plateaus: Capitalism and Schizophrenia* (London and Minneapolis: University of Minnesota Press, 1987), trans. by Brian Massumi, 5.

20 *A Thousand Plateaus*, 5.

21 *A Thousand Plateaus*, 6.

22 *The Silly Little Girl and the Funny Old Tree*, in *Images at the Margins: A Collection of Kuo Pao Kun's Plays* (Singapore: Times Media, 2000), 104.

23 This synonymity can also be found in English slang.

24 Goenawan Mohamad, "An Admiral, a General and a Notion of Home", in *Two Plays by Kuo Pao Kun: "Descendants of the Eunuch Admiral" and "The Spirits Play"*, ed. by C. J. W.-L. Wee and Lee Chee Keng (Singapore: SNP editions, 2003), 126.

25 *Two Plays by Kuo Pao Kun: "Descendants of the Eunuch Admiral" and "The Spirits Play"*, 38.

26 The phrase "cultural orphan" was coined by Kuo Pao Kun and used frequently in his writing outside of plays. See the interview with Kuo in *Interlogue: Studies in Singapore Literature* (Singapore: Ethos Books, 1998), ed. by Ronald D. Klein, 117.

27 *Zaijian, Selamat, Vanakkam* mean "farewell" in Mandarin, Malay, and Tamil. See *Two Plays by Kuo Pao Kun: "Descendants of the Eunuch Admiral" and "The Spirits Play"*, 66.

28 *Two Plays by Kuo Pao Kun: "Descendants of the Eunuch Admiral" and "The Spirits Play"*, 66.

29 Elizabeth Grosz, "The Natural in Architecture and Culture", in *Architecture from the Outside: Essays on Virtual and Real Space* (Cambridge, Mass.: MIT Press, 2001), 92.

30 *Two Plays by Kuo Pao Kun: "Descendants of the Eunuch Admiral" and "The Spirits Play"*, 54.

31 "General Introduction", *Journeys: Words, Home and Nation: Anthology of Singapore Poetry (1984–1995)*, xxvi.

32 A void deck is "the sheltered space in the ground floor of [a] block [of flats]. It is among the most frequently used public space in housing estates, since it is both a throughway and stopping place in a high-rise block. Its importance as a locale to residents is evident from the different types of people who frequently use it for a variety of activities; for example, for casual gatherings, festivals and rituals (weddings, funerals and religious rites) as well as activities organized by agencies (e.g. Residents' Committee gatherings)." See Ooi Giok Ling and Thomas T. W. Tan, "The Social Significance of Public Spaces in Public Housing Estates", in *Public Space: Design, Use and Management* (Singapore: Singapore University Press, 1992), 70.

33 "2 mothers in a h d b playground" by Arthur Yap in *Down the Line* (1980) is an early lonely instance.

34 "Preserve old flats and familiar sights to keep memories alive", *The Straits Times* (2 December 2002).

35 Daren Shiau, *Heartland,* 5. "Point block" flats refer to flats in which staircases provide access to only two units on each floor to allow for greater privacy, as opposed to staircases which access about ten units per floor, all linked by a common corridor. See C. W. Teh, "Public Housing in Singapore: An Overview", in *Public Housing in Singapore* (Singapore: Singapore University Press, 1975), ed. by S. H. K. Yeh, 1–21.

36 Since the early 1990s over 86 percent of the population has been housed in public housing. See *Singapore: A Developmental City State* (Sussex, England: John Wiley & Sons, 1997), ed. by Martin Perry, Lily Kong, and Brenda Yeoh, chap 8.

37 *The Straits Times* (2 December 2002).

38 Daren Shiau, *Heartland* (Singapore: SNP Editions, 1999), 30.

39 John Phillips, "Singapore Soil: A Completely Different Organisation of Space", in *Urban Space and Representation* (London: Pluto Press, 2000), ed. by Maria Balshaw and Liam Kennedy, 175–195.

40 See Chua Beng-Huat and Wei-Wei Yeo, "Singapore Cinema: Eric Khoo and Jack Neo – Critique from the Margins and the Mainstream", *Inter-Asia Cultural Studies*, 4(1), forthcoming.

41 "Eric Khoo: Dude in Toyland", *Big O* (March 1991), no. 63, p. 29.

42 Dave Chua, *Gone Case*, 139.

43 Daren Shiau, *Heartland*, 94–95.

44 Colin Cheong, "Void Decks", in *Void Decks and Other Empty Places* (Singapore: EPB, 1996), 1.

45 *The Straits Times* (30 September 2002).

46 "Foreign architects make their mark", *The Straits Times* (1 February 1998).

47 Robbie Goh, "Ideologies of 'Upgrading' in Singapore Public Housing: Post-modern Style, Globalisation and Class Construction in the Built Environment", *Urban Studies* 38:9 (2001), 1597.

48 Ryan Bishop, "Births of Nations: Narrativity, Nativity, Naivete, and Postcolonial Historical 'm'm'ry' in *Finnegans Wake* and *Shame*", in *Complicities: Connections and Divisions* (New York: Peter Lang, 2003), ed. by Robbie Goh, Rajeev Patke, and Chitra Sankaran. 107–118.

Chapter 3: Toward a Spatial History of Emergency: Notes from Singapore[1]

Gregory Clancey

I want to trace a relationship, as yet little examined, between architecture and the condition of emergency. I'll do so mainly from Singapore, where the nexus seems particularly compelling. It does not occur here uniquely, however, nor did it arise here originally. This essay will thus work its way back toward the city-state from distant but related places. My concerns are chiefly historical, because *emergency* bespeaks an event, and events are the peculiar province of history. *Emergency* cuts across *process* and *design* – or the *design process* – and shifts readily between the "natural" and the "man-made", the political and the personal, conditions subject to description and those which approach the sublime. It suggests the possibility of deception through the manipulation of speed. In these and other senses it seems very much a keyword for the modern condition.

THE EMERGENCY AND THE PLAN

Architecture, at first glance, seems far from the set of actions, emotions, and representations which cluster around *emergency*. In fact the two are rarely encountered in close proximity, at least in English sentences. The exceptions are *emergency shelter* and *emergency exit* and the set of catastrophes they anticipate. Accidents, moreover, are commonly located at the opposite pole – etymologically, spatially, and chronologically – from constructive acts. Architecture has had a more self-conscious relationship with monumentality, a condition that seeks to transcend the sudden and the temporary, and, more mundanely, requires long cycles of design and execution. But not even anti-monumental architecture has resorted to emergency as a semantic or theoretical inspiration. Modern architecture has been temporary, collapsible, transparent, and metabolic. But it's rarely been framed as arising, unexpectedly and disturbingly, outside of a normalized order of hierarchal relationships. In fact architecture normally constructs that order. Emergency calls it into question.

Architectural Modernism was a form of historical determinism which borrowed freely (yet selectively) from the language of Hegel, Marx, and Lenin. A central concept was *the plan*. In socialist discourse, History itself was a plan, segmented into world-changing events by *Five Year Plans* beginning with the original Soviet one of 1928. Long before socialism, however, *the plan* had existed as the most mundane of architectural objects – a drawing on paper – and this may be one reason so many young architects were instinctively drawn to Marxist-Leninist discourse, which is famously resplendent with architectural metaphors. Architectural Modernism might be seen, in fact, as the expansion of the 'normal' architectural practice of planning buildings into an enlarged (and charged) political space opened by the plan-laden language of twentieth-century socialism.

The plan (as *Five-Year Plan*, *Master Plan*, *Urban Plan*, etc.) was constructed as a rational, deliberate, and responsible answer to the chaos sprung from the self-interest that was capitalism. Given the current normalization of *planning* across corporations and bureaucracies of all types, it is hard to recapture the excitement which the concept of *the plan* still had as late as the 1960s, let alone its revolutionary, take-no-prisoners flavor in the 1920s and 1930s. One delegate to a 1968 housing conference in Singapore spoke of the need for *planification*, which, had it migrated from French to English, might have served as a descriptor for that era as *globalization* does ours.[2]

The plan, however, was the artifact of a global imaginary distinctly bipolar. While *the plan* had strong identification with the Left, the language of *emergency* and *crisis* was identified for most of the twentieth century with the Right. Indeed a common descriptor for the Right, among those of the Left, was *reaction*: a set of instinctive, if not panicked responses to the Left's deliberate emergence. Along a continuum ranging from politics to architecture to social science, *the plan* and *the emergency* were thus framed as antithetical in nature.[3] The one was destiny, the other desperation. The *productiveness* of emergency, or its incorporation into the plan – as in *emergency planning* – was a possibility (or condition in practice) long masked given their dichotomous political meanings.[4]

"The time of destruction is at an end" declared the De Stijl *Manifesto V* of 1923, "a new age is dawning: the age of construction".[5] How wrong they were. De Stijl can be forgiven for failing to predict the next war, but less so for masking the essential relationship between architectural design and demolition. It is architecture's problem that, alone among the arts, it needs to physically destroy in order to make. Paintings, sculpture, and music can be infinitely produced without disturbing existing objects. Buildings have to smother something, if only a patch of ground (but usually something more). Le Corbusier may have been the first to actively anticipate and expose the act of destruction which design presaged. His *Plan Viosin* of 1922–1925, which illustrated the obliteration of central Paris from aerial perspective, is only the most famous of many subsequent collages and drawings which unflinchingly dropped planned objects on already densely-built urban sites. Planning for some people was destined to be emergency for others.

HOUSING AS A CRISIS

Inordinately influenced by monumentality, the professional culture of architecture entered the twentieth century initially ill-prepared to face the condition of emergency. This is yet another way it differed from engineering, which was conceived and long nurtured under wartime conditions. It was architecture's twentieth-century encounter with *housing*, more than any other object-type, which brought that discipline into closer dialogue with the speed of *crisis*. The *housing crisis* (the quickened manifestation of the *housing problem*) was a something already out of control that required accelerated action to set right. *Housing* was also ubiquitous, and unbounded: a potential *tabula rasa* extending in an immense arc around the pinpoint monumental sites to which academic architecture had previously been restricted. It proved a wider target for an *avant-garde* with increased spatial ambitions.

An historic explanation for the *housing crisis* is that industrial capitalism created abysmal housing conditions for the poor which had to be mediated in the interests of social justice and stability. While the condition of injustice is beyond question, sensitive chroniclers of housing reform have recognized other controlling agendas.[6] It is perhaps futile to decide whether it was concern for the poor or fear of them which most fueled *housing reform*. It was clearly both. The act of demolishing a neighborhood and building a new one was often aggression and philanthropy as a continuous act. In any case, the *housing crisis* was an apt descriptor of both instincts.

The continuing ubiquity of obviously terrible living conditions in many parts of the world into the twenty-first century suggests we move cautiously in interpreting the *housing crisis* as something other than "real", and desperate. It is not to deny the reality of desperation, however, to be precise about the history of description, and particularly of those descriptions crafted by people who were not themselves desperate. Within the very substantial literature of the nineteenth- and twentieth-century *housing crisis*, it is surprisingly difficult to find the voices of its victims. Those in crisis emerge mainly as numbers: as quantities of the badly housed and properly re-housed. This is somewhat different from the literature on medical crises, in which people are not only diagnosed and handled (cordoned, disinfected, etc.), but suffer, die, flock to hospitals, and line up for inoculations; in which the subject of the victim is so very much *in action*. The housing crisis is more closely related in this sense to the *population crisis* – with which it was often explicitly linked, particularly in Asia[7] – than the crisis of an epidemic or an earthquake or war, each of which summons up (indeed often requires) full-blooded popular texts. As we'll subsequently see, however, *housing crisis* sometimes achieved an enhanced illustrative reality by co-opting other types of crisis narratives. The one original "popular" text of housing crisis may be the "before and after" set of photographs, in which the people in the "before" image often seem unaware that they exist in that chronological condition, and "after" is too often a shining kitchen with no one in it.

The commonly-told lesson in official histories of nations, municipalities, political parties, and housing boards that "people *demanded* better housing" is too rarely documented by the historical record which the *housing crisis* itself produced. In labor history accounts of poor people rallying together in the nine-teenth and twentieth centuries to demand change, a need for different housing is not something that commonly receives articulation (as opposed to a reduction in rents, or the ability to keep the house one had).[8] In some of the bloodiest labor actions in the United States – and America has one of the bloodiest strike histories in the developed world – the discontented marched out of "model" industrial villages like Pullman, Illinois, filled with comparatively well-built houses.[9] The same was apparently true in the Welsh coalfields.[10] Exceptions exist: Peter Marcuse has described mass rallies around housing issues in interwar Vienna.[11] But overall, radical protest by the poor or working class has too rarely coincided with the poor condition of their housing – as poor as that often was – in a way that would give the *housing crisis* a believable subaltern voice.

Why then, when so few poor people articulated a demand for "better housing", was housing so often provided by twentieth-century political parties and bureaucracies when so many other articulated wants – especially higher wages and increased degrees of control over self and community – were withheld? The question suggests its own answer. Housing was a "good" (as in both "goods" and a moral good) whose provision may have been safely offered precisely because it was not clearly demanded. It was a compromise between the demand for social and economic justice on the part of the poor, and the demand of governments that they decide which *concrete forms* justice take. As both a metaphor and a technology, *concrete* was the agreed-upon compromise solution across many twentieth-century jurisdictions. It had the virtues of being material, of creating value, of creating monuments, and of allowing one to keep track of others through the payment of rents and mortgages. This by no means exhausts the list, and clearly philanthropy was mixed in (sometimes), as was, less often, an element of self-help.

An ambiguous politics was one of the major strengths of the *housing crisis*: its ability to bridge otherwise contradictory political programs and instincts. Marx wrote little about housing, but *housing reform* became a favorite of social democratic parties because it appealed to the middle-class attachment to property and stability. It could be sold to more monied classes as a way of ameliorating the condition of the poor without disrupting the regular functioning of industrial capitalism.[12] It could be done, so to speak, 'off to the side' of the capitalist economy, and, if correctly managed, deliver it direct benefits. It demanded only the sacrifice of urban landlords, the lowest and weakest rung of the capitalist ladder (and the one arguably most despised by the poor).[13] Industrial capitalists, on the other hand, were among the major inventors of reform housing models. "Industrial housing" adjacent to plants – a common feature of modern factory landscapes from the early nineteenth century – is an object-type whose historical relationship to political housing reform has too often been obscured.

For many poor people around the world over the last century and a half, the *housing crisis* actually became most real through the ceremony of eviction or demolition, sometimes as part of a larger campaign of compulsory re-housing. The experience of eviction/demolition and relocation better fits the sense of the word *crisis* – a sudden, unexpected, and powerful event which threatens one's well-being or survival. And here the voice of the subaltern has often spoken, in the body language of his/her resistance to moving. By this definition, *housing crisis* is one of the most persistent trans-national experiences of the twentieth century, but one greatly under-chronicled by the century's historians.[14]

For one thing, the ceremony of eviction produces relatively few records. Both in spite of and because of its shocking reality, there are shockingly few images, either graphic or narrative, of even the largest and most sustained of the world's many modern clearance campaigns.[15] This absence of image-making seems often to have had an element of planning. Photographs of destroyed buildings are dwarfed in the historical economy of images by photographs of newly-finished ones, which literally cover and render invisible sites of often forced removal.

HOUSING CRISIS AND WAR EMERGENCY

I've suggested that the discipline of architecture first encountered – and helped perpetuate – the modern condition of emergency in its targeting of *housing*. But there were related vectors. One was war. In the course of the twentieth century, the *housing crisis* developed an affinity with the *war emergency*, and both with architecture, which has gone largely unremarked.[16] Housing reform indeed became most visible in the twentieth century in the context of armed conflict, and in what Paul Virilio has called, in another context, "the passage from wartime to the war of peacetime".[17]

When Le Corbusier wrote polemics against war, he was still writing positively about a distinctively wartime condition: *mobilization*. In that he was a man of his time. Twentieth-century city planning, which almost by necessity meant city-destruction and city-rebuilding on an unprecedented scale, helped to bring the languages of architectural and military action into close convergence:

> The mobilization of the land, the people, and the means of production in order to realize the plan . . . Equipment: the word of command, armaments, machines, and circulation, discipline? EXACTLY THE SAME AS FOR THE WAGING OF WAR.[18]

Kenneth Frampton refers to this as a *pacifist mobilization*.[19] In modern war, civilian populations were mobilized to fight, produce, escape, or be killed. In modern architecture, the same populations were mobilized to vacate or occupy. Architecture indeed developed many of its new forms and patronages in war- and post-war zones.[20] Total war production required huge displacements of civilians and thus intensely accelerated evacuations and occupations. Almost half of the American population is estimated to have changed locations during the Second World War and its immediate aftermath (and there was no actual fighting in America).[21] In the wake of twentieth-century wars, returning soldiers had also earned a warrior right to be re-housed (or such a right was suggested to them by new political programs).

To continue with the American case, the first re-housing of citizens by the state occurred congruently with First World War mobilization. Colonial-style brick towns, complete with church and central square, were produced under the heading *war emergency housing* by the Emergency Fleet and US Housing Corporations. *War worker* was the original category of person to be housed by government policy. This was also the case in wartime Britain.[22] The second and more extensive mobilization of residents by the American state occurred through the Federal Emergency Administration of Public Works during the inter-war depression. Now the categories eligible for re-housing expanded from war-related labor to armies of the unemployed, although it was the need to employ, more than the will to re-house, which actually drove the program. Through state incentives to suburbanization in the Cold War period, such as the Defense Highway Act and the GI Bill, re-housing was eventually extended to a middle class newly reconceived as *war veterans*. The same Defense Highway Act obliterated acres of poor and minority neighborhoods, resulting in large-scale compulsory re-housing in segregated conditions.[23] The point of this thumbnail sketch (which admittedly leaves out the economics as econometric accounts edit out the martial) is that declarations of emergency by the State (whether military, or economic, or both) came to be consistent preludes to new mobilizations of designers, builders, writers, photographers, and populations newly eligible for (or subject to) re-housing. By the Second World War, and into the Cold War, the process had been institutionalized, and thus regularized, and eventually rendered a part of everyday life.[24]

It's true that many architects who worked inside *emergency housing* regimes, whether in the US, Britain, the USSR, Japan, Finland, or Singapore, were never fully comfortable there despite the massively increased opportunities for employment. Tension often arose because of architects' continuing loyalty to *the plan*. For studio-trained architects, *the plan* meant thought and creativity, which required care, resources, and above-all time. But the logic of emergency, which had made States suddenly interested in *planning* (and in employing large numbers of architects) often increased speed and scale to the point where other values in architect culture were alienated and threatened. Architects (at least famous ones) regularly stormed away from re-housing regimes. Yet not before providing many of the necessary prototypes.

If we organize the *history of housing* by form, as is typical, then it seems so multifarious as to defy description. If we organize it as a series of social and political thrusts and parries (and by people who were themselves already well-housed) then it begins to have a more fundamental relationship with historical events. There is a social category especially close to the word *housing* which remains under-defined and under-noticed: poor people who have been coercively de-housed, and/or re-housed at some point in their lives (or at many). This category of person, though existing throughout time, has a special relationship with the twentieth century, where violence targeted and smashed through the previous safety of homes on scales unimaginable to previous eras. If the *history of housing* shifts its attention from forms, often bereft of people, to the drama of mass-scale de-housings and re-housings (and the prefixes are important because everyone is housed somewhere originally) then it necessarily becomes something violent and anxious as well as hopeful and consuming, something to do with justice and injustice and the often hurried assembly of one's possessions.

HOUSING CRISIS AND NATURAL DISASTER

A last understudied link I want to make, before turning to Singapore, is that between *housing crisis* and *natural disaster*. From nearly its beginning, housing reform had a close relationship with fire (combustibility) and epidemics (contagion), but actually with a whole flexible list of susceptibilities to pathological events strategically located in nature. Thus originally it was the expertise of the doctor – that arch-responder to emergency, and a direct mediator between society and nature – rather than that of the architect, which was most often called upon in the event of *housing crisis*.[25] Indeed it was public health officials, who, well into the twentieth century in Britain and elsewhere, normally performed the ritual of condemning inhabited houses and neighborhoods to demolition.

The link between *housing reform* and *emergency medicine* is well-documented. Less so is the convergence between housing and the more heroic (and theatrical) realm of *emergency rescue*. The first state re-housing agency in Japan, the *Dojunkai*, was established in the aftermath of the Tokyo earthquake and fire of 1923. *Fire victim* was thus the first category of person susceptible to state re-housing in Japan. This linkage between the housing crisis and crises of nature soon converged with that of war. Twentieth-century war would not only create many *fire victims*, but the language and forms of *civil emergency* and *war emergency* would increasingly become interchangeable, so that natural and human causes would form continuous sets of explanations.[26] As the geographers of emergency Zelinsky and Kosinski have put it: "during the course of the (twentieth) century, the universe of disasters has increasingly come to form a single interactive system."[27]

SINGAPORE IN A STATE OF RE-HOUSING

Having introduced a set of working theoretical concerns – really generalizations drawn from a myriad of empirical studies – I want to turn to Singapore as one place where the *housing crisis* played out in time. The *local* story of Singapore's re-housing might be productively set, I'll argue, in a wider historical and spatial context of emergency conditions characteristic of the last century. And by the same token, a wider spatial history of emergency, if such is narratable, must inevitably chart Singapore as an important, perhaps crucial, site.

Singapore is one of few nations in the world to have re-housed virtually its entire population in one sustained, if lengthy, campaign. In 1960, one year after the start of self-rule, the government began relocating its poorer citizens from squatter camps, rural villages (called *kampungs*) and inner-city slums with unusual speed and single-mindedness. By 1965, almost twenty-five percent of the island's population was living in government-built high-rise housing estates, a figure unparalleled in Asia. By 1974 the proportion was forty-three percent, exceeding rates of state-managed re-housing anywhere in the world (the only comparative figures being from the nearby colony of Hong Kong). At this moment in time (the mid-1970s), when mass public re-housing policies began to be questioned or abandoned elsewhere, Singapore's program not only survived but accelerated. By 1989, eighty-seven percent of the nation's citizens lived in housing estates built and in most cases administered by the state.[28]

There is a very large literature on what this most total of national re-housings means, the tone of its discussion ranging from the cautiously celebratory to the Machiavellian. None of it, however, is dismissive. There is wide recognition that HDB (Housing Development Board) housing was the foundational infrastructure on which the rest of modern Singapore was subsequently built. Its close identification with the PAP (People's Action Party) state – monumentally and instrumentally – gives Singapore's housing a political significance, for many commentators, comparable to that of the *Wohnhofe* of Red Vienna or the *projects* of New Deal America. It has an inescapable attraction, to many, as a metaphor for control (although the widespread individual ownership of units through 99-year leases raises issues of clientage as much as coercion).[29] Singapore's re-housing also holds deep fascination, given its near-totality and longevity, for students of social process, model-builders, and statisticians. HDB personnel have themselves presented Singapore's infrastructure to overseas audiences as "an urban laboratory unique in the world . . . [because] people are housed on a massive scale in a high-rise, high-density environment".[30] To Rem Koolhaas, the program of this laboratory represents, "the ideological production of the past three decades in its pure form uncontaminated by surviving contextual remnants". But as Koolhaas concedes elsewhere in his sparkling text, Singapore's HDB is deeply grounded in a mid-twentieth-century planning ideology, a "contextual remnant" which has little stake in revealing its own historicity.[31]

Treating HDB housing as a "process" can too easily obscure its identity as a series of events. My purpose in this section and those which follow is to re-excavate its *event-ness,* not only to provide "context", but to write it into other, more event-laden narratives. When Singapore's re-housing took wing in the 1960s, it was one act of a complex and highly spatial political drama which included street riots, detentions, the city's merger with Malaya, the city's "eviction" from Malaysia, and the eventual consolidation of Singapore as a tightly demarcated one-party state. All of this occurred in just a single decade, and most of it before the completion of the HDB's original Five-Year Plan. But the re-housing of that decade had a history as well as a future, one widely understood at the time but forgotten in many contemporary accounts. In Singapore, as elsewhere, *the plan* and *the emergency* had a more than intimate relationship.

The first Five-Year Plan (1960–1965) saw the socialist leadership of the PAP government fighting for its life against the party's communist faction, whose major strength lay in the slums of the center city (Chinatown), and the rural *kampungs* and squatter communities that ringed it. "Radical left-wing organizations", pointed out one contemporary observer, were "firmly woven into the fabric of slum life".[32] Such was the urban fabric targeted for early clearance and resettlement.[33] In the course of the 1960s the ruling People's Action Party split, the dominant Lee Kwan Yew faction taking full and permanent control of the state, and the communists forming a separate party (the *Barisan Socialis*) which was run to ground by the end of the decade. Throughout this period of struggle, and well into the 1970s when politics had all but ceased, the poorer areas of the island were systematically cleared (or "decanted", to use a contemporary descriptor) and their residents relocated to high-rise HDB housing estates.

It would be far too simplistic to portray the HDB as a winnowing tool designed to cut down political opponents. For one thing, the PAP government clearly took a political risk in dislocating people who had the ability not only to resist (as some did), but to vote. Indeed over the long run, the government would tie its fate quite closely to its ability to provide an ever-increasing standard of living, a "standard" largely set by the infrastructure of HDB housing.[34] The "risk" of mobilization was, in that and other senses, carefully calculated. Dramatic and overwhelming acts of re-housing have always had the potential to at least divide, perhaps neutralize, and at best co-opt. Given the socialist credentials of *housing reform*, re-housing could not be effectively opposed by the PAP's communist opponents except in matters of detail (particularly, it turns out, in the uprooting of farmers). Communism as an ideology lacked arguments against the movement of people from slums, villages, and squatter camps to high-rise (high-tech) housing, especially when presented as a planned *developmental process* transcending the immediate logic of capitalism.

In Singapore, the Cold War term "hearts and minds" is commonly used, even today, to describe the parts of the citizen which the government feels compelled to capture and hold. But the act of re-housing was so very bodily, the physical movement and re-containment of hundreds of thousands of bodies whose hearts and minds, at least initially, lay unrevealed. These bodies were with some risk set in motion – "a population movement on the scale of an exodus" in the words of one academic who chronicled the phenomenon in 1965.[35] But the motion had already received its direction, and at least some of its momentum, before the coming to power of the PAP. This citizen mobilization originated not in the policies of Singapore's post-colonial government, but in British policies enacted under a late-colonial *state of emergency*.

THE MALAYAN EMERGENCY AND SINGAPORE'S IMPROVEMENT

Emergency has, of course, an explicitly political meaning: i.e. the suspension of civil liberties during a government crack-down on internal dissent. *States of emergency* are popularly associated with Third World dictatorships, but they are in fact equally British. In the British Empire which re-emerged stumbling and vulnerable from the Second World War, *emergencies* had soon to be declared from Palestine, to India, to Kenya, to Nyasaland, the internal equivalents of international *crises*. The counter-insurgency campaigns which they signaled had been pioneered in pre-war Ireland and, before that, South Africa, although the use of the term *emergency* – rather than *war* or *rebellion* – only became general in the self-consciously "back to normal" conditions following the Second World War.[36] Emergency indeed constructs *normality* the way *war* constructs *peace*. While war and peace are mutually exclusive, however, and thus chronological, the strategy (or hope) behind colonial emergencies seems to have been that they would be *synchronic* with normality, in the manner of policing. The longest and most contested of these synchronic states – referred to in much of the literature simply as *The Emergency* – happened in Malaya (including Singapore) between 1948 and 1960.

Being campaigns against popular insurgencies, emergencies necessarily developed an intimate relationship with houses – as structures in which hostile populations lived and insurgents found shelter. In full-scale war, houses are treated, symbolically and semantically at least, as objects to be incidentally swept around or through by invading armies intent on taking more monumental sites. In truth, of course, large numbers of houses have been deliberately targeted for destruction by aerial bombing for as long as that strategy has existed. In politico-military *emergencies*, however, houses have played a more public or self-consciously strategic role, because the unit of concern is a *population* conceived of as *households*. Thus did the British army in colonized Ireland begin targeting and blowing up specific houses at one point as a retaliation for the killing of soldiers, and the IRA in turn blew up two houses owned by Loyalists for every one dynamited by the British. So did there begin a series of ceremonial retaliations against houses in the British Empire that continues to this day in places like Israel/Palestine, at least partly conditioned by colonial-period emergency strategies.[37] The *architectural* character of political emergencies, one might argue, came to be defined by the house. Its most dramatic manifestation was the *forced re-housing* of entire civilian populations.

The Malayan Emergency involved one of the greatest forced re-housings in the history of modern colonialism, or for that matter in the history of East and Southeast Asia. In the twelve years of The Emergency, close to a million people, most of them Chinese "squatters", were resettled under military supervision in over 600 *new villages* in all parts of the peninsula (though not in Singapore itself). The motto of the campaign, according to one of its historians, was "speed at any cost", and its character was "the wholesale and occasionally forcible resettlement of frightened, largely alien populace into hastily-contrived barbed-wire enclosures". In one year alone, 1951, close to 400,000 people were re-housed in 350 new containments.[38] An additional 600,000 were ultimately "regrouped" (re-housed in new, defensible areas) on rubber estates and mining camps.[39] This emergency re-housing campaign came to be known, after its military author General Harold Briggs, as *The Briggs Plan*.

Although "the actual process of moving was unpleasant and distressing", in the words of an historian not unsympathetic to the project, the re-housed were given "title" (10- to 99-year leases) on their new land, and provided with schools, medical clinics, and even electricity tapped from generators whose principal purpose was to power searchlights.[40] Most of the re-housed were also re-categorized in the course of their move from "agriculturalists" to "wage-laborers", an identity which stuck because the re-housing coincided with a rubber and tin boom linked to the Korean War.[41] Thus, although military strategy drove the project throughout, it could also be presented as *developmental*. General Sir Gerald Templar's coining of the term *new villages* (to replace *resettlement camps*) in 1952 semantically linked the containments to the physically very different *new towns* then being erected throughout Britain.[42]

The same year that Emergency was declared in Malaya (1948), an accelerated campaign of slum clearance and attendant re-housing began in Singapore, then Malaya's principle port, and the largest concentration of overseas Chinese in Southeast Asia.[43] Action in Singapore (a separately-administered colony) was not carried out under the new banner of *emergency*, however, but a pre-existing one of *improvement*.[44] The Singapore Improvement Trust (SIT)[45] promised that the initial demolition of 102 dwellings and shops was "only the first installment of a program for dealing with all such slum properties".[46] In 1949, 1,207 families were evicted from Upper Nankin Street, one of the most crowded areas of Chinatown, and the SIT announced the following year that Chinatown itself was "scheduled for demolition".[47] Chinatown was not the only site to be targeted; one British report estimated that as much as a third of the total population of Singapore were "squatters" requiring eventual relocation.[48] In 1951, the year the British governor of Malaya was assassinated by communist guerillas, and the most intensive year of resettlement on the Malayan peninsula, the Improvement Trust began building nine-story slab-blocks, prototypes for what would become Singapore's dominant house-form.[49] In 1952, the Trust partitioned to become a "development authority", anticipating the post-independence HDB.[50]

As its improvement campaign accelerated, however, the SIT began to face stubborn resistance from squatters, some of them organized into an "Attap Dweller's Association" (*attap* being the large palm leaves traditionally used to roof farmhouses, as thatch was used in Britain). The showpiece of the British program, the *new town* of Queenstown with its fourteen-story tower blocks (the blocks increased in height on an almost yearly basis), had "come to a standstill" by 1954 "because of the difficulty of removing attap dwellings". Work at the site was "immobilized" according to the SIT, by "the reluctance of 266 families to accept the very reasonable conditions of resettlement", which involved removal to a relatively remote part of the island.[51] By the following year, 1955, "it was practically impossible to find sites for public buildings that were not encumbered with clusters of attap dwellings or agricultural settlers" and the entire island-wide re-housing program began to critically slow.[52] One senses from this and related passages that it was not just a problem of "clearing" existing settlements, but stemming a vigorous movement that was continuing to occupy vacant land. "There is a constant threat of new structures", reported the SIT in 1959; "it is only with extreme vigilance that the inspectorate assisted by the watchmen are able to detect and demolish new structures".[53] The "squatters", in other words, were in the midst of their own *housing reform movement*, which involved building or expanding single-family houses on land the British had slated for high-rises. And all of this was occurring, at least from 1954, against a larger backdrop of anti-colonial protests, strikes, and riots, which the authorities were attempting to contain through a gradually-expanding electoral process.

By the mid-1950s the British had been forced to change tactics, paying compensation and establishing a new Resettlement Department within the SIT, partly staffed by "resettlement inspectors" from Malaya.[54] The model of the Malayan Emergency's *new villages* (which had themselves begun as *resettlement camps*) was now to be exported more directly to Singapore as an alternative to high-rise *new towns*. The matter was so politically sensitive that in 1958 the Resettlement Department, alone among the seven departments of the SIT, was made an agency of the colonial government, in order to subject each clearance action to political vetting. Yet squatter resistance still arises continually in the SIT's late-colonial reports as "an extremely difficult problem", with inspectors "intimidated in the execution of their duties and enforcement of instructions becom[ing] a dangerous process". Even the attendance of police constables at the serving of demolition orders was sometimes "insufficient in the first instance to prevent a disturbance of the peace".[55] This willingness to resist offered one major contrast to the campaign in Malaya, where resettlement had been conducted as an overtly military action backed by the threat of overwhelming force and the possibility of deportation. In Singapore, the presence of associations, landowners, politicians (communist and non-communist), and the growing anti-colonial street actions encouraged squatter communities to sometimes stand up to the police.[56]

The British stopped the process altogether in advance of the landmark 1959 elections to, in the SIT's own words "prevent disturbance and maintain good public relations".[57] With the election of the PAP government, however, and the beginning of the end of colonial rule, the English-language *Straits Times* was certain that the squatter problem was finally on the verge of being solved:

> Squatters and other resistance to site-clearing has been a serious brake on at least two years of SIT endeavor . . . this [PAP] government is strong enough to take obstacles of this nature in its stride.[58]

Indeed it would prove to be.

Links between the various "emergency" re-housings in Southeast Asia (and one might include the subsequent one in South Vietnam, which was based partly on the example of Malaya) have rarely been drawn. It may be that the resulting building forms seem so various (*new towns* of high-rise flats in Singapore v. *new villages* of simple wooden houses in Malaya), or that the overtly military and colonial identity of the Malayan project seems dissimilar to the political (and partly post-colonial) character of the Singaporean one.[59] Many details indeed differed, as did outcomes. Yet the rolling emergency re-housing on the Malayan peninsula shared a common context – the Cold War – as well as a common subject or target – Chinese "squatters" (and slum-dwellers in the Singaporean case) whose natural sympathies were believed to lie with the militant left.

In fact the geography of re-housing campaigns in East and Southeast Asia is largely the geography of the post-war British Empire in crisis – perhaps a set of local crises each with their own peculiarities, but commonly conceived by policy-makers as generated by events in China. The massive re-housing of the Malayan Chinese population in The Emergency can be taken as the first example. The second is the Emergency-period work of the Singapore Improvement Trust, from which the HDB directly evolved. The third is the re-housing program in Hong

Kong, which came to rival the efforts of Singapore, and was directly responsive to the crisis of war refugees and the delicate diplomatic relationship with the mainland.[60] All of these projects began in earnest in the late 1940s or early 1950s. In the rest of East and Southeast Asia, with the exception of wartime Vietnam, government re-housing was pursued much less insistently, or affected far fewer people. Japan, which was never colonized, likewise remained ambivalent about bureaucratic schemes to directly re-house large segments of its population. Communist (and Nationalist) China had other priorities. When "squatters" were re-housed elsewhere in Asia – the Philippines, Thailand, Korea, and Indonesia – it was normally to move them out of the way of development projects (which became a key component of the Singaporean re-housing as well, but was not its original motive).[61] Mass re-housing was thus not a ceremony indigenous to East and Southeast Asia, despite its present association with the region. It was a European one, first deployed in Asia at a specific time, in specific circumstances, and among a particular category of British subject.

The 1950s was also a decade when the British metropole, under both Labour and Conservative governments, was re-housing its own population to a degree unprecedented in the West or even the communist world, under a planning regime inherited from the Second World War. What was happening on the Malayan peninsula, the site of Britain's "dollar arsenal", thus made sense from the standpoint of contemporary British domestic politics. When Harold Wilson tried to convince other Labour leaders to delay the British military pullout from Singapore in 1966, he cited Lee Kwan Yew's credentials as a houser, saying "his social record, in his housing programme for example, defies challenge in anything that has been done in the most advanced social democratic communities".[62] Indeed, in the matter of housing, Lee would surpass the Europeans.

Yet this project of challenging, if not surpassing, European re-housing goals began in Singapore under British governors-general. By the time Singapore achieved self-rule, in 1959, almost ten percent of its population had already been re-housed by the colonial administration, a figure then uniquely large either in Asia or the colonized world.[63] In fact, only in select municipalities of Europe itself had such figures been achieved before the late 1950s. Frankfurt's famous housing program under the Weimar Republic affected only eleven percent of that city's population.[64] The government of "Red Vienna" managed to house the same percentage. This achievement of British colonial re-housing has been largely underrated because the post-colonial HDB took the project so much further, numerically speaking. The colonial project also came to be ritualistically denigrated by its post-colonial successor for "failing to meet its targets", etc. and for demonstrating the "neglectful" attitude of the British compared to the caring attitude of their successors.[65] In truth, however, the British were hampered from driving harder by opposition from below.

What most unifies the *new villages* of the Malayan Emergency and Singapore's *new towns* is the identity of the re-housed and the act of their mobilization. The dramatic difference in the forms of the Malayan villages and the Singaporean housing estates mask what were actually great similarities in the forms of the pre-existing settler communities cleared in the two places. Indeed they were hardly "two places" except in the strictest of political senses. Some of the most intensive and extensive resettlement of squatters into *new villages* occurred in the Malayan province of Johor, just across the causeway from Singapore.[66]

The coercive nature of much of the re-housing, the extension of "title" (99-year leases) to the relocated, the emphasis on getting the population "inside the wire" (the element of speed) in order to "drain the communist swamp", the near totality of the program, and the re-categorization of the re-housed from subsistence farmers to wage laborers were all elements of the Malayan Emergency which would find some degree of reflection in Singapore's improvement campaign, which entered its final form (the first Five-Year Plan of the post-colonial government) the year that the official emergency was declared at an end.

"SQUATTING" AS EMERGENCY RESPONSE

The term "squatter" evokes (and designedly so) the image of someone inert, and thus needful of being set in motion. An official account of Singaporean squatters from 1968 paints "the far too familiar picture of an inert community who would not think of moving from their unpleasant and dangerous surroundings until a disaster makes the decision for them".[67] There is much circumstantial evidence, however, that squatter communities in what the British termed the "Black Belt" around the central city, were actually the result of a spontaneous (yet fully conscious, and not irrational) movement from the "unpleasant and dangerous surroundings" of Chinatown in the brief period between the Japanese collapse and the re-imposition of authority by the British.[68] They were themselves an *emergency response*, in other words, and perhaps an opportunistic one as well; a seizure of more space and slightly better living conditions by occupying and erecting shelter on vacant land temporarily unguarded.[69]

The same text which describes squatters as an "inert community" elsewhere admits that most such settlements "sprung up after the Japanese occupation".[70] Historian Paul Kratoska's research on Malaya during the war and immediate post-years suggests that the Japanese colonizers indeed gave squatting an impetus, indirectly through their draconian control over food supplies (yet *laissez-faire* attitude toward property rights), and more directly through the forced resettlement of some urban-dwellers in new agricultural villages. People took (or were taken) to the countryside on the city's fringes, or even well beyond, in order to grow their own food. Others actually came into the city from the countryside in order to join the rationing system (from which the countryside was excluded), presumably joining urban squatter settlements.[71] The labeling of squatter communities in subsequent accounts as relics of the Japanese occupation, however, was meant to construct their abnormal nature, and thus suggest post-war *re*settlement as a natural response.

Squatting in the twentieth century often converged with warfare, and both with political re-housing campaigns. Besides post-Second World War Singapore, another site where this convergence was particularly marked was post-First World War Vienna. Recent scholarship on the famous re-housing campaign in "Red Vienna" stresses its beginnings in the out-migration of hungry people in the aftermath of military collapse. Viennese constructed "wild settlements" (*wilde* being the ironically opposite-sounding Austro-German synonym for the English *squat*) around the activity of survival gardening.[72] The fate of the squatters under the two postwar governments differed, however. In Vienna, many were allowed to stay on the land they'd occupied, and worked alongside local politicians and progressive architects to make a *fait accompli* into a *status quo*. The political identity of the squatter communities was always contestable – were they "wild" radicals (because of their squatting) or petit-bourgeois (because of the little houses they built)? – but the city nonetheless distributed building materials.[73] In British and post-British Singapore, the premium was on clearing squatter communities entirely, as they were cast by the authorities as illegitimate (and thus monstrous) products of war. Another difference was that in Vienna the subsequent urban re-housing program was made with the intention of lowering working-class rents, often drastically.[74] In Singapore, rents were almost always increased, the intention being to reconstruct "underemployed" squatters as a rent-paying working class.[75]

The war-time squatter settlements in both Vienna and Singapore, far from being pathological, were a rational response to crisis through 'self-help'. Marcuse calls Vienna's wild settlements "probably the most widespread example of physical self-help in the twentieth century in an industrialized nation".[76] In "developing" nations, of course, self-help of this sort is a standard developmental strategy of the poor. Because we cannot know the full set of feelings people experienced in becoming squatters, we cannot impose upon them, at least without evidence gleaned from them, a sense of tragedy or despair. We do not have a squatter discourse which is as coherent or powerful as that of the legally-housed classes who defined and managed the "squatter" identity. The fragmental evidence we do have suggests, in Singapore and elsewhere (though not everywhere), a strong community sense, determination, and an active marshaling of resources in the midst of emergency conditions.[77]

Squatter settlements were also vernacular architecture.[78] They cannot be defined merely by what they lack or lacked (the familiar litany of "toilets, electricity, tap-water", etc.). That they lacked these things was partly the result of their being construed as "temporary" (and alien) by those who controlled technological systems and determined where and on what terms these would be extended. Spontaneous settlements (a term increasingly used in preference to "squatter settlements" from the 1970s onward) were sites in which people, however poor, became architects of at least their immediate surroundings, and were not under compulsion to explain or justify their own architecture to anyone in particular. It was this, as much as anything, which made them "wild".[79]

Such settlements also constructed for many of their vulnerable inhabitants a sense of security lacking in other environments. In his study of Hong Kong's spontaneous settlements in the 1960s, anthropologist Otto Golger found crime rates to be lower there than in the rest of the city, and mortality rates virtually the same (but much lower than in "resettlement areas" the government provided). "Low living standards and bad housing can be coped with", Golger noted, "as long as the individual or group is an integral part of [settlement] society." There was also considerable variety in building types. While some dwellings were badly-built huts, others had porches, and some "the appearance of weekend houses, solidly built and cleanly kept". The greatest bane of Hong Kong's squatters was not their own existence, but the threat of the government bringing it to an end. "No fear is more widespread", he wrote, "than finding oneself forced out of a condemned building."[80]

CLEARANCE

At least through the end of its first Five-Year Plan, the PAP government faced squatter resistance seemingly indistinguishable in scope and character to that faced by the British. In Singapore newspaper accounts of the great post-colonial clearances of the 1960s, this resistance was quite prominently reported as constituting "a major obstacle" to redevelopment plans.[81] Compensation had to be increased in 1964. "Under the new plan", wrote the *Straits Times*, "there will be no room left for pro-Communist elements to instigate the farmers and the squatters against the government", echoing words the British had themselves used after beginning the compensation program seven years before.[82] Work on the huge Tao Payoh satellite town, one of the largest in the world, had "been blocked because of organized resistance and obstruction instigated by pro-Communist elements" according to a press report of 1965, but "this organized obstruction", the paper went to on to say, "has now disappeared".[83] Indeed, reported acts of resistance become more fragmented and less frequent under the second Five-Year Plan, although the scale of the resettlement had vastly increased. The HDB was becoming a well-oiled re-housing machine.

Resisting squatters were never assumed in written accounts to be acting in their own interests, but generally as dupes of "agitators", "people out for mischief", "pro-Communist elements", or, in one colorful phrase, "evil-wishers".[84] Indeed, the re-housed's small and ineffectual acts of resistance were seen almost exclusively in party political terms – as the clash of two incommensurable ideologies backed by trained and committed cadres – and never as the legitimate concerns of powerless people faced with the emergency of displacement.

In the West, Modernist multi-story housing was generally associated by both its proponents and detractors with communalism. The prototype slab-blocks were developed, after all, by Left-leaning architects in the spirit of "world war against the domination of the individual", to return again to the language of De Stijl. In the United States, whose powerful real-estate interests felt deeply threatened by New Deal public housing, the equation of multi-family blocks with "communism" was perhaps most persistent, and ultimately effective in limiting their "spread" (and crippling their design and management). That the earliest housing estates in Europe were sponsored by socialist parties added to the sense that the slab-block was the physical expression of communal ideals, while the single-family house was its opposite – the natural container of individualist, bourgeois values.

Given the popularity of this perception, the relative absence of expressions of social collectivism in Modernist architectural manifestos, compared to their enthusiastic discussions of the *dwelling* and its bio-inhabitant, can come as startling. Modern architecture shared with many governments a deep aversion to *the street*, on which crowds gathered. Beaux-Arts architecture, ironically, may have been the true architecture of revolution, with its large squares and broad avenues which channeled crowds directly toward palaces. Modernist slab-blocks with green spaces between them eliminated all focal points that a crowd might gravitate toward – all possibility of identifying an architectural target for the redress of grievance. Had they been designed by capitalists or colonels, Gropius' slab-blocks and Le Corbusier's towers in a park could not have more strongly symbolized the curtailment of revolution. Socialism had been born in crowded conditions – the street, the tenement, and the dormitory – and, in order to continually recreate itself, it needed to architecturally reproduce community. In that it largely failed. In making the *housing cell* the *nucleus of town planning*, CIAM's Charter of Athens of 1933 forgot that the street and the square, not the house, was the natural environment for the politics of progressive reform. The *cell* was also the nucleus of the prison. By the time the Left "took to the streets" of Singapore in a last bid for power in the mid and late-1960s, "the street" was in the process of disappearing.

Singapore's multi-story housing of the 1960s was purposely anti-communal. Although there were many ritualistic references to "building new communities" in early HDB literature, the far more urgent problem was the breaking up of an existing communalism seen to be identical with slums, *kampungs*, and squatter camps (all composed of single-family dwellings). The HDB's policy of purposely mixing "races" in housing estates and even individual buildings has been well-documented and well-discussed.[85] But this policy of mixing extended also to pre-existing communities of the same "race". In an article entitled "The Problem of Tenants in Flats", HDB head Lim Phai Sam wrote in 1966 of the need "to avoid large concentrations of a particular community in any one estate such as happened in Bukit Ho Swee for the fire victims" (who were almost exclusively Chinese). The HDB system would in effect atomize pre-existing sub-racial communities "even though the policy *may eventually slow down clearance*" (italics mine).[86] This was virtually the only reported policy consideration which slowed down the HDB of the 1960s.

FIRE EMERGENCY

The origin stories of state re-housing in Singapore and Hong Kong, like the much less determined effort made in Japan, include dramatic fires. Public housing in Hong Kong is said to have started after conflagration in the squatter camp of Shek Kip Mei in 1953. In Singapore, a very large fire in the squatter village of Bukit Ho Swee occurred in 1961, one year into the first Five-Year Plan.[87] Re-housing narratives in both Singapore and Hong Kong have used the emergency of fire to help explain either the origin of the re-housing, the determination with which it was carried through, or at least its overwhelming necessity. In this sense the fires compete as an explanatory device with "before and after" pictures of squatter settlements and high-rise flats. The fires gave a crucial *non-political* substance to the discursive link between housing and emergency.

As sociologist Chua Beng-Huat has pointed out, the conjuncture of the great fire with the building of the PAP-government's first large housing estate on the same site "imparted to Bukit Ho Swee a symbolic place in the history of Singapore, as the quintessential urban slum and squalor in official terms".[88] In fact, the HDB wrote "The Bukit Ho Swee Story" in 1967 as the introduction to a pictorial book describing the new *Bukit Ho Swee Estate*. The estate "was literally born out of fire", the history begins, consuming a site from which, it later tells us, "the outbreak of infectious diseases . . . could quickly spread throughout the island". The fire was also accorded a pedagogical function in this and other accounts, dispensing "a lesson for all those living in such dangerous and appalling conditions to co-operate with the government".[89] A similar narrative structures *The Emergence of Bukit Ho Swee Estate: From Desolation to Progress*, produced cooperatively with the HDB in 1983, and whose cover-shot is a crowd of homeless people milling before a towering cloud of black smoke.[90]

The crowd on the cover of *The Emergence* looks helpless, even indifferent. But sociologist Chua, who also once lived in Bukit Ho Swee, has provided a contrasting picture of squatter settlement response to the emergency of fire:

> At the slightest indication of a fire breaking out, the village men would be there attempting to put it out rather than rushing home to help their own families prepare for evacuation . . . in both policing and fire prevention, the unemployed men of the village were indispensable.[91]

At Bukit Ho Swee in 1961, this emergency-response system somehow broke down.[92] The village burned and 6,000 of the homeless were, within the year, resettled into the HDB flats that soon covered (quite literally) the fire site. A rump portion of the village which survived the fire itself burned down in 1968.

In the story of Bukit Ho Swee, the *housing crisis* develops victims who are more clearly drawn than the merely badly housed. One result is that fire and bulldozer would thereafter be unevenly balanced in narratives of squatter clearance. Although a comparatively small percentage of Singaporeans were ultimately re-housed because of conflagration, the prominence of the Bukit Ho Swee Fire in histories of the HDB could make self-conflagration seem, to the casual student of the event, the principle agent of slum-clearance.[93] "Special demolition squads", which were actually just as prominent in period newspaper accounts, are rarely given form in retrospective narratives.[94]

An example of how meanings could subtly shift between crises natural and political is the *emergency flat* in which most of the inhabitants of Bukit Ho Swee were re-housed. When HDB flats were introduced in 1960, *emergency* and *standard* were the names given their two variants. The nomenclature suggested, perhaps, that unsettled conditions might be normalized at a higher level of quality; that one might migrate to a better and more secure (standard) place after passing through the space of emergency. Exactly what the emergency was, however, had not been clearly articulated when the government began building *emergency flats* on a site adjacent to Bukit Ho Swee village in 1960. The fire of the following year, and the well-publicized re-housing of the *fire victims*, gave the *emergency flat* a new and clearer meaning. In some subsequent narratives, official and popular, the chronology of the *emergency flat* and the fire would be reversed, so that the vaguely political descriptor would appear to have been specifically generated by the circumstance of natural disaster.

MONUMENTALIZING EMERGENCY

Singapore has emerged internationally as a metaphor for total planning, of which HDB housing is often taken to be exhibit A. To its most vocal critics in the 1960s and 1970s, however, Singapore's HDB represented the opposite of planning – the institutionalization of the ad hoc in an atmosphere of crisis. Many of these critics were from the first generation of native-born Singaporean architects, or at least those among them who were working outside the HDB system. *The plan* which was then fully believed in by many of Singapore's young designers, as by young architects around the world, was to be the best product of their own creative energies, backed by data provided by a whole range of like-minded specialists. It was to unfold, in the words of young architect E. J. Seow, in an atmosphere of "love, hope, and a spirit of analysis, history, and imagination".[95] The HDB's emergency planning campaign caught them unprepared.

In the accounts of period policy-makers, the language of *housing crisis* merges almost seamlessly with the language of crisis politics. HDB Chief Howe Yoon Chong, speaking to delegates of an international housing conference in Singapore in 1967, rejected "ideal solutions" to housing design, because "urgent problems need immediate attention before they get completely out of hand". Housing programs, he said, should thus be "action-oriented", a phrase contributed to local planning discourse by UN advisors, but not coincidentally evocative of the People's *Action* Party.[96] Writing five years later in 1972 in an official HDB history, *Homes for the People*, Howe was somewhat more reflective on the consequences of speed. The HDB of the 1960s "was well aware", he wrote, "that there would arise immense social, cultural, and psychological upheaval among the families re-housed or re-settled. However, time and urgency of the problems did not permit detailed and sophisticated socio-economic surveys and studies into the likely emotional and mental effects which such mass resettlement could cause."[97]

The mobilized – even the reluctantly mobilized – were sometimes memorialized in the midst of their journey. Deputy Prime Minister Dr Toh Chia Chye told Singapore Polytechnic students in 1966 that the HDB system "shows the readiness with which the people of Singapore can adapt themselves to changing conditions". He went on:

> these flats would not have sprung up if the people who were evicted from the slums and the attap hut settlements had not understood that eviction from their familiar surroundings was not a punishment but was a preparation for a better life.[98]

But just as the presence of both *eviction* and *better life* create tension in this passage, so *the plan* and *the emergency* were always more difficult to resolve discursively than in practice. As the HDB's chief architect described his own reality in a radio address of 1969:

> the factors on which the design is based are constantly changing . . . We cannot adopt the approach of preparing a Master Plan to base our future designs. Therefore, we have to evolve a comprehensive design and planning technique which is flexible and adaptable and able to accommodate itself to the fast changing situation.

Although the condition of design was to be *fast-changing*, the results were to be monumental. "The buildings constructed will last for a hundred years", he added in the same radio address.[99] Here was a logic which drove the HDB's architect-critics almost wild: the proposed *monumentalization of emergency*; the refusal to organize *crisis response* as a temporary project phase.

The government's theme of emergency was seized upon, in the midst of the first Five-Year Plan, by one young architect-critic in a student-edited Singapore Polytechnic journal. The state should "search, analyze, synthesize, and plan", wrote Tan Cheng Siong in 1962, rather than "rave about a superficial phenomenon of an emergency". Tan's equation of *superficial* with *emergency* (and both with "political parties which deal in the *awesome* and the *spectacular*" [italics mine]) illustrate the difficulty, in 1962, of recognizing *emergency* as a condition of *productive power*. This was to be a fatal oversight in the Left's critique of the new planning regime. "If it is an emergency", continued Tan, "temporary means would suffice and not building up neighborhood after neighborhood of regimented, inhuman blocks of one-room cells!"[100] CIAM's *housing cell*, the product of idealist architects of the interwar period, was now poised to lock out their idealist successors on the other side of the world under the slogan *action plan*.

Architects were destined to remain among Singapore's most critical voices, despite (or perhaps because of) the ever-increasing strength and spatial powers of the HDB. Planning should be based on "national wants", said young architect Edward Wong to students at Singapore Polytechnic, rather than "the assumption that people should be given what they ought to want".[101] William Lim would caution in 1968 that "the displacement of large numbers of the underprivileged members of the community is unlikely to be an acceptable solution for the more progressive social oriented governments".[102] And always *speed* was the factor which Singapore's architect-critics most consistently associated with the strategy of their marginalization. "The Architecture of Rapid Transformation" is the name of an article describing – and critiquing – the dynamic then constructing his cityscape by Singaporean architect Tay Kheng Soon.[103]

But the HDB system was not just a monument to its own efficiency and fleet-footedness, as Tay also recognized. *Speed* was its instrumentality, but not its goal. If the housing estates monumentalized anything by the end of the 1960s it was the government's successful *emergency response* to an historically-specific political crisis. In the slums and kampungs of the early 1960s "criminal elements bred and thrived; Communism found new adherents", remembered the HDB in its memorial publication *First Decade of Public Housing, 1960–1969*. "The final measure of Singapore's low-cost housing success", wrote the Board, "is the total failure of Communist and communalist appeals in the Board's estates".[104] Translated into a more de-politicized and de-historicized language in the 1990s, this would be rendered in a commemorative article in Singapore's *Straits Times* as:

> Built nationalism has been the medium of nation-building. The Housing Board is therefore more than a board, and is more than housing: its blocks are the nation made concrete, Singapore made home.[105]

THE EMERGENCY OF WOMEN

Women have been crucially affected by policies aimed at *homes*, and, in the history of *housing crisis/reform*, women of the middle and upper classes, at least, have played key roles as both proponents and critics. Housing has been an arena in which it is often "safe" for women to speak politically, taking advantage of their centrality to the *family life* which *home* ideally contains. On the other hand, "breaking the back of the housing problem", a British phrase commonly used in Singapore as well, was overwhelmingly an opportunity for male display.[106]

The book *Report on New Life in New Homes* of 1965 is a statement by a committee of politically-active, English-educated Singaporean Chinese women of how they expected the re-housing program to affect impoverished Chinese women from the slums. The social gulf between the writers and their subjects was immense, and *New Life* can be read in that sense as a document of class assumptions irrespective of gender. But there also exists in *New Life* a critique of the Chinese family system absent in accounts authored by male re-housing proponents. While the break-up of the extended Chinese slum- and *kampung*-family-community is implicit in the HDB program, *New Life* makes it explicit, and gives it sanction.[107]

New Life expects re-housing to alleviate the gender segregation "common among families of the oriental races". Poor Chinese men, according to the writers, spend almost all their time together, "discussing such topics as business, sports, or girls", and even taking their meals separately from the women. "The husband does not come home to his wife, he comes home to the menfolk in the household and usually discusses his problems with them." There is much gender-segregated community in the slums, but not nuclear families, and that's the problem. "Family units comprising father, mother, and children do not exist . . . the married couple does not share each others' joys or sorrows, nor do they solve the family problems together." *New Life*'s discussion of poor Chinese society revolves consistently around the issue of female marginalization and irrelevance.[108]

The HDB slab-blocks, for the authors of *New Life*, will empower poor women by breaking the bonds of extended family and gender-segregated community. Alone with her newly-constituted nuclear family in the HDB unit, the woman finds herself consulted and respected, the only immediate community her husband and children have. But the re-housing, in this account, does not change the wife as much as the husband. "The new pattern of the HDB flats compels the husband to feel responsibility for his [nuclear] family", where little or none was felt before. In Chinatown or the *kampung*, "there were always other members of the household [to rely on] whenever an emergency arose".[109]

Emergency arises in this passage in the unexpected guise of opportunity for female empowerment. The absence of community means individual women will have to be relied upon in a crisis. The wife is now an integral, crucial member of a much smaller crisis-management team. While the HDB's own literature celebrates its having "broken the backbone of the housing problem", *New Life*'s HDB is "giving [young couples] a backbone, a sense of responsibility, freedom, and self-confidence".[110] "The strong [extended] family ties among the Chinese" lurk, in the *New Life* text, as an antiquated enclosure the HDB will puncture. Young people suffer "repression and frustration" living among parents and siblings. In one word picture which seems a testimony of the writer's own experience, a young woman's efforts to decorate "are destroyed in a few minutes by the innumerable nieces and nephews over whom one has no control". "There is less friction and tension", the writers are sure, when large families are re-distributed in smaller, spatially-distant units.[111]

In the ceremony of escape which *New Life* lays out, however, freedom does not play so constructive a role as a sense of danger. In a section of the book entitled "New Sense of Possession", Chinatown is pathologized as a place where "the joy of possessing is unknown and the question of responsibility for *safeguarding one's possessions* does not arise" (italics mine). The *New Life* of the title is presented as a new relationship with private things which others covet. "The need to *protect* one's possessions becomes more real when one realizes one is now *surrounded by strangers instead of friends*. This is the beginning of house-pride" (italics mine). Or later: "It seems paradoxical that in spite of the extra living room available and *the security of strong doors with reliable locks*, tenants, especially from Chinatown, feel a certain amount of confinement, insecurity, and loneliness in the Housing Estate Flat" (italics mine). That this outcome was seen by the writer as "paradoxical" may strike us now as the greater paradox. It illustrates the perceptual gap not only between the English-speaking Chinese women who wrote *New Life* and their Chinese-speaking subjects (or at least their own perception of that gap), but between ourselves (or at any rate, most of us) and the extraordinary instinct for spatial containment – of oneself and others – more natural in a period of riot and emergency.[112]

Singapore's re-housing campaign produced as a byproduct – and eventually as a systemic component – much sociological research on the condition of the re-housed. *Report on New Life in New Homes* was followed by extensive surveys conducted by the HDB itself, and parallel efforts by professors and students at Singapore's two universities. The HDB-commissioned surveys found people were, on the whole, satisfied. The professors and students often found them not to be, documenting (and one senses, deliberately so) the social and individual costs of the re-housing. This was particularly evident in the work of Pakistani-born sociologist Riaz Hassan, whose *Families in Flats* (1977), although organized in the statistical, quantitative frame common to social science of that era, adds up to a narrative of displacement and confusion.[113]

Families' interviews agree with *New Life's* prediction that "in the case of emergency" the re-housed HDB tenants were thrown back largely on themselves. If a "sudden minor illness or injury" arose, only eight percent of flat-dwellers would turn to neighbors, they said, as compared to forty-three percent who said they would have relied on friends in their former neighborhood or *kampung*. Over a quarter of respondents told Hassan and his graduate students that they would turn to "former neighbors", spatially distant, as compared to those they currently lived among. In the slums and *kampungs*, only six percent said they relied on "immediate family only" in the event of emergencies. The number in HDB flats who claimed to have adopted this fall-back strategy was triple that amount.[114] Concludes Hassan:

> The perceived insecurity of the surroundings further reinforces the "need" for
> personal privacy, which in fact is really the need for personal security in an
> impersonal and insecure environment . . . Their perception of the "outside"
> environment is that of increasing constraints which are gradually narrowing the
> margins which they can manipulate in order to obtain a certain degree of
> freedom . . . a cognition of the environment which is ever restricting and over
> which they have little control. They seem to accept but still remain hopeful about
> the future.[115]

The HBD's own poll of residents in 1968 records, under the heading "environmental conditions", that the largest "unsatisfactory" response was in the category "nearness to a police station" (35.7 percent) (Tan Tsu Haung in Chua). It is hard not to conclude that the growing sense of national security which the re-housing represented to its leadership, was mirrored by new forms of insecurity in many of its subjects. Everyone acknowledged this condition, at the time, even many in the leadership. But no one expected it to last.[116]

HOUSING AS TECHNOLOGY

Housing in the 1950s and 1960s evoked *technology* in a sense now difficult to re-capture, given the intervening shift of that word away from the architectural, and toward the computational and informational. But in Singapore, Tokyo, Liverpool, and the suburbs of Long Island in those decades, the ceremony of being re-housed was portrayed as a transit not only to a more *secure* world (if one often mediated by locks), but a more *technologically advanced* one. It was an invitation to enter the Space Age in the form of advanced living space. The full discursive power of *high technology* was thus brought to bear as an explanation for why radical changes in personal environments were not only desirable, but inevitable. That slab-blocks could be set down on any site at any time only helped to cement their relationship to other forms of space technology. The status of the slab-block as a type of transfiguring machine remained of deep relevance to those who promoted, designed, and built them long after Gropius and Le Corbusier had turned away from their early prototypes. This was especially true in places like Glasgow, St Louis, and Singapore, fearful of being left behind in the Space Race, and determined to re-launch themselves with bold ceremonies of spatial repro-duction. What was unique in the case of Singapore was perhaps only the numbers of people strapped to the rockets, and the mission's eventually stellar success.

Singapore could not, in the 1960s, create from whole cloth its own indus-trial revolution. The government realized that it needed foreign corporations in order to do that. But it could – and did – cover its landscape with tall building-machines and begin re-locating its population inside, thus symbolizing the depth of its technological aspirations both to itself and off-shore investors. The clear-ances of the slums and *kampungs* also cleared space for land on which to build the city's present high-rise skyline (although Urban Renewal was a strategic late-comer, beginning half-way through the second Five-Year Plan). The econometric reasons for the re-housing have been well-discussed elsewhere. But business is also about marketing, and marketing about branding, and branding about signs. Slab-blocks were never really as high-tech as their proponents would have wanted them to be. Prefabrication, for example, was initially tried in Singapore but rejected in favor of low-tech and labor-intensive concrete casting.[117] But the build-ings were, at the time, unmistakable aspirations to a condition which transcended mere nation-building. The growing popularity of the term *satellite town* in press reports of the late 1950s and 1960s (as opposed to the older *new town*) is one example of this cultural framing. Queenstown's description in one newspaper article of 1958 as a "down-to-earth satellite town" made the linkage explicit.[118]

If one accepts the results of sociologists' detailed interviews with HDB resi-dents about their likes and dislikes, then it was precisely the *technologies* of the flats which most consistently symbolized anxiety to the first generation of their inhabitants/users. The two most objectionable features of their new living space, according to residents polled in social science surveys, were the *noise* and the *lifts*. *Noise* would seem a surprising objection coming from former slum and squatter camp inhabitants. Were not those places noisy? *Noise* in the HDB flats turns out to have described a new technologically-generated aural environment. It was the neighbor's television and radio which could be heard but not turned down because (presumably) one did not know one's neighbors, and the sound of strangers' children, beyond one's ability to discipline, playing in the echo chamber of the adjacent corridor. The new anti-communal privacy ironically generated "the invasion of privacy" as more and more people turned to television and radio as a substitute for conversation – the alone irritating the alone through the manipulation of disembodied electronic voices. Sound-proofing had been sacrificed in the new emphasis on speed, as partitions were made lighter in order to increase their quantity and ease of erection.[119]

Lifts were the first pieces of complex machinery that many of the re-housed had ever found themselves dependent on. But their novelty and complexity made them a principal target of teenage vandalism. The result was that they often failed to work, trapping people on the upper or bottom floors.[120] This problem of attacks on lifts had actually begun in the British SIT estates, and occurred, of course, almost everywhere in the world that tower blocks first sprung up.[121] As late as 1973 the efficiency of lifts was judged by Singapore's planners "the most inadequate condition" in the housing estates, a view also held by the residents they surveyed. The HDB responded by establishing a *Lift Emergency Unit*.[122]

The most widespread objection was to the cost of running water, which, among all the technologies of the flats, would seem to be most deserving of welcome. *Kampung* and slum dwellings were without household taps. In their nearly universal complaints about utilities charges, however, the residents seemingly turned on the sinks (and electrical outlets) as among their principle banes. In the *kampungs*, water had been distant (at pumps and taps) but virtually free, and distance was not necessarily an inconvenience to adults where fetching water was the task of children. Having one's water close at hand was thus not considered enough of an improvement, by many, to warrant the high mandatory charge. This charge was significant enough, to a poor family, that it often meant foregoing other things judged necessary.[123] Indeed, writing in 1972, Buchanan estimated that a quarter of HDB tenants were still living "either in poverty or close to poverty – despite physically sound housing conditions".[124]

Certainly the residents learned to self-regulate technological noise, to prevent their children from short-circuiting the lifts, and to enjoy the convenience of running water. But their initial reactions to all these things call into question the universality of technological enthusiasm in 1960s and 1970s Singapore, especially among the poorest and least willingly re-housed.

CONCLUSION

With the problem of non-operating lifts this essay has arrived full-circle, back to the *emergency exit*. In some of the literature Singapore's re-housing has generated, there is a suggestion that historical dislocations matter little, because everything turned out to be all right in the end. Eviction is treated as incidental to the overall success of re-housing, a success measured by the numbers of the re-housed, or by subsequent social-science surveys which find populations "on the whole satisfied" with what happened. The habitation of HDB flats was indeed a benchmark for national development, as their subsequent ownership became the concrete evidence for Singapore's arrival in the First World. The lifts of Singapore are now an unproblematic component of daily life, here as elsewhere. For some commentators and inhabitants, however, there is no clear exit from the condition of emergency which helped generate the flats, and which they in turn help generate. They embody for some a loss of public architect-ness to the ongoing demands of crisis-management.

From its first "Great War", the twentieth century was characterized by a sense of constant crisis which the existing term "emergency" was increasingly pressed into service to describe, and in many cases direct. It directed policies, but it also directed masses of people about. The twentieth century's concern with housing most often discussed using words such as "process" or "provision" – is also capable of politico-military analysis. This is not to suggest that housing produced in the context of emergency forever encapsulates martial values. The trajectory of internet technology from ARPANET to Napster has taught us that artifacts are capable of remarkable and unpredictable transformations in the course of successive handlings. The state-built housing that Singaporeans, Americans, Venezuelans, and Scotsmen were hurried into during the twentieth century, sometimes consensually and sometimes not, has been the setting for millions of subsequent lives – lives too diverse and anonymous to be woven into any meta-narrative.

This essay has argued, more simply, for considering de-housing and re-housing as part of the larger history of mobilization, which taken in its broadest meaning – to render mobile – was among the most common state-citizen interactions of the twentieth century. It has suggested an underappreciated convergence between the politics of space and the politics of emergency around the act of habitation. The subject is too vast and multi-chambered, empirically and theoretically, to be adequately dealt with in a single essay. But moving toward a history of emergency may be moving toward a fuller understanding of our present condition, when emergency threatens to replace even the fiction of "normality" as the officially-sanctioned texture of everyday life. In the normal-ization of emergency conditions, if that is indeed our trajectory, the seemingly mundane object of housing might be an underappreciated portal.

NOTES

1 I'd like to express my gratitude to Jordan Sand, Chua Beng-Huat, Paul Kratoska, Tim Barnard, and Ryan Bishop for commenting on earlier drafts of this chapter. I'd also like to thank Jim Warren and Tony Reid for allowing me to present some of these ideas in a seminar at the Asia Research Institute of the National University of Singapore.

2 Saba George Shiber, "Era Ahead for Planning and Housing", *Proceedings of the Second Afro-Asian Housing Congress* (Singapore, 1967) v. 2, p. 92

3 This seeming duality of images helps explain why references to haste, speed, and spontaneity are so rare in Modernist architectural manifestos, excepting those of the Futurists. Even in Futurist writing, however, a premium is placed on control, or as Rowe and Koetter describe it, "the celebration of force". Colin Rowe and Fred Koetter, *Collage City* (Cambridge, Mass.: MIT Press, 1978), p. 30.

4 The geographers Zelinsky and Kosinski, writing in the context of their work on emer-gency evacuations, note that "social scientists tend to be wary of unique events, the traditional domain of historians, who, as we have seen, have somehow overlooked emergency evacuations . . . Thus one will search in vain for even the barest mention of emergency evacuations in geography or demography textbooks." Wilbur Zelinsky and Leszek A. Kosinski, *The Emergency Evacuation of Cities: A Cross-National Historical and Geographical Study* (Savage, Md.: Rowman & Littlefield Publishers, Inc., 1991), p. 13.

5 De Stijl, *Manifesto V* in Ulrich Conrads, *Programs and Manifestoes on 20th-Century Architecture* (Cambridge, Mass.: MIT Press, 1991), p. 66.

6 A landmark article in this regard is Peter Marcuse, "Housing Policy and the Myth of the Benevolent State", which originally appeared in *Social Policy*, Jan./Feb. 1978, and was reprinted in Rachel Bratt, Chester Hartman, and Ann Meyerson (eds) *Critical Perspectives on Housing* (Philadelphia: Temple U. Press, 1986), pp. 248–263.

7 For example J. M. Fraser, the head of Singapore's colonial-period re-housing agency, The Singapore Improvement Trust, presented his work in the British journal *Town and Country Planning* under the title "Singapore, a Problem in Population", *Town and Country Planning*, 139 (Nov. 1955).

8 Stieber makes this point in discussing turn-of-the-century housing reform in The Netherlands (Nancy Steiber, *Housing Design and Society in Amsterdam: Reconfiguring Urban Order and Identity, 1900–1920* [Chicago: U. of Chicago Press, 1998], p. 33). Karolak, referring to the US, writes of "the long-standing consensus among large sections of the industrial working class that homeownership diminished labor's independence" (Eric J. Karolak, " 'No Idea of Doing Anything Wonderful': The Labor-Crisis Origins of National Housing Policy and the Reconstruction of the Working-Class Community, 1917–1919" in John F. Bauman, Roger Biles, and Kristin M. Szylvian (eds) *From Tenements to the Taylor Homes: In Search of an Urban Housing Policy in Twentieth Century America* [Univ. Park, Penn.: Pennsylvania State University Press, 2000], p. 71).

9 One of the reasons for the Pullman Strike of 1894 was the cutting of wages without a reduction in rents. It was the high cost of good (*model*) housing, and the coercion this allowed the company during wage disputes, rather than the condition of *slum housing*, which caused worker anger to boil over, eventually leading to a national railroad strike and one of the earliest invocations of emergency powers by an American president. See Peter Marcuse, "Housing Policy and City Planning: the Puzzling Split in the United States, 1893–1931" in Gordon E. Cherry, *Shaping an Urban World* (London: Mansell, 1980).

10 Peter Saunders, *A Nation of Home Owners* (London: Unwin Hyman, 1990), p. 34

11 Peter Marcuse, "A Useful Installment of Socialist Work: Housing in Red Vienna in the 1920s" in Bratt, Hartman, and Meyerson, p. 569.

12 As Stieber writes in her detailed study of social housing in Amsterdam, "housing offered the option of reform without structural, social or economic changes" (Strieber, p. 33). Peter Rowe agrees, writing that "contrary to some interpretations of the modern period, the interest in housing aimed more at achieving social stability than at radical reform" (Peter Rowe, *Modernity and Housing* [Cambridge, Mass.: MIT Press, 1995], p. 159).

13 As Marcuse puts it "in a crisis, real estate interests are expendable" ("A Useful Installment of Socialist Work . . ." in Bratt, Hartman, and Meyerson, p. 583)

14 Examples of recent attempts to catch up include Raymond A. Mohl, "Planned Destruction: The Interstates and Central City Housing" in Bauman, Biles, and Szylvian; Roger Biles, "Public Housing and the Postwar Urban Renaissance, 1949–1973" in Bauman, Biles, and Szylvian.

15 Jordan Sand has pointed out (private correspondence) that the archetypical visual medium of clearance may be the map, among the most bloodless of all graphic forms.

16 One historian who has remarked on this omission is Karolak; Marcuse makes a link between American housing reform and riot ("Housing Policy and City Planning: The Puzzling Split in the United States, 1893–1931" in Cherry, pp. 23–58).

17 Paul Virilio, "The State of Emergency" in James van Derian (ed.) *The Virilio Reader* (Oxford: Blackwell, 1998), p. 50.

18 Kenneth Frampton, *Le Corbusier: Architect and Visionary* (London: Thames & Hudson, 2001), p. 119.

19 Ibid. On the politics of Le Corbusier, see also Charles Jencks, *Le Corbusier and the Continual Revolution in Architecture* (New York: Monacelli Press, 2000).

20 To take just a single high-art example, Le Corbusier's *Unite d'Habitation* project began with plans for temporary housing in Vichy France in 1944. Its most famous realization, commissioned in Marseilles by the Ministry for Reconstruction in 1946–1952, housed over 1,600 of the *displaced* (the war-related homeless).

21 Rowe (p. 175) citing figures from Mel Scott.

22 The First World War is usually dealt with in passing in social histories of housing, but even passing comments by scholars of housing, architecture, and urban planning suggest a more fundamental relationship. See for example Steve Schifferes, "The Dilemmas of British Housing Policy" in Bratt, Hartman, and Meyerson, p. 51. Saunders agrees that rent controls, the cornerstone of modern British housing policy, began as "a stop-gap, emergency measure", a "response to the exigencies of running a semi-

controlled war economy" (Saunders, p. 22). In the case of the Netherlands, Stieber finds that the "emergency measure" of a "limited wartime socialism" helped clear political ground for that country's famous state housing efforts (Stieber, p. 25). Waswo finds, in the case of Japan, that "the first urban rent disputes" accompanied the First World War boom (Ann Waswo, *Housing in Postwar Japan: A Social History* [New York: Routledge Curzon, 2002], p. 43). Marcuse writes that in Vienna, "the war accentuated the housing crisis and changed its political character entirely" (Marcuse in Bratt, Harman, and Meyerson, p. 559). For additional details on Austria see Eve Blau, *The Architecture of Red Vienna, 1919–1934* (Cambridge, Mass.: MIT Press, 1999).

23 See especially Mohl, who documents that "at least 330,000 urban housing units were destroyed as a direct result of Federal highway building between 1957 and 1968" (p. 227).

24 The Second World War as a context for housing policy is as understudied as the First, although the post-war planning regimes in many countries were themselves products of war. See for example G. E. Cherry, *Town Planning in Britain since 1900* (Oxford: Blackwell, 1996). Even in pacifist Sweden, Appelbaum notes that one root of its noted public re-housing program lay in cessation of private building brought on by wartime (Richard P. Appelbaum, "Swedish Housing in the Postwar Period: Some Lessons for American Housing Policy" in Bratt, Hartman, and Meyerson).

25 The medicalized language of housing reform was more specifically the language of *emergency medicine*. The condition is never stable but is always *spreading* or *festering* and the whole body is threatened with infection. This is the epidemic-centered language of public health, and not that of general practice or even hospitalization. The housing crisis is never about *sickness* but immanent *fatality*.

26 Tokyo Municipal Government, *Tokyo's Housing Problem* (Tokyo: TMG, 1972), pp. 134–135. The *Dojunkai*, established to re-house earthquake victims, would eventually be folded into the *Jutaku Eidan* (Japan Housing Corporation) established in 1941 to house war workers.

27 Zelinsky and Kosinski, p. 301.

28 About 95 percent of Singaporean households were technically eligible for public flats by the early 1980s. Liu Thai Ker, Lau Who Cheong, and Loh Choon Tong, "New Towns in Singapore" in Y. M. Yeong (ed.) *A Place to Live: More Effective Low-Cost Housing in Asia* (Ottawa: International Development Research Centre of Canada. Report No 209e, 1983), p. 36.

29 For a sophisticated discussion of this issue, see Chua Beng-Huat, *Political Legitimacy and Housing: Stakeholding in Singapore* (London: Routledge, 1997) and, more succinctly, Chua, "Public Housing Residents as Clients of the State", *Housing Studies*, vol. 15, n. 1 (2000), pp. 45–60.

30 Liu, Lau, and Loh, p. 27

31 Rem Koolhaas, "Singapore: Portrait of a Potempkin Metropolis"/"Songlines: Thirty Years of Tabula Rasa" in Jennifer Sigler (ed.) *Small, Medium, Large, Extra-Large* (Rotterdam: O10 Publishers, 1995).

32 Iain Buchanan, *Singapore in Southeast Asia* (London: G. Bell and Sons Ltd., 1972), p. 239.

33 Linda Lim writes that "particularly in the early days, compulsory urban resettlement provided the PAP with the opportunity of breaking up established and potential opposition electoral communities". (Lim, "Social Welfare" in Kernial Singh Sandhu and Paul Wheatley, *Management of Success: The Moulding of Modern Singapore* [Singapore: Institute of Southeast Asian Studies, 1989]).

34 See Chua.

35 Anne E. Wee, Foreword in Seow Peck Leng, *Report on New Life in New Homes* (Singapore: Persatuan Wanita Singapura, 1965), p. 1. Wee was a lecturer in Social Studies at the University of Singapore.

36 The term "emergency" actually has too complex an etymology to be fully treated here, but according to my search through a number of major library catalogs, its historical usage was relatively sporadic or episodic prior to the twentieth century. A major event in the history of its popularization was surely the First World War, when the numbers of laws, enactments, reports, and administrative rules with the word "emergency" in their titles increases exponentially. "Emergency" was used in the same period to describe

natural disasters and accidents, but not, it seems, as commonly as it is used for such purposes today. The references to "emergency medicine" are particularly sparse before mid-century. While the First (and Second) World Wars begat many "emergency" regulations and rules, which sometimes referred to these armed conflicts as "war emergencies", the use of the term "emergency" as a substitute for the word "war" (rather than to supplement or modify it) only became common following the Second World War.

37 See Colin Campbell, *Emergency Law in Ireland, 1918–1925* (Oxford: Clarendon Press, 1994).
38 John Weldon Humphrey, "Emergency Resettlement and the Chinese in Malaya", unpublished manuscript, Singapore-Malay Collection, National University of Singapore (ca. 1973), pp. 1, 12.
39 Kumar Ramakrishna, *Emergency Propaganda: The Winning of Malayan Hearts and Minds, 1948–1958* (Richmond, Surrey, UK: Curzon, 2002), p. 94.
40 Ibid., p. 12; Richard Stubbs, *Hearts and Minds in Guerilla Warfare: The Malayan Emergency, 1948–1960* (Singapore: Oxford University Press, 1989), pp. 102–103; Humphrey, "Emergency Resettlement . . .", p. 12; ibid., "Population Resettlement in Malaya" (Ph.D. Thesis, Northwestern University, 1971), p. 226.
41 Stubbs, pp. 103, 108–110, 262.
42 Ramakrishna, p.126; Humphrey, "Population Resettlement . . .", p. 127.
43 Colonial Singapore had been shaped in a contestive environment from its beginnings, a story told in length by Brenda S. A. Yeoh in *Contesting Space: Power Relations and the Urban Built Environment in Colonial Singapore* (Kuala Lumpur; New York: Oxford University Press, 1996). See particularly her fourth chapter for a discussion of housing regulations and urban planning prior to the period I consider (Yeoh's account ends in 1930).
44 The Emergency-period re-housing campaign had some local antecedents, but was based most directly on a report by the 1947 Singapore Housing Committee. The declaration of Emergency in 1948, just as the Committee's report was circulating, seems to have rapidly moved its recommendations forward on the list of colonial priorities (*SIT Annual Report,* 1957, pp. 2–3).
45 The Singapore Improvement Trust had been founded as a quasi-governmental organization in the 1920s and began building housing before the war, mostly for civil servants and other members of the non-British middle class. In 1948, however, it began receiving substantial loans from the British colonial government (a total of $140 million between 1948 and 1957) and turned its attention toward low-income housing (*SIT Annual Report*, 1957, p. 2). Thus did the SIT become the de facto housing and planning ministry of the colonial government in Singapore. For a discussion of the SIT's origins, see Yeoh, pp. 164–167.
46 Singapore Improvement Trust (hereafter SIT), *The Work of the Singapore Improvement Trust* (Singapore, 1948), pp. 3–4.
47 Ibid. (1950), p. 21.
48 Ibid. (1954), p. 14.
49 Ibid. (1951), p. 14. It is worth noting that the first ten-story tower blocks in London had appeared only three years before, in 1948 (Glendenning and Muthesius, p. 53). Judging from the plans and illustrations in its annual reports, the SIT's architects stayed in close touch with design developments in the metropole.
50 SIT, *The Work of the Singapore Improvement Trust* (1952).
51 Ibid. (1954), p. 14.
52 *SIT Annual Report*, 1957, p. 28. Although statistics show that the SIT re-housing program did not seriously slow until 1955–1956, planning began to be affected much earlier. T. P. F. McNeice, Chairman of the SIT, wrote as early as 1953 that "improvement schemes which involved the wholesale demolition of insanitary and overcrowded property are not possible in present circumstances" (SIT, *The Work of the Singapore Improvement Trust* [1953], preface).
53 *SIT Annual Report*, 1959, p. 27.
54 Ibid. (1957), pp. 28–29.
55 Ibid. (1958), p. 35
56 Indeed, the squatters gained friends in high places as the colonial period ratcheted to a finish. A *Straits Times* editorial of Sept. 12, 1958 complained that "So little do

some of Singapore's legislators understand the problem [of clearance] that in the Assembly debate there were complaints once again of the disturbance of squatters".

57 *SIT Annual Report,* 1959, p. 27.

58 "A Colossal Effort" [Editorial], *The Straits Times*, Sept. 19, 1959.

59 One of the few to make this linkage (among many other useful ones) is Christopher Tremewan, *The Political Economy of Social Control in Singapore* (New York: St Martin's Press, 1994), p. 45.

60 The political nature of the Hong Kong program is most forcefully stated by Alan Smart, "Hong Kong's Slums and Squatter Areas: A Developmental Perspective" in Brian Aldrich and Ranvinder S. Sandhu, *Housing the Urban Poor: Policy and Practice in Developing Countries* (London: Zed Books, 1995). See especially his discussion on p. 106.

61 Brian Aldrich, "Habitat Defense in Southeast Asian Cities", *Southeast Asian Journal of Social Science*, vol. 13, n. 2 (1985).

62 Quoted in Lee Kwan Yew, *From Third World to First: The Singapore Story: 1965–2000* (Singapore: Singapore Press Holdings, 2000), p. 50.

63 *The Straits Times*, Feb. 2, 1960. The same article points out that the housing of 150,000 Singaporeans by the SIT had "no parallel elsewhere in Asia".

64 Peter Rowe, p. 12.

65 Hassan is one of few commentators to stress continuity between the two planning regimes, noting the "fairly entrenched public housing bureaucracy, which the present [post-colonial] government inherited in 1959": Riaz Hassan, *Families in Flats: A Study of Low Income Families in Public Housing* (Singapore: Singapore U. Press, 1977), p. 12.

66 Humphrey, "Population Resettlement . . .", pp. 77–78. Humphrey notes that Johor and Perak were the two Malayan states with the largest squatter populations, and that the first large-scale resettlement occurred in the former state, just north of Johor Bahru.

67 HDB, *The Bukit Ho Swee Estate* (Singapore: HDB, 1967), p. 39.

68 The *SIT Annual Report* of 1958, discussing "the early post-war years", describes how "much of the Trust land prepared before the war was requisitioned by the War Department, and a great deal of what remained was covered by unauthorized attap huts – a legacy of the Japanese occupation" (p. 2).

69 Smart discovers a similar history in Hong Kong. "Squatting in the prewar period", he writes, "was not a serious problem, but difficulties of making land available for development [after the war] were blamed on the illegal occupation of vacant land in the disorder following the [Japanese] occupation" (p. 102). Cho and Park trace the squatter phenomenon in Korea to a similar dynamic occurring in the same (post-war) period, which merged with the refugee crisis of the Korean War (Cho Jaesoon and Park Jeonghee, "Slums and Squatter Settlements in South Korea" in Aldrich and Sandhu, p. 113).

70 HDB, *The Bukit Ho Swee Estate*, p. 5.

71 Paul H. Kratoska, *The Japanese Occupation of Malaya, 1941–1945: A Social and Economic History* (London: C. Hurst and Co., 1998), chapters 9 and 11.

72 Marcuse, "A Useful Installment of Socialist Work . . ." in Bratt, Hartman, and Meyerson, pp. 558–585; Blau, especially chapters 2 and 3.

73 Marcuse, ibid., pp. 568–569; Blau notes that by 1921 some squatter settlements had "stabilized into more permanent communities with their own systems of cooperative self-government" (p. 95).

74 See Blau.

75 Alan Choe, head of the Urban Renewal Dept. of the HDB, made this policy explicit in a speech before an international housing conference in 1968. "Underemployment thrives in the central area slums", he said, "because of the presence of cheap poor accommodations, affording negligible overhead." Choe, "Slum Clearance and Urban Renewal in Singapore", *Proceedings of the Second Afro-Asian Housing Congress, Singapore* (1968), p. 5.

76 Marcuse, "A Useful Installment of Socialist Work . . .", p. 565.

77 Social scientists of the 1960s to 1970s left us more descriptions of life in Singapore's high-rise flats than in the *kampungs* and squatter camps they replaced. At least part of the reason is suggested by geographer Iain Buchanan, who recognized that *kampung*-dwellers were better-placed to avoid participation in social science surveys than those living in government-managed flats (especially door-to-door surveys administered with the cooperation of estate managers) [see Buchanan, below]. Our most

vivid accounts of *kampung* life in this period are by sociologist Chua Beng-Huat, based partly on his own experience of growing up in the urban village of Bukit Ho Swee See Chua, *Political Legitimacy and Housing*, chapter 8; ibid., "The Business of Living in Singapore" in Sandhu and Wheatley; and ibid., "That Imagined Space: Nostalgia for *Kampungs*" in Brenda Saw Ai Yeoh and Lilly Kong, *Portraits of Places: History, Community, and Identity in Singapore* (Singapore: Times Editions, 1995). See also field-work-based accounts in Robert E. Gamer, *The Politics of Urban Development in Singapore* (Ithaca: Cornell University Press, 1972), and in Iain Buchanan, *Singapore in Southeast Asia* (London: G. Bell and Sons Ltd., 1972).

78 On squatter settlements as vernacular architecture, see Amos Rapoport, "Spontaneous Settlements as Vernacular Design" in Carl V. Patton, *Spontaneous Shelter: International Perspectives and Prospects* (Philadelphia: Temple University Press, 1988); see also Aldrich and Sandhu (1995).

79 For the history and justification of the term "spontaneous settlement", see Elizabeth Kubale Palmer and Carl V. Patton, "Evolution of Third World Shelter Policies" in Patton.

80 Otto Golger, *Squatter and Resettlement, Symptoms of an Urban Crisis* (Weisbaden: Otto Harrassowitz, 1972). Golger conducted his fieldwork in 1966–1967. Chua and Buchanan make similar points regarding Singapore's *kampungs*. Both point out the variety of housing types (and associated levels of status, income, and material comfort), and the lack of crime. Chua's accounts are careful, however, to foreground the dark (and merely mundane and repetitive) aspects of squatter life which Golger, in his enthusiasm to correct stereotypes, tends to downplay. Nonetheless, Chinese squatter life turns out, in these and the few other accounts we have of it by academics, to have been not only more complex than its parodied portrayals, but more "settled" and routinized than the label "temporary" would allow.

81 "Squatters, Illegal Houses Set a Problem", *Straits Times*, June 10, 1962.

82 "New Deal for Squatters", ibid., January 7, 1964.

83 "50,000 Homes to Go Up", ibid., January 2, 1965.

84 "Stay-put Squatters: Agitators Blamed", *The Straits Times*, July 9, 1962; "The Squatters", ibid., July 11, 1962; "50,000 Homes Go Up", ibid., Jan. 2, 1965. The phrase "evil-wishers" appears in Seow, *Report on New Life in New Homes*, p. 59, who speaks of the need to protect "illiterate women" from such people.

85 See, for example, Chua Beng-Huat, "Race Relations and Public Housing Policy in Singapore", *Journal of Architectural and Planning Research*, vol. 8 (1991), pp. 343–354.

86 Lim Phai Sam, "The Problem of Tenants in Flats", *The Straits Times*, Oct. 4, 1966.

87 This fire/re-housing was actually preceded by an earlier one, which happened soon after the start of self-rule in 1959, at Kampong Tiong Bahru. The "emergency arrangements" made by the outgoing SIT for the several thousand people displaced by this fire may have served as a dress rehearsal of sorts for the HDB's later performance at Bukit Ho Swee (*SIT Annual Report*, 1959, p. 42).

88 Chua Beng-Huat, "The Business of Living in Singapore", pp. 1009–1010.

89 HDB, *The Bukit Ho Swee Estate*, pp. 1, 4, 39.

90 Archives and Oral History Dept., Kim Seng Citizen's Consultative Committee, and Bukit Ho Swee Area Office (HDB), *The Emergence of Bukit Ho Swee Estate: From Desolation to Progress* (Singapore: News and Publications Ltd., 1983).

91 Chua, "The Business of Living in Singapore", p. 1008.

92 In one official narrative of the fire, village men rush to help, but "the eagerness of the people hampered the work of the experienced firemen" (HDB, *The Bukit Ho Swee Estate*, p. 8).

93 Hassen found that "The majority of the households, 61%, were relocated as a result of urban renewal, and 21 percent moved because of better housing environment provided by the HDB flats." Only 3 percent were rehoused because of "natural disaster", meaning mainly the fires, (p. 39).

94 See for example *Straits Times*, June 10, 1962; ibid., June 1, 1964.

95 E. J. Seow, writing in *Rumah: Journal of the Society of Malaysian Architects*, vol. 3 (Nov. 1960), p. 21.

96 *Proceedings of the Afro-Asian Housing Congress* (Singapore, 1967), vol. 1, p. 3.

97 Stephen H. K. Yeh and the Statistics and Research Department (HDB), *Homes for the People: A Study of Tenants' Views on Public Housing in Singapore* (Singapore: HDB and Economic Research Centre, NUS, 1972), p. i.

98 Toh Chia Chye, Foreword, *Architecture 1 17' N" : Journal of the School of Architecture of the Singapore Polytechnic Institute*, vol. 1 (1966/67), p. 5.

99 The Cheang Wan, "Public Housing – The Next Efforts" in J. F. Conceicao (ed.) *A New Environment for Singapore* (Singapore: Joint Committee for Radio Courses, ca. 1969), p. 17.

100 Tan Cheng Siong, "The Housing Problem" in *Dimension: Annual Journal of the Singapore Polytechnic Architecture Society* (1962), p. 12.

101 Edward Wong, "Talk to Singapore Polytechnic Architectural Students" in *SPUR*, 65/7.

102 William Lim, "Rehabilitation: A Possible Solution to Urban Slums in Developing Countries", *Proceedings of the Second Afro-Asian Housing Congress, Singapore* (Singapore: 1967), p. 4.

103 Tay Kheng Soon, "The Architecture of Rapid Transformation" in Kernial Singh Sandhu and Paul Wheatley, *Management of Success: The Moulding of Modern Singapore* (Singapore: Institute of Southeast Asian Studies, 1989).

104 HBD, *First Decade of Public Housing in Singapore: 1960–1969* (Singapore: HDB, 1970).

105 "HDB as Nation-Building and Built Nationalism", *Sunday Straits Times*, Sept. 28, 1997.

106 Wrote Felix Frankfurter [Chairman of the US War Labor Policies Board] in 1918: "the housing problem – even in its emergency aspects – is a family problem". Quoted in Karolak, p. 71.

107 Seow Peck Leng and Pan-Pacific South-East Asia Women's Association, *Report on New Life in New Homes* (Singapore: Persauan Wanita Singapura, 1965). Seow was one of five women elected to Singapore's legislative assembly in 1959. She was defeated in the 1963 election.

108 Ibid., p. 38.

109 Ibid., pp. 38–40.

110 Ibid.

111 Ibid., pp. 40–41.

112 Ibid., p. 26.

113 Riaz Hassan, *Families in Flats* (Singapore: Singapore U. Press, 1977).

114 Hassan, pp. 68–69.

115 Hassan, p. 201.

116 Writing in 1983, HDB planners problematized elements of their estates which *Report on New Life in New Homes* had earlier celebrated: "The government's effort in curbing population growth emphasized the setting up of small nuclear families. The physical design and configuration of the HDB flat complement this type of family unit. As a result, the extended family system is slowly being eroded . . . (while) lack of social integration among the residents on various floors and within the estate itself results in a general lack of communal identity and attachment" (William S. W. Lim *et al.*, pp. 55–56).

117 Tan Tiang Beng, "The Experiment with the Industrialized Method of Construction of Multi-Story Flats in Singapore", *Proceedings of the 2nd Afro-Asian Housing Congress, Singapore*, vol. 3.

118 "Down to Earth Satellite Town of Queenstown", *Straits Times*, Apr. 29, 1958.

119 Hassan, Table 4.15 shows that what residents "dislike most [about] living in flats" was "noise" (32 percent), p. 59; Tan in Chue Peng Chye, Table 5.2, p. 50, combines the results from two surveys undertaken by the HDB in 1968, which show that 25.22 percent of residents found "unsatisfactory" the "amount of noise" and 27.92 percent criticized the "efficiency of lifts". Only 6.62 percent found the lifts "satisfactory".

120 Teh Cheang Wan, "Public Housing – The Next Efforts" in J. F. Conceicao (ed.) *A New Environment for Singapore* (Singapore: Joint Committee for Radio Courses, ca. 1969), p. 22: "The frequency of breakdowns of the lifts is still quite intolerable. It must be noted however that vandalism accounted for substantial part of the breakdown of the lifts."

121 *SIT Annual Report*, 1959, p. 39.

122 Tan in Chua Peng Chye, p. 49.

123 Hassan writes: "They complained of the increase in rent and PUB bills, even though there was a great deal of convenience in the availability of water and electricity . . . hence they were forced to reduce the number of times they could go out and enjoy themselves because of budget constraints" (p. 207).

124 Buchanan, *Singapore in Southeast Asia*, p. 195.

Chapter 4: "The Vertical Order Has Come to an End": The Insignia of the Military C³I and Urbanism in Global Networks

Ryan Bishop

> Technique itself . . . must be seen as an inseparable link in the continuum joining architecture and all other aspects of design to the world around it (to bodies and human-motor fields, in particular) for technique is the foundation of all overcoding, indeed, technique is the architecture of architecture. – Sanford Kwinter

> City planning is – once more – an adjunct to the science of war. – Le Corbusier, *The Radiant City*[1]

Saturday afternoons in Singapore bring mobilization exercises for all male citizens who remain in reservist units even after the mandatory full-time military stint known as National Service. Male civilians are both citizens and standing military reserve, much as the *miles* were. Not all reservists are mobilized, but all are potentially mobilized and mobilizable on any given weekend exercise and at any time for military conflict. In an "open mobilization exercise," battalion code names are broadcast over cable TV stations, broadcast television, radio stations and in cinemas. Global Positioning Systems (GPS), developed by the US military to track and co-ordinate terrestrial positions from space, also relay messages to reservists via Short Message Service (SMS) systems or through mobile phone calls from commanders. If a reservist in the center of the city is without a hand phone or is away from immediate broadcast equipment, all he need do is glance at one of the ubiquitous TV screen façades of buildings positioned along the main shopping artery of Orchard Road or near the Convention Centre and Suntec City. The heart of Singapore's financial, commercial, shopping, and entertainment districts is littered with such screens, allowing broadcast commands to go out rapidly to the entire standing military force. With this brief broadcast, the civilian becomes the military in a matter of seconds. Much of the urban environment is just as easily convertible. The highway system along which the reservists speed to their designated military camps also has military implications. As is the US highway system, the highways connecting Changi Airport and the commercial center of town have been designed as emergency landing strips for air force fighter planes as well as the easy circulation of conscripts. Hausmann's wide boulevards for soldiers to march down have been updated in cities around the world. The Singaporean Saturday open mobilization broadcast, or call to arms and readiness, displays a densely interwoven and interdependent system of information technologies, broadcast capabilities, urban space, infrastructure, architecture, commercial and financial interests, and nation-state security interests, all ultimately under the command and control of military demands. From geo-orbital space to one's living room and hand phone, the built and un-built environments of the city-state, at all levels, can be understood as bearing the imprimatur of militarization that marks global cities around the world. That, in Singapore, this stamp is beamed electronically bespeaks its status as a Broadcast City, the most recent and advanced manifestation and articulation of militarization in an urban setting. That it is used most overtly for military purposes *every* Saturday bespeaks its embeddedness in daily life. The Broadcast City and the trajectory from its earlier incarnations to its present form are the foci of this essay.

C³I, MILITARIZED CITIES, AND GLOBALIZATION AS WE KNOW IT: AN INTRODUCTION

> The bank towers loomed just beyond the avenue. They were covert structures for all their size, hard to see, so common and monotonic, tall, sheer, abstract, with standard setbacks, and block-long, and interchangeable, and he had to concentrate to see them . . . They were made to be the last tall things, made empty, designed to hasten the future. They were the end of the outside world. They weren't here, exactly. They were in the future, a time beyond geography and touchable money and the people who stock and count it. – Don DeLillo, *Cosmopolis*

The co-ordinated set of military strategies that emerged during the Cold War known as C³I – command, control, communications, and information (also, intelligence) – dominated US policy throughout the last half of the twentieth century in all its varied but deeply interconnected facets: military, political, business, and academic. The goal of this highly articulated, codified, and technologically sophisticated set of strategies was containment, specifically of communism. Global in scope and quotidian in its enunciation, C³I revealed an intensification of practices that gained specific shape and mobilization during the Second World War but which predate that event. No part of the world went untouched by C³I, and it delineates the organizational, economic, technological, and spatial systems that derive from, rely on, and perpetuate military strategy. The "insignia of the military," then, manifests itself in a myriad of ways in global urban sites.[2] The technologies alone bespeak this impact: satellites, mobile phones, digital computers, computer graphics, jet airplanes, autonomous and semi-autonomous systems, the Internet, "real-time" technologies (including television), to name but a few examples. The technicity does as well: e.g. logistics, mobility, speed, circulation, control, surveillance, monitoring, deterritorialization, simulation, game theory, and organizational modeling.

As can be readily noted from these examples, current globalization processes rely heavily on C³I technologies and technicity, which have accelerated in the post-Cold War world of global capital and which seem likely to accelerate and intensify even more in the age of the global "war against terror." The meshing of these technologies and technicity with state economies and military bodies further reveals the ways in which the insignia of the military continues to shape daily existence, daily space, and urbanism. The urban center-qua-global city, in fact, is largely the result of this historicity and these technicities. The global city would not be a global city, as we have come to understand the phenomenon, without being deeply embedded in these processes. If Singapore manifests them, it does so because it could not have emerged as "a global city" during the Cold War (when cities became global, in the terms we use now) if it had not done so. That is, in order to be a global city within the various global orders following the end of the Second World War, Singapore had to embrace the historicity and technicity of C^3I, and this embrace is demarcated in every dimension of its urban landscape.

The Cold War's C^3I has had profound impacts on the explicitly modernist "vertical order" (in both built and un-built environments) of colonialism and early postcolonialism. The "vertical order," as used by Paul Virilio and other urban theorists, invokes the modernist move toward greater architectural verticality (e.g. skyscrapers and high rises) in urban areas. This move marked a shift away from the horizontality of early urban architecture and largely defined the modernist movement as such. The term, however, also invokes hierarchical power structures made manifest in the built environment of cities. Therefore, it contains literal and figurative meanings of verticality, as well as a conflation of the literal and figurative in which the hierarchical power of a corporation or a governmental authority, for example, is found in the vertical hierarchy of its skyscraper. (As we will note later, the "vertical order" invokes a number of other related structures of power and control, including capital, business mergers, organizations, institutions, urban–rural relations, nation-states, geopolitical orders, information flows, and the military.) The extent to which optoelectronics (e.g. lasers, fiber optics, image sensors, optical discs, LED and LCD displays), tele-optics and "real-time" technologies inscribe a new military insignia on urban sites and create new models for global cities has been interpreted by some as signaling the end of "the vertical order." But, from a more sustained analysis, it seems that they might instead provide a reconstitution and update of it. The constant refinement and acceleration of C^3I provide us with synchronic and diachronic elements to explore architecture and spatial orders in the historicity of the present, which demands both a looking back and projecting into the future.

Mobility and the triumph of the eternal "now" of "real-time" technologies integral to C^3I have merged with business, architectural, and spatial practices in ways that have made the divisions between military, economic, and political domains remarkably fluid (if discernible at all), allowing one to fold into the other as the need arises. The deterritorialization of economic regimes thrives through military technicity and is coupled with the C^3I of the Cold War and post-Cold War construction of mobile sovereignty. The demand for global surveillance that characterized the Truman doctrine and the Cold War revealed the extent to which sovereignty no longer necessarily demanded attachment to territory. Mobile sovereignty in the postcolonial era, however, reiterates the mobile sovereignty of colonialism, which maintained sovereignty over non-contiguous terrain while simultaneously extending it in new, accelerated ways. This deterritorialization of economic, military, and state apparatuses, therefore, has altered significantly our understanding of built and "un-built" space, and has done so by combining the vertical order of discipline and accumulation with the horizontal order of dispersed control. (Dispersal had a Cold War function, as well, specifically as a shield against nuclear attack through the decentralization of industry and workforces, not to mention urban populations, as Norbert Weiner's MIT urban designs highlighted.)

In other words, it is worth remembering that the explicit goal of C^3I was *containment,* managed and controlled under a centralized command although implemented under the guise of liberation and the rhetoric of freedom. The goal was *not* dissemination, dispersal, or autonomy, but the necessity of the incalculable for determining the calculable means that these other unintended results could and did occur. As such, the modes of C³I's enunciation in global urban space reveals a historicity in which the horizontal order poses no challenges to the vertical order's hierarchical goals of command and control. Rather, the horizontal aids and abets the vertical.

We will see how this situation manifests itself in a trajectory from the "linear city"(of the late nineteenth and early twentieth centuries) to the "ballistic city" (as discussed by Virilio and manifested in the mid and late twentieth century) and, finally, to the "broadcast city," as exemplified by contemporary Singapore. The broadcast city links the horizontal with the vertical order through electromagnetic and optoelectronic technologies in the generation, management, and experience of urban space and design. The logic of the broadcast city facilitates C³I in every dimension of urban and civic life. This trajectory provides a means for accessing the performative technicities of the military enunciated in daily urban experience. The trajectory also displays an intensification of these technicities in each stage – a *surenchère* of sorts (an increase of existing conditions but also a raising of the stakes).

BROADCASTING IDEOLOGY: THE VERTICAL ORDER AND COMMUNICATIONS TECHNOLOGY

> To the maximum extent possible, machines should do the talking so that horizontal integration results in a cursor over the middle of the target, and the technology becomes transparent. – Air Force Chief of Staff Gen. John P. Jumper, before congressional and defense industry leaders 16 October 2001, at an aerospace power seminar on Capitol Hill

> [T]hey were able to get a partial view of the electronic display of market information, the moving message units that streaked across the face of an office tower . . . This was very different from the relaxed news reports that wrapped the old Times Tower . . . These were three tiers of data running concurrently and swiftly about a hundred feet above the street. Financial news, stock prices, currency markets . . . Beneath the data strips, or tickers, there were fixed digits marking the time in the major cities of the world. – Don DeLillo, *Cosmopolis*

The term "broadcast" as linked to technologies that send out messages without receiving replies, responses, queries, or objections entered the English language in the first years of the 1920s, and broadcast technologies, due to their unremittingly unidirectional communicative nature, have ever since held a peculiar spot in the history of communications. The ebb and flow of language or information assumed by the term "communication" and its cognates ("common," "community," "commerce," etc.) has no real bearing on broadcast technologies. Nonetheless, these assumptions remain the mainstay of the utopian and emancipatory rhetoric about what communications and information technologies allow us in an age dominated by the pursuit of information: namely participatory politics, economics, and cultures. While the promise of communications technologies remains that of the dialogue, the vast majority of communications technologies are decidedly monologic. Loudspeaker technology provides a useful example. In the 1920s and 1930s, the loudspeaker represented aural technology for outdoor use in transition from the factory whistle to the air-raid siren. Loudspeaker technology made it possible to produce live events attaining the status of aural spectacles that manifested "mass culture" and "mass movement," if not crowd control and crowd manipulation. "The logistical achievement that underlay these spectacles," argues Sanford Kwinter, "was redoubtable, and the extension of military techniques of planning and control to the civilian multitudes was undoubtedly but a felicitous side-effect from the viewpoint of the fascist regimes."[3]

But was it just a felicitous side-effect? Then, in the 1930s, for fascist regimes? Or, later during the Cold War and its redeployment as the air-raid siren? Or even more importantly in the post-Cold War era, for those regimes that steadfastly define themselves as the very antithesis of fascism or totalitarianism? The seeds of the Cold War's C^{3}I can be found in the technicity of the loudspeaker, just as they can in the air-raid siren or, as Paul Edwards argues, the computer.[4] The loudspeaker and the air-raid siren are both aural broadcast media deployed largely in urban centers for one-way communication from authorities (of a sort) to the masses.[5] We find in these broadcast technologies the emergence of the "control" and "contain" attributes of communication, as well as of the geo-political and local–social organization in which the communication functions, that characterized the post-Second World War world. Paul Bracken, a contemporary historian of the Cold War, has argued that the terms "command and control" form an arrangement of technologies, information gathering, processing, and dissemination for use by "a commander in planning, directing and controlling military operations," thus rendering the additional terms in C^{3}I (i.e. communications and information/intelligence) "redundant."[6] And although the command and control qualities inherent in terms such as communication and intelligence became codified and intensified in Cold War institutions and applications, the histories of these terms denote such meanings much earlier. Similarly the institutional and militaristic history of the term "control" can be found in its earliest cited *OED* usage as meaning "the fact of controlling, or checking and directing action," when in 1784 it was used in relation to a Board of Control supervising the East India Company in the governance of British India. The related communications term, "network," has its earliest use in 1825 when military engineers approved it for designating the connections between fortresses, fortifications, underground galleries, and routes of communication. From the outset, and inextricably woven into the historicity of these terms and concepts, are the notions we find operative in C^{3}I as strategy for containment.

The shift from disciplinary power to control power, as discussed by Gilles Deleuze, emerges through the intricate interlinking of technology, policy, and economics operative in the Cold War, especially C^{3}I.[7] What Kwinter calls "a felicitous side-effect" is actually the explicit, strategic, and central effect of geopolitical strategy for "free" governments in the latter part of the twentieth century (who fought fascism, of course) found in the ideal of C^{3}I. The marks, legacies, and technicity of C^{3}I, as has already been noted, are everywhere around us, no more so than in global cities-as-broadcast cities poised not just on, but *as,* networked nodes of circulating capital, information, images, hardware, materials, *matériel,* and (to a certain extent) personnel.

The emergence of video façades on buildings in the last decade of the twentieth century is only an updated version of the loudspeaker, augmented with animated visual images and advertising. The end of the Cold War saw the full implementation of C³I in the private sector and realization in the dominant neo-liberal democratic/capitalist understanding of "the new world order." Under-girding this moment is the terrain-less flow of information, goods, capital, and sovereignty facilitated by and put into operation through the technologies developed for the Cold War C³I demands. The video screens that pass as the architectural façade of global cities in Asia, Europe, and North America broadcast the triumph of this "new world order" onto the streets and over the heads of civilians, creating a means of mass crowd control and manipulation so overt that it has become oblique and background: the *actual* façade of life and buildings. It has become architecture: the technique, or rather technicity, of architecture and of dwelling.

"The vertical order," therefore, has both militaristic and social/economic institutional meanings. When Virilio applies the phrase to architecture, it quite obviously gestures towards Le Corbusier's modernist vertical visions. The phrase, then, describes the integration of a certain type of militaristic strategy into architecture: specifically, the desire to overcome horizontal limits, gain the high ground, and accelerate ballistics and "project(ile)s"[8] of all kinds. Le Corbusier well understood the inseparable military dimensions of city planning and architecture, as exemplified in *The Radiant City* and *Towards a New Architecture*. He even argues that city planning should mobilize its resources accordingly: "Equipment: high command and army, machines and transportation, discipline – ALL EXACTLY THE SAME AS FOR WAGING WAR."[9] That the direct audience of *The Radiant City* was the Vichy government, and an indirect one was Mussolini, indicates that Le Corbusier's rhetoric and urban/military analogies were not arrived at haphazardly. Following a trajectory that made cities and architecture more amenable to circulation and mobility, Le Corbusier saw the Futurist embrace of military technicities as the future of the built environment within urban planning, and the cities we live in today bear this out.

The military implications of the "vertical order" are clear in both command structure and battlefield strategy as it sought to gain ever-greater visual control of the battlefield. The penultimate move in the trajectory toward "gaining the higher ground" for military strategy resulted in airplanes and their general impact on geopolitical space. The romanticized effects of this move for architecture and urban planning are outlined in the visionary volume by Le Corbusier on vision and perspective, *Aircraft: A New Vision*. The period from 1870 to just prior to the First World War saw the various European states trying to limit the effects of air power and their potentially catastrophic impact on cities and civilian populations.[10] Their inability to so contain air warfare can be found in the concept of "total war," which made all civilians potential targets while simultaneously providing the impetus and momentum for the next move in the struggle to gain the higher ground. The ultimate step in this desire to break the existential clench of the horizon for military strategy emerges as war in space, which was temporarily halted by the 1967 Treaty on Principles Governing the Activities of States in the Exploration and Use of Outer Space, but vigorously pursued by US administrations from Reagan onward.

But the term "vertical order" also bears upon the "New Economy" discourse of the post-Cold War era. Modeled on the supposedly decentralized circulation of information provided by the Internet, which presumes to undermine hierarchical arrangements, this discourse employs such phrases as "horizontal integration" or "horizontal organization" in a depreciatory sense to express the end of top-down controls in institutions, systems and economies. That the Internet, as well as the language of decentralization regarding command and control systems that emerges from it, is a technology designed for military application, might indicate that the challenge to hierarchies IT and other "new economy" technicities purportedly pose might be somewhat ameliorated. Even those terms and models meant to liberate us from the sedimentary hierarchical influences of institutions apparently past, simply repeat the order they are said to undermine. The shift to horizontal patterns of architecture (the oblique function and topological expansion), economics (the "New" economy and IT revolution), management systems, and communications systems bear the imprint of the very hierarchy they purport to overturn, and, in fact, reveal an interrelatedness by which the existence of one necessitates the existence of the other. The dispersal of control mechanisms does not mean the loss of centralized control, but rather guarantees its survival, as the initial design of the Internet reveals (i.e. as a communications system designed to withstand and survive nuclear attack). The vertical and the horizontal orders, in other words, are complementary, not contradictory, and might even be synonymous, linked as they are by the electromagnetic realm and the technologies that produce it. General Jumper's epigraph found at the start of this section evocatively makes this very point.

In this enlightening statement by the current US Air Force Chief of Staff, we find the full complementary nature of vertical and horizontal integration. The higher ground is achieved by machines talking to one another, freed of "the human factor" that weapons systems since the Second World War have sought to minimize, in such a manner as they create horizontal integration – that is complete control over the visual field, so that the horizontal plane of the earth emerges *without* horizon through the co-ordination of horizontal planes above the earth. The field of perception essential to warfare loses the limits imposed by the horizon. The same principle guides Global Position Satellite systems (GPS): that is, the flattening of the earth's sphere into a two-dimensional surface. General Jumper further delineates what this means for those involved in this most ideal of battle scenarios: the placement of the cursor over the target, "and the technology becomes transparent." Horizontal integration results in the imposition of the mark from the vertical order on the target, and does so with such speed, efficiency, and clarity that the technology disappears into the action it enables. The goal of these ultra high-tech weapons systems is their disappearance into the manifestation of the combatant's orders, which, of course, come from above. This is why the move to high-tech weaponry in the military from the 1950s onward was resisted by many professional officers who felt their autonomy for battlefield decision making was being systematically removed from them and centralized in the upper echelons. They were right.

CITIES OF CIRCULATION: FROM LINEAR TO BALLISTIC CITY

Ever since the advent of the mechanistic model of organization, notions of crisis and management of crises in complex situations had been linked to those of communication and information. They would become more and more central to the degree that the informational model was approached, with the latter ultimately supplanting the former at the end of World War II. The origin of the shift from the mechanistic model to the model characterized by electronic transport of information and action, or the "control revolution," lies precisely in the fact that the techniques of information and communication instituted in the course of the nineteenth century proved insufficient to administer accelerated circulation of production and distribution. – Armand Mattelart

[W]e have enriched our sensibility with a *taste for the light, the practical, the ephemeral, and the swift* . . . [The Futurist city must be] like an immense and tumultuous shipyard, agile, mobile and dynamic in every detail. – Sant'Elia, *The Manifesto of Futurist Architecture* (emphasis in the original)

The vision of cities, governments, and architecture that facilitate the circulation and movement of commodities, goods, population, images, information, and capital has been essential to urban planning throughout the twentieth century, building upon and expanding models and technologies developed in the nineteenth. No single model has emerged as triumphant in this desire, as the Garden City and the Radial City prove, but the enunciation of this urbanist mode reveals the technicities that drive it in an ever-increasing fashion. The vision of urban design that facilitates circulations parallels the exponential growth in the numbers deployed in standing armies, which went from tens of thousands in the nineteenth century to several million in the twentieth, and the boulevards have been cut ever-wider to accommodate them. This growth would lead to the primacy of *logistics* in military strategy, especially with the innovations of Napoleon, who placed speed and mobility of an army over its size, thus making his first modern, "nomadic" military co-opting of the war machine by the state. The service industry known as logistics is about just this perpetuation of the flow and movement of goods, capital, information, and images to maximize efficiency in areas such as "last-minute production," copying real-time innovations in IT as well as strategies for feeding, outfitting, and arming soldiers in the field in the most efficient manner possible.

The emphasis on circulation is also, and obviously, an emphasis on speed. Architecture, for centuries, was supposed to resist destruction, and therefore provide a monumentality that stood in opposition to speed and temporality. Yet, now, in the US, Europe, and Asia, some cities demand a demolition permit to be acquired along with the building permit. The building has become a material image and manifestation of immateriality, of evanescence. As such, architecture moves even closer to the Futurist manifesto by Antonio Sant'Elia, in which he argues an inherent relationship between buildings and speed that not only reveals the increased mechanization of society and culture, but also the increased militarization of buildings and society through the incorporation of speed. "*The house will last for less time than we will*," Sant'Elia writes on the eve of the First World War; "*each generation must build its own city.*"[11]

Military architecture, as Paul Virilio points out, has a ballistic dimension; that is, it is "not static and is not interested in the resistance of materials," and thus for this type of architecture, "the act of destruction is part of the construction."[12] Cities within global networks, then, have mandated, at times, that buildings be militarized, and at others have merely incorporated buildings that are militarized: temporary, mobile, and dynamic. The materials deployed to achieve these qualities are the ones the Futurists fetishized, as did Le Corbusier, in a similar embrace of the military: glass, reinforced concrete, steel, textile fiber, and the other substitutes for stone, wood, mortar, and brick. These materials, of course, dominate recent and current construction projects in many global urban sites. The first dean of MIT's Humanities and Social Sciences division, John Ely Burchard, wrote in 1954 that the modernist, militarized mobility found in architectural evanescence linked it to the threat of nuclear weapons. "Historians trying to generalize from our buildings," he said, "may develop elaborate hypotheses to explain the metal and glass cages as the expression of the feeling of a society with a sense of death, 'ephemera, ephemera, all is ephemera,' in which building for permanence was obviously futile and for which there was something symbolic in using fragile and transitory materials."[13] Burchard, sensitive to the geopolitical moment, attributes current design issues to an existential despair in the face of atomic warfare. But a better explanation, one ineluctably connected to the military as well, could reside in the nearly half-century interest in facilitating the speed of buildings and the circulation of urban systems in which they are situated.

Despite the modernist preoccupation with the individual living unit – or "the cell" – disconnected and decontextualized from the systems that support it, the Futurist city of Sant'Elia, and more importantly Le Corbusier's adaptation of it, is the one most readily realized in contemporary global urban sites: designed in ways to accelerate, and not overturn, the Beaux Arts fixation on circulation. "Sant'Elia," Kwinter asserts, "was the first to establish movement or circulation as a first principle that does not so much act upon the substratum as meld with and mobilize the city's actual substance (including its architectural elements)."[14] If Sant'Elia was the first, then Le Corbusier was not far behind, and they both merely intensified urban processes already begun and accelerated throughout the nineteenth century. Both Sant'Elia's Futurist city and Le Corbusier's "Radiant City" depend on maximizing the horizontal flows of energy, transport, people, communications, and information through ever faster materials working on interlinked planes stacked vertically – which, of course, is the configuration of GPS and other vertical–horizontal interconnected military technologies of centralized command discussed in the previous section.

The vertical stacking of complementary horizontal planes finds early textual articulation in Le Corbusier's celebration of planes, or more specifically airplanes, *Aircraft: The New Vision,* published in 1935. This work expresses Le Corbusier's strong affinity for Futurist obsessions, rejections, and delights, including a deep romanticism of the machine. But, more importantly for the historicity being delineated here, *Aircraft* reveals the ways in which the horizontal and the vertical orders conjoin. In the text that accompanies picture 96, in a publication without standard pagination, Le Corbusier waxes futuristically enthusiastic about what the new vision from the air allows and portends:

THE BIRD'S EYE VIEW.
THE EYE NOW SEES IN SUBSTANCE WHAT THE MIND FORMERLY
COULD ONLY SUBJECTIVELY CONCEIVE.
IT IS A NEW FUNCTION ADDED TO THE SENSES.
IT IS A NEW STANDARD OF MEASUREMENT.
IT IS A NEW BASIS OF SENSATION.
MAN WILL MAKE USE OF IT TO CONCEIVE NEW AIMS.
CITIES WILL ARISE OUT OF THEIR ASHES.[15]

The arrangement of the typography highlights the vertical dimensions of the page, not the standard horizontal construction of typeset prose, thus making the layout mimic both modernist/futurist manifestos and the architectural agenda. At the same time, the text enunciates the effects that the technology of flight will perform on humans, the sensorium, judgment, and urban redesign (in much the same way that D. W. Griffith and Dziga Vertov contemporaneously argued would happen due to the technology of the cinema camera and analytic/montage editing). The grim irony in Le Corbusier's prognostications is that his glorified aircraft would also rain down the destruction necessary for urban reconstruction to occur. The aircraft revving up on the European continent, the UK, and North America would provide Le Corbusier with the means to have his cities literally turned into the ashes out of which his new urban plans will arise. Le Corbusier gives this point little attention, though the attention he does extend to aerial warfare is sufficient to deduce that he had some inkling of the grimmer consequences of embracing the new vertical order wrought by aircraft.[16]

As Le Corbusier sought to decongest the city, his radiant vision of complete urban planning led to a series of concentric rings that resembled a bull's eye target, which the city in the age of aerial warfare had become and which Le Corbusier argued his design, in fact, could protect against. More importantly, though, the "Radiant City" cleared space between high-rise, "horizontal skyscrapers" to facilitate the circulation of that which the city would be required to circulate. That this circulation supported the arbitrary divisions created between civic, military, political, and economic domains is inscribed in Le Corbusier's name for his foundational buildings: "horizontal skyscrapers," which presage the complex task of merging and integrating the vertical order with its supposed-antithesis, the horizontal order. The immediate post-Second World War world saw numerous such "horizontal skyscrapers" emerge from the rubble of war, and Singapore contributed its own version of these in the massive rehousing project undertaken by the HDB.[17] These vertical slabs of reinforced concrete (the foundational material of choice for the Futurists and Le Corbusier) remain the most memorable and visible dimensions of the Singaporean built environment.

Le Corbusier took Sant'Elia's concerns further than the idealistic Futurist was able to ever concretely realize in such constructions as "the aerohabitat" in Algiers (Fig. 4.1) which embeds family dwelling units within roads leading to different levels and layers of transport connection. While also recalling the late Renaissance bridges that allowed stone roads to pass over the fluid roads of rivers while also accommodating living spaces, "the aerohabitat" is most reminiscent of the dream-like "Station and Airport design" (Fig. 4.2) of 1914 proposed by Sant'Elia.

When the vertical order manages and controls the horizontal one, then we get the ballistic trajectory delineated explicitly in Le Corbusier's "Obus" plans for Algiers. (Plan B is featured in Fig. 4.4, and resembles quite markedly Sant'Elia's Futurist City found in Fig. 4.3.) The "Obus" plans explicitly articulate their ballistic inheritance and intent, for they are named after the shell fired by a cannon or other projectile accelerator. These plans layer the city of Algiers on several planes that merge the horizontal flow of traffic and pedestrians with the vertical order of the marina high-rise – another of LC's horizontal skyscrapers – while also intersecting with the building itself at several different vertical heights.

Figure 4.1
Le Corbusier's "Obus" plan for Algiers – horizontal layering of circulatory routes

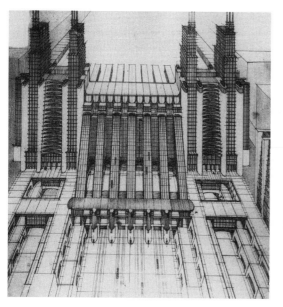

Figure 4.2
Sant'Elia's Station for planes and trains

Figure 4.3
Sant'Elia's Futurist City – vertical integration of horizontal layers

Figure 4.4
Le Corbusier's ballistic vertical integration of horizontal layers for Algiers

As Sant'Elia's manifesto argues, the ideal analogy for the Futurist City (read here as the direct antecedent for the Ballistic City) is the shipyard, or port, with its emphasis on speed, mobility, and dynamism in every detail, to echo his words. Singapore's colonial past and postcolonial present have depended on its port. The military and communications extensions of that port have been involved in the technicities of urban design as the city has moved through the colonial, postcolonial, Cold War, and post-Cold War eras, transforming the geographical, territorial port into the deterritorialized "hub" of the "Intelligent Island." The explicitly material nature of the Ballistic, Obus urban site has been gradually trans-mogrified into the even more circulatory and flow-driven electromagnetic realm of the Broadcast City. The speed of the port, which accommodated an astonishing 146,000 ships in 2001, and the hundreds of logistics companies that facilitate the port, is outpaced only by the city-state's real-time capital and financial services circulating through the wired island and its building-nodes.

Le Corbusier's and Sant'Elia's urban designs create buildings as nodes in networks of circulation, as do the urban designs present in global cities today. The segregation of horizontal planes for different circulating entities (e.g. planes, trains, cars, pedestrians, communications systems, electricity, sewage) comes under the control of a highly articulated vertical order. The horizontal "street" as a site of neighborhood culture, communal interaction, and, potentially, political action, is neatly contained and made vertical, through high-rise living accommodations. The military combination of horizontal and vertical integration can be found in the enunciative modalities of circulation updated materially and intensified through the performative dimensions of the materiality of urban design as articulated by Sant'Elia and manifested by Le Corbusier.

The contemporary global urban site reveals intensification in the deterritorialization of the city begun in the nineteenth century with mechanical transportation systems, industrial production, explicit decongestion urban designs, and telecommunications systems. Hausmann's wide Parisian boulevards were updated to grids in the US, which in turn led to Arturo Sora y Mata's 1880s model of the lineal garden city. This shaped the Russian linear city of the 1920s that influenced Le Corbusier's linear and ballistic Obus plans. A particular trajectory can be delineated that moves from the linear city, to the ballistic city, to its next "logical" step that incorporates and articulates the explicitly militaristic dimensions of deterritorialization implicitly enunciated in Sant'Elia and Le Corbusier: the broadcast city.

The Futurists best conceived of and envisioned our current urban moment, but the results have been far less utopian. Striving for dynamism in plastic forms, Boccioni writes: "My inspiration moreover seeks through assiduous research a complete fusion of environment and object by means of the interpenetration of planes."[18] This interpenetration of planes that allows for increased circulation in urban sites originally held, in the Futurist manifestos, liberatory potential for the working classes. But their application instead yielded their performative powers to the insignia of the military. In fact, they came to comprise that insignia in their *surenchère* from the First to the Second World War and into the Cold War. The intensive rationalization of interpenetrating planes became the grid of networks circumscribing the bifurcated Cold War globe, allowing mobile sovereignty to enact itself through the technicity and logic of the nomadic and deterritorialized modalities of the war machine. In this intensification of a specific urban trajectory, the ballistic city becomes our contemporary broadcast city.

CLOSING WINDOWS: FROM BALLISTIC CITY TO BROADCAST CITY

> Architecture will have to come to terms with the problem of "hosting" virtual space within its concrete spatiality. Just as, in the seventeenth century, it absorbed the fictitious spatiality of mirror, it will, in the twenty-first century, absorb the far-more fictitious, and yet very real presence of virtual spaces. – Paul Virilio

> Countries are driven by their need for accurate visual information. – Conrad Mueller, V-P of Global Alliances of Space Imaging

> STRICOM is enhancing its support to Security Assistance by exporting the corporate vision it maintains for supporting the US Soldier. We envision ourselves as an enabler to the identification of quality "Simulation Solutions" to support training, testing and warfighting experimentation. By relating this strategic vision and our Security Assistance mission we can now assist our security partners in determining where they want to be in the domains of Live, Virtual and Constructive simulation. – http://www.stricom.army.mil/STRICOM

So we arrive at the city-state of Singapore, a broadcast city in full beam. The creeping urbanism begun in the nineteenth century – simultaneously in seemingly diverse sites such as Singapore, London, Paris, and Hanoi[19] – has accelerated through colonialism, the Second World War, the Cold War, postcolonialism, the post-Cold War Global order, and the War on Terror. Each stage is archived and intensified in various systems, circulations, and technicities distributed throughout the ever-shifting urban site. The architectonics of architecture no longer conform or cohere to the tectonics of the island, as the latter metamorphoses under explicit fauna engineering – through the transplanting of trees and plants as well as the very soil in which they grow – and the literal expansion of the island's land mass. The buildings must be mobile, transient, nomadic, ballistic, and deterritorialized for even the ground beneath their very foundations is in flux, and not due to the shifting of the earth's plates that plagues nearby archipelagos, but rather due to urban planning meant to keep the city-state relevant in the urban trajectory this article has been delineating.

This trajectory from linear city to ballistic city to broadcast city mirrors in Singapore, as it does for many global cities, the trajectory of architectures of the horizontal order (the *Kampong*) to one in which the horizontal is managed by the vertical order (the high-rise blocks of condos and the modernist verticality of HDB buildings). Then the explicitly complementary combination of the two emerges, in which circulation, communication, surveillance, and logistics are simultaneously built into urban design and architecture, as well as business, political, and military practices, through and by the technologies and technicities of the electromagnetic realm and optoelectronics. In another set of analogues directly related to this trajectory, Virilio delineates three stages of weapons, each of which corresponds to the three stages of the urban site and its attendant orders: weapons of obstruction (e.g. battlements, shields, helmets, ramparts, and bunkers), weapons of destruction (e.g. arrows, bullets, shells, and missiles), and weapons of communication (e.g. spies, satellites, information systems, unmanned aircraft, and spy planes – or, in essence, C^3I).[20] The weapons of obstruction are deployed in the horizontality of the linear city, those of destruction in the vertical order of the ballistic city, and those of communication in the integrated horizontal and vertical regimes of the broadcast city.

In each of these mutually dependent and inextricably interrelated enunciations of specific technicities – cities, spatial orders, and weapons – we find an archiving, speeding up and *surenchère* at work, so that each successive stage attaches to and detaches from specific elements, techniques, and strategies found in earlier stages: never erasing (completely) nor only making a palimpsest of the specific historicity at work. Geopolitical space in Singapore, as elsewhere, has become also time-space, speed-space, logistics-space, and broadcast space. The IT realm demanded by the military spills over into the ubiquity of video screens in business, pedestrian, and urban life. The video screens that function as a building's façade, as a result, now return in the *surenchère* of this article's argument (so that the rhetoric and logic of the article embodies the operations of the *surenchère* found in these trajectories).

Video screens-as-façades of buildings in numerous urban areas function as "a third window," according to Paul Virilio.[21] The first was the door, which allowed for entry into a structure, and the second was the one that let in light and air, to more closely connect interior space with exterior space. But Virilio's account of video screen façades as the next step for buildings to accommodate shifting notions of spatiality ignores the fact that doors and windows allow things into *and* out of buildings, whereas the video screen merely broadcasts. The window further provides a framing that allows for distinguishing between inside and outside, marking space in each in specific and privileged ways. The video screen does none of this, though the discursive field in which it operates pretends that it prosthetically extends the optic gaze of the serene and rational interior beyond the limits of the physical window and the biological eye.[22] Instead, the video screen merely extends the network and movement of circulating images, advertisements, cybercapital, currency market updates, TV programs, etc. and actually often has little to do with accommodating cyberspace or virtual space *as* space beyond the two-dimensional screen. In this manner, the video façade rearticulates the mode of enunciation found in broadcast technologies delineated earlier. Buildings merely carry and transmit messages, without providing any input. They become another node in the general network of C^3I. Materially and symbolically, as Paul Edwards has argued, the centralization of C^3I has become equated with computers and computerization, despite, as we have already discussed, the rhetoric of decentralization and horizontal integration meant to overturn vertical hierarchies.[23] With the architectural incorporation of the video monitor, the physical, spatial, and ideological control of Cold War strategies materialize in the urban landscape as innovative, cutting-edge, emancipatory technology, while actually being none of these. The video screen façade provides the perfect melding of technology and architecture with the control dimensions of control society, as outlined by Deleuze.

The logic and technicity of C^3I clearly determine urban and business design that relies on and perpetuates communications and information. The technologies of nuclear weapons paralleled and depended upon communications systems: emission, transmission, dispatching, and delivering – but they did so *in a singularly unidirectional broadcast manner* (or so the military planners hoped, despite the deterrence posited by Mutual Assured Destruction). Although Bracken argues otherwise, communications is the essence of C^3I because it ensures, in theory, that politicians and military commanders (central command and control) speak to each other knowledgeably and rationally, thereby averting all-out nuclear conflagration. But, as we have noted, the goal of C³I was/is containment, so the type of communications operative within it more closely resembles that found in broadcast teletechnologies than that in dialogical communication models. Communication and information became essential dimensions of Cold War military strategy, and migrated rapidly from there to government, business, and polity strategy with information becoming the ground upon which all sufficient reasons for action were based. But, as Martin Heidegger noted, but a decade into the Cold War trajectories so concretely realized around us,

> while information in-forms, that is apprises, it at the same time forms, that means, arranges and sets straight. As an appraisal, information is also an arrangement that places all objects and stuffs in a form for humans that suffices to securely establish human domination over the whole earth and even over what lies beyond this planet. In the form of information, the powerful Principle of providing sufficient reasons holds sway over all cognition and thus determines the present world-epoch.[24]

The "ballistic" attribute that Virilio notes in contemporary buildings emerges from their circulation of information that in-forms and sedimentizes even as it circulates, following the Sant'Elia and Le Corbusier plans. The IT 2000 vision of Singapore as an "intelligent island" makes clear this point. "In effect," Peter Droge writes, "buildings function as computer-aided information processing nodes on the urban grid."[25] The network nodes, flow, and circulation of information essential to the operation of C³I have become essential to governmental and business practice globally, just as C³I provides us the model for all globalization projects. The ballistic dimension is intensified in communications-and/as-broadcast practices and technicity that lead to the video façade, which embodies this technicity and its enunciation in the broadcast city. (That Sant'Elia's "New City" included an apartment building with a cinema screen for advertising – that is, a precursor of the video façade as well as revelation of its primary function – displays both his prescience and, more importantly, the historicity of the conditions that currently prevail.) The broadcast city enables and informs broadcast in all its varied manifestations, and is both the broadcast node and its recipient/projector. In some ways, we are a long way from the loudspeaker but, in other more important ways, we are not. The intensification of modalities of enunciation and performance found in the shifts from linear city to ballistic city to broadcast city mean that the historicity iterates and reiterates itself in ways that are unsettlingly familiar yet also comfortingly new – at least enough of each to make us think we have a past to draw on and that the present reflects this while also providing change, which can also be interpreted as progress. Elements of each city remain in its current avatar as we move along this particular trajectory of the global urban site.

As the vertical order and the horizontal order integrate their own integral patterns in the broadcast city, the horizontal order capitulates to the command and control modes of the vertical order. As the higher ground is more effectively gained, developed, and domesticated, the vertical order flattens the curvature of the earth, and renders the globe the two-dimensional artifact of the cartographer. Space imaging and remote sensing essential to the real-time, global reach of Cold

War surveillance of every part of the earth now play a similarly essential role in business, government, agricultural, meteorological, and disaster planning and responses, while also becoming ever-increasingly important for the military that inaugurated them. The broadcast city is not only broadcast through these systems but is itself broadcast too, as the video façade reveals. The video façade, the very architecture of our cities, and the essence of urban planning is broadcast and projected in and through CCD (charged-couple device) detectors that turn territory, terrain, and buildings into machine-coded images capable of being read only by machines in horizontal integration. The commercial application of these technologies manifests itself all around us, and not only in the broadcast city, but also in the rural areas that surround and support it. One of the leading companies trafficking in space and remote sensing, imaging, and processing lists its various applications as including utilities/telecommunications, government, disaster, real estate, and transportation.[26] One of the centers for processing this imagery is based in Singapore, and the website broadcasts an image of the city to display its product (see Fig. 4.5).

Pictured in the space-imaging photo is a stellar complex of convention/exhibition center, shopping malls, and high-rise commercial buildings called Suntec City (with the War Memorial visible in a carved out swath of greenery amidst the buildings), which John Phillips examines in detail in this volume. This space-image, then, pictures a completely two-dimensional, horizontalized urban space (read, militarized in the technicities delineated by General Jumper in this piece) that Phillips reads in a three-dimensional, archived and archiving manner. But there is, of course, archiving on display here as well: the archiving documented in this photo is the archiving of the trajectory of the technicities operative in urban planning that culminates in the broadcast city. Of specific note about this particular archival document, however, is the technicity by which the technology can be attached to, and just as easily detached from, a myriad of applications – commercial, civil, military, speculative, emergency. This specific detail of the larger space-image of the city center of Singapore further highlights the deeply inter-related nexus of technicities of the military insignia in daily urban space, for not one single dimension of the Suntec City complex is uninfluenced by the space images and their manifold applications broadcast from orbital space to the green space of the War Memorial separating shopping from other types of built aggregations.

Figure 4.5
Satellite image of Singapore, featuring Suntec City and the War Memorial

The horizontal order and the vertical order explicitly interlocked in the broadcast city exhibit the conventions of urbanism that we have come to expect in the global city. Flourishing under the rubrics of freedom, choice, mobility, opulence, freedom, and liberation, global urbanism is constructed out of a complex range of technologies and technicities that result from and perpetuate the *containment* that is the essential and targeted effect of the Cold War's C[3]I. If, as John Phillips argues, modernity produces "islands of possibility within the proscribed yet infinitely reproducible city limits,"[27] then C[3]I provides the techne through which this infinitely reproducible yet constrained global urbanism can and does emerge in global cities. And, if moments of freedom, choice, and liberation do emerge – islands potentially manifest in the conditions that pertain – then they are but the unintended consequences of the technicities of containment, despite the fact that they are articulated *as* the rationale for the technicities. The hinge of the "as" here between the ideological (or designed) and discursive (or designated) operations of C[3]I technicities highlights the permutation of stated effects and/as actual effects, of intended consequences and/as unintended consequences in global urbanism.

The historicity of global urbanism, and the archiving that is the city, allows the Cold War containment dimensions of C[3]I to be stored away, out of view, in contemporary urban space (even though it is often stored out of view *before our very eyes*, much like Poe's purloined letter, as in the case of the video façade). But as with all archived materials, they can be retrieved and put into full, explicit, and marked view if need be, as in the case of the War on Terror. The hinge of the "as" allows the global urban site as free market/free space to become a contained/controlled site under the global surveillance of the opto-electronic realm.[28] The space-image that charts the flow of shoppers on the horizontal sidewalk from the upper reaches of vertical geo-orbital space can also chart the flow of suspect groups and individuals. The cell phones that beepingly broadcast social engagements and allow for the co-ordination of the collection of children from school, can also allow, via GPS, the collection of individuals targeted by the state or international law enforcement agencies/military organizations operating increasingly with mobile sovereignty. (GPS, in military abbreviation, can stand for either Global Position System or Gunner's Primary Sight – targeting is the key to both.) The co-ordinated interlocking of vertical and horizontal space to maximize control over terrain and contain populations as transparently and efficiently as possible is the principle of urbanism, and it is the principle of C[3]I. The global city-as-broadcast city is the product of the *surenchère* of military technicities, and yet we are told that it is the result of benign markets, democratic states, transnational corporations, and research enterprises bringing us all a better and brighter tomorrow.

Seen from space, the city is broadcast back to itself through a video façade on which we can see the horizontal loss of horizon under the vertical order's technicity broadcast onto a vertical façade, high above our pedestrian heads, on the very street we see pictured in the image. Perhaps it is offering us a preview of a film, or advertising new property developments, or news footage displaying the most contemporary of military surveillance techniques harnessed to fight the next war, or an open mobilization exercise call. The image, however, can be, and one could argue *is*, the same one. We can be certain it will tell us which type of image it is when it flashes on the building before our eyes: entertainment, investment, or security. Just as the horizon of the city has disappeared along with the horizon of the globe under the scrutiny of the vertical order, the division, or horizon, between entertainment, product, investment, surveillance, protection, and military target has also disappeared into the frame of the global video node-as-screen. The city speaks to us, as do its buildings, and it tells us how to interpret it and what it says. After all, this *is* broadcast technology.

NOTES

1   I would like to thank Greg Clancey, Nick Cullather, John Phillips, Wei-Wei Yeo, and Bobby Wong for their comments on drafts of this article.
2   See Ryan Bishop and John Phillips "Diasporic Communities and Identity Politics; Containing the Political" in *Asian Diasporas and Cultures: Globalization, Hybridity, Intertextuality,* Robbie Goh and Shawn Wong (eds) Hong Kong University Press pp. 159–173.
3   Sanford Kwinter *Architectures of Time: Toward a Theory of the Event in Modern Culture* (Cambridge: MIT Press, 2001) p. 20.
4   Paul Edwards *The Closed World: Computers and the Politics of Discourse in Cold War America* (Cambridge: MIT Press, 1996).
5   For a discussion of the air-raid siren and its relation to the politics of manufactured and continued emergencies, see Ryan Bishop and John Phillips "Manufacturing Emergencies" in *Theory, Culture and Society* vol.19(4), Fall 2002, 93–104.
6   Paul Bracken *The Command and Control of Nuclear Forces* (New Haven: Yale University Press, 1983) p. 3.
7   See "Control and Becoming" and "Postscript for Control Societies" in *Negotiations: 1972–1990,* Martin Joughin (trans.) (New York: Columbia University Press, 1990).
8   John Armitage's term "project(ile)s" has resonance with the use of ballistics in this chapter, just as his conceptualization of "hypermodernity" as an intensification of modernity that stands in contrast to "postmodernity" has resonance with the use of *surenchère* in this chapter. For a further explanation of these concepts as Armitage uses them, see his *Paul Virilio: From Modernism to Hypermodernism and Beyond* (London: Sage, 2000), and John Armitage and Joanne Roberts, "From the Hyper-modern City to the Gray Zone of Total Mobilization in the Philippines" in Ryan Bishop, John Phillips and Wei-Wei Yeo (eds) *Postcolonial Urbanism: Southeast Asian Cities and Global Processes* (New York and London: Routledge, 2003).
9   Le Corbusier *The Radiant City* (London: Faber & Faber, 1967 (1933)) p. 345, with caps in the original.
10   See Ryan Bishop and Greg Clancey "The City as Target, or Perpetuation and Death" in Ryan Bishop, John Phillips, and Wei-Wei Yeo (eds) *Postcolonial Urbanism: Southeast Asian Cities and Global Processes* (Routledge, 2003), H. Bruce Franklin *War Stars: The Superweapon and the American Imagination* (New York: Oxford University Press, 1988), and Sven Lindqvist *A History of Bombing* (New York: New Press, 2001) for more on the debates about air power and its application to civilian targets.
11   Found on numerous websites, including http://www.unknown.nu/futurism/architecture.html (accessed on 12 Sept. 2002). Emphasis is in the original.
12   See "Paul Virilio and the Oblique: Interview with Enrique Limon" in John Armitage (ed.) *Virilio Live* (London: Sage, 2001) p. 51.
13   "Architecture in the Atomic Age" in *Architectural Record*, Dec. 1954, 120.
14   Sanford Kwinter, p. 91. For further discussion of Le Corbusier's centrality in the emergence of the global city see William Lim's and Heinz Paetzold's articles in this volume.
15   Le Corbusier *Aircraft* (London: Trefoil Publications, 1987 (1935)).
16   Adnan Morshed has examined Le Corbusier's aerial aesthetics and its relation to militarization and urbanization in his article "The Cultural Politics of the Aerial Vision: Le Corbusier in Brazil (1929)" in *Journal of Architectural Education* 55:4, May 2002. Tom Vanderbilt also touches on LC in relation to aerial vision, city planning, and aerial bombing in his book *Survival City* (Princeton: Princeton Architectural Press, 2002).
17   See Gregory Clancey's "Toward a Spatial History of Emergency: Notes from Singapore" in this volume for an extended analysis of emergency, warfare, and housing projects.

Also, see Wei-Wei Yeo's article in this volume for an examination of the representations of HDB complexes in various cultural productions.

18 Quoted from *The Technical Manifesto of Futurist Sculpture*, written in 1912, and widely available on a number of websites.

19 For a discussion of the temporal relations between and simultaneity of urbanization processes on a global scale, see R. Bishop, J. Phillips and W.-W. Yeo, "Perpetuating Cities: Excepting Globalization and the Southeast Asian Supplement" in Bishop, Phillips, and Yeo (eds) *Postcolonial Urbanism: Southeast Asian Cities and Global Processes* (New York and London: Routledge, 2003) pp. 1–36.

20 This is detailed in "On the Strategies of Deception" in *Virilio Live,* p. 169.

21 See "Speed-Space: Interview with Chris Dercon" in *Virilio Live*, p. 69.

22 For more on the window and its relation to inside/outside space and vision, and their relation to the problematic of the transcendental/empirical, being/becoming, optic/haptic categories of knowledge, see John Phillips "Urban New Archiving" in this volume.

23 See Edwards on the material, symbolic, and discursive role played by the computer in relation to C3I, pp. 130–133.

24 Martin Heidegger *The Principle of Reason,* Reginald Lilly (trans.) (Bloomington: Indiana University Press, 1991 (1957)) p. 124.

25 Peter Droge "Future Places" in *Places* vol. 5 no. 3, 3.

26 See www.spaceimaging.com for this and other information.

27 See John Phillips "Archiving Urbanism" in this volume.

28 See Phillips in this volume for the "as" and the hinge. For an extended discussion of the hinge in relation to the military and the military body, see R. Bishop and J. Phillips "The Curious Logic of the Hinge and the (Post) Colonial Military Body" *Body and Society* vol. 9 no. 4 (December 2003) 1–21.

Chapter 5: At Home in the Worlds: Community and Consumption in Urban Singapore

Philip Holden

When I first came to Singapore in 1994, I lived in a rented apartment on Bukit Timah Road close to the seven-mile market. Bukit Timah at that time was a community which had almost completed a profound change from a village on the road to Malaysia to a suburban condominium belt. When I walked to the shopping centre, I would stumble on a pathway still haunted by the presence of now-demolished shophouses. Every few yards, there would be a step down or up, a change of surface from bare concrete to chipped tile: the ghost of the floor of the five-foot way, that contested space[1] of colonial modernity, was all that now remained of buildings swept aside by the modernizing project of nationalism. Six months or so later, the pathway was replaced with a new, even one of textured concrete.

As I walked on, other signs of the past would emerge. The shabby shopping centre where I bought my groceries was called, somewhat bizarrely, Beauty World Centre: the Chinese name, *Mei Shijie Zhongxin*, displayed prominently on the façade, provided no clearer explanation. Besides the supermarket, I went there to have my hair cut, speaking Mandarin in a salon staffed almost exclusively by Malaysians. Across the road from Beauty World was an open field, with a small Urban Redevelopment Authority car park: auctions were held there during the seventh month of the lunar calendar. Beyond this, there was a smaller connecting road, Jalan Jurong Kechil, and then the five-year-old, apathetically postmodern Bukit Timah Community Centre, where I went to apply for classes in Malay, Singapore's national language, and found that none were offered.

Although I didn't realize it at the time, the shopping centre and the community centre, with the empty field in between, were profoundly symbolic spaces in Singaporean modernity, as significant as my own nostalgia for a past I had never known. The shopping centre, at least to all appearances,[2] was a place of hedonism and consumption – albeit of hawker food, sundries imported from China, Korean electronic goods, something of a step down from the global pleasures of Ngee Ann City on Orchard Road – the community centre of production, of leisure time transformed into the discipline of citizenship. The field was the site of Beauty World amusement park, one of Singapore's four Worlds, amusement centres which provided entertainment from the 1920s to the 1980s, and which are still nostalgically remembered by Singaporeans in productions such as Michael Chiang's musical *Beauty World*. Community centre and World, indeed, might be seen as sites of the generation of a Singaporean modernity under capitalism. The community centre, in this reading, is part of a postcolonial narrative of production, of the disciplining of individual citizen subjects in a national modernity which, for all its protestations to the contrary, is in one sense very much the fulfilment of colonial modernity in the fullness of time. The management of leisure time in the centre, and the elaborate regimes of self-improvement and bodily training encouraged within its walls, are part of an ascetic devotion to work which Max Weber identified with Protestantism and which, in the 1980s and 1990s, came to be identified with Confucian and Asian values in Singapore's national narrative. The World, however, reveals the cultural contradictions of capitalism, the necessity of increased consumption to counterbalance every increase in production, and the resultant "tension of asceticism and acquisitiveness":[3] it is a space which is always already postmodern, fractured, globalized. Exploring the community centre and the World as two opposite faces of Singaporean modernity, then, opens up possibilities of viewing Singaporean social history outside of the framework of a progressivist national narrative, the *Singapore Story* of the memoirs of its elder statesman Lee Kuan Yew and of the recent initiative in National Education. Such a revisioning also invites a reimagining of urban space as perpetuating elements of the colonial world which nationalism thought to erase.

CONSUMPTION AND ANTI-COLONIAL NATIONALISM

Understanding the opposed spaces of the community centre and world necessitates a consideration of the place of production and consumption in nationalist narratives of progress and cultural retrieval. In the last twenty years, studies of consumption have moved away from the notion of the consumer as a passive dupe of capitalism, the "empty shell of liberty"[4] preserved in consumer choice serving only to disguise the totalitarian nature of late capitalist society. Consumers may be subcultural actors engaged in subverting hegemonic cultural signifiers through "double inflection,"[5] or even participants in a "semiotic democracy,"[6] in which all consumers have the potential to appropriate or reassign meaning. While many commentators have stressed the need to mediate between the apparent pessimism of the Frankfurt School and the promotion of consumer as unfettered *bricoleur* by semioticians such as John Fiske, it is clear that consumption carries social meaning which is subject to negotiation and change. Consumption thus reflects neither a mirror image of a dominant ideology, nor the autonomous choices of individual actors, but a social space in which hegemonic social forms are negotiated and, at times, contested.

Studies of consumption outside Europe and North America have belatedly followed a similar trajectory. The notion that the "third world" consumer passively acquiesces to – or heroically resists – cultural imperialism has now been discarded, and various commentators have explored how goods such as Coca Cola, McDonalds, and Disney products are resignified as something other than a passive acceptance of American modernity in a variety of social contexts.[7] At the same time, a centre–periphery model persists in many studies of the global nature of consumerism. Consumer society is seen as something recent, a product of postmodernism or post-Fordism which arrives belatedly as an export from the West to the Third World,[8] which in turn attempts to resist becoming "consumerized,"[9] or which then reassigns new meanings. Such a conceptual division has no place for non-Western societies which are not – and have historically not been – "Third World": Japan, for instance. More fundamentally, the Third/First world division involves the acceptance of a certain Gramscian "common sense" regarding the relation of cities to their hinterlands which obscures the intertwined histories of colonialism and consumption. Urban Southeast Asia, in particular, has for the past five hundred years comprised a series of nodes in a dense network of consumption enmeshing East Asia, South Asia, and Europe.

In South and Southeast Asia, indeed, colonialism and consumption have been inextricably linked. Some commentators have argued that consumer culture in Europe was sparked by the availability of goods such as calicoes and muslin from India in the 1690s.[10] Certainly Stamford Raffles' original vision for Singapore was as a commercial "emporium," embedding itself into and strategically realigning pre-existent patterns of trade.[11] The great cities of the colonial world, from the eighteenth through into the twentieth centuries, were port cities, nodes in a world of goods, sites of commerce, of consumption as much as production. What we think of as postmodern culture, Mike Featherstone's "unstable field of floating signifiers" in which individuals move from "unreflectingly adopting a lifestyle, through tradition or habit" to a new "assemblage of goods, clothes, practices, experiences, appearance and bodily dispositions,"[12] might equally describe the juxtapositions of the colonial city, the re-mapping and re-signifying of communities caused by the dislocations of migration and indentured labour. The colonial city, indeed, was a site of "commerce" and consumption. Indeed, J. A. Hobson's liberal critique of Imperialism in the early 1900s was that it was motivated by suppressed domestic and artificially-induced colonial consumption, and was thus "a depraved choice of national life, imposed by self-seeking interests which appeal to the lusts of quantitative acquisitiveness."[13]

Hobson's use of language hints at a key point: while colonialism may have been about consumption, it represented itself, especially under the New Imperialism of the late nineteenth century, as emphasizing production and discipline. Hobson's critique gains rhetorical power because it pictures colonialism, in contrast to its doxological signification, as surrender to acquisition rather than rational asceticism. The project of late nineteenth-century imperialism, indeed, might be described as colonial governmentality, an internalization of disciplinary mechanisms so that each individual would engage in self-regulating devotion to work.[14] In colonial Malaya, thus, Malay "laziness," a refusal to enter a world of alienated production and consumption, was contrasted to Chinese industry by a generation of Malayan Civil Service officers. Yet colonial governmentality always ran up against a fundamental feature of colonial rule: its need to separate colonizer from colonized, to museumize indigenous cultures. Colonial power would thus simultaneously incite colonized subjects to Weberian self-discipline and self-improvement, and condemn those subjects who achieved such discipline as inauthentic and deracinated. The response by nationalist and proto-nationalist groups was to embark on disciplinary projects which won for them the high moral ground, and which realized, through their potential representativeness, the possibility of formation of a modern state.

Within the colonial city, the nascent capital of the new nation, then, anti-colonial nationalism thus paradoxically maintained and amplified late colonialism's distrust of consumption. The liberation of the national territory and building of the nation takes on the significance of a psychic and physical cleansing: it is figured as a restoration of bodily integrity, an expulsion of sickness and disease, the elimination of "poison," the "refusal to accept . . . amputation" of a limb.[15]

The nineteenth-century bourgeois subject saw the aristocrat as an embodiment of excessive, decadent consumption, in contrast to his – or much less frequently, her – devotion to work and self-improvement. The anti-colonial nationalist places the colonialist in the same position: colonialism is a disease which tempts the appetite, which spreads consumption "in order to stimulate the baser instincts of the people" in order to make them "forget the responsibility of national recon-struction,"[16] and which must be resisted. The disciplinary project of anti-colonial nationalism is thus concerned with bodily integrity and single-minded devotion to a cause. It is profoundly production-centred – the project "to lay the foundations for a Malayan culture," for Singapore's first Minister of Culture, S. Rajaratnam, was a component of a national project "to build hospitals, schools and factories for our expanding population,"[17] and consumption, "individual enjoyment,"[18] becomes its disavowed Other. Here the New Jerusalem of an urban environment built by devotion to work drives away the hauntings of the colonial past.

YELLOW CULTURE AND NATIONAL PURITY IN SINGAPORE

Anti-colonial nationalism and later nationalist ideologies in Singapore have, following the contours of the discussion above, always displayed a productivist bias. In the 1950s, much anti-colonial activism by both the Malayan Communist Party, democratic socialist parties, and other organizations, phrased its project as cleansing a Malayan national body debilitated by the addictions "yellow culture" promoted by colonialism. In Singapore in the 1950s, yellow culture was identi-fied with pornographic publications and films, cabarets, and nightclubs, and also "decadent Western culture which comes in the form of rock and roll."[19] In 1957, as Singapore moved towards self-rule in 1959, various leftist and community-affiliated groups set up the "Anti-Yellow Culture Council" at a meeting attended, among others, by future Prime Minister Lee Kuan Yew and his then fellow party member, leftist Lim Chin Siong. Chinese press coverage of the event defined yellow literature, for example, as catering to a "lower taste" and being "full of erotic expressions," and inducing an amoral passivity among the colonized that might be eliminated through the promotion of "healthy recreation."[20]

On taking power in the 1959 elections, the People's Action Party, in its vision of a social democratic future set out, in Lee Kuan Yew's words, to outflank "the communists with puritanical zeal," banning "pornography, striptease shows, pin-table saloons, even decadent songs."[21] Ong Pang Boon, the Minister of Home Affairs, withdrew the permits for the publication of several Chinese magazines which promoted "literary lechery"[22] "in order to correct the degenerate standard of morals in our society, to create a new and healthy vigour in our society."[23] Eight teachers at government schools were suspended for "moral turpitude" in watching an allegedly pornographic film.[24] In the 1960s, as the People's Action Party's vision of modernity embedded in international capital flows triumphed over a more radical leftist alternative, other campaigns were mounted against "hippism" and similar symbols of Western decadence. The ideal citizen of Singapore would be "rugged," a product of "a systematic programme for the inculcation of self-discipline"[25] committed to resisting the excesses of consump-tion in a devotion to unremitting production. And this citizen, again, would realize his potential for discipline in a modern urban environment which stressed efficiency, in which the crooked was made straight.

THE COMMUNITY CENTRE – PRODUCING THE NATIONAL SUBJECT

A key site for the production of national subjects was the community centre. The Bukit Timah Community Centre to which I went when I first arrived in Singapore was a modern building, opened in 1989, one of a network of centres around the island managed by the People's Association, a government statutory board. Community centres seem to have originated from food distribution centres and so-called "people's kitchens" and "children centres" set up by the British military administration immediately after the end of the Second World War. The status of such centres varied widely: some catered largely for the Anglophone middle classes, while others, such as Yio Chu Kang Village Community Centre (see Fig. 5.1), were often in poorer areas, set up by charitable donation. Teo Song Bee, from wealthy Straits Chinese background, for instance, was instrumental in setting up Tiong Bahru Community Centre following a request from a city councillor: he donated some $8000 and took responsibility for the conversion of a Singapore Improvement Trust shelter into the club's first premises. In 1959, however, despite increased government emphasis on the development of community ties in the 1950s, there were only 28 centres.[26] The new Minister of Labour, Kevin Byrne, was shocked to discover that the clubs were havens of "yellow culture," noting with disapproval the "typical nightclub style" of one centre and the fact that children at another were "brainwashed with American propaganda."[27]

After the elections which brought the People's Action Party to power, the centres came under the management of the Department of Social Welfare and then, a year later, transferred to the care of the newly-formed People's Association. This change was political in two senses. First, in attempting to remove an Anglophone elite from the management of the centres and return them to the masses, Singapore's new government was committed to bypassing the bureaucracy of the colonial state[28] and, through "political socialization and nation-building,"[29] realizing the nation as a representative polity in a way that the colonial state could never do. In doing so, the right wing of the People's Action Party consciously used tactics of mass mobilization learned from their leftist, largely Chinese-educated colleagues in the 1950s. The centres, indeed, became the scene of struggles in 1961, after the splitting off of the left wing of the PAP as the Barisan Sosialis: six members of staff were sacked for anti-government

Figure 5.1
Yio Chu Kang Village
Community Centre (1956)

agitation, and a strike by the majority of PA staff was put down.[30] After the referendum on merger with Malaysia, new community centres were opened in largely rural areas with, in all probability, a high Barisan vote. In this sense, the function of the community centres might be seen as narrowly political, promoting the influence of the ruling party.

Community centres, however, were also and more crucially political in a second sense, in their effort to train the energies of anti-colonial nationalism and community-based self-help into work for the development of the nation. The bare concrete architecture of the urban centres, with austere modernist detailing, indicated their alignment with a modernizing project through the medium of the nation. In a speech in 1966, Lee Kuan Yew noted that activities in the community centre marked the beginning of a "long process of identification with the country" for citizens.[31] Cultural performances outside the centres thus contributed, in the early years before Singapore's separation from Malaysia in 1965, to a collective sense of multiracial Malayan culture. More crucially, however, community centres promoted a rationalization of leisure time, a Foucauldian disciplinary regime of self-care or perhaps even the production of a nationalist *habitus*, which prepared the citizen-subject for a role in national development in a Fordist regime of accumulation as Singapore moved from entrepôt trade to the status of a manufacturing centre by attracting multinational capital. Activities in the community centres thus stressed the training of the body, and the production of disciplined individuals for a "rugged society."

The community centre, with its role as a focus for Vigilante Corps and later National Service recruitment, was thus instrumental in the evolution of a new Singaporean subject, whose body stood metonymically for the nation. Singaporeans, Lee noted, should not be a "soft people" with a "lethargic or indifferent approach to . . . life";[32] above all, they should not be "slack."[33] Rather, Lee noted, they should cultivate "physical and spiritual ruggedness."[34] In a recruitment speech held at a community centre, Lee expressed a desire for a "different kind of Singapore citizen[;] . . . not stooping, not weak or flabby but with guts and gusto."[35] What Singapore society needed, Lee had argued a year earlier, were "men of action, sportsmen, gymnasts, rugger players, boxers, airmen, leaders of debating societies, organisers of men" rather than those who were good at "just being clever and writing essays."[36]

The embodiment of citizenship in the new Singapore worked on a variety of levels. The community centres themselves had offices, classrooms, and small halls, but were frequently surrounded by badminton and *sepak takraw* courts. Their organizing committees promoted sports activities amid concerns that urbanized Singaporeans were losing rural vitality. The People's Association Bulletin even ran a "Choose Mr P. A. Bulletin" contest, with a gas stove as first prize (neatly here incorporating a hidden incitement to consumption) in which readers had to nominate one out of five heavily muscled, scantily clad, but racially representative males. At the national level, National Day parades demonstrated individual bodies as components of the national body; in the 1969 parade, students performed a, presumably rather paradoxical, "dance of ruggedness and grace" for an approving audience. Three years earlier, Lord Rhodes, the visiting Parliamentary Secretary to the British Board of Trade, described Singaporeans as a "virile people"[37] and was appreciatively quoted by the Ministry of Culture's weekly *Mirror*. Here we see what John Phillips has called the "empirial" at work, the imperial project merging with the requirements of the postcolonial state which might be thought to stand in opposition to it.

A concrete example of how this process occurred might be the Bukit Timah Community Centre. The centre was opened in 1959, developing out of a youth club which had been started as a community initiative in 1955 at Pei Hwa Chinese School. Bukit Timah Village was at that time a stopping place on the road to Johor and was also a multicultural community. Bukit Timah was also a place in transition towards Fordism: there was a series of factories which drew their labour from the village and surrounding communities, existing simultaneously with Indian labourers' lines and a Malay police compound.[38]

The community centre seems to have been run initially by the English-educated, and to have been viewed with some suspicion by Chinese-educated members of the community. After the 1959 election, the management committee was scrapped, and the management taken over by officers of the People's Association, all of whom were Chinese-educated. There seems to have been some inter-communal tension here. Sports popular among the Chinese educated, such as basketball, were stressed, and new facilities developed, while the football pitch was left unmown, and old footballs not replaced, much to the chagrin of the largely Malay participants in this sport. However, the centre also became the site of an attempt to produce a Malayan culture: films were shown, cultural concerts performed, and the overall participation in community centre activities by all communities seems to have increased.

While the centre had educational, vocational, and recreational elements, it does seem that the recreational element – particularly physical recreation – predominated. The centre seems to have purchased, for instance, a complete set of weights for a bodybuilding club with only twelve members, while choosing not to subscribe to a Tamil newspaper. More subtly, however, the community centre became a site at which leisure time and work time were demarcated, and in which leisure was transformed into a purposeful, disciplined activity. This can be shown in the comments of Sukveer Singh, a University of Malaya sociology student who produced the report which I have been relying upon for much of the information above. Obviously sympathetic to the new national project, Singh was perturbed by the fact that a number of Indian men would gather to drink coffee outside the community centre, but never think to go inside:

> When the writer asked them why do not they go into the centre and sit comfortably instead of standing at street corners they all replied (three of them) that if they were to go there they would not see other friends whereas at the side of the street they can meet friends and crowds moving about.[39]

What the community centre's activities aimed for, above all, then, was an elimination of *jalan jalan*, of purposeless loitering, and openness to random, chance meetings. The rhetoric of the rugged society transformed both leisure and work into a series of disciplinary practices enabling production, channelling the energies of nationhood into a project of self-improvement, and ascetic devotion to work.

The space of the community centre, then, attempted to inscribe a national narrative not just on a landscape, but on the bodies of individual citizens. Named after a location, the community centre aimed to place citizens' bodies within a manufactured neighbourhood whose multiracial nature was a microcosm of that of the nation. The various overlapping affiliations of the colonial world were smoothed out into a series of ever-widening concentric circles, now inscribed on an increasingly urbanized landscape of HDB flats: my body, my family, my neighbourhood, my nation. Untidy corners were eliminated: the individual would maintain an ascetic regime of self-care, devoted to ceaseless production, to support the national development. In the community centre, even leisure time became devoted to self-improvement for increased production. In the 1980s, the two detached halves of a narrative of Malayan cultural specificity and Fordist development met in the notion of Asian values or Confucian capitalism, and ascetic devotion to labour was given a civilizationalist gloss. The community centre thus becomes part of a strategy, "the calculus of force-relationships when a subject of will and power . . . can be isolated from an 'environment'."[40]

In the new millennium, perhaps, the explanatory power of the strategic narrative falters in Singapore, confronted by the tactics of consumption: the shops of Orchard Road, J-pop inspired fashion, body piercing, government scholars breaking bonds with their employers to depart overseas. Yet community centres have also changed over time. Early community centres, we have seen, were often nothing much more than huts in rural kampungs; later structures were either free standing or built into the void decks of HDB blocks. From the 1980s onwards, the physical space of community centres has been transformed. Tanglin Community Club's postmodern mock Tudor architecture, for instance, pastiches the colonial "black and white" mansions still found in the area, attempting to provide an atmosphere of Bourdieuan distinction very different from that of the first centres; even smaller buildings such as Bukit Merah Community Centre have acquired gabled roofs and terracotta roof tiles (see Fig. 5.2). Other community clubs, such as the Marine Parade Community Club, are architecturally significant buildings, and feature elements as diverse as resident theatre companies and Starbucks outlets. As places of increasing consumption they begin to take on other attributes, those previously embodied by spaces "no longer fixed by a circumscribed community,"[41] the submerged narratives of consumption in fairgrounds of the Worlds.

Figure 5.2
Bukit Merah Community Centre

THE WORLDS AND THE PLEASURES OF CONSUMPTION

The Worlds, like the community centres, had origins outside Singapore, here in the great city of Chinese modernity, Shanghai. While China was not formally colonized, Shanghai was, like Singapore, a colonial city, its central district apportioned by the European powers, encircled by a Chinese city with a hinterland behind. The city, Leo Ou-fan Lee has noted, occupies an ambivalent place in Chinese modernity. In parallel to the discursive construction of many colonial cities by diverse nationalisms, its decadence became a sign of China's degeneration and humiliation at the hands of foreign powers for a generation of May Fourth movement writers, who created a sense of nationhood by invoking images of uncontaminated rural simplicity "symbolically invoked as the 'native land' of villages (*xiangtu*)."[42] Simultaneously, however, Shanghai provided a space in which such modern nationalism could be brought into being: as a publishing centre, it was pivotal in the dissemination of such images through the "print-capitalism" in the vernacular (here the common speech, *bai hua wen*, as opposed to Classical Chinese *wen yan wen*) which Benedict Anderson has noted is crucial to the production of a nation as an imagined community.[43]

The Great World amusement park, opened by businessman Huang Chujiu in Shanghai on July 4th 1917, reflected many of the ambiguities of urban Chinese modernity under colonialism. It grew to a five-storey building, featuring distorting funhouse mirrors, cinemas, fast-food shops, theatres, puppet-shows, wrestling matches, songs, and various games. Modernity existed side by side with reinvented traditions. There was, for example, a great deal of regional drama,[44] an example being "Shaoxing opera," originally a rural art form which was refurbished and made more melodramatic in performance to the Shanghai populace.[45] Traditional storytellers were brought in from various parts of the Yangzi valley, speaking in a wide variety of regional dialects. Great World in the 1920s thus epitomizes Grant McCracken's description of consumer goods as "bridges to displaced meanings" in cultures in which these meanings are no longer part of lived cultural realities.[46] Great World would thus parade and shape Chinese nationhood embodied in the *xiangtu* to displaced urban citizens; simultaneously, the modern and internationalist elements of the amusements (the cinema, for instance) provided citizens with access to a global modernity from which the divisions of the colonial city attempted to exclude them.

In the 1920s, Great World in Shanghai was joined by other amusement centres such as New World and *Fuxian Shijie* (World of the Blessed Immortals).[47] Developments in Singapore followed those in Shanghai. In 1923, the brothers Ong Boon Tat and Ong Peng Hock opened the New World amusement park at Jalan Besar[48] and it was followed by the openings of Great World and Happy World (later Gay World), the latter commencing business in 1937[49] (see Figs 5.3 and 5.4). Beauty World, the last and most remotely located of the Worlds, has a slightly more surprising history. It was originally opened as the *Da Dong Ya* or Greater East Asia amusement park during the Japanese occupation, its name suggesting Japanese colonial order's Greater East Asia Co-Prosperity Sphere; after the Second World War ended it quietly metamorphosed into Beauty World.[50]

Spatially, the Worlds in Singapore differed from their Chinese counterparts. Great World in Shanghai was a multi-storey building, while the Worlds in Singapore were large, enclosed spaces filled with booths, stadiums, restaurants, and other structures. Like their Shanghai counterparts, however, the Singapore

Figure 5.3
Entrance to Great
World Amusement Park,
early 1950s

Figure 5.4
Happy World on
Geylang Road, 1949

Worlds offered tradition in modernity, here drawn not merely from a Malayan hinterland, but from countries where much of a migrant population had roots, and from a wider world beyond. Cantonese opera mixed with Malay *bangsawan*, Indian dance, *wayang Peranakan*, wrestling and boxing matches, variety shows, gambling, and later cabaret with Filipino, Goanese, and African American musicians. Once admission charges were paid, the space of the Worlds offered apparently limitless possibilities of consumption. The Singapore Worlds, like the Shanghai Worlds, were a site of displaced meanings, an infinite variety of goods offering the possibility of globalized consumption, unconstrained by the divisions of the colonial world.

For Isa Ibrahim, who came to Singapore to work from a small Malayan town in 1936, the Worlds were part of the "glamour" of the metropolis.[51] Open from six to midnight, the Worlds offered boxing matches, gambling, and eating stalls, while the Ghost Train and Crazy House in New World provided particularly tempting novelties. Others remembered the cabarets – one anonymous interviewee recalled the huge dance floors, and the "taxi dancer" system in which men would buy tickets which they would then use to purchase dances with waiting cabaret girls. Visitors to the cabaret at New World ranged from Chinese businessmen, soldiers and naval personnel to Sultan Ibrahim of Johor. Even during the bleak years of the Japanese occupation, the Worlds offered the pleasures of gambling. Beauty World was no doubt established partly so that the Japanese might cream off gambling revenue, and was surreptitiously patronized by Japanese soldiers changed into Chinese clothes in order to evade the surveillance of their officers.[52]

What the Worlds offered, then, was a particular juxtaposition of tradition and modernity in an urban space. Many events held there, such as the wrestling or boxing matches, or the freak shows witnessed by Rudolph's interviewees, attracted members of all communities, and had international participants. The overall structures of the Worlds were modern: Great World had some of the first Art Deco architecture in Singapore, while New World's ferro-concrete Chinese restaurant and Happy World's immense covered stadium were both impressive engineering feats at the time they were constructed.[53] At the same time, many of the activities carried out in the Worlds were specific to small communities, and were often directed towards the preservation, or reconstruction, of community identities. Matchmaker Lee Guat Kwee, for instance, used the space of New World to introduce prospective marriage partners of a Hokkien dialect group to each other in the 1930s. Peranakan matchmakers offered similar services to their communities. While the audience for *bangsawan* would be both Peranakan and Malay, audiences for such shows as Cantonese opera or Tamil-language drama productions would have largely been restricted to a linguistic community. Rather than being a place of playful hybridity, in this reading, the Worlds become places of community self-identification in opposition to Others, a process at least partly complicit with the racial classification system of the colonial state which mutated into multiracialism upon self-rule.[54] The Worlds were also not insulated from the modernizing projects of both colonialism and nationalism. They were the sites of trade fairs from the colonial period onwards, and Happy World stadium provided the stage for two Malayan victories at badminton in the Thomas Cup in the early 1950s, key events for a nation in waiting for independence.

It would be mistaken, therefore, to see consumption in the Worlds as radically disruptive of disciplinary narratives of colonial and national production, a kind of Bakhtinian Carnivalesque which builds "its own world versus the official world, . . . its own state versus the official state."[55] It would be equally mistaken, however, to see such consumption as entirely complicit with such narratives, a space of release that "serves the interests of that very culture which it apparently opposes."[56] A more nuanced way to approach consumption in the Worlds is indicated by Michel de Certeau's distinction between strategy and tactics. The community centre, we have seen, is part of a strategy of power. A strategy, de Certeau notes, "assumes a place that can be circumscribed as *proper* (*propre*) and thus serves as the basis for generating relations with an exterior distinct from it"; it is the basis for "[p]olitical, economic, and scientific rationality."[57] The disciplinary project of nationalism is thus eminently a strategy. A Foucauldian critique of strategies, de Certeau argues, is certainly powerful, but it may miss examination of also "innumerable other practices that remain 'minor,' always there but not organizing discourses," practices that do not have "their own place."[58] Such practices de Certeau names tactics, part of "an operational logic . . . which . . . has been concealed by the form of rationality currently dominant in Western culture."[59] Tactics do not have their own place, since they occupy "the space of the other" and must "play on and with a terrain imposed . . . and organized by the law of a foreign power."[60]

Crucially, de Certeau notes that while strategy – and analyses of strategy such as Foucault's – stress production, tactics are often expressed through consumption. Within the overall strategy of modernity, then, "the procedures of contemporary consumption appear to constitute a subtle art of 'renters' who know how to insinuate their differences into the dominant text."[61] Consumption occupies the space of the Other, subtly transforming and processing those goods imposed on it through "its ruses, its clandestine nature, its tireless but quiet activity."[62] In a very real sense, the Worlds do not have their own space: the fairground atmosphere, for all the magnificent modern structures, promises impermanence. Unlike the community centre, which roots itself in an imagined social space, and brings a community as a microcosm of the nation into being, the World's space is always unstable. In the heart of the city or the village, it is always already globalized. The World is a place of commerce, spectacle, trade, interchange: it insinuates consumption into a colonial and later a nationalist narrative in which production is paramount. It is a place of both theatricality and spectrality. Pleasure in the world thus worries at, teases out, the bare threads of a nationalist project based upon tightly woven ascetic self-discipline.

THE WORLDS AND NOSTALGIA

The Worlds have now vanished in Singapore: Great World, like Beauty World, has given its name to a shopping centre, while the skeletal remains of Gay World await urban redevelopment. The community centre has, if anything, become naturalized. Rather than constituting free-standing buildings, contemporary community centres are often built as part of a complex with a library, a theatre, or shops. In the 1990s, many community centres gave way to community clubs, in an attempt to imitate the private country clubs to which middle-class Singaporeans aspired before the 1997 Asian crisis. This might, in one reading, bespeak the triumph of the disciplinary project of nationhood as Singapore reaches, by most objective measures, developed nation status. De Certeau, however, offers another possibility. A minor practice, a tactic, he suggests, may begin to "colonize" institutions which embody strategies.[63] Thus "the system of discipline and control which took shape in the nineteenth century on the basis of earlier procedures, is today itself 'vampirized' by other procedures."[64] Consumption in Singapore is increasingly, and ambiguously, engraved on the island's landscape. At times consumption would seem to still fit in with Fordism, the need for Bourdieuan "distinction" driving ever more Herculean efforts in production. Thus the proliferation of condominiums with English or French names – Chantilly Rise, Hillbrooks, Le Wood – distinguished from their Housing Development Board counterparts by a few metres of marble veneer, a swimming pool, a security guard, and a few hundred thousand dollars. Even here, however, there is an ambiguity: the walled-in condominium forms its own community, based upon wealth and social exclusion, not upon citizenship. Consumption becomes self-centred, turning its back upon the nation. The market, so long seen as a "disciplinarian" who must be appeased,[65] now appears more seductive, luring government scholarship holders away from service to the nation, inciting internationalist body projects among younger Singaporeans which draw eclectically upon Japanese and American popular culture.

In this environment, the Worlds become a nostalgic space. Michael Chiang's 1988 musical *Beauty World* mapped the plot structure of a 1960s' Cantonese television serial onto the space of the World, and recollections of the Worlds published periodically in Singaporean newspapers are always nostalgic in tone. Well-known actor Moses Lim remembered the Worlds as a place of simpler entertainment, of relaxed attitudes, and a slower movement of time,[66] while former President Wee Kim Wee described it as the place he courted his future wife, chaperoned by her family.[67] Yet nostalgia in Singapore has a special function. Unlike most other nations, Singapore traditionally had none of the "wilful nostalgia" for an imagined national past which so animated other nations:[68] Singapore nationalism from 1965 onwards was resolutely progressivist, determined to leave colonialism behind, and ancestral pasts before colonialism were largely imagined as being elsewhere – China, India, the Malay Sultanates.

In contemporary Singapore, a nostalgic turn away from the increasing bureaucratization of life is accommodated through references to the private: sepia tinted advertisements of domestic consumption in a quieter, slower age – family meals, children playing in suitably Arcadian landscapes. The public experience of the past outside the embrace of the state, in contrast, is frequently figured as trauma: the Japanese occupation, or race riots in the late colonial period. In this environment, nostalgia for the Worlds may not only be conservative, but also play an admittedly ambivalent role "in social criticism and political protest."[69] What is recalled here is a public space which is neither colonial nor national, a space of safety marked by consumption, not production. Increasingly, such nostalgia is for a past, a safe place, which those who feel nostalgia have never known: a place which perhaps lies in Singaporean futures as much as in pasts, a time when one might be at home in the World, the world now one's home.

NOTES

1   See Brenda Yeoh, *Contesting Space: Power Relations and the Urban Built Environment in Colonial Singapore* (Kuala Lumpur: Oxford University Press, 1996).
2   Daniel Miller notes in *A Theory of Shopping* that while there is clearly a "discourse of shopping" (65) which emphasizes "extravagance and 'mindless' hedonistic materialism" few shoppers display such features in practice, instead enacting shopping as a ritual "transforming consumption into devotion" for loved ones (155). Daniel Miller, *A Theory of Shopping* (Cambridge: Polity, 1998).
3   Daniel Bell, *The Cultural Contradictions of Capitalism* (New York: Basic, 1996): 283.
4   Theodor. W. Adorno, *Adorno: The Stars Down to Earth and Other Essays on the Irrational in Culture*, (ed.) Stephen Crook (London: Routledge, 1994): 44.
5   Dick Hebdige, *Subculture: The Meaning of Style* (London: Routledge, 1988): 18.
6   John Fiske, "The Commodities of Culture" in *The Consumer Society Reader*, (ed.) Martyn J. Lee (Oxford: Blackwell, 2000): 282.
7   See Daniel Miller, *Capitalism: An Ethnographic Approach* (Oxford: Berg, 1997); Chua Beng Huat, "Singaporeans Ingesting McDonalds" in *Consumption in Asia: Lifestyles and Identities*, (ed.) Chua Beng Huat (New York: Routledge, 2000): 183–201; Shunya Yoshimi, "Consuming 'America': from Symbol to System" in *Consumption in Asia: Lifestyles and Identities*, (ed.) Chua Beng Huat (New York: Routledge, 2000): 202–224.
8   John Hannigan, *Fantasy City: Pleasure and Profit in the Postmodern Metropolis* (London: Routledge, 1998): 11.

9   Constance Classen and David Howes, "Epilogue: The Dynamics and Ethics of Cross-Cultural Consumption" in *Cross-Cultural Consumption: Global Markets, Local Realities*, (ed.) David Howes (London: Routledge, 1996): 193.

10   Neil McKendrick, "The Consumer Revolution of Eighteenth-Century England" in *The Birth of a Consumer Society: The Commercialization of Eighteenth-Century England*, (ed.) McKendrick, John Brewer, and J. H. Plumb (Bloomington: Indiana University Press, 1982): 9–33.

11   The short extract from Raffles's letter to Colonel Addenbrooke from Singapore, June 10 1819, quoted in Sophia Raffles's biography, has now become a paradigmatic asser-tion of the rationale for the founding of Singapore. "Our object is not territory, but trade; a great commercial emporium, and a *fulcrum*, whence we may extend our influ-ence politically as circumstances may hereafter require. . . . One free port in these seas must eventually destroy the Dutch monopoly; and what *Malta* is in the West, that may *Singapore* become in the East." Lady Sophia Raffles, *Memoir of the Life of and Public Services of Sir Thomas Stamford Raffles*, 1830 (Singapore: Oxford University Press, 1991): 380.

12   Mike Featherstone, "Lifestyle and Consumer Culture" in *The Consumer Society Reader*, (ed.) Martyn J. Lee (Oxford: Blackwell, 2000): 94–95.

13   J. A. Hobson, *Imperialism: A Study*, 1902 (London: Allen & Unwin, 1954): 368.

14   David Scott, "Colonial Governmentality," *Social Text* 43 (Fall 1995): 191–220. Nicholas Thomas, *Colonialism's Culture: Anthropology, Travel and Government* (Cambridge: Polity, 1994): 41–43.

15   Frantz Fanon, *Black Skin, White Masks*, 1952, trans. Charles Lam Markmann (New York: Grove, 1967).

16   Lee Khoon Choy, Speech in Singapore Legislative Assembly, July 21 1959. *Legislative Assembly Debates, State of Singapore: Official Report*. July 1 1959 to December 29 1959. Singapore: Government Printer, 1964. Col. 330.

17   S. Rajaratnam, *The Prophetic and the Political: Selected Speeches and Writings of S. Rajaratnam*, (ed.) Chan Heng Chee and Obaid ul Haq (Singapore: Graham Brash, 1987): 119.

18   Lee Khoon Choy, 330.

19   Baharuddin bin Mohamed Arif, Speech in Singapore Legislative Assembly, July 16 1959. *Legislative Assembly Debates, State of Singapore: Official Report*. July 1 1959 to December 29 1959. Singapore: Government Printer, 1964. Col. 144.

20   See Colony of Singapore Public Relations Office File 330/56 (Confidential): July 31 1956 – September 22 1956, which contains newspaper articles, reports, and comments from a Special Branch investigation of the Anti-Yellow Culture Campaign. National Archives of Singapore, Microfilm Reel PR027.

21   Lee Kuan Yew, *The Singapore Story: Memoirs of Lee Kuan Yew* (Singapore: Times, 1998): 326.

22   "The Pin Table Culture – By Minister," *Straits Times* (June 25 1959): 1.

23   "Govt. Bans Eight Publications," *Straits Times* (June 9 1959): 4.

24   "Teachers at 'Blue' Show Sacked," *Straits Times* (July 9 1959): 4.

25   "Chan: Discipline's Role in a Rugged Society," *Straits Times* (May 15 1967): 20.

26   Brenda S. A Yeoh, *Community and Change: the Tanjong Pagar Community Club Story* (Singapore: Armour, 1997): 56.

27   *Singapore Standard* (July 19 1959) in Seah Chee Meow, *Community Centres in Singapore: Their Political Involvement* (Singapore: Singapore University Press, 1973): 18.

28   Seah, 18.

29   Seah, 10.

30   Seah, 24–26.

31   "Pay Greater Attention to Your Physical Fitness: P.M. Lee," *People's Association Bulletin* 4.4 (April 1966): 2, 6.

32   "The Thrust Forward," *The Mirror: A Weekly Almanac of Current Affairs* 5.32 (August 11 1969): 4.

33   "From Each His Best," *The Mirror: A Weekly Almanac of Current Affairs* 5.1 (January 6 1969): 1.

34 "Singapore will Climb to Higher Levels of Performance," *The Mirror: A Weekly Almanac of Current Affairs* 5.7 (February 17 1969): 1.

35 Lee Kuan Yew, "The Vigilante Corps Recruitment Campaign at Tanjong Pagar Community Centre, 10 December, 1966," in *Excerpts of Speeches by Lee Kuan Yew on Singapore, 1959–1973*, (ed.) Douglas Koh (Unpublished collection, National University of Singapore Library, 1976): 96.

36 Lee Kuan Yew, "Speech at the Convent of the Holy Infant Jesus, Serangoon Gardens, December 11 1965," in Koh: 88.

37 "Rhodes: A Virile People," *The Mirror: A Weekly Almanac of Current Affairs* 2.49 (December 5 1966): 3.

38 The majority of my information in describing Bukit Timah Community Centre is derived from Singh's 1960 account. While carefully put together, Singh's research paper does reveal certain ideological imperatives. The multiracial nature of the centre seems to be exaggerated: the text maintains the centre, after the People's Association took control, was fully racially representative, but the statistics quoted would suggest that the Chinese community was over-represented, especially among the younger regular users of the centre. Understandably, Singh sees the centre through the lens of a newly emergent Malayan nationalism. See Sukveer Singh, "A Study of the Bukit Timah Community Centre" (Diploma of Social Studies Research Paper, University of Malaya in Singapore, 1960).

39 Singh, 71–72.

40 Michel de Certeau, *The Practice of Everyday Life*, trans. Stephen Rendall (Berkeley: University of California Press, 1984): xix.

41 De Certeau, xx.

42 Leo Ou-fan Lee, *Shanghai Modern: The Flowering of a New Urban Culture in China, 1930–1945*. Cambridge: Harvard University Press, 1999, xi.

43 Leo Ou-fan Lee, 45–46; Benedict Anderson, *Imagined Communities: Reflections on the Origin and Spread of Nationalism* (Revised Edition. London: Verso, 1991).

44 Frederic Wakeman, *Policing Shanghai, 1927–1937* (Berkeley: University of California Press, 1995): 105.

45 Wakeman, 106.

46 Grant McCracken, *Culture and Consumption: New Approaches to the Symbolic Character of Consumer Goods and Activities* (Bloomington: Indiana University Press, 1988): 104.

47 Wakeman, 280–281.

48 Jürgen Rudolph, "Amusements in the Three 'Worlds'" in *Looking At Culture*, (eds) Sanjay Krishnan, Sharaad Kuttan, Lee Weng Choy, Leon Perera and Jimmy Yap. See also the website http://www.happening.com.sg/commentary/amusement.html.

49 Rudolph's article is perhaps the most thorough social history of the Worlds yet published, and I have relied upon some of its contents in the ensuing discussion. Its one weakness is that it was written at the end of a longer project on Peranakan culture. The vast majority of Rudolph's informants are thus male, middle-class Peranakans who provide a detailed but limited perspective on the life of the Worlds. I have thus supplemented Rudolph's account with a variety of oral history sources from the Singapore National Archives.

50 Lim Chok Fui, Interview (August 21 1981) with Mdm Chua Ser Koon, trans. Victoria Wong Kum Oi. National Archives of Singapore, English Transcription of Oral History Recording No. 100: 36.

51 Isa Ibrahim, Interview. National Archives of Singapore, Oral History Recording No. 242: 7.

52 Lim, 39.

53 The Happy World stadium was, if anything, too ambitious. Prior to its opening in 1937, the steel girders of the stadium roof caved in, injuring three workmen. See "Serious Disaster at Happy World," *Singapore Free Press* (April 27 1937): 9.

54 Hirschmann notes that the systems of racial classification used in contemporary Malaysia have their origins in colonial census categories. While racial categories and community identities were certainly not invented by colonial fiat alone, the notion of race as "a pseudobiological concept" with explanatory force evolved during the

colonial period. See Charles Hirschmann, "The Meaning and Measurement of Ethnicity in Malaysia: An Analysis of Census Classifications," *Journal of Asian Studies* 46 (1987): 562. "Race" was made use of in different national projects involving management of ethnicity – both termed multiracialism – in Malaysia and Singapore after independence. In Singapore, all citizens are given their father's race at birth; this is imprinted on their identity cards and determines which language is taught as the "mother tongue" at school. In a certain sense, then, the variety of entertainments in the Worlds might have "staged" an evolving multiracialism in much the same way that Liisa Maalki argues theme parks such as Disney's Epcot Center stage internationalism by stressing "the differences between national units in a way that is dehistoricizing, depoliticizing and ultimately homogenizing of differences that exceed or escape the limits of internationalist 'diversity.' " See Liisa Maalki, "Citizens of Humanity: Internationalism and the Imagined Community of Nations," *Diaspora* 3.1 (1994): 58.

55 Mikhail Bakhtin, *Rabelais and His World*, trans. Hélène Iswolsky (Bloomington: Midland-Indiana University Press, 1984): 88

56 P. Stallybrass and A. White, *The Politics and Poetics of Transgression* (London: Methuen, 1986): 13.

57 De Certeau, xix.

58 De Certeau, 48, 49.

59 De Certeau, xi.

60 De Certeau, 37.

61 De Certeau, xxii.

62 De Certeau, 31.

63 De Certeau, 49.

64 De Certeau, 49.

65 Pang Gek Choo, "PM Renews Call to Japan, US, Europe for Help," *Straits Times* (January 12 1988): 3.

66 Alison De Souza, "Of Fights and Sweaty Diners," *Straits Times* (July 16 1998): 29.

67 Zuraidah Ibrahim, "Together for 60 Years," *Straits Times* (April 7 1996). *Dow Jones Interactive* November 16 2000. http://www.djinteractive.com.

68 See Roland Robertson, "After Nostalgia? Wilful Nostalgia and the Phases of Globalization," in *Theories of Modernity and Postmodernity*, (ed.) Bryan S. Turner (London: Sage, 1990): 45–61.

69 Bryan S. Turner, "A Note on Nostalgia," *Theory, Culture and Society* 4 (1987): 154.

Chapter 6: Evangelical Economies and Abjected Spaces: Cultural Territorialisation in Singapore

Robbie B. H. Goh

> For here have we no continuing city, but we seek one to come.
> (Heb 13: 14, KJV)

RELIGIOUS MOVEMENTS, RELIGIOUS SPACES

Religious practice in Singapore is governed by a fundamental contradiction, consisting in the fact that while it is "constitutionally . . . a secular society" with "no official religion," at the same time it is far from being an "irreligious or an anti-religious society" (Sheares 1974: 3), with a vibrant and pluralistic religious life. In a preliminary report from the 2000 population census, 85 percent of the population professed faith in one religion or another, the religions with the largest followings being Buddhism (43 percent), Christianity (15 percent), and Islam (15 percent; Leow 2000: H7). While this flourishing of (multiple) religions is seen as offering a "richness to individual life" capable of creating a "better citizen," on the other hand it is also seen as posing a potential threat to social unity and harmony, an anxiety reflected in the passing of the Religious Harmony Act in November 1990, an Act which makes it an offense to "cause ill-feelings between different religious groups" (Ministry of Information and the Arts 1992: 1). Religious harmony is governed by guidelines which, rather than defining the legality/illegality of precise acts per se, speak to the "feelings" and attitudes ("tolerance and understanding" of other religions, avoiding "ridiculing," "persuasive" manners), which are supposed to guide the interaction of the different races on religious matters (Jayakumar 1987: 6).

If religious movements are subordinated to the "feelings" of individuals outside the religious group, then the strategy of religious practice tends towards the creation and consolidation of safe spaces for that practice, rather than the unguarded circulation and dissemination of credos and texts in a campaign of free expansion. In other words, space becomes the consolidation and definition of a particular religious identity which is at some risk in the multiculturalism of Singapore. Religious spaces manifest and contain the religious-cultural motivations and anxieties which create them. It is not surprising that the discussion of religious harmony often turns on metaphors and considerations of space and building: according to then-Minister for Home Affairs S. Jayakumar, the need for religious harmony is justified in part by the fact that we live in a "small, multi-racial densely populated society" (Jayakumar 1987: 6). Religious harmony is then meant to function as an "essential pillar for our stability and nation-building," containing religious-cultural difference just as the analogy of the building houses difference by assigning it specific spaces or rooms. Similarly, the late President Sheares spoke of the "faith that our efforts today will make not only a bigger and wealthier but a better Singapore," the spatial measurement a metaphor not only for the spiritual enrichment which active religions are supposed to confer, but also for the impression of roominess which religious-cultural "tolerance" will bring (1974: 4). Not surprisingly, the recurrent symbol of this tolerance, for Sheares, is "our oldest [religious] buildings" whose endurance is testimony to their acceptance within a multi-religious society.

The paradox of a religion which is free, but nevertheless circumscribed by multiculturalism and considerations of political stability, is displaced from the overt social and political sphere (where its anxieties cannot be articulated), onto the landscape as a complex social code, as an overdetermined product of historical and cultural influences. In the case of Christianity in particular, the paradox is complicated in the Singapore context by its status both as colonial inheritance and progressive cultural force, as both history and global future, sign of power and the abnegation of worldly power, the religion perceived as being aligned with commerce and bourgeois materialism, while it preaches the renunciation of riches. This paper is thus interested in what, with Kristeva (1982: 22), might be called the "atopic" qualities of the Christian religion in Singapore. For Kristeva, Christianity is a symbolic system which abjects the undesirable (sin, defilement, idolatry, unclean food) by means of a social logic and narrative of the "chosen people" of the true God. Kristeva's overarching concern is with cultural scapegoating, and she thus places Hebraic abjection within the context of other related phenomena like the ritual sacrifice in the Hellenic world-view, the Hindu caste system, instances of misogynistic construction in general, and racial hatred. Yet the theoretical framework she establishes – the anthropology of cultural production in terms of scapegoating, abjural, repudiation, their displacement in overdetermined and complex social symbolism – has implications for the study of postcolonial spaces and globalization with which Kristeva is less concerned. Specifically, abjection as a cultural logic which tends towards atopia, and which relies on a metaphysical order which is meant to shape and ultimately supplant the material one, establishes useful terms for the analysis of evangelical Christianity and its cultural-spatial strategies, particularly in the competitive domains of global cities. We might thus conceive of the postcolonial city in the condition of global competition as being driven by a logic of infrastructural "sacrifice" (Bataille 1992: 45), in which a certain cultural and historical signification is elided and suppressed within a motivation of progress and development. Yet elision is not eradication, and suppression leaves textual and physical traces or remainders. In the Singapore context in particular, abjection raises crucial issues of colonial remainders, the ambivalence of history, the Christianity–Commerce–English Language nexus and its ramifications for nationhood and global positioning.

THE CIVIC AND THE SACRED: TEXTUAL AND IDEOLOGICAL MIXTURES IN THE COLONIAL CITY

The first scene of cultural abjection that one might speak of in the context of the colonial city, is the loss of the integrity of denominational traditions and their architectural symbolism, within colonial planning and construction processes.

Christianity in Singapore is on the one hand a cultural force coeval with colonial-ism, whose influence is inextricably bound with the history and power of the British administration of its empire. On the other hand, however, Christianity is governed by an independent body (the Established Church of England, the various mission organizations in England and America responsible for the commissioning of missionaries), with a discourse and organizational structure distinct from that of the colonial government. At the same time, this split within the hegemonic order is further complicated by the difference constituted by the colonial land – its geographical, climatic, racial, cultural, linguistic, and other differences from the centre. Finally, Singapore's different immigrant populations also create a cultural differentiation with the ranks of the colonial concept of the "native" as well. The result is on the one hand a multiple layering of meanings upon the landscape, in which the political order imposes a public code, which negotiates with and shares its meanings with the other cultural elements within the dominant (a process which might be termed the "condensation" of mean-ings); and on the other hand an abjection or dislocation of meanings from colonial to native realms, in which cultural adaptations cross over the seemingly inviolable line between master and subject ("displacement").

In terms of the European–native, colonizer–colonized relationship, Chris-tianity played the role of a textual influence (via discourses, values, liturgies, institutions, and spatial forms) not unlike Harold Bloom's (1975: 9, 11) account of poetry as the influence of a patriarchal "strong poet" against which succeeding poets "wrestle." The psychoanalytic model is appropriate in many ways, not the least of which is the overdetermined nature of architectural production and the ways in which this is capable of concealing and overwriting certain cultural influences which then stand in the place of an unconscious. Also useful is the diachronic element in Bloom's model of cultural history, which does not subscribe merely to the "passing-on of images and ideas" through time, but instead sees the process as an active and "dialectical" engagement between received textual elements and "revisionist" readings (Bloom 1975: 4, 5). The hermeneutic contexts under which even historical and inherited spaces are read change significantly over time, particularly in the transition from colonial to independent states; at the same time, this new hermeneutics also encounters what (with Lecercle, 1990: 5) we might call the "remainders" of spatial forms: not just edifices, but ideas of spatial organization and utilization, stylistic elements, countering and conflictual ideologies, which run beneath the surface of the dominant codes.

Historically, the psychological landscape of the colonial city is implicit in Raffles' organization of the early port of Singapore, a model which is in turn based on the colonial organization of Calcutta, where Raffles was "partly resi-dent" (Lim 1991 I: 33). Written into this landscape is the more obvious split between colonizer and colonized, inscribed in the town plan of 1822, which allowed for a "European Town" comprising the Civil Station, residences of the important British administrators and merchants, and cultural and religious spaces; and a "native town" separated by the Singapore river to the south, the Esplanade to the east, and the "Old Lines" (an ancient Malay wall) to the north. In effect, as Lim (1991 I: 35, 70–75) observes, this was the "maidan" mentality of eighteenth-century Calcutta re-inscribed onto Singapore, with the distinct "separation of the military, civil and native requirements," and the creation of an "imposing symbol" of colonial supremacy.

Christianity, as the religion of the colonizer, played a complex role in this colonial city. On the one hand, it sits at the heart of the European town as symbolic project. The "mitred front" of religion, as Edmund Burke saw it – the pomp and social pre-eminence of the English church, but also its riches, its establishment in property – played a crucial role in the cultural identity of the nation, and certainly in the conservative politics of the monarchy and aristocracy. A few decades after the articulation of Burke's reactionary arguments, Georgian imperialism and its spatial forms – including the architecture and social position of the church – were exported to the settlements of Penang and Singapore by way of India. In Singapore, key landmarks of the mid-nineteenth-century European town were religious edifices like St Andrew's Cathedral (1835–1836), the Cathedral of the Good Shepherd (1846), and the Armenian Church (1835). In this imposition of a symbolism of cultural domination onto the colonial cityscape, the architectural heritage of the imperial centre played a crucial role. Lim (1991 I: 51) argues that the dominant church style exported to a majority of the British colonies in the late eighteenth and early nineteenth centuries was the Palladio-inspired classicism of the "Gibbs' type church in the fashion of St Martin-in-the-Fields," with its "pedimented façades" and hexa- or tetra-style columns. Underlying this style is the older architectural symbolism and structure of the Norman church, with its gothic ornamentations, arches, prominent buttresses, and related features: the present St Andrew's Cathedral, built by Macpherson in 1856–1862 after two previous edifices on that site were destroyed by lightning, is based on the popular ruins of Netley Abbey in Hampshire (*History* 2001).

On the other hand, however, this use of religious spatial forms to reinforce the cultural dominance of the colonial government is fraught with intertextual borrowings and ideological admixtures. This is inherent in the form of English classicism which was codified in the eighteenth century, and which borrowed heavily from Palladio's own reinterpretations of classical architecture. The Palladial façade is thus the sign of a number of different social values: civic republican virtue and justice, Renaissance cultivation and learning, the social pretensions of the urban rich in the eighteenth century, and the accommodation of these meanings into a neoclassical religious form appropriate to the metropolitan centre of the expanding English empire. It is thus hardly surprising that the symbolic function of religious edifices in the colonial city is inextricably linked with a larger civic project. The colonial church structure inherits from the imperial centre an already-hybrid model, a composite of classical and gothic styles, sacred and secular symbolisms, and in turn adapts this mixed model in response to the landscape and culture of the colony. In the first place, colonial church styles to a significant extent blur denominational distinctions within the singleness of civic planning and implementation. This is perhaps best seen in the Armenian Church, which departs in a number of points from the characteristic features of Orthodox Church architecture, particularly in the absence of rotundas, archways, and ornate carvings, and in its use of classical (Doric) columns and pitched, tiled roofs. Designed by George Coleman (who also designed the first St Andrew's Cathedral), the Armenian Church was incorporated into a unified colonial town plan, and made to serve a project of cultural influence. As Lim (1991 I: 117–118) points out, the main churches of the European town in Singapore had no steeples until after the 1840s, when they were all (regardless of denomination and liturgical tradition) given essentially similar steeples based on the Gibbs model. This was part of a project of cultural and religious display which (as the method of implementation shows) is inherently a political intention and civic act – no less than the engineering of structures of dominance.

Furthermore, the use of neoclassical architecture to denote civic order and prosperity, as well as the colonial government's practice of centralized town planning and design, resulted in a blurring of religious and secular building styles and symbolisms. Many of the prominent buildings in Singapore's European town were designed by George Coleman, the architect from Calcutta "who was responsible for most of the settlement's building programme between 1826 and 1844" (Lim 1991 I: 111). The result was a pervasive Palladial style not only in the principal churches (the first St Andrew's, the Armenian Church), but also in the chief government buildings (the Court House, originally built as John Argylle Maxwell's villa), and residences of the settlement's leading citizens (Sir J. P. Grant, Coleman's own villa, and other homes on what eventually became Coleman Street; Lim 1991 I: 111–115; *History* 2001; *Singapore Places* 2001). This pervasive style, mutatis mutandis, was also applied to other parts of the colonial city, either by direct and personal influence (for example, Dennis McSwiney, Coleman's clerk, built the Cathedral of the Good Shepherd in Queen Street), or else as part of a general adoption of neoclassical style to denote civic grandeur and majesty (for example, the pedimented and columned portico of the Supreme Court, the "last classical building to be built in Singapore" in 1939; *History* 2001).

From one point of view, the colonial town plan with its fostering of semantic equivalents between civil and ecclesiastical spaces was merely a reflection of the civic will of the imperial centre, which borrowed from the architectural symbolism of classical civilization and incorporated this into a project of national and metropolitan aggrandizement. As Jane Jacobs's (1996: 51) analysis of London's historically-redolent Bank Junction shows, both the Bank of England and St Paul's are integrally linked in this symbolic "heart of the empire," the complementarity of their social functions reflected in their spatial complementarity and contiguity. Yet from another point of view, the structure and symbolism of religious spaces in the colonial context are submitted to additional pressures and influences, which ultimately create fissures in the edifice of the colonial cityscape. One of these pressures is that of topology: thus in the case of St Andrew's Cathedral, the traditional cruciform layout and terminology of the Norman church is modified by the contours of the Singapore river which determine the general orientation of streets and city blocks. Thus the "North Transept" of the cathedral really faces north-west, or west-north-west, and the "South Transept" and "West Door" are accordingly off their traditional orientations. Climate and socio-political factors also result in structural changes: the cathedral was built by Indian convict labour, using in substantial quantities a material known as "Madras chunam" (a mixture of shell lime, egg white, sugar, water, and coconut husk) borrowed from another part of the empire. This fact about its construction leads the *History of Singapore* webpage, in what might be seen as a remaindered colonial cringe, to declare that the cathedral "lacks the fine details of its early 13th century English prototype" (*History* 2001).

The immigrant peoples and cultures of the colony, too, exerted a modifying pressure on received imperial ideology and its spatial expression. This was particularly true of evangelical Christianity, with its mission to preach the gospel to these unreached masses, a mission which could only be accomplished by a degree of cultural and linguistic accommodation. One of the earliest mission schools in Singapore was the Anglo-Chinese School, founded by the Methodist mission in 1886. As its name suggests, it attempted to forge a compromise with the Chinese families whose sons it expected to form the bulk of its students. It conducted classes in both English and Chinese, made religious instruction purely voluntary, and tried (not always successfully) to avoid the controversies that might attend a strong proselytizing programme. Its school buildings (particularly in the earlier years) reflect this accommodation of Chinese culture: the original school was a Straits Chinese-vernacular shophouse on Amoy Street, and in the 1924 plans for a larger school at Cairnhill Road, elements of this vernacular ("Chinese tiles," louvred folding wooden windows and doors, and stylized internal court-yard) still feature prominently (Swan and MacLaren 1924). In subsequent and other school edifices, however, the vernacular elements give way to modernist blocks (Anglo-Chinese Junior College) or stylized versions of classical architecture (the old Barker Road campus); ethnicity, once written onto the physical landscape itself, recedes to a nominal history in the naming of parts of the campus after Chinese philanthropists (Tan Chin Tuan, Tan Kah Kee, Lee Kong Chian).

POSTCOLONIAL "GRANDEUR" AND COLONIAL REMAINDERS

The ideological collusions and accommodations represented by civic-religious neoclassicism, while marking imperial culture's rapprochement with the colonized landscape and culture, also established a civic will with an enduring influence on the postcolonial, independent nation. If the colonial religious building sets up the grounds of its own decommissioning (of specific signification) by its accommo-dation of a broader imperial grandeur, in the same gesture it also ensures its continuing dominance even within the logic of national development. This is another cultural abjection, the differential logic which appears to be at work in urban redevelopment and conservation projects, in which the religious desacral-ization of Christian spaces goes hand-in-hand with a cultural preservation and aggrandizement.

Singapore's push to become a global city, boasting an attractive lifestyle capable of drawing both tourist revenue and corporate re-location, has involved a policy of selective re-development of its downtown area, balancing the need to maximize limited land space (hence producing megalithic shopping malls like Ngee Ann City on Orchard Road) with the conservation of historic low-rise struc-tures (for example, in the Emerald Hill and Boat Quay areas), the creation of new structures with state-of-the-art facilities (Theatres on the Bay) with the retention of refurbished old structures (the Singapore Art Museum). The cosmopolitan city, so conceived, is driven by a certain spatial logic – a packaging of space for visual and experiential consumption, an aesthetic discourse which is ultimately a commercial one as well – which, in the context of the postcolonial city, comes with a certain cost.

While the commercial logic is obvious in most of the high-rent downtown areas in major cities, in Singapore's case it acts as a particular discourse which re-writes historical and religious signification. This may be contrasted with an opposing gesture, i.e. the re-creation of historical and/or religious symbolism in new buildings which invoke and complement existing historical buildings in a neighbourhood or district. Thus, for example, the Harold Washington Library

Center in Chicago, built in 1991 but designed to evoke "a classicism that . . . is all Chicago" (Rogers 1998); or the Paternoster Square project in London, a collection of buildings designed as shopping arcades, all of which refer to the classical style of older surrounding buildings, and some of which are "a direct response to Wren's architecture at St Paul's" (Papadakis 1992: 39). The Singapore Art Museum is quite a different strategy, capitalizing on colonial religious symbolism via refurbishment and re-presentation. The museum occupies what used to be St Joseph's Institution, the oldest Catholic school in Singapore, founded in 1852 and designed largely by Father Charles Benedict Nain around the turn of the century. The creation of the Art Museum (which took place from 1992, after the school vacated its premises on Bras Basah Road, to 1996 when the museum opened) was not simply a matter of retaining the shell of the building and stripping it of its colonial and religious symbolic structures. Significantly, the Art Museum retains and even capitalizes on elements of religious spatial form, in the crucifixes prominently situated on the cupola, the series of arches in the façade strongly evocative of a cathedral arcade, the ambience and acoustics of the Auditorium which used to be the school chapel (Singapore Art Museum 2001). These features are packaged and advertized collectively as the "grand" and "impressive" structure which (together with the historical points of information of the building's religious past) commend it as a tourist attraction, as well as a collection of facilities available for rental (Singapore Art Museum 2001).

Thus while the Paternoster Square arcades shape new commercial spaces to the idiom of neoclassical imperial-ecclesiastical architecture, a project like the Singapore Art Museum neutralizes the imperial-ecclesiastical import of such architecture by accommodating it within the nation's commercial-tourist enterprise, and by emphasizing a countering culture of the local and regional. The columned façade and imposing dome are thus expressly packaged as part of an "impressive entrance for arriving guests," the museum's display galleries exist side-by-side with spaces reserved for commercial use ("cocktails, dinners, weddings, or business functions") such as the Glass Hall and the Auditorium (Singapore Art Museum 2001). In addition to this commercial discourse, the signification of colonial-religious architecture is also contested by aesthetic content and function: the museum boasts a permanent collection which is "the largest collection of twentieth-century Southeast Asian art in the region" (Singapore Art Museum 2001). Temporary international exhibitions of Western art (the Guggenheim collection; Leonardo da Vinci) are balanced with "country focus exhibitions" featuring the art of neighbouring countries like Indonesia and Malaysia. In so doing, the museum positions itself dually, on the one hand as an attraction of international calibre (wherein the style and historical significance of the building play crucial roles), and on the other hand as a collector of and commentator on a specifically Southeast Asian cultural wealth (for which the building can be no more than a neutral display space).

The former St Joseph's Institution thus becomes one of several historical edifices de-commissioned of their religious function and signification, and converted into tourist spectacles and commercial structures; a group which includes the former Convent of the Holy Infant Jesus (whose chapel was also designed by Father Nain) which has been converted to a collection of "premiere lifestyle" restaurants, bars, and event facilities collectively known as CHIJMES; the old Kampong Kapor Methodist Church building on Waterloo Street, used at various times as a car workshop and exhibition centre (Leong 2000: 53); and churches like the Armenian Church and the Cathedral of the Good Shepherd, which no longer hold services but are featured as prominent tourist attractions. In the process, this urban policy unconsciously reiterates manifest features and ideological assumptions of the colonial city. The chief areas of the old European town become the hallmark cultural zone of the modern city, where neoclassical architecture and colonial-mission history are packaged as accessories to an attractive "premiere" lifestyle featuring the visual and performing arts, fine dining, black-tie corporate events, and private events of the upper classes. In this region – roughly bounded by Bras Basah Road, the Singapore river, the Padang, and Fort Canning Hill – colonial remainders are simultaneously invoked and repudiated, elevated for their "historical" and "social" importance while neutered of their specific political-cultural signification. This is true of buildings in this area like CHIJMES and the Singapore Art Museum (and to a certain extent even St Andrew's Cathedral, the Armenian Church, and the Cathedral of the Good Shepherd), together with others of secular provenance like The Fullerton (the upscale hotel occupying the refurbished General Post Office), the Victoria Concert Hall, Raffles Hotel, and the like.

In contrast, the native areas of colonial times – both the older ethnic settlements around the Chinatown area, as well as outlying areas such as Geylang, Serangoon Road, and elsewhere – are often the subject of more radical rebuilding, with the replacement of vernacular building forms with modernist high-rise buildings, and the confirmation of a more socially-open or plebeian character. While ethnic religious buildings are also often designated as tourist attractions (the Hindu temple on Tank Road, the Tan Si Chong Su Temple on Magazine Road), here the sacred symbolisms inherent in traditional architectural forms are preserved, if also exoticized within tourist discourses as "local colour." The social mix is facilitated by the proliferation of the local equivalent of the classical "agora" – the market, hawker centre, or combination bargain shopping-centre and foodcourt (the Ellenborough market, and the numerous bargain shops in malls like People's Park Complex and Pearl's Centre on Eu Tong Sen Street, are just some examples).

The contrast with the hallmark civic district is often striking. Where neoclassical edifices (both in the imperial centre as well as in the postcolonial city) are generally afforded a kind of reverence which recognizes the commercial value of grand architectural style and civil–religious history, commercial development elsewhere is often at the cost of vernacular style. This is seen for example in the Overseas-Chinese Banking Corporation (OCBC) headquarters, whose site was recently declared a national landmark (Cheong 2001: L4). The bank's origins (it began as the Overseas-Chinese Bank, founded in 1919 by a Hokkien family, before it merged with other small banks also serving the Chinese community) are narrated in the six glass panels in the building's lobby, which tell a story of immigrant labour and gradual infrastructural progress, and implicitly celebrate the bank's role as facilitator of this work ethic and history. The glass panels belong to the old bank headquarters, known as "China Building," which was in vernacular style, evocative of the pagoda and Chinese roofs. The new building, a concrete tower designed by I. M. Pei with absolutely no concession to that vernacular style, presents an entirely different symbolism, of impersonal solidity and a towering presence suited to the bank's present drive to become an international financial corporation. It is thus fitting that what the historic landmark commemorates is not the building and its historical and social function, but rather the site itself, an abstract and perhaps arbitrary locus which commemorates Raffles' first landing site in Singapore.

Attached to the phenomenon of decommissioned and re-utilized colonial religious spaces are thus the overtones of Anglophone culture, cosmopolitan outlook, and social elevation which are inextricably involved with Christianity in Singapore. Despite its relatively modest following of 15 percent of the Singapore population (especially when compared to Buddhism's 43 percent), Christianity continues to be the religion most "positively associated with the level of education," with the highest proportion of university graduates of all the religions (Kuo and Tong 1995: 20). The preliminary data from the 2000 population census also suggests that "the Christian faith . . . [seems to] go hand in hand with the English-speaking" (Leow 2000: H7). Yet more than these specific educational or linguistic markers, Christianity in Singapore has wider and often less easily-defined connotations of cosmopolitanism, upward social mobility, and access to a Western intellectual and cultural tradition which serves to differentiate its believers from the local, vernacular, and traditional elements of Singapore society. As one informant puts it, "to think of what 'Christian' means in Singapore, is to think of someone English-speaking, middle- or upper-middle class, well-educated. . . ." While few of the other religions operate in anything other than their respective vernacular languages, Christianity operates largely within a liturgical, social, and educational network based on the English Language.[1] Given these perceived and felt connotations, it then becomes easy for Christianity to become associated with what Prime Minister Goh Chok Tong, in his 1999 National Day Rally, calls the "cosmopolitan" element in Singapore: those "able Singaporeans" who "speak English, have talents and skills, and are totally mobile," and thus play a frontline role in advancing Singapore's global position and stake. They are thus contradistinguished from the "heartlanders" who, while equally important to the nation, are assigned a conservative cultural role: they aid in "maintaining our core values and social stability," and very likely would have "studied in Chinese, Malay or Tamil schools" (Goh 1999).

The spectacular display of colonial church architecture in the downtown area may thus be related to a larger project, the new phase of Singapore's global competition in the years approaching the millennium, marked for example by the opening up of the local retail aspects of the banking industry to competition from offshore banks, and the call for Singapore companies to become not just regional but global in their operations and outlook. Within this project, cultural remainders occupy an ambivalent position: on the one hand tokens of a pre-modernist history which must be repudiated in the name of progress, on the other hand they form part of the eclectic sign- and spatial-system of the global and flexible machinery. Colonial-ecclesiastical-missionary remainders are thus used within an overdetermined signifying system which can (variously) repudiate or counterbalance ethnicity (as the mark of a pre-national, pre-multicultural society), evoke historical weight and particularity (as the counterbalance to an anonymous cosmopolitanism), represent a classical grandeur in a new nation without a clear classical tradition of its own, and so on.

POSTMODERN URBAN FORMS AND THE EVANGELICAL IMAGINARY

Singapore as postcolonial city thus inherits a religious culture which is venerated and preserved as a sign of something other (global rather than local, historical rather than recent, grand and exclusive rather than demotic), at the same time that its specific sacred meanings are neutralized and overwritten by other significations. Cultural veneration and spiritual abjection thus go hand-in-hand in the conservation projects of the downtown area. Outside the historical downtown area – for example, in the public housing flats and their attached amenities in which some 80 percent of the population lives – this is complemented by the incorporation of architectural forms loosely derived from ecclesiastical traditions, as one element within an eclectic postmodern style.

Cultural remainders would seem to be accommodated the more easily in a postmodern urban landscape, with its "playfulness," "openness," and "pastiche," its selective and revisionist use of history, which Jameson (1991: 21–25) sees as defining qualities of "late capitalist" cultural expression. There are arguably postmodern elements in the most recent of Singapore's building plans, particularly in the housing estates designed and built in the latter part of the 1990s such as parts of Hougang, Sengkang estate, and Punggol 21 (Goh 2001: 1597–1598). Yet the "pluralism" of postmodern aesthetics is, at least according to certain theorists, underpinned by a political intention which is "populist," "subversive" of institutions and conventions, and celebrates "dissensus rather than consensus" (Jameson 1991: 2; Hutcheon 1988: 5, 9; Ellin 1996: 110). Thus Hutcheon's discussion of Charles Moore's Piazza d'Italia in New Orleans centres on its evocation of the "social and political function" of the "res publica," which is in turn rooted in notions of "communal power" and a "public idiom" (Hutcheon 1988: 32–33). Somewhat differently, Ellin (1996: 104–112) argues that dominance of the media has "reinforced differences" and installed an ethos of "privatism" which is actually at odds with the notion of a homogenous and shared "public sphere." Nevertheless, Ellin agrees with Hutcheon in invoking a demotic, inclusive, and anti-hegemonic political current underlying postmodern urban forms.

This politics of difference is difficult to reconcile with the strong tradition of patriarchal governance which manifests itself in so many aspects of Singapore society. I argue elsewhere (Goh 2001: 1597) that recent stylistic elements in Singapore public housing, which are arguably postmodern in influence, actually play a crucial role in the contained expression of "upgrading" desires and ambitions to own private property, in a land-scarce country where about 80 percent of the population lives in high-rise public housing. Thus the ostensibly postmodern style of more recent public housing arises, not from any demotic impulse and participation from the different elements and groups of the res publica, but is imposed upon the urban landscape by a central planning body, the architects of the Housing Development Board which has charge of all public housing space in Singapore.[2]

In respect of space for the construction of religious buildings, the scarcity of land together with the need to preserve "religious harmony" and thwart potentially divisive relations between the different races in Singapore have resulted in a policy whereby the state has "direct control" over the allocation of land for religious purposes in new estates, and may also "influence" the activities of religious groups in "converting existing buildings from secular to religious use" (Kong 1993). New land for religious purposes is allocated by the HDB in a pre-established ratio which allows one place of worship within the dominant religions (i.e. Church, Chinese Temple, Mosque, and Hindu Temple) per number of dwelling units (du) in that area, the ratio varying according to the relative dominance of each religion. The land is then opened to tender, but only by groups within the allotted religion; thus while this policy "has prevented competition among religious groups," it has increased competition among groups within each religion, for example among the different Christian denominations (Kong 1993). With regard to changes in the use of existing space, application must be made to the Urban Redevelopment Authority (URA).

Christianity's unofficial role in the Singapore context, as the religion most clearly associated with cosmopolitan citizenship and a higher educational and social status, must thus be located within this central control of religious spaces and an allocation policy based on mathematical proportions. As a consequence, spatial markers of Christian culture (removed from their religious connotations) are seen to manifest themselves in public spaces, as one means of adding to the pool of stylistic elements which are meant to signify cosmopolitan eclecticism. Like the art deco, English Tudor, classical republican, gothic revival, and other architectural styles imitated by the HDB in newer housing estates, cathedral tropes become desacralized (Kong 1993) intertextual elements used to evoke a sense of an international mix. Thus, for example, the moulding on the side of a block of flats in Hougang, which owes itself to nothing so much as the similarly raised, four-lobed mouldings known as "quatrefoils," and found in many Norman-style churches. Of course the stylistic element, abstracted from its structural and semiotic context (the tops of church windows, where they framed stained glass and thus added to the grandeur of the Chancel and the Sanctuary in particular; Cunningham 1999: 26), creates an altogether different, ambivalent effect: on the one hand it declares its pronounced difference from the original, in its secularity, its difference of medium (lack of glass) and placement. On the other hand, however, it also mockingly gestures to the original, in its position at the top of a vertical panel, and in its attempt to be a secular version of a similar grandeur of ornamentation.

Elsewhere, public housing recreates and retains religious architectural forms which become increasingly difficult, if not impossible, within Singapore's modernization process and limited land area. Thus, for example, the church tower, which is only infrequently seen in Singapore, and seldom survives unless it is in a protected building such as St Andrew's Cathedral and such churches. Older mission schools such as St Andrew's and the Anglo-Chinese School also incorporated functional bell towers on their premises, which have either been scaled down or become more ornamental and stylized in the process of rebuilding and expansion.[3] As the tower decreases in size and significance in religious spaces, it re-appears in the secular landscape, for example in the ornamental tower in Ang Mo Kio; lacking the scope and function of the church tower (i.e. to "demonstrate man's heavenward aspiration," and to house the bells which ring services and warn the village of danger; Cunningham 1999: 59), this tower becomes a deliberate mimicry of the religious symbol, down to the mock buttresses which spread outwards, ostensibly to bear the weight of the tower.

Even as desacralized tropes of religious spaces are projected onto the secular cityscape, this contributes to a contrary pressure exerted upon the Christian religion in Singapore: the tendency to align itself with a larger organizational identity which transcends national borders and local traditions and forms. Thus the theatrilization of church spaces, the imitation of newer and expanding evangelical centres in larger Anglophone cities, the move to modular spaces which are capable of fulfilling a variety of uses (including being rented out to other organizations) – all of which involve a cost, the removal and decontextualization of such church spaces from an evolving local tradition of spatial and social organization.

In one sense, this is an inevitable dualism caused by an inherent Christian hermeneutic. Fostered by a narratology of parables, analogies, and a symbolism which is often complex if not mystical, this hermeneutic facilitates the imposition of spiritual typologies of space ("the promised land," the "New Jerusalem," "Babylon," the "Kingdom of God") onto geopolitical particularities. The duality (as well as the typological hermeneutic) is expressed in explicitly spatial/urban terms by Augustine, when he says that "God's city lives in this world's city, as far as its human element is concerned; but it lives there as an alien sojourner" (Augustine 1984: 761). Earthly cities imperfectly manifest the spiritual perfection of God's city, these spiritual germs existing in isolated spots (for Augustine, the various basilicas in Rome which were the sites of an unlikely charity and mercy during the sack of that city) likened to the marginal and transient space of the "alien sojourner." Yet on the other hand, this marginal and unstable position within the earthly city, is rooted in the "glorious" and eternal perfection of the divine city, "as it stands in the security of its everlasting seat" (1984: 5). Thus what characterizes this Christian hermeneutic and perspective is the constant juxtaposition of two spatial orders, the dominant with the marginal, the earthly with the divine, the present with the possible.

It does seem accurate to suggest, however, that the duality is more evident and pressing in the vibrant and fast-growing urban ministries which are, to various degrees, impatient with the socio-political and geographical limits of their local context. On the one hand, it is understood that the Christian organization occupies a concrete site or edifice, and works within the geographical, socio-economic, and political parameters of the city. On the other hand and at the same time, the organization also maps its position and praxis in a proleptic and imaginative vision at some odds with the concrete map, overlaying that map with an alternative spiritual territory. Thus the Without Walls International Church in Tampa, Florida, founded in 1991, which met first "in a strip mall, then a local high school auditorium, and later in a south Tampa warehouse," before finally acquiring an office in 1995 (Gillespie 1998: 32). The mission and goals of the Church belie this search for a physical headquarters, since they conceive of "the lost" of the entire city as their proper congregation, and rely on a mobile ministry which (for example) has "a convoy of trucks that bring Sunday school and food and supplies to inner-city children five days a week" (Gillespie 1998: 32). In a real sense, then, the church sees its premises as the entire city of Tampa itself. The expansive geographical territorialization of the church without walls need not stop at the city limits, either; founder Randy White maintains that the church has been called to the specific "geographical area," but that subsequently, "God will expand your horizons" (1998: 32). Accordingly, the ministry is now "reaching . . . the nation and the world through . . . their preaching, television program and pastors training sessions."

Christian evangelical hermeneutics tends to overlay geopolitical space with alternative signification, a cultural technique with heightened implications in the tightly governanced space of Singapore. Thus the case of Sengkang estate, a new public housing development touted as the "21st-Century Township." With an expected 95,000 residential units when it is completed around 2014, Sengkang is expected to be one of the most heavily-populated towns in Singapore (Tee 2000: 2). Accordingly, the HDB's attempts to advertize Sengkang as a desirable residential area have emphasized not only its many recreational facilities and amenities, but above all the comprehensive and sophisticated transportation network – the first instance in which "the transport system is being built at the same time as the town is being planned" (Tee 2000: 2).

The Methodist Church in Singapore has successfully bid for the plot allocated for a Christian church in Sengkang, and its own representation and charting of Sengkang town reveals a semiology of projecting religious significance onto existing sites, of (as it were) creating space for religious signification out of the interstices of the site.

Thus the map in the newspaper article emphasizes Sengkang as a town of "seamless travel," with a close-up of fairly broad and uncluttered roads and a town centre placed in relation to the rail network (source: *Sunday Times* 24 September 2000, p. 2). This compares in many respects to the map produced by Centrepoint Properties in conjunction with their marketing of the private housing project Compass Heights, in which clean, clear transportation lines (Centrepoint Properties takes the liberty of squaring the angles of junctions and making all roads seem equally broad) are supplemented by little symbols showing the proliferation of amenities (shopping, schools, parks, clubs) in the area. In contrast, the map produced in the Methodist Message (which appeared just four months before the newspaper map) takes a higher, more distant perspective than both these maps, which locates Sengkang in relation to surrounding areas, including Hougang, near the bottom of the map, which is the location of the Gloria Methodist Church family service centre and thus the base of operations for the Methodist "expansion" into Sengkang (Lai 2000: 1). One strand in its textual representation is thus of Sengkang as a borderland to existing Methodist territory, ready to be claimed in an operation described in quasi-military terms: the article speaks of "three main thrusts," "community penetration," "to march ahead," "training camp" (Lai 2000: 20).

Another textual strand is the agricultural one, in which Sengkang is seen as "a great harvest field, waiting for the CAC [the Chinese Annual Congress which governs the Chinese- and dialect-service Methodist churches] to plough, sow and reap souls for Christ" (Lai 2000: 1). The Methodist map exercises a kind of imaginative regression or erasure, so that the town site as a whole appears open, prospective, as yet undeveloped. Thus while the Centrepoint Properties map is highly stylized with an even coloured background filled up with amenity symbols, and the *Sunday Times* map is in black-and-white and highlights chiefly transportation details such as train stations, the Methodist map attempts to include some topographic/geographical detail, in the highlighting of areas already developed or being developed, in the swamp or foliage surrounding the Punggol river, and the crude indication of shallows in the river. Such details (together with the inclusion, whether intentional or otherwise, of the "Seletar East Farmway" roads to the top left of the map) create a ruralization of the area when compared to the other two infrastructural/progressive maps. This topographical differentiation is all the more marked considering the other similarities that the Methodist article bears to the newspaper report: both use similar statistics (the figure of 95,000 homes), both mention the history of the settlement ("Kangkar," the fishing village at the "foot of the port"), both locate Sengkar within the "riverine frontage" that is planned for the neighbouring Punggol 21. Yet while the newspaper article incorporates these details into a story of prospective infrastructural development, the Methodist article instead overlays these details with a narrative and topography of need, opportunity, and lack.

These textual strands of military and agricultural endeavour, not incidentally, echo St Paul's well-known descriptions of the Christian life and calling in verses like 2 Timothy 2: 3–6 and elsewhere. More than a textual echo for its own sake, these narrative and topographical strategies re-write Sengkang as spiritual space (marked by Biblical echoes, proselytizing opportunities, pre-developed openness), rather than the already-filled, materialistically rich, Enlightenment-progressive towns depicted in the other maps. This creation of a materially underdeveloped topography as an opposition to and critique of a Singapore society and cityscape perceived as too crowded and commercialized, is also evident in the Singapore poetry written in English, which is a manifestation of the strong influence on many of these poets (Edwin Thumboo, Lee Tzu Pheng, Arthur Yap, Oliver Seet, Robert Yeo, and others) of either a practising Christian faith, or a mission school upbringing, or both. Thus there is a recognizable topography in many such poems, which turns attention away from the busy city, the rich financial district, the developed waterfront, and the resorts like Sentosa, which form the backdrop of many touristic representations of Singapore. Instead, nature reserves, the unscenic topographies of mud flats and wild grass patches, pockets of undeveloped rural spaces, and the like, become sites invested with a spiritual signification, a valorization or emphasis alternative to the codes of money, social status and power evident in the developed city. This alternative hermeneutic becomes pertinent to the extent that it is influential – to the extent that it is linked to a culture which may, despite its lack of official representation or numerical dominance, nevertheless be capable of exerting influence on the praxis in and attitudes to the landscape.

CONCLUSION: ABJECTION AND ATOPIA IN THE POST-COLONIAL CITY

An urban structure like Singapore offers a different understanding of the "dual city," which as Mooney and Danson (1997: 73) point out, "has long been a classic theme of urban sociology. While the dual city is often understood in terms of "spatial divisions," i.e. sociological differentiation in distinct spaces within the city ("inner city" v. "affluent middle class districts," city and suburbs etc; Mooney and Danson 1997: 73, 74), the post-colonial city, the city with a strong central governance and planning, or the city without a hinterland often necessitate a different understanding of space and sociological relationships. An urban imaginary is possible and relevant to cities in general, of course, and arises out of the different hermeneutic, representational, and socio-political orders at work in each situation – arises, that is to say, out of the gap between a dominant order at the material and planning levels, and an order of signification which has the means of textual expression but not socio-political representation. What is interesting about Christianity in Singapore is not, however, such a marginalized or ephemeral culture; rather, it is the way in which Christianity's atopic strategies and tendencies figure a vital quality of the spatial organization of the city itself, in its attempts to juggle differing demands within limited available space, to tolerate and even encourage religious observance while remaining strictly a secular government, or to accommodate the colonial past within a project of national progress and development.

In this perspective, the atopic spiritual strategies of Christianity and the utopian progressivist vision of the secular state become uncanny doubles of each other. Bataille's analysis of the act of sacrifice as mythic production and ritual – an act which is a "negation of the real order," to create an otherwise inconceivable or suppressed relationship of "intimacy" (1992: 43–45) – sketches the basis of an urban cultural mechanism of repudiation in order to re-incorporate, of a ritualistic rupturing or sundering of material processes and relationships, to enable a visionary order which in turn sustains or justifies new material production. Singapore's national discourse of grandeur and cosmopolitan style, itself an element within a larger commercial-global ideology, is thus built in part upon strategies of spatial re-organization and the manipulation of cultural signs; in this process originary meanings are abjected for the sake of new cultural and spatial formations intended to reinforce a centralized government's initiative of global competition. The Christian spatial and hermeneutic order is peculiar in its collaboration in this project, both historically and in its present forms. Yet this collaboration is also a strategy of continuation and re-emergence, in processes of alternative interpretation, in overlays and over-writings of official-commercial landscapes.

NOTES

1   Historically, the larger Christian denominations in Singapore have founded churches catering to vernacular congregations, but these churches over the years have typically seen a decline in the vernacular congregations, and the institution of English worship services with rising congregation sizes, especially as the speaking of Chinese dialects is discouraged among younger generations by the Singapore education system's insistence on Mandarin as the definitive Chinese language, and by rising competence in and exposure to English.

2   There are, of course, particular exceptions to this rule – opportunities for individual customization of housing units, and a greater consultative atmosphere in the management of the HDB, particularly in recent years. Thus in 1991 the HDB initiated a scheme which allowed private architectural and construction firms to bid for contracts to build new apartment blocks, and has also solicited public feedback in the construction of newer estates like Punggol 21 (Goh 2001).

3   The fate of the clock tower at the Anglo-Chinese School (Barker Road) is typical: during a recent plan (begun in 2000) to re-develop the school site, the school's Board of Governors decided (in the face of opposition by a number of alumni) to "sacrifice the old Clock Tower for a new rebuilt facsimile" (Home Page 2000: 3). The Board cited (among other justifications) "serious implications for function and design" of retaining the existing tower.

REFERENCES

Anglo-Chinese School. *Family Traditions* (Special Publication of the ACS Family to Commemorate its 115th Birthday). Singapore: ACS Board of Governors, 1 March 2001.

Augustine. *Concerning the City of God against the Pagans*, trans. Henry Bettenson, ed. John O'Meara. Harmondsworth: Penguin, 1984.

Bataille, Georges. *Theory of Religion*, trans. Robert Hurley. New York: Zone Books, 1992.

Bloom, Harold. *A Map of Misreading*. Oxford: Oxford University Press, 1975.

Burke, Edmund. *Reflections on the Revolution in France*, (ed.) J. G. A. Pocock. Indianapolis: Hackett Publishing, 1987.

Cheong, Suk-Wai. "Where Raffles Landed," *Straits Times* 17 February 2001.

Cunningham, Colin. *Stones of Witness: Church Architecture and Function*. Phoenix Mill: Sutton Publishing, 1999.

Ellin, Nan. *Postmodern Urbanism*. Cambridge, MA: Blackwell, 1996.

Gillespie, Natalie Nichols. "Building a Church Without Walls," *Ministries Today* September/October 1998, 30–35.

Goh, Chok Tong. "First-world economy, world-class home," National Day Rally speech delivered 23 August 1999. Reprinted in *MITA webpage* http://www.gov.sg/mita/pressrelease/99082202.htm [date accessed: 24 February 2000].

Goh, Robbie B. H. "The Mission School in Singapore: Colonialism, Moral Training, Pedagogy, and the Creation of Modernity," paper presented at conference on Immigrant Societies and Modern Education, 31 August – 3 September 2000, Singapore.

Goh, Robbie B. H. "Ideologies of 'Upgrading' in Singapore Public Housing: Postmodern Style, Globalisation and Class Construction in the Built Environment," *Urban Studies* 38: 9 (2001): 1589–1604.

Harvey, David. *The Condition of Postmodernity: An Enquiry into the Origins of Cultural Change*. Oxford: Basil Blackwell, 1989.

"History in Glass," *Straits Times* 7 April 2001.

History of Singapore. "St. Andrew's Cathedral." http://library.thinkquest.org/10414/andrewcat.html [date accessed: 30 March 2001].

Home Page. "Why ACS Clock Tower Has to Go," *Methodist Message* 102: 5 (May 2000), 3.

Hutcheon, Linda. *A Poetics of Postmodernism: History, Theory, Fiction*. New York: Routledge, 1988.

Jacobs, Jane. *Edge of Empire: Postcolonialism and the City*. London: Routledge, 1996.

Jahn, Graham. *Sydney Architecture*. Sydney: Watermark Press, 1997.

Jameson, Fredric. *Postmodernism: Or, the Cultural Logic of Late Capitalism*. Durham: Duke University Press, 1991.

Jayakumar, S. "Opening Address" at the Parliament of Religions, 21 February 1987, in *Harmony Among Religions*, Singapore: Inter-Religious Organisation, 1987.

Kong, Lily. "Ideological Hegemony and the Political Symbolism of Religious Buildings in Singapore," *Environment and Planning D: Society and Space* (1993) 11.

Kristeva, Julia. *Powers of Horror: An Essay on Abjection*. New York: Columbia University Press, 1982.

Kuo, Eddie C.Y. and Tony Chee Kiong. *Religion in Singapore*. Singapore: SNP Publishers, 1995.

Lai, Choy Fong. "CAC to Build Church in Sengkang," *Methodist Message* 102: 5 (May 2000), 1, 20.

Lecercle, Jean-Jacques. *The Violence of Language*. London: Routledge, 1990.

Lefebvre, Henri. *The Production of Space*, trans. Donald Nicholson-Smith. Oxford: Blackwell, 1991.

Leong, Weng Kam. "Church to Car Workshop . . . to Historic Site," *Straits Times* 27 January 2000.

Leow, Jason. "Christianity Popular Among Chinese Here," *Straits Times* 18 November 2000.

Lim, Jon Sun Hock. "Colonial Architecture and Architects of Georgetown (Penang) and Singapore between 1786–1942." 5 vols. Thesis submitted for degree of Ph.D. Architecture, NUS, 1990.

MacPherson Secondary School. "School History." http://www.moe.edu.sg/schools/ms/school history.htm [date accessed: 30 March 2001].

Ministry of Information and the Arts. *The Need for the Maintenance of Religious Harmony Act*. Singapore: MITA, 1992.

Mooney, Gerry and Mike Danson. "Beyond 'Culture City': Glasgow as a 'Dual City'" in Nick Jewson and Susanne MacGregor (eds) *Transforming Cities: Contested Governance and New Spatial Divisions*. London: Routledge, 1997.

Papadakis, Andreas C. (ed.) *Paternoster Square and the New Classical Tradition*, Special Issue of *Architectural Design* 97 (1992).

Rockefeller Memorial Chapel. *Rockefeller Memorial Chapel Webpage*. http://rockefeller. uchicago.edu [date accessed: 29 March 2001].

Rogers, Christy. "Harold Washington Library Center." *Galinski Webpage*, http://galinsky. com/buildings/hwcpl [1998; date accessed 11 May 2002].

Sheares, Benjamin. "Speech at the Opening of the Seminar Organised by the Inter-Religious Organisation and the Society for Spiritual Culture, 30 October 1972," in *What Religions Mean Today*, Singapore: Educational Publications Bureau, 1974.

Singapore Art Museum. "Museum Facilities" http://www.nhb.gov.sg/sam/profile/facilities. shtml [date accessed: 9 April 2001].

Singapore Places of Attraction. http://asiatravel.com/sinplac2.html [date accessed: 30 March 2001].

Singapore Tourism Board. *Official Guide Singapore*. Singapore: Singapore Tourism Board, 1999.

Solomon, Robert. "Worship in Culture of Entertainment," *Methodist Message* 100: 22 (November 1998), 2.

St. Andrew's Cathedral Online. http://www.livingstreams.org.sg [date accessed: 29 March 2001].

Straits Times, "History in Glass," 7 April 2001.

Swan and Maclaren Architects. *Cairnhill Road Singapore: Proposed New Unit Anglo Chinese School*, 1924. National Archives microfilm NA 309.

Tee, Hun Ching. "Life Behind the Vale," *Sunday Times* 24 September 2000, 2–3.

Venturi, Robert. *Learning from Las Vegas: the Forgotten Symbolism of Architectural Form*. Cambridge, MA: MIT Press, 1977.

Chapter 7: Singapore: A Skyline of Pragmatism

Kwek Mean Luck

[The major buildings of Singapore] collectively symbolise the aspirations, the values and the levels of aesthetic appreciation of the Singapore society, especially its decision-makers . . . [Singapore's] recent architecture only reflects the dominance of the business community and its material wealth.[1]

THE BIRTH OF SINGAPORE AND PRAGMATISM

On 9 August 1965, Singapore was thrust into independence. The new island state measured 23 km from north to south and 42 km from east to west. Its total area was a mere 646 square kilometres.[2] It had joined the Federation of Malaysia two years earlier in the hope that this would provide an economic hinterland for an island lacking in natural resources, with 75 percent Chinese in a population of two million while surrounded by more than a hundred million Malay and Indonesian Muslims. With separation, Singapore was now on its own.

The historical circumstances of Singapore's birth, and its geographic limitations, shaped the priorities and outlook of its leaders. Economic survival was the clarion call of the day, and the ostensibly socialist People's Action Party eschewed ideological approaches to problems, seeking instead to deal with them by way of practical methods adapted to the circumstances. Through the years, this approach has acquired the label 'pragmatism'. The central doctrine of pragmatism is the primacy of economic growth[3] and, in the pursuit of this, an admittance of only 'concrete' evidence of a statistical type and no qualitative or 'soft' evidence or 'in principle' arguments.[4]

Though born out of a desire to avoid ideological solutions, pragmatism has over the years become an ideology in itself,[5] ingrained in the bureaucracy,[6] and informing domestic thought in fields such as economics,[7] foreign affairs,[8] law[9] and urban planning.[10] It might very well be, that such an ideological framework, created in a time of crisis, and seeping over the years into many areas, means different things in different fields. Whether there is a kernel of consistency in the many applications of pragmatism, or whether such consistency in application is at all realistic and possible, is a matter deserving consideration but beyond the scope of this study. The focus of this paper is much narrower, on pragmatism as applied to urban planning, and in particular to heritage conservation.

It argues that pragmatism in urban planning creates a bias towards land use for economic development, and in the land use allocation process, a bias towards land use with the highest economic return. One consequence of this is the low priority accorded to conservation in the 1960s and 1970s. Conservation was given a new lease of life from the mid-1980s onwards; however, this was not a result of a change in policy, but was in fact a continuation of pragmatism. That the same ideology can give rise to two different sets of directions within a short span of time highlights the limitations of pragmatism as a working ideology. Pragmatism places a premium on what is quantifiable. What is unquantifiable at the time of the decision-making is left out of the equation, even though it has an economic impact. Consequently, what appears to be a rational economic decision in the face of a limited set of quantifiable factors, may be far from so when the totality of factors reveals itself in due course. This has implications on the utility of pragmatism not just in relation to urban planning and conservation, but as a general framework.

PRAGMATISM IN URBAN PLANNING

The stark strategic constraint on urban planning in Singapore is its size limitations, and this is reflected in the literature in this field. In the conclusion of his comprehensive study on urban planning in Singapore, Ole Johan Dale observes that the limited land area has necessitated careful planning and use of land. It has also made land a valuable asset.[11] The limited land space in Singapore sets boundaries for what can be achieved, and affects the evaluation of options in urban planning. It is a key strategic constraint that operates regardless of the ideological framework adopted for urban planning, and is, in that respect, distinct from pragmatism. The interaction between land area as a strategic constraint and pragmatism can be seen from the thoughts of former Chief Executive Officer and Chief Planner of the Urban Renewal Authority in Singapore, Liu Thai Ker, in respect of whether Singapore can afford conservation. He stated in 1992 that Singapore can afford conservation since, with large-scale reclamation in the Marina areas adjacent to the financial district, Singapore has enough land to satisfy its commercial requirements in the city centre well into the future.[12]

Implicit in this are two strands of thought. First, there is the recognition of strategic constraint in available land area. Second, given the limitations of space, land should be used first for commercial development, and conservation can be afforded only if the land needs for commerce have been satisfied. The impact of pragmatism on urban planning lies in the second strand of thought, on the *priority allocation* for land use, in the light of the strategic constraint.

The operation of pragmatism on priority allocation takes place at two levels. On the first level, it creates a bias towards land use decisions that will enhance the overall economic development of Singapore. One example of this is the redevelopment of the central district in the 1960s and the 1970s. By 1957, the population had reached 1,445,929, of which 78.6 percent were living in the city area.[13] Social surveys by Goh Keng Swee[14] and Barrington Kaye[15] revealed overcrowding, poverty and slum-like housing conditions throughout the centre of the city. A report by a team from the United Nations Development Programme noted that in spite of this, there was tremendous vibrancy in the community.[16] Nevertheless, the final assessment was that there was a need to relocate the city dwellers to alternative housing and, more importantly, a need to redevelop the land space in the city area for economic purposes. A publication of the Housing Development Board in 1966 captures the spirit of the time:

What is Urban Renewal and why the need for it in Singapore? In Singapore, Urban Renewal means no less than the gradual demolition of virtually the whole 1,500 acres of the old city and its replacement by an integrated modern city centre worthy of Singapore's future role as the New York of Malaysia. Apart from the slums in the city centre, there is the problem of traffic congestion. The whole road system will have to be boldly and drastically redeveloped.[17]

Ultimately, the demands of a rapidly developing economy, on housing, transportation and social services for the population, and the facilitation of employment, dictated the urban planning agenda in the city district.[18] In so doing, the needs of economic development were given a wide conception. At a time when most developing countries did not, Singapore poured its energies into greening the city.[19]

On a second level, pragmatism creates a bias in the priority allocation process, in favour of land use with the highest economic return. The stated aim of urban renewal was to 'rejuvenate the old core of the city by making better economic use of the land by rebuilding the city completely in stages'.[20] The criticality of the economic benefit arising from land use is best seen in the area of conservation. Liu Thai Ker noted that conservation 'should not be an economic burden to the government. Instead, its economic success will go a long way towards furthering the cause of conservation.'[21] William Lim observed that while conservation programmes in many advanced countries are often subsidized or accorded concessions, such as direct grants, tax rebates and compensation in the transference of development rights, Singapore cannot afford and need not follow these examples, and some new and better suited mechanisms should be introduced to encourage the private sector to participate actively in conservation.[22] The translation of such thinking into practice can be seen from the *Bu Ye Tian* proposal. In 1982, a small group of individuals presented an unsolicited report to the government to retain and revitalize a built area of the Central Business District along Boat Quay, traditionally known as *Bu Ye Tian*. Emphasis was placed in the report on proving that the preservation and adaptive re-use of this traditional environment could be made economically viable, without the need for any government subsidy.[23]

PRAGMATISM AND CONSERVATION

One consequence of pragmatism's emphasis on land use for general economic development and the maximization of economic return from the land use was the low priority accorded to conservation in the 1960s and the 1970s. This was despite the establishment of the Preservation of Monuments Board (PMB) in January 1971. The PMB had four statutory objectives: (a) the preservation of monuments of historic, traditional, archaeological, architectural or artistic interest; (b) the protection and augmentation of the amenities of those monuments; (c) the stimulation of public interest and support in the preservation of those monuments; and (d) the taking of appropriate measures to preserve all records, documents and data relating to those monuments.[24]

To achieve these objectives, the government was given, amongst other powers, the overriding power to place a 'monument' under the protection of the PMB, through a preservation order issued by the Minister on the advice of the PMB.[25] Objections to the making of the preservation order may be submitted in writing to the Minister within three months of its publication. Any refusal by the Minister to revoke the order would be final. Where a preservation order is in force, the monument to which the order relates shall not without the written consent of the Board (which consent shall not be unreasonably withheld), be demolished, removed, altered or renovated or have any addition made except in case of urgent and immediate necessity for the safety of persons or property.[26]

This power was used sparingly in the early years of the PMB, and few buildings were placed under the protection of preservation orders.[27] This was not because of any legal restraints on the exercise of its powers. The PMB can advise the Minister to issue a preservation order in respect of a 'monument', and the definition of a 'monument' has been drafted in an extremely wide manner, essentially placing a great latitude of discretion in the PMB. Section 2 of the Preservation of Monuments Act (Cap 239) defines a 'monument' as including:

(a)   any building, structure, erection or other work whether above or below the surface of the land, any memorial, place of interment or excavation and any part or remains of a monument; and

(b)   any land comprising or adjacent to a monument which in the opinion of the Board is reasonably required for the purpose of maintaining the monument or the amenities thereof or for providing or facilitating access thereto or for the exercise of proper control or management with respect thereto, *which is considered by the Board to be worthy of preservation by reason of its historic, traditional, archaeological, architectural or artistic interest.* (Emphasis added.)

In effect, the PMB has the power to advise the Minister to place under a preservation order, any building, structure, and the adjacent land, which *the PMB itself* considers to be worthy of preservation by *reason of historic, traditional, archaeological or artistic interest.* That demolition and redevelopment continued at a relentless pace, despite the introduction of the PMB and the wide ambit of its legal powers, is an indication of the hold of pragmatism on urban planning.

The introduction of the Urban Renewal Authority also failed to bring about any change. In 1974, the Urban Renewal Department of the Housing Development Board was reconstituted as a statutory body and renamed the Urban Redevelopment Authority (URA).[28] It inherited its existing objectives from its days as the Urban Renewal Department and acquired two new ones: the construction of more open space and landscaped pedestrian malls, particularly in the central city area, and the preservation of Singapore's historical and architectural heritage.[29]

The stated objective of heritage preservation was not, however, translated into any substantive action in the immediate years following the URA's creation. The primary focus remained the demolition of old buildings, clearance of slums, resettlement of the population from the central city area, and the erection of new buildings, despite the efforts of planners in the URA and the Planning Department of the Ministry of National Development to retain traditional shophouses for conservation.[30]

Several factors combined in the 1980s to create a reversal in thinking and push conservation up on the priority list. One factor was the oversupply of commercial facilities in the mid-1980s. In 1980, it was reported that 'the critical shortage of prime office space is expected to worsen soon'.[31] Projections of demand by various consultancy firms forecast a shortage of between 200,000 and 500,000 square metres over the next five to six years.[32] By 1982, some 700,000 square metres worth of projects, largely in the office district in the Golden Shoe area, had been approved. From 1979 to 1982, the URA also offered for tender about 10 hectares of land predominantly for office development. These projects, on completion, were to supply a total of 284,000 square metres of office floor space.[33] In addition, the URA and the HDB were also directed to build 100,000 square metres of office rental space.[34] By 1983, real-estate firms were projecting an oversupply of office space over the next few years.[35] In 1985, the government-appointed Property Market Consultative Committee reported that the excess of supply over demand by 1990 would range between 500,000 square metres and 950,000 square metres.[36] In consequence, commercial use, which had been delivering the best economic returns, became less of a competing factor in priority allocation on land use.

A related factor was the realization that the government had accumulated, through land acquired under the Land Acquisition Act (Cap 152) and the reclamation efforts in the Marina area, sufficient unreleased land stock to last well into the twenty-first century. This reduced the pressure to demolish quality old buildings for new developments.[37] The third, and probably the most influential factor, was the decline in tourist arrivals. Annual growth rate in tourist arrivals experienced double-digit growth in the 1970s and, by the 1980s, tourism had become the third most important sector after manufacturing, and transport and communication, contributing 16 percent to Singapore's total foreign exchange earnings.[38] In 1983, however, tourist arrivals dropped by 3.5 percent over the previous year. It was Singapore's first decline in tourist numbers since 1965. The sense of crisis was heightened in 1984 when the annual increase in business visitors exceeded for the first time the annual increase in recreational visitors.

To rejuvenate the tourist industry, the Minister for Trade and Industry formed the Tourism Task Force in August 1984. The Tourism Task Force comprised four permanent secretaries as well as representatives from the hotel sector and the Singapore Tourist Promotion Board (STPB).[39] The Tourism Task Force took the view that Singapore should present itself both as the epitome of oriental mystique and a high-tech entertainment centre. It noted that as a result of the efforts to construct a 'modern metropolis', 'we have removed aspects of our Oriental mystique and charm which are best symbolised in old buildings, traditional activities and roadside activities such as the *pasar malam*'. Amongst its key recommendations was the conservation of Chinatown and other historical sites.

Pannell Kerr Forster was commissioned to follow up on the work of the Tourism Task Force. The Pannell Kerr Forster team recommended the:

> conservation of historical and cultural features to provide a remarkable contrast to the urban setting of this dynamic commercial city/state. Conservation of the suggested areas will provide a focus of attractions which will bring to life the historical and cultural heritage of the nation.

According to its calculations, the 'preliminary computations show that the enhancement of Chinatown and the Singapore River as historic preservation districts can increase potential occupancies of hotels by 369,000 room nights in 1988. The impact on the Singapore economy in total expenditure would apportionate $70 million.'[40]

In October 1986, the government released the Tourism Development Plan. Under the plan, $187 million would be spent on building, preservation and restoration projects, $260 million on upgrading historical areas and landmarks, $30 million on redeveloping Fort Canning Park and $480 million on developing Sentosa and Lazarus Islands.[41] Concurrent with these developments, in 1984 the URA completed its restoration efforts in Emerald Hill, along the shopping district of Orchard Road. This was followed by conservation studies in respect of Chinatown, Singapore River, Little India and Kampong Glam in 1985.[42] These were culled together into the URA's Conservation Master Plan, which was publicly released in December 1986. A Master Plan for the Civic and Cultural District was published in 1988. On 17 February 1989, Parliament passed the Planning (Amendment) Act. The amendments came into operation on 31 March 1989 and made substantial changes to the Planning Act (Cap 232). Pursuant to the Act, the URA was appointed the national conservation and central planning authority, and statutory recognition was given to the tasks that the URA had been doing over the last four years, namely the identification and designation of any area of special architectural, historic, traditional or aesthetic interest as a 'conservation area'.[43] The most important provision related to the institution of planning control for works carried out within a 'conservation area'.[44] Any person who wishes to carry out any works within a conservation area must have the written permission of the URA. In granting permission, the URA may impose conditions to require compliance with any guidelines it had issued.[45]

Conservation, which was largely ignored in the 1960s and the 1970s, was thus given a new lease of life from the mid-1980s onwards. Interestingly, the reversal in policy was not because of the demise of pragmatism. It resulted from a continued application of it. The central emphasis of pragmatism in urban planning, land use for economic development and the maximization of economic return from land as such, remained as forceful as ever. There were two main arguments in favour of conservation in the mid-1980s, both economic. First, conservation was deemed necessary for Singapore's economic development, in particular for the tourism industry. The prevailing mood was aptly captured by an editorial in *The Business Times*, which said:

> We tore down old buildings unselectively before various groups pressed for their preservation. It was all in the name of development and urban renewal. But we have to make up our minds what we really want. If we do not care for the tourist industry, fine.[46]

In line with this, 81.9 percent of the respondents in a survey of popular attitudes identified the attraction of tourists to Singapore as a prime motivation for urban conservation.[47] In Ole Johan Dale's analysis:

> Conservation of the historic areas now presented itself as a major growth sector. While the old shophouse areas had previously been razed, they now became an asset. Studies on the tourism sector had clearly shown the vital need for the retention of historic areas . . . The problem with historical conservation is that it has become a sort of consumption good. The genuine historical and cultural value in terms of people and

buildings is becoming subsidiary to the commercial needs of the tourist industry . . . The effort to re-create the atmosphere of the old Chinatown, for example, is a weak effort in recapturing the past for the sake of tourism. The result is a synthetic patchwork and 'gimmicks' that smack of artificiality. What is lost can sometimes never be regained.

Second, there was no competing use for the land that would yield a higher economic return. With the oversupply of commercial land on the market, and a more than sufficient land stock to meet future commercial needs, the opportunity cost of using land for conservation was much lower. Hopes of tourist arrivals also created a sense in the government that conservation could bring about financial returns. Twenty years after independence, conservation had become economically acceptable.[48]

The question that follows though is this: if it was pragmatic in the mid-1980s to emphasize the conservation of our architectural heritage, why was it not pragmatic in the 1960s and 1970s to do so? The short answer may be that it was not pragmatic because the two conditions which caused the shift in emphasis, decline in tourist arrivals and sufficiency of land for commercial use, were not in existence in the 1960s and the 1970s. Such an explanation is, however, hardly satisfactory. Arguably, with better assessment and projections, this could have been avoided. For example, it could be said that, given the utter lack of natural tourist attractions in Singapore, it should not have been hard to see the value that conservation would bring to the economy through tourism. In this sense, the fault was not with pragmatism as an ideological framework, but in the imperfect execution of it. However, while such an assessment seems plain with the benefit of hindsight, is it ever realistic to expect such prescient evaluation? But, if not, what does that suggest about the adequacy of pragmatism as an ideological framework?

PRAGMATISM OF HERITAGE CONSERVATION

Although the late shift towards conservation may salvage the tourism industry, in one aspect, it might already be too late. Twenty years of demolition and redevelopment has destroyed much of our architectural heritage and the communities that were built around them. Could this have been avoided if the dominant focus was not economic development, as demanded by pragmatism? Chua Beng-Huat has said that, in Singapore, the economic is privileged over the cultural because economic growth is seen as the guarantee of social and political stability necessary for the survival of the nation.[49] Could this have been avoided if there was a change in ideological focus, if the cultural was allowed from time to time to trump the economic?

Yet, on the other hand, is a change in ideology necessary before the importance of heritage can be accepted? Is heritage conservation truly incompatible with pragmatism? After all, as S. Rajaratnam, former Senior Minister has said:

A nation must have a memory to give it a sense of cohesion, continuity and identity. The longer the past, the greater the awareness of a nation's identity . . . A sense of a common history is what provides the links to hold together a people who came from the four corners of the earth.[50]

More recently, Prime Minister Goh Chok Tong emphasized: 'The story of Singapore needs to be a key part of the psyche of every citizen, which motivates him to excel and bond him to Singapore'.[51]

Heritage conservation helps to provide the people of the present with an insight into and experience of the past. It grounds the memory of the nation, the story of Singapore, into something concrete and visual. In the process, it aids economic development in at least two ways. First, the awareness of the nation's past helps to provide a common identity, thereby strengthening the social stability of an island of disparate peoples, filled with descendants of migrants, and with the prevailing emphasis on foreign talent for survival, an island of migrants for a long time to come. Second, it helps to create a mental and emotional bond to Singapore, providing an anchor against the lure of the international metropolises, a lure which has been heightened by the wave of globalization. In a society more conscious than any of the criticality of human resource, and of the leavening effect that talented individuals could have on the economy, such an anchoring effect on those contemplating distant shores is invaluable.

That heritage conservation has an impact on economic development and survival is undeniable. Why then was there no emphasis placed on it? One response is that it was not pragmatic then to do so. Back then, it was a question of economic survival. There was an urgent need to clear the slums, to find space for commercial development, to create jobs. Those immediate needs had to be met first, before conservation could be considered. This line of argument presupposes that conservation is incompatible with survival, and that wholesale demolition of old buildings was necessary for economic development. It is an unjustified assumption. In early 1962, Erik Lorange, a United Nations consultant, conducted a six-month study on urban renewal in Singapore. Among his recommendations was that redevelopment should start at the core of the central area, where there was a large portion of state land that would be easier to clear and to reparcel. His strategy of moving from the periphery to the core would allow for the potential conservation and rehabilitation of Chinatown.[52]

In 1963, a United Nations team arrived to follow up on Lorange's work. They emphasized that urban renewal should not lead to wholesale demolition of existing buildings. The team referred to the similarity in arguments for urban renewal in Singapore and those in other countries, particularly the United States, namely the desire to clear slums, improve central neighbourhoods, free the traffic flow and make land available for business and growth. They observed, however, that Singapore was unique, as there was an inflow of people into the city. The renewal districts were thriving, not decaying. Furthermore, the people's economic wealth and success were based on the proximity of their residential accommodation to trade and small services. The United Nations team recommended that 'a commitment be made to identify the values of some of Singapore's existing areas and build and strengthen these values'.[53]

While many of the specific recommendations of Lorange and the United Nations team were implemented, their recommendations in respect of conservation were ignored. Ole Johan Dale offers two possible reasons for this. One reason may be that both politicians and administrators looked upon the traditional shophouse areas as unbecoming of Singapore. Instead of being looked upon as potential assets, they were considered slums that had to be cleared and rede-veloped. Another reason relates to the nature of ownership. Many of the properties were in private ownership and the government's stand had been that any maintenance or upgrading is the owner's business. Subsidy for conservation of private property was thus rejected. Meanwhile, properties in state ownership were provided minimum upgrading or improvement, in the belief that these buildings would be demolished sooner or later.[54]

The thrust of Ole Johan Dale's analysis, then, is that heritage conservation was not given due regard by the administrators and the politicians because no economic value was placed in them. That, however, serves only to provide an indication of the prevailing mindset. It still begs the question: in view of the impact that heritage conservation could have on economic development, why did the administrators and politicians accord such little value to heritage conser-vation? One possible reason is the nature of pragmatism. The fundamental goal of such an ideological framework is the pursuit of economic growth, which is measured quantitatively by the annual percentage growth in Gross Domestic Product (GDP). Success is measured solely in terms of quantitative increases, and the evaluation of policy options is invariably dictated by the quantitative impact a policy choice will have on the fundamental end-goal of GDP growth. It is, however, incredibly hard to quantify the value that heritage conservation could add to the economy, through the creation of a common identity and its anchoring effect. The result of this is that what is unquantifiable at the time of the decision-making is left out of the equation, even though it has an economic impact. Where this occurs, what appears to be a rational economic decision in the face of a limited set of factors may turn out quite different when the totality of factors reveals itself in due course.

PRAGMATISM AND QUANTIFICATION

Pragmatism's problem with quantification is not limited to conservation. Consider the issue of home ownership in Singapore. Mechanisms in the public and private sector have provided adequate housing for the population.[55] The high valuation of property has also created a sense of prosperity and progress. In quantitative terms, such as the percentage of the population housed and the value extracted from residential property, the housing programme in Singapore has been an unmitigated success for its citizens. However, what about the impact of such home ownership and the high property valuation on other unquantifi-able aspects, such as a culture for entrepreneurship? The Economic Review Committee has identified the creation of an entrepreneurial economy as a key thrust of Singapore's economy.[56] The Minister of State for Entrepreneurship, Raymond Lim has observed that a key missing ingredient is an entrepreneurial culture among Singaporeans.[57] Whether there is a dampening effect on entre-preneurial culture will require more detailed study but, on first blush, there is a case that a culture focused on the acquisition of residential property as a sign of progress and as a financial investment, and the corresponding commitment to large monthly mortgage payments, reduces the incentive to venture out. The difficulty of quantifying such a dampening effect makes it easy to ignore it, even though, if true, it would affect an extremely important aspect of our economy.

CONCLUSION

One consequence of pragmatism in urban planning has been the pursuit of certain governmental interventions in land use, which had to be changed when unforeseen conditions arose, leading to a policy reversal, perhaps too late in time. It may yet be true that economics is the wellspring of all others, including the social and the cultural. Nevertheless, in the pursuit of the economic, it may serve us to take heed, that the seemingly social or cultural may have an impact on the economy. It is just that, at least for now, you cannot measure it. We have remembered this in the past, in our efforts to green the city. It would be a pity to forget it now.

NOTES

1   William S W Lim, *Cities for People: Reflections of a Southeast Asian Architect*, Singapore: Select Books, 1990, pp. 117–118.

2   As a point of comparison, the total area of Hong Kong is 1,092 sq km. Further territorial details of Hong Kong are available at http://www.graphicmaps.com/webimage/countrys/asia/hkcia.htm.

3   'The overriding goal of PAP pragmatism is to ensure continuous economic growth. This singular goal is simultaneously the singular criterion for initiating and assessing all government activities, in terms of how an act will aid or retard this growth'; Chua Beng-Huat, *Communitarian Ideology and Democracy in Singapore*, London: Routledge, 1995, p. 68.

4   *Ibid.*, p. 70.

5   For a detailed study of the ideology of 'pragmatism', see Chua Beng-Huat *supra* n. 3. Another interesting study is that of Professor Edgar H. Schien, who described the cultural paradigm of the Economic Development Board in terms of 'strategic pragmatism'; Edgar H. Schien, *Strategic Pragmatism: The Culture of Singapore's Economic Development Board*, Singapore: Toppan Company, 1996.

6   Mr Lim Siong Guan, Permanent Secretary in the Prime Minister's Office and Head of the Civil Service, observed in 1996 that one of the traits of Singapore's public service was 'judging effectiveness by results achieved with pragmatism and a sense of urgency; Lim Siong Guan, 'The New Public Administration: Global Challenges, Local Solutions – the Singapore Experience', *Ethos*, Civil Service College, 1996. See also Ho Khai Leong, *The Politics of Policy-Making in Singapore*, Singapore: Oxford University Press, 2000, p. 116, where it is said: 'policy initiation and formulation in the developing states is not undertaken to seek maximum political support but rather to acquire the best possible solutions to significant social and political problems. State elites prefer to call this approach pragmatism.'

7   The early problems confronting the leaders of the newly independent Singapore included unemployment, a high birth-rate, a lack of infrastructure, political instability, housing shortages and labour unrest. Its ideology became economic pragmatism for survival; see Goh Keng Swee, 'A Socialist Economy that Works', in C. V. Devan Nair, *Socialism That Works: The Singapore Way*, Singapore: Federal Publications, 1976, published more recently in Goh Keng Swee, *The Practice of Economic Growth*, Singapore: Federal Publications, 1995, pp. 94–106.

8   The collection of speeches and writings by Professor Tommy Koh, one of Singapore's most distinguished diplomats, is entitled, 'The Quest for World Order: Perspectives of a Pragmatic Idealist'.

9   In his lecture, 'The Confluence of Law and Policy: The Singapore Experience', Minister of Law Professor S. Jayakumar identified five key principles which have guided the development of Singapore's legal system. The first principle is that of pragmatic adaptation of the common law to serve the changing needs of Singapore; see *The Singapore Conference: Leading the Law and Lawyers into the New Millennium @ 2020*, Singapore: Butterworths, 2000, pp. 5–8.

10 Mr Liu Thai Ker, former Chief Executive Officer and Chief Planner of the Urban Redevelopment Authority of Singapore, noted in 1992: 'there is no single method to charting a course for conservation for all cities. The lesson we have learnt in Singapore is that it is possible to aspire to a world-class professional standard in conservation, but the approaches to it must be pragmatic to suit the local environment'; Liu Thai Ker, *Charting A Course for Conservation in Singapore*, paper delivered in September 1992 at Conference on Building Conservation in Hong Kong – In Search of Times Past.

11 Ole Johan Dale, *Urban Planning in Singapore: The Transformation of a City*, New York: Oxford University Press, 1999, p. 243.

12 See *supra* n. 10. Liu also raised the point that 'one can argue that even without Marina reclaimed land, we have to try to conserve our heritage anyway. Although we do not have architectural masterpieces, these old buildings provide a different kind of accommodation from the large modern edifices for offices, shops, hotels and residence. They enrich our urban life and add identity to the image of our city.'

13 Ministry of National Development, Planning Department, *Master Plan, First Review 1965: Report of Survey*, Singapore, 1965, p. 37.

14 Goh Keng Swee, *Urban Incomes & Housing, A report on the Social Survey of Singapore, 1953–54*, Singapore: Government Printing Office, 1958.

15 Barrington Kaye, *Upper Nankin Street, Singapore: A Sociological Study of Chinese Households Living in a Densely Populated Area*, Singapore: University of Malaya Press, 1960.

16 'Vitality is the theme and leitmotif of the Central Area. Mixture, movement and change were everywhere; United Nations Development Programme (Singapore), *Assistance in an Urban Renewal Development Project, Part Four, The Central Area*, Singapore, 1970, p. 4.

17 Housing and Development Board, *50,000 Up: Homes for the People*, Singapore, 1966.

18 Lily Kong and Brenda S. A. Yeoh, *Urban Conservation in Singapore: A Survey of State Policies and Popular Attitudes*, Urban Studies, Vol. 31, No. 2, 1994 247–265 p. 249.

19 Greening was 'good for morale, for tourism, and for investors'. Singapore's botanists brought back 8,000 different varieties and got some 2,000 to grow in Singapore; Lee Kuan Yew, *From Third World to First: The Singapore Story: 1965–2000*, Singapore: Times Media Private Limited, 2000, p. 204.

20 Housing and Development Board, *Annual Report 1963*, Singapore, 1964, p. 2.

21 Liu Thai Ker, *supra* n. 10.

22 William S. W. Lim, *supra* n. 1, p. 156. Lim's proposals for financing conservation are discussed in William S. W. Lim, 'Financing Conservation', *Singapore Business*, March 1982, p. 31. In essence, the specific proposal is for all rents of rent-controlled premises in designated conservation areas to be decontrolled within a specific period. Tenants should be compensated by the landlords generally along lines similar to the compensation paid to tenants under the Land Acquisition Act. However, the landlords must, at their own cost, restore their premises back to their original conditions making as few changes as possible. If the landlords do not wish to fulfil the stipulated conditions for restoration, the tenants should have the option to take over the premises, which can be valued in accordance with the Land Acquisition Act. If the tenants do not wish to take over, the authorities can do so. Any landlord may offer his premises to the authorities to be included for conservation. If accepted, the premises will be preserved under similar conditions as those in the designated conservation areas.

23 Bu Ye Tian Enterprises Pte Ltd, *Singapore River – A Conservation Proposal for Boat Quay, Boating Activities and Floating Chinese Restaurants*, November 1982; described in William S. W. Lim, *supra* n. 1, p. 135.

24 Section 5 of the Preservation of Monuments Act (Cap 239).

25 *Ibid*. at section 8. For the bulk of the PMB's existence, this would have been the Minister for National Development. With the transfer of the PMB from the Ministry of National Development to the Ministry of Information and the Arts on 1 April 1997, the power is now exercised by the Minister for Information and the Arts.

26 *Ibid*. at section 9.

27 The first exercise of the powers conferred by s. 8 of the Preservation of Monuments Act was on 8 July 1973. Eight buildings were placed under protection: Thong Chai

Medical Institution, Armenian Church, St Andrew's Cathedral, Telok Ayer Market, Thian Hock Keng Temple, Sri Mariamman Temple, Fatimah Mosque and Cathedral of The Good Shepherd. Since its inception, over the course of the last 30 years, the PMB has placed 42 buildings under the protection of s. 8 of the Preservation of Monuments Act (Cap 239). Notably, no vernacular shophouse has been placed under the PMB's protection.

28   The Urban Redevelopment Authority Act (Cap 340) was promulgated by Parliament on 28 January 1974 and became operative from 1 April 1974.

29   Urban Redevelopment Authority, *Annual Report*, 1974, Singapore: URA, pp. 2–3.

30   See Ole Johan Dale *supra* n. 11, p. 156.

31   Interviews with real-estate firms in *The Straits Times,* 'Squeezed for Office Space', 27 June 1980.

32   Jones Lang Wootton, *South-East Property Review*, London, 1980. Jones Lang Wootton estimated that the supply of space in prime locations was likely to fall short by about 250,000 square metres over the next six years. See also 'Running Short of Prime Space', *Business Times*, 3 March 1980.

33   Urban Redevelopment Authority, *URA Chronicle of Sale Sites*, Singapore, 1985.

34   Khoo Teng Chye, 'Organisational Analysis and Proposed Changes for Organisational Development in an Urban Redevelopment Agency', MBA thesis, National University of Singapore, 1984, pp. 140–141.

35   See Richard Ellis (Pte.) Limited, *South East Asia: The Property Market 1982/83*, Singapore, 1983; and Simon Lim, Oh & Partners, *Property Market Review 1982/83*, Singapore, 1983.

36   Ministry of Finance, *Report of the Property Market Consultative Committee: Action Plan for the Property Sector*, Singapore, 1986, p. 46.

37   See Liu Thai Ker *supra* n. 10; and Ole Johan Dale *supra* n. 11, p. 155.

38   Ministry of Trade and Industry, *Report of the Tourism Task Force*, Singapore, November 1984.

39   It is now renamed the Singapore Tourism Board.

40   Pannell, Kerr, Forster, *et al.*, *Tourism Development Plan for Singapore*, Singapore: Singapore Tourist Promotion Board, June 1986. For a comparison of differences in approach of the Pannell Kerr Forster team with that of the Tourism Task Force, see T. C. Chang and Peggy Teo, 'From Rhetoric to Reality: Cultural Heritage and Tourism in Singapore', in Linda Low and Douglas M. Jonhston (eds), *Singapore Inc.*, Singapore: Asia Pacific Press, 2001, at pp. 277–279.

41   Ministry of Trade and Industry, *The Tourism Product Development Plan*, Singapore, October 1986.

42   Urban Redevelopment Authority, *Annual Report 1984*, Singapore, 1984 cited in Lily Kong and Brenda S. A. Yeoh *supra* n. 18, p. 249, which contains a more detailed account of the changes to the URA during this period in relation to conservation.

43   Section 6A of the Planning Act, 1990 (Revised Ed.).

44   *Ibid.* at section 10A.

45   To enforce planning control, section 10A(6) of the Planning Act, 1990 provided that any person who does not apply for permission before carrying out works of conservation shall be guilty of an offence and liable on conviction to a fine not exceeding $3,000. Section 10A(7) provided that any person who fails to comply with any condition imposed by the URA shall be guilty of an offence and liable on conviction to a fine not exceeding $3,000. Section 10A(8) provided that the URA may cancel the permission of any person who fails to comply with the condition imposed.

46   Editorial, *Business Times*, 4 September 1984.

47   See Lily Kong and Brenda S. A. Yeoh *supra* n. 18, p. 255.

48   The redevelopment–conservation conflict has not, however, been fully resolved. Instances where buildings of historical and/or architectural significance have been demolished to make way for more 'pragmatic' use of the land attest to that. For example, Eu Court, a building with 'landmark qualities' located in the Civic and Cultural District, was torn down in early 1993 to make way for the widening of Hill Street; see Lily Kong and Brenda S. A. Yeoh *supra* n. 18, p. 251. Chua Beng-Huat notes that in spite of the plans for conservation, 'the government continues to be of two minds regarding heritage preservation and encouraging cultural developments: it

wants to get the best financial returns for its land holdings but conservation and cultural developments do not usually even pay for themselves'; Chua Beng-Huat, *Political Legitimacy and Housing: Stakeholding in Singapore*, London: Routledge, 1997, p. 42. The continued vitality of pragmatism can be seen from the observations of the Chief Planner of the URA, Mr Khoo Teng Chye, in 1994: 'We take a pragmatic approach in implementing the conservation programme. Two elements are critical in our implementation approach: harnessing the private sector to undertake conservation, and encouraging new commercially viable uses in the restored buildings to give the commercial incentive to conserve.' This has prompted the response that such 'an approach based on the economic rationale is undoubtedly useful as a guiding principle, if only to instil a sense of responsibility and accountability to the conservation process, and on those involved in it. However, if applied rigidly and without exception, many of the best examples of our living heritage could be in danger of being lost to economic pressures'; Malone-Lee Lai Choo, 'Heritage and Planning', in Kwok Kian-Woon, Kwa Chong Guan, Lily Kong and Brenda Yeoh (eds), *Our Place in Time: Exploring Heritage and Memory in Singapore*, Singapore: Singapore Heritage Society, 1999, p. 184.

49   Chua Beng-Huat *supra* n. 3, p. 59.
50   Quoted in Brenda Yeoh and Lily Kong, 'The Notion of Place: In the Construction of History, Nostalgia and Heritage', in Kwok Kian-Woon, Kwa Chong Guan, Lily Kong and Brenda Yeoh (eds), *supra* n. 49, p. 141.
51   Reported in *The Straits Times*, 22 July 1996.
52   Erik Lorange, *Final Report on Central Redevelopment of Singapore City*, Report prepared for the Government of Singapore, 31 July 1962.
53   C. Abrams, O. Koenigsberger and S. Kobe, *Growth and Urban Renewal in Singapore*, Report prepared for the Government of Singapore, Singapore: United Nations Programme of Technical Assistance, November 1963.
54   Ole Johan Dale, *supra* n. 11, p. 125.
55   For a comprehensive study on the public housing programme in Singapore, see Chua Beng-Huat, *supra* n. 49.
56   See Report of Economic Review Committee. The report is accessible via the internet through the MTI website at: http://www.mti.gov.sg/public/ERC/frm_ERC_Default.asp?sid=150&cid=1487.
57   See The Raffles Conversation – The entrepreneur's entrepreneur, *Business Times*, 12 April 2003.

Chapter 8: The Axis of Singapore: South Bridge Road

Robert Powell

South Bridge Road runs due south from the first bridging point of the Singapore River and is deeply embedded in the collective memory of the island's population.[1] In this essay I identify the origins of the urban artery and the historic events that have been associated with it in its 170-year history. In the last decade the Singapore Government and the Supreme Court have consolidated their presence at the northern end of South Bridge Road, and I speculate whether this will in the future create a new focus and orientation away from the padang and towards "The Axis of Singapore".

At the outset of the twenty-first century, on an island where practically every physical feature has changed beyond recognition, South Bridge Road is an urban space which has retained much of its original form and where one's imagination is constantly stirred by the memories that are indelibly imprinted in the fabric.

It is a road steeped in the history of the ordinary Singaporean, far more so than the creations of post-independence planners of the URA and HDB. It is etched deeply in the collective memories of many Singaporeans. It links them to the privations and suffering of the indentured labourers and migrants from southern China and to the successful entrepreneurs among the diaspora. And the memories are not just of the early Chinese immigrants but also of the Indian Muslim and Hindu community and to a lesser extent of the European administrators and engineers in colonial times.

South Bridge Road dates from 1833 and it was built employing convict labour transported from India. It is one of the oldest roads on the island and runs south from what was the very first bridge over the Singapore River erected by Lieutenant Philip Jackson in 1822–1823 and known officially as Jackson's Bridge. It was also referred to as the Presentiment Bridge or the Monkey Bridge. Before Raffles' arrival in Singapore the river was a refuge for the sampans of the *orang laut* or sea pirates but they soon gave way to the trading vessels of the East India Company.

The wooden footbridge was repaired several times and eventually replaced by yet another wooden footbridge designed by J. T. Thomson in 1843 and promptly renamed the Thomson Bridge. This was widened in 1845 to take carriages but subsequently demolished in 1862 and replaced with an iron bridge imported from Calcutta and named after the Governor General of India at the time, Lord Elgin.

Widened yet again in the 1870s it still proved inadequate and was demolished in 1927 to make way for the present bridge linking the growing Chinese community south of the river with the Indian merchants in the High Street on the north side of the river. This bridge, which was opened in May 1929, is a modest structure by today's engineering standards but perfectly serviceable with high arches and slender suspension columns to support the carriageway. The old cast iron lamps with decorative work were made by Cavalieri Rodolfo Nolli (Fig. 8.1). The bridge overlooks the crescent-shaped Boat Quay. In the 1860s three-quarters of all shipping business was done on Boat Quay. Lighters known as *tongkangs* and *twakows* ferried goods from ships in the harbour to the godowns which lined the river bank (Fig. 8.2).

South Bridge Road starts here on the very edge of the colonial administrative core of Singapore indicated on Lt Philip Jackson's map of June 1828, where the major government buildings such as the Court House and later City Hall were located (Fig. 8.3). It terminates at the Jinricksha Station (1903) in the heart of Chinatown where it splits to form Tanjong Pagar Road and Neil Road, which run on either side of Duxton Hill (Fig. 8.4).

This is the area I worked in when I first came to Singapore in February 1984. I would make my way, through jostling crowds, to lunch in Telok Ayer Market (before it became an upmarket food centre), or to swim in the pool at Yan Kit Swimming Complex.

ACCESS TO CHINATOWN

Older Chinese Singaporeans knew South Bridge Road as Ta Ma Lo (Great Horseway) or Chat Bok Koi (Paint Wood Street) and it provides access to the distinctive areas of Chinatown namely South Boat Quay via Circular Road, Kreta Ayer with its colourful Sago Street, Smith Street, Temple Street, Pagoda Street and Mosque Street, and to Cross Street, Chin Chew Street and Ann Siang Hill which originally housed many of Singapore's clan associations (Fig. 8.7).[2]

Telok Ayer was the original coastline until 1843. Trading junks, slave traders and passenger boats from China landed here and discharged their cargo of humans and goods. Teochews settled nearest to the Singapore River and along Boat Quay; Hokkiens congregated in the Amoy Street area; Hakkas favoured Tanjong Pagar; and the Hainese settled in Tanjong Pagar. Many of the early arrivals from China came as indentured labour and would be housed in "kengs" or "coolie quarters" in Pagoda Street that runs off to the west of South Bridge Road.[3] Until the early 1980s the street was still referred to by older residents as Kwong Hup Yuen Kai after one of the slave traders.

Pagoda Street was also a street of tailors while Mosque Street was famous for tim sum, tea houses, bakeries and *karang guni* men.[4] The latter recycled newsprint and cardboard long before it was accorded the respectable description of "sustainable use of resources".

Sago Street was initially associated with sago mills located in the area but for decades was known as the street of "death houses". All the shops had something to do with funerals – wreaths, joss sticks, paper money, candles, black-dyed mourning wear, embalming services, paper effigies of ships and cars. In the upper rooms of the house were dormitories where the old of Chinatown spent their last years (Figs 8.6, 8.8 and 8.9).

Temple Street was famous for its blacksmiths, tin smiths and pottery. According to Geraldine Lowe-Ismail some of the old families are still in business: Sia Huat sells household and kitchen ware, Bao Yuan Trading sells wholesale porcelain and Too Foong is an old antiques dealer.[5]

Figure 8.1
Elgin Bridge (1929). The cast iron lamps were
made by Cavalieri Rodolfo Nolli

Figure 8.2
The Singapore River. Until 1983 it was thronged with
lighters used to transport goods to the godowns along
South Boat Quay

Figure 8.3
City Hall

Figure 8.4
The Jinricksha Building (1903) designed by
Samuel Tomlinson and D. M. Craik

Figure 8.5
Shophouses at the corner of Trengganu Street and Smith Street in 1984

Figure 8.6
A paper effigy of a ship waits to accompany the deceased

Figure 8.7
Letter writers' premises in Sago Street

Figures 8.8 and 8.9
In the upper rooms of the houses in Sago Street were dormitories where the old of Chinatown spent their last years

The area had a thriving night market or *pasah malam* but also earned a dubious reputation as a "red light" area in the early twentieth century. Sago Lane had more than a dozen brothels and Smith Street more than twenty-five, which persisted until 1930 when they were brought under tight control. Spring Lane was once known as *Phan Tsai Mei* or Lane of Foreign Prostitutes on account of the many Japanese prostitutes found there (Fig. 8.10).

On the opposite side of South Bridge Road, Chin Chew Street housed a community of *samsui* women. Older Singaporeans will remember them because of their distinctive red hats and dark blue trousers and top. Tough and hard working, many of these women ran away from poverty or arranged marriages in China and found work in the construction industry in Nanyang (the South Seas). They could often be seen early in the morning, squatting at the junction of Chin Chew Street and South Bridge Road awaiting their transport. In the 1980s they were still seen though less and less as the demographic profile of Chinatown changed.[6] Their distinctive headgear was said to have come from the Sam Sui district of Guangdong Province and to have been originally worn by Chao Yun, the mistress of the poet Su Tung Po.

TRANSPORT IMPROVEMENTS

When the first steam tramway commenced operations in Singapore on May 3 1886, it was intended to link the town with the new harbour at Tanjong Pagar and it followed the route of South Bridge Road. But apparently it could not compete with the rickshas, which were imported from Shanghai from 1880 onwards, and the tramway ceased to operate in 1894. By 1919, an estimated 20,000 ricksha pullers were pulling 9,000 rickshas in the colony, the administrators of this tough trade working in the modest building at the end of South Bridge Road known as the Jinricksha Station (1903), designed by Samuel Tomlinson and D. M. Craik of the Municipal Council. Most of the early jinricksha pullers were immigrants from southern China who stayed in densely populated row houses such as Sago Street and Banda Street. After the Second World War, rickshas were confiscated and trishas were used instead. The Jinricksha Building has been used for several purposes since the Jinrickshas departed: at one time it was a family planning clinic and in 1990 it was bought by a developer for S$1.76 million who refurbished it into a restaurant and nightclub.

Figure 8.10
Street vendors in Trengganu
Street in 1984

The Singapore Electric Tramways Company started operations on five tramway routes in 1905 and included Tramway No. 2, which ran along South Bridge Road from Tanjong Pagar Dock to Jalan Sultan. The trams ceased operating in 1927 and in 1929 trolley buses were introduced. There was also a version of the "jeepney" that one still sees today in Manila. Trolley buses lasted until 1962 when they were displaced by the motorbus system. Today, South Bridge Road is still a major bus route.

INDIAN ENCLAVES

Two buildings that stand out in this road of predominantly Chinese owned shophouse are the Jamae Mosque (1830–1835) and the Sri Mariamman Temple (1827–1843), which is the oldest Hindu place of worship in Singapore.

The Jamae Mosque is also referred to as the Chulia Mosque, as it was established by Chulia Indians from the Kalinga Empire on the Coramandel Coast. These were mainly Tamil Muslims who came to Singapore as traders and money-changers.[7] Under the leadership of Anser Saib the mosque started in 1826 but the present building dates from 1835.

The Sri Mariamman Temple was built by Naraina Pillay, who accompanied Sir Stamford Raffles to Singapore in 1819. The *gopuram* was designed and built by craftsmen from India. According to S. Dhoraisingam Samuel, the boat caulking Indian community who had migrated from Poigaiyur in Nagapatanam installed their village deity Thirobathi Amman in the temple.[8] The temple is widely known for its annual Thimithi festival when devotees walk over red-hot embers in honour of the goddess Droba-Devi.

To the Tamils, South Bridge Road was known as *Kalapithi Kadei Sadakku* (Cawkers Shop Street). The nearby Upper Cross Street was also known as Kling Street (Kiat Leng Kia Koi Street) in the early twentieth century and was occupied by a Tamil school. There was once a thriving goat milk business here.

EMBRACING CHANGE

South Bridge Road is 1.2 kilometres in length and one can walk briskly from the Elgin Bridge to the Jinricksha Station in fifteen minutes but the many activities and shops along the way make it an urban space in which one always finds distractions, so that this time can easily be doubled or trebled. There are shops selling Chinese medicines and herbs, the best known being the Eu Yan Sang Company premises (1910), established by Eu Tong Seng who was born in Penang in 1877. Its main business is retailing Chinese medicines but it also has a separate division dealing in remittance of money to China (Fig. 8.13).

Another established company is the Wing Soon Medical Hall, while Heng Fatt Yong Kee Pawnshop dates back to before the Second World War and is still in business in the same premises (Fig. 8.14). In the back lane between South Bridge Road and Club Street is a modest "thieves market", a memory of the economy in second-hand goods that has always existed in this area (Fig. 8.11).

South Bridge Road is a comfortable scale for pedestrians. It is approximately sixteen metres wide and now has four lanes of traffic with a narrow pedestrian pavement on either side. The height of building on either side varies from three-storey shophouses to eighteen-storey housing blocks above four-storey podiums

Figure 8.11
"Thieves market" in a back lane behind South
Bridge Road

Figure 8.12
Elegant SIT apartments at the corner of Upper Pickering Street
and South Bridge Road were constructed between 1950 and 1958

Figure 8.13
The Eu Yan Sang Building (1910) in
South Bridge Road

Figure 8.14
Renovated shophouse in South Bridge Road including the Heng
Fatt Pawnshop Pte Ltd enjoying a new lease of life

in the Hong Lim Complex. There is a sense of enclosure that is not found in the New Towns or along the modern highways.

The Pickering Street Flats were added to the landscape by the SIT between 1950 and 1958 (Fig. 8.12). They were the highest apartments in Singapore in the 1950s and are a simple and uncluttered, indeed elegant, design. Looking at the flats reminds me of some of the earliest SIT Commissioners: Sir Percy McNeice who in his nineties (he died in 1997) still walked with a straight-backed bearing, and J. P. Rajah, the respected lawyer who in his later years could often be observed quietly watching cricket on the verandah of the Ceylon Sports Club.

The SIT apartments were cleared of their tenants in 2002 and now stand empty, their future uncertain. They overlook another landmark, Hong Lim Green, one of the earliest public parks in Singapore that occupies a site donated by Cheang Hong Lim in 1876. Hong Lim Green was used as recreational ground by the Straits Chinese Recreational Club, which opened in 1885 and was the first Chinese club where western games were played.[9] I have friends in the Singapore Cricket Club who recall playing here in the post-Second World War years. It has also been a site for Chinese Opera and was witness to some of the early rallies of the PAP. It has served more recently as a venue for a Speakers Corner.

Many of South Bridge Road's traditional shophouses and businesses remain, although some traditional services have been displaced by modern activities related to media and information technology (Figs 8.15, 8.16, 8.17, 8.18 and 8.19). There is, for example, a WH Smith bookshop opposite the Sri Mariamman Temple.

The scale of the road has altered, but only modestly and hardly at all as one moves to the southern end. If a jinricksha puller of the early twentieth century were to return there would be sufficient of the fabric remaining for him to recognize and orientate himself even though one hundred years have elapsed (Fig. 8.20). Temples and bridges are intact and even the old Jinricksha Station has survived as has Maxwell Market, though it has been upgraded. One day, perhaps, the Jinricksha building will become a museum documenting the period of Singapore's history from 1880 to 1947 for the benefit of future generations.

Figures 8.15 and 8.16
Renovated shophouse in South Bridge Road

Figure 8.17
Fook On Co (Pte) Ltd in South Bridge Road curiously advertising "winterwears"!

Figure 8.18
Shing Lee Hardware (Pte) Ltd

Figure 8.20
Tourists at the entrance to the Hindu Sri Mariamman Temple (1827–1843) at the corner of Pagoda Street

Figure 8.19
Yoo Yuen and Co Ltd

THE AXIS OF SINGAPORE

If I were pressed to predict what future changes might take place, it would be that the High Street Centre might one day be demolished to form a large Parliament Square flanked by Parliament House, the new Supreme Court, the Ministry of Information and the Arts, and the Ministry of Finance.

This new public space at the beginning of South Bridge Road would emphasize its importance as the true "axis" of Singapore in much the same way that the Champs Elysees has been termed the "Axis of France". Perhaps the functions of the High Street Centre and its predominantly Indian traders, who are also an integral part of South Bridge Road's memories, could go underground like the Forum des Halles or Louvre in Paris or a larger version of the air-conditioned underground link from Raffles Station to Marina Square.

But whatever changes are planned it seems that the "indelible imprint" of South Bridge Road will resist any attempt to erase its memories.

NOTES

1   This essay is an extended version of a paper presented at the Great Asian Streets Symposium, Centre for Advanced Studies in Architecture (CASA), Department of Architecture, School of Design and Environment, July 25–26 2002.
2   Sumiko Tan, *Streets of Old Chinatown Singapore* (Singapore: Page Media Publications, 1990).
3   Geraldine Lowe-Ismail, *Chinatown Memories* (Singapore: Singapore Heritage Society, 1998).
4   Ibid.
5   Ibid.
6   Ibid.
7   Sumiko Tan, *Streets of Old Chinatown Singapore*
8   S. Dhoraisingam Samuel, *Singapore Heritage* (Singapore: Elixir, 1991).
9   Ray Tyers (Updated by Siow Jin Hua), *Singapore Then and Now* (Singapore: Landmark Books, 1993).

Chapter 9: Modernist Urbanism and its Revitalization

William S. W. Lim

INTRODUCTION TO WILLIAM S. W. LIM

John Phillips

Emerging out of a distinguished career as one of Asia's most adventurous and committed architectural thinkers, urban activist William Lim is now building on an impressive body of writing that aims to address the fraught issues of Asian urbanism within the tensions created by development and modernity. William Lim's commitment to the welfare of communities in developing areas is built on a solid understanding of rapidly changing global conditions. Local communities, for instance, cannot thrive without an understanding of the global conditions upon which they inevitably and increasingly depend. This dependency should not become a kind of passive credulity to the ideology of globalization, as William Lim puts it, to "the false expectations and images of *a good life* of consumer-oriented modernization and economic progress."[1] Nor can the values associated with the conservation of cultural history be separated from the demands of cosmopolitan expansion. In the rhetoric of resistance, these forces and interests might have been understood as being irremediably opposed – with local cultures at risk from various kinds of oppression or even extinction by malign global forces. In the rhetoric of modernity, on the contrary, an idealized version of the local (with its fully market-able ethnic iconicity) comes under the umbrella of benign global capital (as the worldwide advertising campaign for HSBC puts it: "your local bank").

So William Lim's address aims at a doubled form of critique: at once affirming the actively creative forces available to local cultures and communities and adding to the growing number of voices who represent a global community of serious postmodern thinkers. This doubled form of critique is the key to understanding the precise nature of William Lim's engagement. In this way he disentangles the aims and values of resistance from the impasses inherent in many forms of postcolonial theory – which often remain focused too uncritically on (post)-colonial dichotomies – and he re-traces them instead along the fault-lines of modernity. For William Lim, the potential for cultural and social development lies not within the geographical boundaries of new nations and new economies. These remain dependent on the historical forces of global expansion. The potential lies instead in the creative possibilities inherent in what is already institutionally antithetical to the forms of technological modernity that now dominate in the Asian region – in the curious logic of the postmodern.

We have to distinguish carefully between a slack postmodernism, defined by Frederic Jameson in terms of the forms that rise up from the economic basis of late capitalism, and a more philosophically rigorous notion of postmodernism introduced, for instance, by Jean-François Lyotard and developed by Heinz Paetzold. Jameson's argument has been powerful. Cities in Asia sometimes seem to highlight symptoms that fit Jameson's diagnostic: the loss of a sense of historical *content*; a corresponding nostalgia for past *forms*; fixation on the intensities of the present; and the overwhelming dominance of electronic media technologies. The arguments of Lyotard and others help to qualify and complicate the argument. To distinguish too sharply between a slack postmodernism and a rigorous one would be to fall rather smartly back into the modernist paradigm of dichotomous values. William Lim seizes instead on the Lyotard concept of the *différend*. Lyotard develops this French legal term into a fully-fledged ethical/political concept in his book of the same name. The word is used in legal contexts for disputes that have no just or rational solution – in such cases an adjudicator is responsible for making a decision where, strictly, none is possible. The *différend* is thus the legal equivalent of the philosophical notion of the undecidable. For Lyotard, modernity's failure is bound up with its aspirations to *solve,* through technical and rational means, the various forms of conflict, dispute, discrepancy and, at base, all *differences* in society through its own peculiar vision. William Lim regards this failure as having been forcefully demonstrated by the economic realities of globalization, that is, by the economic and foreign policies of modernity failing, "to effectively translate the enormous wealth generated by incredible economic development for the common good, particularly for the poor in the less developed economies."[2]

So Lyotard is important for William Lim's project. The classical Marxist line would be constrained to see the relationship between the economic success of the west and the impoverishment of developing countries in dialectical terms, in terms of exploitation and alienation. To be sure, the neo-Marxist position represented by Jameson complicates matters enough to show how the prevalence of consumerism effectively destroys any will to resistance or rebellion. One of William Lim's chief imperatives remains the need for a creative rebelliousness in the character of the social and political agent. But it is with notions like the *différend* that the possibility or space for such agency can be located as part of the postmodern condition. A *différend* imposes on the agent the requirement that he or she make a decision in the face of the undecidable, in short, that they make a decision and take full responsibility for it. No technology or rationally calculable answer lies ready to hand in such cases. In the field of architecture, where William Lim's experience and track record command great authority, the point is relatively easily made: "In design terms, postmodern architecture accepts the absence of rigid aesthetic guiding rules and, therefore, everything becomes permissible. Some of the experiments may even appear nihilistic, whimsical or irrelevant; but they are not, as the designer must exercise strict self-discipline and take full responsibility in applying his own aesthetic judgment."[3] It is where these aesthetic principles translate into socio-economic ones that William Lim's take on postmodernity gathers most force.

William Lim's interest in postmodern thought leads him to formulate a range of arguments that address the ways in which peculiarly Asian and Southeast Asian sites have been able to respond to the expansion of global capital. The condition that William Lim calls postmodernity signifies a kind of concrete (rather than abstract) potential that outstrips modernism in urban planning, still marked as it is by "Corbusier's sanitized urbanism and automobile city."[4] Against the slack postmodernism identified by Jameson, with its loss of history and its fetishism of commodities, William Lim posits a postmodernity that is "all embracing." But the nature of this ubiquitous postmodernity is fundamentally that of the *alternative*: a response that can change as quickly as the conditions it responds to, a fleet contingency grounded not on fixed values but on principles of trans-valuation.

The alternative, in this actually rather precise sense, does not mean just another of globalization's possibilities amongst others. It would be more a matter of identifying a kind of condition – the possibility of the alternative or the condition that grounds all possibility *as* alternative. In other words, the alternative can emerge wherever modernity fails to produce a saturated and fully calculable totality – the fully functional efficient city. In this sense the limits of modernity are nothing other than the resources of postmodernism. The alternative inevitably manifests as concrete social reality, and William Lim's discussion of urban "spaces of indeterminacy" demonstrates how. These spaces emerge whenever an urban area or property falls out of economic favour. With dilapidation comes a level of chaotic freedom, which gives these spaces the flexibility to withstand rapid changes in use. The "fragmented idiotic design expressions and uncompromisingly irrational space arrangements," which can develop if allowed to, provide "alternative lifestyles and a natural resistance to the Fordist and global forces of rational conformity."[5] By focusing on such spaces William Lim can address issues of social justice outside the paradigms and rhetoric of technological progress.

William Lim's ability to combine broken images creatively exemplifies the trends he advocates. In this sense he is clearly a member of a "coming community" in the sense defined by the Italian philosopher Giorgio Agamben.[6] The *Coming Community* would not oppose itself to any form of the state but would be composed of evolved singularities, unforeseeable and open to as yet undetermined futures.

INTRODUCTION

Modernity is understood in the West as the process of historical transformation that has taken place in Europe and later in the United States and other white Commonwealth countries.[7] It includes the concepts of freedom, human rights and individuality as well as democracy and the rule of law.[8] However, its encounter with civilizations of different religions and value systems often resulted in disastrous and tragic consequences. It is therefore important to put on record that the democratic applications of modernity in the West were only practiced within the boundaries of their nation-states, and did not apply in any effective manner to the non-Western "Other".

In the last few decades, we have experienced incredible scientific development and rapid economic growth. There is also increasing income disparity between countries and more recently within countries. The modernist planning and architectural theories have increasingly become effective tools of globalization and consumerism for US-style late capitalism. In the meantime, there have been many serious shifts in the culture, value and lifestyle as well as ethic and aesthetic particularly of the younger generation. It is in this context that I wish to speak about modernist urbanism and its revitalized possibilities. This article will deal with three interrelated issues. They are: 1) Where we are; 2) Challenges and critical voices; 3) Postmodern imagery.

WHERE WE ARE

In Europe, the intellectual discourse on modern architecture continued with great vigor during the inter-war years. CIAM (Congrès Internationaux d'Architecture Moderne) was established at the meeting in 1928 in La Sarraz, Switzerland. The fourth CIAM meeting, in 1933, produced the Athens Charter.[9] The break with the past was intended to be absolute. Modernist urbanism must liberate us from history. The most important exponent of CIAM principles was Le Corbusier. His seminal text entitled *The Radiant City* demonstrated his passion: "the rationalist metropolis that resulted was a city that dehistoricized the particular; it was a city distilled into an universal model".[10] In the meantime, the increasing pace of technical and economic development and the secularization of Western thought have progressively eroded the status of the sublime of modernity.[11]

Since the mid-twentieth century, modernism has been the dominant force in mainstream urban planning and architecture. In the process, it has molded much of the urban visual environment in major cities and particularly in cities with explosive population expansion of the rapidly developing economies.

The urban reconstruction of the Second World War's destruction in Western Europe was executed with the intellectual tools of modernism. It was often done with strong socially-oriented expectation towards building a brave new world. This was carried out in the context of an ideological commitment of the population to conserve the traditional cities, and to meet the increasing pressure and demand for commercial spaces by intensive high-density development of new areas in close proximity to the traditional urban centers.

In contrast, the US government since the 1950s supported urban renewal programs in American cities as an effective instrument to promote economic activities and to accommodate the increasing demand of the financial sector. Tall office buildings, higher plot-ratio, major road widening, expensive highways and supporting infrastructure were introduced. These were super-imposed onto the traditional environment. This process resulted in large-scale clearance and displacement of the subalterns, the minorities and the poor. Existing communities and much of the traditional urban fabric were badly fractured.

With US dominant economic and cultural influences, many developing countries have assumed there is no other alternative but to follow the American method of regenerating their traditional centers. In the process, many valuable traditions and irreplaceable complex memories are destroyed. With the rapid expansion of the global financial sector, the need for physical spaces downtown in close proximity increases dramatically. This has further strengthened the attractiveness of the Wall Street imagery beyond the global financial centers of New York, London and Tokyo. Cities everywhere have followed to build similar global city images.

It is interesting that only three major city-scale projects based on Le Corbusier's urban planning model have been implemented, and they are all located in developing countries. The projects are located in Chandigarh, Brazilia and Singapore. In Chandigarh,

> Corbusier's greatest impact in retrospect was that he instantly solved the debate between the revivalist and the modernist – the modernist won! Le Corbusier's designs became an image and symbol for the modern India of Nehru's imagination – for Corbusier's progressive social ideals and architectural ideas fitted neatly with Nehru's ambitions for India.[12]

Interestingly, Brazilia was planned and executed by persons with antagonistic social and political agenda. However, all supported the project as it symbolized "the break with a colonial past and the leap into the future".[13] Singapore is the *developmental state*[14] par excellence. Since the mid-1960s, its vigorous *Tabula Rasa* style – the idea of starting from scratch, of renewal and reconstruction programs – is described as "uncontaminated by surviving contextual remnants . . . if there is chaos, it is *authored* chaos; if it is ugly, it is *designed* ugliness; if it is absurd, it is *willed* absurdity".[15]

Since the 1950s, mass production of cars, construction of highways and active government supports in America have resulted in large-scale suburbanization of the middle-income families. These suburbs all have their own orientation, preferences, prejudices and exclusions, particularly in relation to race, religion, education and marital status. Extensive suburban developments are soon followed in other affluent economies, particularly countries with low population density. In the last two decades, they are spreading everywhere, even in many developing economies.

With better employment opportunities for women and increasing numbers of high-earning singles, there is now escalating demand by the young and more affluent generation for urban living in the form of gated urban condominium developments. Their exclusivity varies, but most are based essentially on income and affordability of the occupants. In the meantime, New Urbanism,[16] a new phenomenon in America, attempts to inject new activity and energy into the existing boring suburbs and the new gated township, but without changes to their main exclusion rules and within the restricting nostalgic and spatially limiting parameter.

With US late capitalism and aggressive consumerism, large demand for commercial spaces is still generated, particularly in major urban centers. Many new developments, based on out-dated modernist planning theories and compromised by market-driven forces of profitability, are being planned and constructed. They are often missed urban opportunities. Important recent examples include London's Docklands – Canary Wharf,[17] Melbourne's Docklands[18] and Shanghai's Pudong.[19]

CHALLENGES AND CRITICAL VOICES

Since the 1960s, the US-led cultural liberation, particularly in relation to women, race and gays, has resulted in major changes in the cultures, values and lifestyles of the younger generation. Many of their symbolic modes have been recast, adopted and co-opted into the cultures of mainstream consumerism. However, their essence and spirit have continued to develop and broaden in many directions, including gender and race equity, gay rights, consumer rights, environmental awareness, sustainable development and the green movement.

Rapid development of IT together with the new cultural orientation of the new generation as well as the increasing pace of globalization and mega-mergers have revolutionized traditional concepts of work and locations of work places. Many are working at home, while others are located in offices around peripheral and convenient transport modes. Furthermore, the countless and increasing number of self-employed do not work in expensive downtown offices. Collectively, these phenomena require a completely new mind-set in the planning of cities and to seriously examine the implications of greatly reduced demand for high-density and high-rental spaces within most city cores. Furthermore, multi-usages with mixed income activities after office hours need to be introduced urgently. In most cases, specialized and well-regulated zones for shopping, entertainment and tourism will become increasingly unattractive and economically non-viable, unless there is serious restructuring to generate vibrancies and attractions with complexity, uncertainty and chaos.

The incredible pace of physical development linking Hong Kong to Guangzhou with a continuous belt of high-density urbanization and powerful multi-faceted manufacturing activities known as the Pearl River Delta region must be the most spectacular demonstration of time–space–urbanity compression in the history of the twentieth century.[20] This huge urban venture is carried out with total pragmatism and with minimum planning strategy and regulations. However, without handphones, email and computers, this extensive development just cannot be realized within two decades. Even today, there are still no effective and reliable postal and telephone services. It is therefore important to conclude – and more research is no doubt needed – that the increasingly affordable and easy-to-use IT is a vital tool for the progressive developing economies to *bridge the gap* with less pain, cost and time. Another successful example is Bangalore, India, which is now already an important center of software production and innovation, and is considered to be the second Silicon Valley. The tremendous implications of IT and its combination with the borderless world of manufacturing and servicing locations and the reduction of trade barriers have clearly not been fully appreciated or understood. These are unprecedented conditions that have generated a new unstructured and dynamic urbanism particularly in the densely populated and rapidly developing economies.

Physically dilapidated and densely populated, many traditional areas in urban centers are identified as *slums*. However, these areas provide employment for the unskilled, the handicapped and the subalterns. They offer staging and work facilities for rural immigrants and the poorer new immigrants. The scale of such spaces varies greatly. Some occupy large areas such as the informal *bazaar city* of Mumbai[21] with several million residents. What looked like chaos was complexity with a multi-layered order and systems superimposed on each other or existing next to each other. These ordering systems were totally comprehensible to those participating in them and frightening to those outside.[22]

Modernist planning theories, such as Le Corbusier's sanitized urbanism to the automobile city are now widely discredited. Since the early 1990s, many theorists and others seriously challenge the very definition of what constitutes planning, and the necessity to go beyond mathematical systems and intellectualized rationality. We need to re-define planning as community-driven, people-oriented and accepting the radical interpretations of differences and pluralism. In this context, Leonie Sandercock has severely criticized the mainstream analysis of Peter Hall's *Cities of Tomorrow*.[23] Edward Soja further deepens the urban discourse, particularly on issues relating to spatial justice and their specificities:

> Entwined with this refocusing of critical studies of cities and regions and the concurrent spatial turn so integral to it has been the onset of something even more significant, the emergence of an active and situated practice of a cultural politics that is consciously driven by increasingly spatialized notions of social justice, participatory democracy, and citizenship rights and responsibilities.[24]

On the theoretical discourse of critical voices, we must now recognize the essentiality of meaningful local inputs to achieve viable globalization, the need to accept the interdependency of globality and its urban discontents,[25] the importance of investigating the implications of grassroot globalization[26] and alternative postmodernity,[27] and the urgency to accelerate a global environmental awakening towards a sustainable eco-economy.[28] Enforcing the concern of many theorists, Joseph E. Stiglitz has recently presented an insider's account that critically exposes the vast shortcomings of US-dominated globalization and their related institutions.[29] In the meantime, there is an increasing awareness of the *Modernity of the Other*[30] and the necessity to identify the special characteristics of *Asian New Urbanism*[31] that requires out-of-the-box analysis beyond the distortion by Eurocentric modernity.[32]

POSTMODERN IMAGERY

The word postmodern displays a diversity of meanings, particularly when it is applied over several decades in various academic disciplines from art and literature to cultural studies, architecture and urbanism. Its definition has evolved and developed over time. Whatever definition one prefers to adopt, the main characteristics of postmodernity are pluralism, tolerance of differences and creative rebelliousness. A key factor of the postmodern is the centrality in the concept of space in social theory. I refer particularly to Henri Lefebvre's brilliant and definitive work *The Production of Space*,[33] and David Harvey's two recent books entitled *Spaces of Hope*[34] and *Spaces of Capital*[35] which challenge the claim of ethical neutrality and define the importance of geographical space and its urban implications.

In the 1990s, intellectual discourse of the postmodern has greatly intensified. Convergent as well as divergent views of various theories have been identified and critically examined. Notwithstanding increasingly indefensible and often disastrous consequences of modernist urbanism, there were no obvious viable alternatives to modernism until recently to substitute for its well-established theories and practices. Fortunately, frontiers of discourse, particularly in relation to urbanity in the context of global–local hybridity and eco-sustainability, have been substantially broadened to embrace ethic and aesthetic from art, architecture and urbanism to social, environmental and spatial justice as well as the marginalized other.

For the first time, we can now start to formulate a realistic, equitable, sustainable and people-oriented alternative agenda, which can dramatically revitalize and restructure the present decadent drifts of late-capitalist priorities, with vigorous intentionality of the postmodern. Let me quote Michael Dear's courageous statement: "Our ability to choose, to act, even to speak about the future depends on how we adjust to the altered intentionality of a postmodern age."[36] However, this is not an attempt to take-over the much besieged modernity, as I completely concur with Leonie Sandercock that a *postmodern utopia* can never be realized, but is always in the making.[37] It is in this context that I wish to highlight selected contemporary urban conditions that can collectively provide further important signposting for the rapidly evolving postmodern urbanism. They are spaces of indeterminacies, transgressive activities, ethnics beyond lifestyles, and over the edge.

Spaces of indeterminacy exist in all major cities.[38] They are pluralistic, fuzzy and chaotic. They are democratic spaces that users and participants, particularly the marginalized communities, can identify with and even take psychological possession of, without the need for legal ownership. The scale of such places varies greatly, from substantially large areas to many urban run-down locations, what planners often describe as *Dead Zones*[39] or derelict areas, as well as the countless in-between spaces located in the cracks and gaps of new urban projects and major infrastructure development. These complex environmental areas have historically been the breeding ground for great innovative and creative energy. Collectively, they provide unique urban character to and energize the spatial quality of all that already exists much more radically than any rationally planned creation.[40]

Demonstrations, festivals, art performances and cruising or public sex are transgressive activities that constantly test the original boundary set for the usages of streets and public spaces. In recent years, many countries have shown better flexibility and understanding towards these intrusions. Since the massive global events of anti-Vietnam war demonstrations in the US, Chinese students demonstrating in Tiananmen Square and the numerous street protests in East Europe, the demonstrations against US-style globality, poverty and inequality are still continuing in different times and places after their first success in Seattle. These radical global demonstrations and street performances[41] will continue to test the limit of democratic tolerance of differences, the ability to understand the increasingly pluralistic and complex contemporary world, and the active supports for an ethical approach with global responsibility.

A recent article by Richard Florida on *The Rise of the Creative Class*[42] has stimulated much discourse and may even induce some countries such as Singapore and Hong Kong to relax strict policies governing social behaviors from gays to unmarried mothers. The emphasis of the article is essentially about advantages in expanding easy availability of pleasure, leisure and desire in order to enrich lifestyle options. However, this is not enough. In this era beyond the capitalist modernity, we must aim to establish a creative environment not just for the creative class, but for the whole community. The agenda must be firmly anchored to a contemporary ethics that transcends personal greed and excessive consumerism. It must include the ever-more-exciting and varied art creation in order to stimulate our multiple-senses and intellectual appetite, as well as meaningful and active citizen participation from numerous local issues to major global concern.

Today, cities are sites of new contestants whose expectations differ substantially from what modernity offers. These over-the-edge postmodern contestants are the contemporary *flaneurs*, the new bohemians, the graffitists and the skate-boarders. Their interventions have often posed serious challenges for policy-makers as well as other urban inhabitants. As Walter Benjamin explained, the *flaneur* always seeks to scrutinize the city in search of experience not knowledge. Although the *flaneur* takes the distancing position of the visual observer, he always seeks to evoke the essence of his urban explorations. In the present context, the contemporary *flaneur* must glocalize his timeless gaze and energize his understanding of the subalterns and the marginalized other, in order to give new meaning to his existence amidst the time compression of global-cosmopolitan late capitalism.[43]

Historically, the spiritual site of bohemia is strongly associated with the Latin Quarter in Paris. The bohemian's way of life has a scale of values beyond money and material well-being. He works when he wants and adapts his life to the consequent revenue.[44] The image of the bohemian is expanded with the Beat Generation of the 1960s in America. Bohemianism today is a universal phenomenon and its rebelliousness has sometimes been credited with generating energy for contemporary art creation.

Modern graffiti art originated in New York city in the 1960s. There are various forms of graffiti. They are often individual illegal markings in public places. As such, it can be called vandalism. The majority of graffitists enjoy what they do and find it to be fun, rewarding and exciting. Furthermore, the graffiti artist takes his art work very seriously. In recent years, there are increasing instances where the art world has recognized graffiti art as art. The recognition prevents the sweeping generalization that graffiti is vandalism and therefore something that always should be eradicated.[45]

Skateboarders are an increasingly common feature of the urban environment. They create for themselves an alternative reality and change the nature of their urban experiences. They continue to transgress the boundaries of convention, but do not commit crime or confront the authority. This sub-culture of the young clearly demonstrates its importance in the current discourse of contemporary cultural theories. As Iain Borden argues "street-style skateboarding, especially of recent decades, conducts a performative critique of architecture, the city and capitalism".[46]

In conclusion, this paper attempts to raise many serious questions in the deficiencies of the present modernist planning model as well as in the importance of identifying alternatives and scopes for its revitalization. In the urban context, spatial justice provides one such effective tool to achieve an urban ethics with equity and active citizen participation. In the process, it must ensure that land speculation is strictly controlled, and public facilities such as libraries, health clinics and recreational spaces as well as public transport etc. are easily accessible and affordable. With the increasing pace of change in values and lifestyles, urban instability and uncertainty will escalate. They necessitate continuous dynamic re-invention of planning rules and regulations in response to demands and challenges of the new emerging pluralistic creative environment.

NOTES

1   William S. W. Lim. *Alternative (Post)Modernity: An Asian Perspective*, Select Books, Singapore, 2003, p. 122.
2   Ibid. p. 51.
3   Ibid. p. 69.
4   Ibid. p. 123.
5   Ibid. p. 13.
6   See Giorgio Agamben. *The Coming Community*, Minneapolis, University of Minnesota Press, 1993. Here Agamben argues that, "the novelty of the coming politics is that it will no longer be a struggle for the conquest or control of the State, but a struggle between the State and the non-state (humanity), an insurmountable disjunction between whatever singularity and the State organization."
7   A different version of this article was presented as a keynote speech for the Conference on Urbanism Downunder 2003 organized by the Centre for Continuing Education (University of Auckland), 20–22 March 2003, and was subsequently published, also in a different form, in William S. W. Lim. *Alternative (Post)Modernity: An Asian Perspective*, Select Books, Singapore, 2003.
8   William S. W. Lim. "The Dynamics of East Asian New Urbanism". In *Back from Utopia, The Challenge of the Modern Movement*, Hubert-Jan Henket and Hilde Heynen (eds), 010 Publishers, Rotterdam, 2002, pp. 198–205.
9   Eric Munford. *The CIAM Discourse on Urbanism*, MIT Press, Cambridge, Mass., 2000.
10 Michael J. Dear. "Reading the Modern City: A Colonial History of Los Angeles, 1781–1991". In *The Postmodern Urban Condition*, Blackwell Publishers Ltd, Massachusetts, 2000, pp. 91–116.
11 Heinz Paetzold. "Lecture 2: Lyotard's Definitions of the Postmodern Status of Knowledge". In *The Discourse of the Postmodern and the Discourse of the Avant-Garde: A Series of Ten Lectures concerning the Link between Social Philosophy and Aesthetics under the Conditions of Postmodernity*, Jan van Eyck Akademie, Maastricht, 1994, pp. 14–20.
12 Rahul Mehrotra. "Introductory Essay: The Architecture of Pluralism – A Century of Building in South Asia". In *World Architecture: A Critical Mosaic, 1900–2000*, vol. 8, South Asia, Springer-Verlag Wien, New York, 2000, pp. 17–31.
13 J. Holston. *The Modernist City: An Anthropological Critique of Brasilia*. University of Chicago Press, Chicago, 1989.
14 Manuel Castells. "The Network Enterprise: The Culture, Institutions, and Organizations of the Informational Economy". A state is developmental when it establishes as its principle of legitimacy its ability to promote and sustain development, understanding by development the combination of steady high rates of economic growth and structural change in the economic system, both domestically and in its relationship to the international economy. In *The Rise of the Network Society*, vol. I, Blackwell Publishers Inc, Massachusetts, 1996, pp. 151–200.
15 Rem Koolhaas and Bruce Mau. "Singapore Songlines: . . . or Thirty years of Tabula Rasa". In *S,M,L,XL*, Rem Koolhaas, The Monacelli Press Inc., New York, 1995, pp. 1008–1089.
16 David Harvey. "The Spaces of Utopia". In *Spaces of Hope,* Edinburgh University Press, Edinburgh, 2002, pp. 169–173.
17 Janet Foster. *Docklands: Cultures in Conflict, Worlds in Collision,* UCL Press, London, 1999.
18 Kim Dovery and Leonie Sandercock. "Hype and Hope: Imagining Melbourne's Docklands". In *City: Analysis of Urban Trends, Culture, Theory, Policy, Action*, vol. 6, no. 1, April 2002, Bob Catterall (ed.), Carfax Publishing, Oxford, pp. 83–101.

19 Hou Hanru. "Shanghai Spirit: A Special Modernity". In *The Prince Claus Fund Journal*, 6, 2001, pp. 60–65.

20 Bernard Chang, Mihai Craciun, Nancy Lin, Yuyang Liu, Katherine Orff, Stephanie Smith. "Pearl River Delta (Harvard Project on the City)". In *Mutations*, Rem Koolhaas, Actar, Barcelona, 2000, pp. 280–337.

21 Rahul Mehrotra. "Bazaar City – A Metaphor for South Asian Urbanism". In *Visions of the 21st Century*, Goldschmeid Marco (ed.), Virgin Publishing Ltd, London, 2002.

22 Ramesh Kumar Biswas. "One Space, Many Worlds: Bombay". In *Metropolis Now!*, Ramesh Kumar Biswas (ed.), Springer-Verlag/Wien, Austria, 2000, pp. 46–61.

23 Leonie Sandercock. Introduction – Framing Insurgent Historiographies for Planning". In *Making the Invisible Visible*, University of California Press, L.A., 1998, pp. 5–6.

24 Edward W. Soja. "Postscript: Critical Reflections on the Postmetropolis". In *Postmetropolis: Critical Studies of Cities and Regions*, Blackwell Publishers Ltd, Oxford, 2000, pp. 396–415.

25 Saskia Sassen. *Globalization and Its Discontents*, The New Press, New York, 1998.

26 Arjun Appadurai. "Grassroots Globalization and the Research Imagination". In *Public Culture*, vol. 12, no. 1, Winter 2000, pp. 1–19.

27 Arif Dirlik and Xudong Zhang (eds). *Postmodernism & China*, Duke University Press, Durham, 2000.

28 Lester R. Brown. *Eco-Economy: Building an Economy for the Earth*, W.W. Norton & Company Inc., New York, 2001.

29 Joseph Stiglitz. *Globalization and Its Discontents*, W.W. Norton & Company Inc., New York, 2002.

30 William S. W. Lim. "Modernity of the Other". In *Alternative in Transition: The Postmodern, Glocality and Social Justice*, Select Books, Singapore, 2001, pp. 34–48.

31 William S. W. Lim. "Asian New Urbanism". In *Asian New Urbanism*, Select Books, Singapore, 1998, pp. 14–32.

32 Enrique Dussel. "Beyond Eurocentrism: The World-System and the Limits of Modernity". In *The Cultures of Globalization*, Fredric Jameson and Masao Miyoshi (eds), Duke University Press, Durham, 1998, pp. 3–31.

33 Henri Lefebvre. *The Production of Space*, Blackwell Publishers Ltd, Oxford, 2000.

34 David Harvey. *Spaces of Hope*, Edinburgh University Press Ltd, Edinburgh, 2000.

35 David Harvey. *Spaces of Capital: Towards A Critical Geography*, Edinburgh University Press Ltd, Edinburgh, 2001.

36 Michael J. Dear. "Epilogue: Beyond Postmodernism". In *The Postmodern: Urban Condition*, Blackwell Publishers, Oxford, 2000, pp. 317–318.

37 Leonie Sandercock. "Towards Cosmopolis: A Postmodern Utopia". In *Towards Cosmopolis*, John Wiley & Sons, England, 1998, pp. 163–200.

38 William S. W. Lim. "Spaces of Indeterminacy". In *Bridge The Gap*, Miyake Akiko and Hans Ulrich Obrist (eds), Center for Contemporary Art, Kitakyushu, 2002, pp. 377–397.

39 Gil M. Doron. "The Dead Zone and the Architecture of Transgression". In *City: Analysis of Urban Trends, Culture, Theory, Policy, Action*, vol. 4, no. 2, July 2000, Carfax Publishing, Taylor & Francis Ltd, Basingstoke, pp. 247–262.

40 William S. W. Lim. "Conservation & Spaces of Indeterminacy". Keynote speech for Symposium on Urban Development in South East Asia organized by Goethe-Institut Hanoi, Vietnam, 4–5 December 2002.

41 Jan Cohen-Cruz (ed.). *Radical Street Performance: An International Anthology*, Routledge, London, 1998.

42 Richard Florida. "The Rise of the Creative Class: Why Cities without Gays and Rock Bands are Losing the Economic Development Race". In *Washington Monthly*, May 2002, Washington DC.

43 William S. W. Lim. "The Contemporary Flaneur and Spaces of Indeterminacy". Lecture delivered to the Urban Architecture Laboratory Masters Programme at Royal Melbourne Institute of Technology, Melbourne, 10–12 May 2002.

44 More information about the subject of the bohemian spirit can be obtained at: http://www.bohemiabooks.com.au/eblinks/spirboho/index.html.

45 George C. Stowers. "Graffiti Art: An Essay Concerning the Recognition of Some Forms of Graffiti as Art". The essay can be viewed at http:graffiti.org/faq/stowers.html.

46 Iain Borden. *Skateboarding, Space and the City: Architecture and the Body*, Berg, Oxford, 2001.

Chapter 10: Post-functionalist Urbanism, the Postmodern and Singapore

Heinz Paetzold

Today we are acquainted on a worldwide scale with the successes, the failures and the problems caused by functionalist urbanism. What can be said about post-functionalist urbanism? This is an open question. At any rate, any answer given to this question has to be linked with the postmodern. In this article, I would like to single out some crucial elements of post-functionalist urbanism. I take as my point of departure the revaluation of architecture, which occurred in postmodern discourses, and then turn to questions of urbanism proper. Eventually I shall sketch some elements of an Asian model of post-functionalist urbanism, as suggested by William Lim, and which is strongly related to and informed by the Singaporean urban fabric. The main drift of my essay is that we should conceptualize the move from modernist functionalist to post-functionalist postmodern urbanism under the heading of the *cultural turn* of urbanism. This seems the appropriate umbrella under which we can gather all the various elements of an emerging post-functionalist urbanism we notice during the past three decades or so.

I

In postmodern discourses *architecture* has attained a *new rank* in the system of the fine arts. The nineteenth-century philosopher G. W. F. Hegel, exponent of cultural modernism, had attributed the lowest status to architecture on the grounds that it does not express fully the essence of the human spirit, but only prepares the external surrounding for the appearance of that spirit. In post-modern theory, on the contrary, it was precisely architecture that stood as model for the paradigmatic expression of the new cultural spirit. Charles Jencks, one will recall, explained postmodern style in architecture in terms of double coding. Indeed, double or, even better, multiple coding has become the hallmark of post-modern architecture.[1]

Talking about postmodern architecture exclusively in terms of style, however, does not really bring to the fore the cultural shift implied in the move from modernism to postmodernism. This shift, I contend, is essentially based on the revaluation of the city. All those stylistic features which we may single out as specific for postmodern architecture – its historicism, its narrativity, its eclecticism, its irony, its being pastiche – in one way or another intentionally offend the assumption that form follows function. This creed was the core of modernist urbanism and subsequently of modernist architecture. The creed says that urban design and architectural form are completely determined by function. We can distinguish basic social functions, and forms are supposed to articulate them.

Figure 10.1
Skyline of Singapore: chaos or well-ordered?

Figure 10.2
Street corner near
Raffles' Place

The *form–function axiom* is the foundational basis of Le Corbusier's cele-brated "Urbanisme" (1925) which has been translated to English as "The City of Tomorrow and Its Planning" (1987). Here we can find Le Corbusier's model of zoning the city. According to this model the city has to be divided into four zones: the business and residential centre; the industrial city; the garden city; and transportation.[2] To these urban zones the functions of working, housing, recre-ating and moving about are coordinated, as the "Charter of Athens" (1933) has pinned down.[3] Le Corbusier's vision was an equally successful international eye-opener as were Ebenezer Howard's "To-morrow" (1898) and Camillo Sitte's "The Art of Building Cities" (1889) some decades earlier.

Le Corbusier's approach took shape during the 1920s; it was refined in the 1930s and 1940s and was brought to political influence worldwide, as Manfredo Tafuri in his "Progetto e utopia" (1973) has shown. This model of city design presupposed three steps:

(i)   the theoretically clear identification of social functions,
(ii)   their being made operational in determined architectural forms,
(iii) the application of the zoning-model in city planning.

As Tafuri has argued, house, street, block, city were treated as constituting one homogeneous totality.

One only understands the overpowering influence of Le Corbusier and the CIAM during the 1930s and 1940s appropriately if one realizes that functionalist city design was part and parcel of an *avant-garde concept*. It implied a link

Figure 10.3
Verticality exemplified

Figure 10.4
Old Chinese Temple against the backdrop of Capital Tower with a roof in the shape of a Chinese lantern

Figure 10.5
Wak Hai Cheng Bio Temple

Figure 10.6
Malabar Muslim Jaina-Ath Mosque

between artistic sensibility, on one hand, and political as well as economic and technological operations, on the other. Le Corbusier's real impact derived not from cities he designed and built himself but from cities built by others incorporating the planning principles that he pioneered. Not only by virtue of complete examples like Brasilia and Chandigarh but rather in that his principles were adopted after the Second World War by several governments, Le Corbusier became "a true prophet of modern urbanism".[4] It is really not an overstatement for LeGates and Stout to say that the "Le Corbusier vision has truly transformed the global urban environment".[5]

II

This seems the appropriate place to interrupt my discourse for a short moment. As mentioned above, talking about postmodernity exclusively in terms of style does not bring to light sufficiently the impact of cultural change that is implied in the shift from modernity to postmodernity. It is primarily a distancing from modernist creeds such as the *form–function axiom*. This applies to architecture and urbanism alike.

Here I can introduce an observation by Fredric Jameson and furnish my own discourse with it. According to Jameson, genuinely postmodern buildings have in common the fact that they try to create a new category of *urban space*. Their general denominator is the pretension to articulate a "complete world", "a kind of miniature city", as Jameson has put it.[6] This qualification applies to buildings such as the Beaubourg in Paris, the Eaton Centre in Toronto as well as John Portman's Bonaventure Hotel in Los Angeles and his Marina Mandarin Hotel in Singapore. These buildings achieve a "placeless dissociation . . . from (their HP) neighbourhood".[7] As Heinrich Klotz has argued, postmodern buildings aspire to confuse the spatial orientation of the individual experiencing "postmodern hyperspace".[8] In this case, though, a reductive reference to single buildings is maintained and the city is present only, as it were, as a kind of negative instance.

III

Post-functionalist urbanism emerged during the last four decades. I would like to distinguish between a genuinely urbanistic and a more architectural approach. The first puts stress on the urban cultural features characterizing the city. The second looks at the city from the viewpoint of the building and the built environment. Let me begin with the first kind, ranging from Jane Jacobs through Joseph Rykwert, Colin Rowe and Fred Koetter and leading to Hoffmann-Axthelm and William Lim. At the end of the article I shall make a few remarks on the second kind of approach, which raises the question of the contemporary vernacular and includes architects such as Aldo van Eyck, Rem Koolhaas and Aldo Rossi.

Jane Jacobs attacked Le Corbusier's functionalism by debunking its central presuppositions. *Urban vitality*, according to her view, cannot be guaranteed by separating rigidly basic functions and then zoning urban regions accordingly. On the contrary, a viable urbanism implies a *multiplicity* of uses of city spaces, a *diversity* of functions in one and the same region, the rehabilitation of *street-sidewalk*s by reclaiming them for children while not excluding grown-ups, and a concern of *security* for women and, again, children. These are but a very few of the issues that Jacobs argued for in *The Death and Life of Great American Cities*.[9] Note Jacobs' starting-point, as follows: because we use cities, we have already experience with and tacit knowledge of them. Theoretically the city should be rethought as a "structural system in its own right";[10] it is an "organized complexity".[11] Jacobs charged Ebenezer Howard and Le Corbusier alike with thinking the city through a reductive set of variables (just housing and working in Howard's case, though they were more varied in Le Corbusier's)[12] rather than through its complexity and processuality. We have to think of cities to such an extent that it covers both, the increasing dangers of the decline of urbanity as well as the innate abilities to overcome difficulties.[13]

Jacobs' *The Death and Life of Great American Cities* became an international eye-opener as influential as Le Corbusier's vision. We can find traces of Jacobs' thought in German urbanistic reflections ranging from Alexander Mitscherlich's "Die Unwirtlichkeit unserer Städte" (1965; "The Inhospitality of our Cities") to Heide Berndt's "Architektur als Ideologie" (see note 3) and her "Die Natur der Stadt" (1976; "The Nature of the City") from the 1970s. Even the later Kevin Lynch is close to Jacobs' inspiration when he states that a good city form as a normative concept could derive neither from ancient cosmology nor from Le Corbusier's machine-model, but rather it should be rethought in terms of the organic.[14]

In Jacobs' as well as in Lynch's case we may speak of their urbanism in terms of culture insofar as they both refer to the culture of using a street, the culture of utilizing public squares and the culture of neighbourhoods. Urban culture in this context means that the physical environment which a city is, has a meaning for people that is expressed in the way they live in it, stroll, hang around, and perform the urban drama (to use Lewis Mumford).

IV

Jacobs and Lynch had related the urban fabric to everyday culture. Joseph Rykwert with his *The Idea of a Town* (1976, 1989) addressed all those *deep cultural layers* that had been forgotten by functionalist city planners, which had happened as a consequence of their preoccupation with questions of housing and economic calculation. In Rykwert's view, what functionalism missed was that the city is primarily a "symbolic pattern".[15] Symbols, however, cannot be reduced to their cognitive meaning. They have above all an evocative function. They are embedded in the larger realm of collective ritual practices from which they receive their significance.

Rykwert's *The Idea of a Town* disclosed a broader perspective on the city and true urban life by referring to foundational rituals in ancient Rome. The book offers an *anthropological outlook* on urban form in that parallels are drawn from Roman antiquity to ancient China and India, Africa and America. However, looking back to antiquity does by no means imply nostalgia. The closed world of the ancient Roman city cannot be a rational option for modern people used to the open city. Quite the opposite is to be assumed.

Rykwert's approach is relevant to my own discourse because it corroborates my basic assumption: breaking through the narrow confines of functionalism basically requires the cultural turn of urbanism. Such a turn implies an address to the urban form from an angle that accounts for the economic along with the

Figure 10.8
Hawker Center "Market Place" at Bedok Road (designed by Tangguambee Architects)

Figure 10.7
Barbershop in Chinatown

Figures 10.9, 10.10 and 10.11
People's Culture Center (designed by William S. W. Lim)

historical, the religious, the juridical and the political dimensions of urban life. It would be tempting to discuss in more detail the fascinating narrative of ancient Roman, ancient Chinese or ancient Indian rites and ceremonies accompanying the foundation of the city. Instead of following such a temptation I restrict myself to a very few remarks.

First, the *iron grid* plan of the city is not a US invention; it is neither an ancient Roman invention nor did it originate from modern colonialism. Its origins can be traced back to ancient Sumer. Although the grid of urban design is often called the Roman grid plan, Sennett writes, and Rykwert agrees, that the

> oldest known cities in Sumer were built according to it, as were Egyptian and Chinese cities thousands of years before Roman dominance. In Greece, Hippodamus designed checkerbord cities, as on the Italian mainland did the Etruscans. What matters about grids, as about any elemental image, is the way a particular culture uses them.[16]

Second, the specific ancient Roman use of the grid plan was related to *foundational rituals*.[17] Above all the site of the new city had to be determined. Herein rational considerations were always mingled with magical and religious regards. The augur, the ancient Roman priest, had to perform the ritual of inauguration. Watching carefully the flight of birds, he was empowered to decide where to place the *templum*, the sacred site of the city. He pinned down the diagram of the various city regions. The augur drew the cross of *cardo* and *decumanus*. Afterwards followed the *haruspication*, that is the necromantic inquiry of the liver of the sacrificed animal. Then the surveyors came in to the action, dividing the land in determined parcels.

The most important part of the founding ceremonies was the drawing of the initial furrow, in order to establish the city's boundaries. Such an act had to be performed by the founder using a bronze plough to which a white ox and cow were yoked, the ox on the outside of the boundaries, the cow on the inside. When he came to places on the boundary where the gates were to go, he took the plough out of the ground and carried it over the span of the gate.

Third, the logic of rituals implies that they are not acted out once, but that they be repeated again and again in order to give actions, regions and sites a sacred meaning. Antiquity was familiar with *labyrinth* or *maze dances* in front of the gates to the new city. Since Rykwert is not at all clear in this point, I am referring briefly to the German scholar Hermann Kern. According to him the labyrinth is a very ancient symbol originating from Minoan culture.[18] Historically it is prior to ancient Greek civilization. Originally the maze dance was a group dance which followed a labyrinthine pattern. Its symbolic meaning was to initiate young girls and young boys into adult culture, thus making them adults. The examinee had to undergo a complicated examination. He/she had to move through a maze, in order to find a new self. Important in this context is that the individual had to entrust him/herself to the group in order to reach eventual salvation, that is to say, to endure the move through the labyrinth.

According to Kern it was the genius of the ancient Romans, not the ancient Greeks, to apply the maze dance to the *realm of the city*.[19] They coded it as maze dance, to be exercised by horsemen in front of the city gates. The symbolic meaning of this dance was both a magical protection of the city and a regeneration of it. Renewal and protection were maze dances' functions.

V

As I said, Rykwert's approach is completely misunderstood if it is conceived of as a direct device for understanding contemporary urbanism. Hannah Arendt looked back upon the ancient Greek *polis* in order to regain a full notion of politics because it was obscured in and by modernity. Similarly Rykwert looked back to the ancient culture of Rome as well as to ancient Chinese and Indian cultures in order to pose more fully questions about urbanism today.

To lay bare the cultural dimensions of today's urbanism is the aim of Colin Rowe's and Fred Koetter's *Collage City* which was reprinted several times after 1978.[20] (Rowe, by the way, was Peter Eisenmann's teacher.) Le Corbusier understood the role of the urbanist in terms of a "social engineer". Rowe and Koetter reinterpreted the architect's and city planner's activity as that of a *bricoleur*. Indeed, this role truly recuperates the function of the contemporary urbanist. He/she no longer designs whole cities but rather sections of the urban texture. The notion of the *bricoleur* belongs to the idiom of the anthropological structuralism of Claude Lévi-Strauss. Just as the anthropologist no longer disposes of stable images of man, but can only concentrate on the metamorphosis of the human race, the city planner, too, can no longer assume that he disposes of a total image of the city as functionalism presupposed.

Contrary to the totalized image of the city in functionalism and contrary to a technological methodology derived therefrom, the post-functionalist architect is endowed to offer interventions into sections of the city. As a skilful *bricoleur* the post-functionalist urbanist operates with several tools. Among them is the cultural interpretation of a specific urban site. The urbanist has to know something about the meaning of urban landscapes for their inhabitants. He has to become familiar with the specific rules of political participation of the urban population in the processes of decision-making in city planning.[21] Instead of global utopian solutions that have been the aim of functionalists, within the changed context of post-functionalist urbanism piecemeal ameliorations are required along with pragmatic adaptations of the design to specific localities of the city.

To sum up, post-functionalist city design no longer offers overriding solutions to the architectural problems of the whole city, but is engaged in interventions which are comparable with *collage-technique*. The reading of the urban texture, the care for the plurality of structures, the trial to connect what appears to be dissimilar and heterogeneous are key notions for describing the

FIGURE 10.12
Indian Temple

Figure 10.13
At Race Course Road

new virtues of the urbanist. Philosophically speaking, the collage-approach of the post-functionalist city design breaks with an understanding of architecture and city design in the sense of fundamentalism and foundationalism. Both were hallmarks of functionalism. The collage-approach, on the contrary, favours a design that remains open to the various historical and social layers of a given city. They all can exist side by side. They should even coexist with each other. History is no longer brought to its final end. It is not originating from a completely new base, but history is just to be continued.[22]

VI

Contemporary societies all over the world have to face new conditions of producing and distributing goods which are leading to more and more global-ized economies. Enormous streams of immigration, the mixture of peoples from divergent parts of the world, and multiculturalism are unavoidable consequences of the emergence of new information technologies. In what follows in this section and the following ones I am sketching just two convincing models of post-functionalist urbanism. In his book "Die dritte Stadt. Bausteine eines neuen Gründungsvertrages" (1993; "The Third City. Bricks of a New Agreement of Association") the city planner Dieter Hoffmann-Axthelm argues that contempor-ary cities are confronted with two urgent problems. On one hand, we notice the waves of *immigration* to the rich societies of the West. On the other hand, the *environmental crisis* can no longer be neglected. Neither of these urban prob-lems can be coped with adequately by functionalism.

Hoffmann-Axthelm takes a postmodern stance, which he argues implies looking back at historically earlier urban *forms* in order to find starting points for reorientation but without accepting their former *substance*. Note here, that such a reflection is methodologically very close to Rykwert. From an ecological point of view the European medieval city has been much more successful than the modern industrialized city. Functionalism with its preference for increasing car transportation has disastrous ecological effects.

On this view, immigration can best be tackled by a city that has areas with diverse functions, so immigrants are more likely to find a shelter in order to

Figure 10.14
Chinatown

Figure 10.15
Chinatown

Figure 10.16
People's Park Complex

survive. The functionalist separation of the functions presupposes the participation of the whole city population in the official economy. Newly arrived immigrants, however, often have only limited access to this economy. Hoffmann-Axthelm claims that with regard to the ecological problem we have to accept the premise of a halt to the city's spatial expansion. A sustainable environment demands limits on uncontrolled expansion of the city. The new methods of computer-supported production in much administrative work as well as in the sections of design-related work allows many jobs to be done at home. For that reason the functionalist separation of production and housing loses its rationale.

Given the condition that the city may no longer expand spatially, the question emerges: how is it possible to link the two problems, increasing immigration on one hand and ecological sustainability of the environment on the other? This link is best established through a method of urban planning which guarantees that each section (parcel) of a city already contains all the ingredients of the urban as such. This device requires the urban planner to deal with issues of planning and structure to the extent that they are understood as just two sides of the same coin. It means adopting a method of urban planning which had horrified the modernists, namely the nineteenth-century urban planning of the Berlin-based James Hobrecht. Hobrecht's method implies undoing the difference between the exciting cultural centre of the city and the boring suburbs.[23]

I would like to add just two minor points that remain unclear in Hoffmann-Axthelm's discourse.

First, along with William Lim I would like to stress the fulfilment of environmental justice for all areas of the city.[24] This demand becomes urgent precisely if we in a post-functionalist urbanism favour the mingling of the functions in one and the same urban region. That is to say, if we neglect the demand of ecological justice we lose the historical advantages of functionalist urbanism, which had offered comparatively cheap and healthy housing for the poorer city population.

Second, the cultural turn in post-functionalist urbanism that I am advocating in this essay requires coping more adequately with immigration. We have to introduce what Will Kymlicka has dubbed cultural membership.[25] This concept allows immigrant minority groups to keep the culture of their upbringing alive in their new surroundings, especially their native language and their historical memory. The liberal state – which is the central idea of the concept of cultural membership – is only allowed to intervene in the community life of immigrant groups if their officials prevent their members from free choice of their own individual life perspective. In this sense a Dutch court was right in punishing both a Turkish father and his son. The father had incited his son to kill his sister's Dutch lover because he had had sex with her. In this case the Turkish father had to be punished because under the guise of cultural membership he had tried to withhold the right of sexual self-determination from his daughter by forcing the Islamic value of virginity before marriage on her.

VII

Hoffmann-Axthelm's post-functionalist urbanism articulates European experiences, though his model is not restricted to this pretext. The Singaporean urbanist William Lim proposes a genuinely *Asian model of city planning*. His approach

Figure 10.17
Opposite to Robertson Quay

Figure 10.18
Thain Hock Keng Temple

Figure 10.19
In the neighbourhood of Jalan
Besar

claims to meet the demands and the conditions of the *globalized city*. Singapore is, for sure, one outstanding example of the global city.

In William Lim's view, a viable Asian urbanism has above all to balance the requirements and forces of globalization with the demands of local cultures. "Glocalization" is the new catchword termed by the geographer Edward Soja[26] as well as by the sociologist Roland Robertson.[27] William Lim provides an urbanistic understanding of this term. The blending of the local and the global is necessary in order to maintain the values shared by local cultures and to resist the unfettered commodification of culture brought about by untempered capitalistic globalization. According to William Lim, genuinely "Asian" values that are still shared by most Singaporeans are community and family centredness of the individual, community support for the individual, consensus instead of contention, and racial and religious harmony.[28]

The stress on the (Asian) logic of *fuzziness*, remarkably evident in the urban lay-out of Tokyo, is intended to achieve two different aims. One aim is to oppose and to overcome the International Style's exclusion of climatic and cultural components.[29] The other aim is to introduce an attitude that is more adaptive to the complexity of contemporary city environments into the rigid modernist rationalism that orders and zones the urban fabric.[30] Diversified usage of regions, which has already been championed by Jane Jacobs, is also strongly required today instead of "zoning by classified usage"[31] since the "established principles of modernist planning theories from zoning to land use and transportation are no longer valid".[32]

Le Corbusier had conceived of the *streets* as "place(s) for trucks and taxis".[33] According to William Lim, the urban planner today should, on the contrary, pay more attention to both main streets and secondary streets in order to stimulate "street activity" in its full range, including walking and strolling, in order to meet the "community of strangers".[34] William Lim refers explicitly to Singapore's traditional Chinatown. As a consequence, the author pleads for the rescue of Singapore's Chinatown, which came under pressure a couple of years ago. Against any plan to demolish the houses or to devote them exclusively to retail he argues that a mixed population, and diversified uses and activities would be the appropriate ways of sustaining residential life in the city centre.[35]

Figure 10.20
Fencing around a
building site

Here we find an outstanding instance of how a contemporary urbanism could function, an urbanism that has an eye for the complexities of urban culture. Such an urbanism should engage in an urban politics that structures the environment to the extent that its places meet the *desires* and *memories* of its inhabitants. Memories, however, are not quantifiable. They are completely personally bound. Although memories are ephemeral and evanescent they are nevertheless necessary for constituting a rich personal and social urban identity. The city planner should have a more elaborate cultural and social knowledge of the part of the city he/she is concerned with than is often the case. Decisive points of reference herein are the memories of the inhabitants. The logical conse-quence of this argument is that local communities and civil groups have to be involved in the procedures of city planning in order to adapt urban design to the expectations and desires of the local people.[36]

Taking people's memories and their social culture seriously into account opens up a fresh view on that dimension of city planning which is concerned with *cultural heritage* and *conservation*. It is, in fact, a viable alternative to the theme-parkism exemplified in Singapore by the failing Tang Dynasty City and Haw Par Villa or by Asian Village on Sentosa Island.[37] William Lim goes straight to the point:

> Conservation is definitely not a nostalgic retreat into the past. It is an effective
> urban instrument to preserve visual memories and our heritage. Adaptive reuse is
> an economically viable option for environmental conservation. The present western
> model of "theme-parkism" with its fantasy images is not.[38]

VIII

Before I reach my conclusion, I have to concentrate on one other point. It is well known that Kenneth Frampton's essay "Towards a Critical Regionalism: Six Points for an Architecture of Resistance", first published in Hal Foster's influential *The Anti-Aesthetic. Essays on Post-Modern Culture* (1983) and later in a different version added as the final chapter to the revised and enlarged edition of Frampton's book *Modern Architecture: A Critical History* (1985), played an import-ant role in postmodern discourses on architecture.[39] William Lim has shifted the meaning of the concept of Critical Regionalism by giving to it, as it were, an Asian twist. Frampton argues for a postmodern architecture under the umbrella of Critical Regionalism. William Lim has transformed the scope of this concept to the extent that it now engages the question of the *contemporary vernacular*.

Within an Asian context, the issue of the contemporary vernacular is related to a bulk of architectural works. Among them are remarkable works by Charles Correa from India, Mathar Bunnag from Thailand, Ernesto Bedmar from Singapore, Kazuhiro Ishii from Japan, Geoffrey Bawa from Sri Lanka, Yoshio Kato from Japan, Kerry Hill from Singapore, Richard Ho from Singapore, as well as William Lim himself. William Lim has provided the following definition of the term:

> The notion of a contemporary vernacular can . . . be defined as a self-conscious
> commitment to uncover a particular tradition's responses to place and climate, and
> thereafter to exteriorise these formal and symbolic identities into creative new forms
> through an artist's eye that is very much in touch with contemporary realities and
> lasting human values.[40]

From the outset it has to be kept in mind that the concept of contemporary vernacular is neither nostalgia nor a return to regional practices as such. On the contrary, the contemporary vernacular describes an architectural practice that attempts to rearticulate regional culture from the viewpoint of the existing world culture today. The choice of specific practices and customs worth being maintained is implied. A particular past thus is disclosed and defended vis-à-vis an evolving world culture. Questions of scale are decisive. It is important to distinguish the contemporary vernacular from mere replications and "superficial historicism" (Frampton) in order to demarcate it from historical, romanticizing or just fake repetition. In a word, the concept of the contemporary vernacular is above all a critical and, as it were, a dialectical concept. The contemporary vernacular, then, is an attempt to reappropriate valuable but historically marginalized cultural traces doomed to commercialization by the powers of global culture industries and thereby threatened to become merged in the trivialities of Disneyland or theme parks.

IX

This is the appropriate place for a summarizing conclusion and a qualifying addition. My point in this essay has been to show that we should gather the elements of an emerging post-functionalist urbanism under the heading of the cultural turn of urbanism. This turn is the marker of the move from modernist functionalist to postmodern post-functionalist urban design. In summarizing we can say that post-functionalist urbanism places stress on the multiple uses of one and the same urban region, on mingling of functions, on a vivid street-life. It reminds us of the various cultural deep-structures of urban design. Post-functionalist urbanism, furthermore, identifies the urban architect not as the social engineer, but rather as the cultural tinker, whose interventions into the urban fabric are collages instead of an overriding design for the whole city. Post-functionalist city design enables us to cope with the problems that emerged on an unprecedented scale in postmodern times. They challenge most contemporary cities worldwide: immigration and ecological problems. Post-functionalist city design eventually attempts to find a balance between the global and the local by strengthening particularly valuable local cultures without losing sight of universalizing forces. To use an idea from Adorno: the particular has to be rescued from the dominating power of the universal.

Indeed, to walk about on the Singaporean streets and squares makes one immediately aware that in this city quite different layers of urban sensation converge. The architecturally impressive skyline in a decidedly modernist style and the elegant shopping malls on Orchard Road, on the one hand, coexist with the labyrinthian network of streets and by-streets as well as the various hawker centres of Little India, Chinatown and the Arab Street on the other hand. This has already a clearly postmodern touch insofar as the urban design brings together completely divergent strands of contemporary urban culture. Mohamed Sultan, however, is in itself one marker of outstanding genuinely postmodern urban culture in Singapore. To use for the last time William Lim's phrasing:

> Perhaps the most interesting facet is the social and cultural phenomenon enacted every night. The spontaneous and unregulated energy of the young, the hip and the

Figure 10.21
Façade of a shophouse

Figure 10.22
Altar for the moon-cake festival

Figure 10.23
Mail-box

deviant coexist with fuzzy, invisible and undefined boundaries. Office boys rub shoulders with the new technology elite. Middle-aged businessmen and their female companions share crowded dance floors with gay men cruising each other. Perhaps this reflects the spirit of pluralism, tolerance and rebelliousness of postmodernism, as well as being an indicator of the demand for more space, cultural or intellectual, within our urban environment.[41]

X

There remains one qualifying addition. I am advocating an understanding of post-modern post-functionalist urbanism that does not put aside the avant-garde element of architecture and urbanism altogether. On this point I completely dis-agree with Andreas Huyssen, who identified in his "After the Great Divide" (1988) postmodernism with the farewell to any avant-garde what so ever. On the contrary, I do believe that a certain degree of social and political commitment is still alive among contemporary architects although a deep transformation has taken place.

I will sketch only two different possibilities of how architects today can react to the questionable aspects implied in the avant-garde pretension in modernist urbanism. The concern with the single architectural building does not necessarily lead the architect to the denial of the building's embeddedness in the urban fabric.

Aldo van Eyck, the recently deceased dissident of CIAM, who together with others caused CIAM to fall,[42] maintained the presumption that there must still survive a link between the architectural building on the one hand and the city on the other. A retreat from any urban engagement was not the conclusion van Eyck drew from the failure of modernist functionalism. This stance is graspable in his assertion that relationship between the house and the city should be brought under the poetic heading of a "labyrinthian clarity".[43] I don't have to mention that this formula inspired many of his pupils, such as Herman Hertzberger, Lucien Lafour and Piet Blom.

Rem Koolhaas has always been and still is a strong opponent to Aldo van Eyck and his school. Nevertheless Koolhaas expressed his own reliance upon, as well as his distance from, the avant-garde element in modernist urbanism with the following *manifesto-like sentences*:

> If there is to be a "new urbanism" it will not be based on the twin fantasies of order and omnipotence; it will be the staging of uncertainty; it will no longer be concerned with the arrangement of more or less permanent objects but with the irrigation of territories with potential; it will no longer aim for stable configurations but for the creation of enabling fields that accommodate processes that refuse to be crystallized into definitive form; it will no longer be about meticulous definition, the imposition of limits, but about expanding notions, denying boundaries, not about separating and identifying entities; but about discovering unnameable hybrids.[44]

The notion of cultural hybridity is one of the key notions in contemporary discussions about multiculturalism, intercultural reorientation of philosophy, etc.[45] This dimension has from the very beginning been implied in debates on the postmodern condition but it did not find enough attention. Post-functionalist urbanism, at any rate, is intrinsically related to this favouring of cultural plurality, otherness and heterogeneity.

XI

As a footnote I would like to add that the voice of Aldo Rossi may not be missing from our discussion if we consider the debunking of the modernist creed that architectural as well as the urban form follow from their function. Rossi, on the contrary, argued convincingly in his "L'architettura della città" (1966) that there is enough historical evidence for the opposite thesis. Excellent urban and architectural forms can absorb quite diverse social functions instead of being coordinated with stable and fixed functions.[46]

NOTES

1   Charles Jencks, *The Language of Postmodern Architecture*. London: Academy Edition 1977.
2   Le Corbusier, "The City of Tomorrow and Its Planning". Translated from the eighth French Edition of *Urbanisme* with an Introduction by Frederick Etchells. New York: Dover Publications 1987, pp. 163–178.
3   Heide Berndt, "Ist der Funktionalismus eine funktionale Architektur?" (Is Functionalism a Functional Architecture?) in H. Berndt, A. Lorenzer and K. Horn, *Architektur als Ideologie* (Architecture as Ideology). Frankfurt am Main: Suhrkamp 1968, pp. 9–50, here: p. 11.
4   Richard T. LeGates and Frederic Stout, "Modernism and Early Urban Planning, 1870–1940" in *The City Reader*, (eds) Richard T. LeGates and Frederic Stout. London and New York: Routledge 2nd edition 1999, pp. 298–313, here: p. 309.
5   R. T. LeGates and F. Stout, "Introduction to Le Corbusier: A Contemporary City" in *The City Reader*, p. 336.
6   Fredric Jameson, *The Cultural Turn. Selected Writings on the Postmodern, 1983–1998*. London and New York: Verso 1998, p. 12.
7   Jameson, *The Cultural Turn*, p. 13.
8   Jameson, *The Cultural Turn*, pp. 13–14. Compare Heinrich Klotz, *Moderne und Postmoderne. Architektur der Gegenwart 1960–1980* (Modernity and Postmodernity. Contemporary Architecture 1960–1980). Braunschweig Wiesbaden: Vieweg 1985 2nd edition.
9   Jane Jacobs, *The Death and Life of Great American Cities*. New York: Vintage Books 1961.
10 Jacobs, *The Death and Life of Great American Cities*, p. 376.
11 Jacobs, *The Death and Life of Great American Cities*, pp. 429–443.
12 Jacobs, *The Death and Life of Great American Cities*, pp. 435–436.
13 Jacobs, *The Death and Life of Great American Cities*, pp. 439–448.
14 Kevin Lynch, *A Good City Form*. Cambridge Mass. and London England: MIT Press 1996 10th printing, pp. 73–108.
15 Joseph Rykwert, *The Idea of a Town. The Anthropology of Urban Form in Rome, Italy and the Ancient World*. Cambridge Mass. and London England: MIT Press 1989, p. 23.
16 Richard Sennett, *Flesh and Stone. The Body and the City in Western Civilization*. New York and London: Norton 1994, p. 106.
17 Rykwert, *The Idea of a Town*, pp. 41–68.
18 Hermann Kern, *Labyrinthe. Erscheinungsformen und Deutungen. 5000 Jahre Gegenwart eines Urbilds* (Labyrinths. Appearances and Interpretations. The Presence of an Archetype in 5000 Years). München: Prestel 1999 4th printing, pp. 26–33; pp. 54–56. Compare my essay "Walter Benjamin and the Urban Labyrinth" in *Filozofski Vestnik* Vol. XXII, 2001, no. 2, Ljubljana, pp. 11–126.
19 Kern, *Labyrinthe*, pp. 113–117.
20 Colin Rowe and Fred Koetter, *Collage City*. Cambridge Mass. and London: MIT Press 1993.
21 Rowe and Koetter, *Collage City*, pp. 36; 41–42.
22 Rowe and Koetter, *Collage City*, pp. 118–149.

23 Compare my analysis of Hoffmann-Axthelm's urbanism, "Zentrum, Peripherie, Zone, Globalisierung" (Center, Periphery, Zone, Globalization) in *Thesis. Wissenschaftliche Zeitschrift der Bauhaus-Universität Weimar*, 4./5. Heft, 2000, 46. Jahrgang, pp. 90–103.

24 William Lim, *Asian New Urbanism and Other Papers*. Singapore: Select Books 1998, p. 104 and William Lim: *Alternatives in Transition. The Postmodern, Glocality and Social Justice*. Singapore: Select Publishing Pte. Ltd. 2001, pp. 136–140.

25 Will Kymlicka, *Multicultural Citizenship. A Liberal Theory of Minority Rights*. Oxford: Clarendon Press 1996, pp. 84–106. Compare my essay "Von der Multikulturalität zur Interkulturalität (From Multiculturality to Interculturality) in Wolfdietrich Schmied-Kowarzik (ed.) *Verstehen und Verständigung. Ethnologie, Xenologie, Interkulturelle Philosophie* (Understanding and Agreement. Ethnology, Xenology, Intercultural Philosophy). Würzburg: Königshausen & Neumann 2002, pp. 343–358.

26 Edward Soja, *Postmetropolis. Critical Studies of Cities and Regions*. New York: Blackwell Publishers Inc. 2000, p. 199.

27 Roland Robertson, *Globalization: Social Theory and Global Culture*. London: Sage 1992.

28 William Lim, *Asian New Urbanism*, p. 223. William Lim, *Alternatives in Transition*, pp. 41–44.

29 William Lim, *Asian New Urbanism*, p. 65, p. 71.

30 William Lim, *Asian New Urbanism*, pp. 24–25; pp. 132–137.

31 William Lim, *Asian New Urbanism*, p. 62.

32 William Lim, *Alternatives in Transition*, p. 163.

33 Richard Sennett, *The Conscience of the Eye. The Design and Social Life of Cities*. New York and London: W. W. Norton & Company 1990, p. 172.

34 William Lim, *Asian New Urbanism*, p. 64.

35 William Lim, *Alternatives in Transition*, pp. 78–84.

36 William Lim, *Alternatives in Transition*, pp. 62–72.

37 William Lim, *Alternatives in Transition*, p. 91.

38 William Lim, *Alternatives in Transition*, p. 94; compare p. 175.

39 I have discussed Frampton's Critical Regionalism to some extent in my book *Profile der Ästhetik. Der Status von Kunst und Architektur in der Postmoderne* (Profiles of the Aesthetics. The Status of Art and Architecture in Postmodernity). Wien: Passagen Verlag 1990, pp. 151–170.

40 William Lim and Tan Hock Beng (eds), *Contemporary Vernacular. Evoking Tradition in Asian Architecture*. Singapore: Select Books Pte Ltd 1998, p. 23; compare William Lim, *Asian New Urbanism*, pp. 198–214.

41 William Lim, *Alternatives in Transition*, pp. 155–156.

42 Klotz, *Moderne und Postmoderne*, pp. 105–107.

43 Aldo van Eyck, "Labyrinthian Clarity" in *Situationist Times*, No. 4, October, 1963, p. 84.

44 Rem Koolhaas, "Whatever Happened to Urbanism?" from Rem Koolhaas and Bruce Mau, "S, M, L, X L" (1995) in *The City Cultures Reader*, (eds) Malcolm Miles, Tim Hall and Iain Borden. London and New York: Routledge 2000, pp. 327–329, here: p. 328.

45 Compare *Debating Cultural Hybridity. Multi-Cultural Identities and the Politics of Anti-Racism*, (eds) Pnina Werbner and Tariq Modood. London and New Jersey: Zed Books 1997.

46 Compare Klotz, *Moderne und Postmoderne*, pp. 262–264.

Chapter 11: The Tropical City: Slippages in the Midst of Ideological Construction

Wong Chong Thai Bobby

"The Tropical City" is none other than the tropical city of Tay Kheng Soon, a Singapore architect who first came into prominence during the 1960s. He was one of three founding partners of Design Partnership. The practice designed many architecturally significant buildings of the time. One notable piece of work is the People's Park Complex located in Singapore's Chinatown. In the late 1960s and early 1970s, Tay was instrumental in the formation and the operation of SPUR (Singapore Planning and Urban Research Group), an independent think-tank. With SPUR, Tay commented on many urban issues, ranging from the cultural to the technological. Often Tay's articles were directed at the policies of the Singapore Government agencies.

During the 1980s, Tay turned his attention to a project called "Mega-Cities in the Tropics." In a seminar held under the auspices of the Institute of Southeast Asia Studies in 1989, Tay theorized what he meant by the Tropical City. For Tay, the tropical city first came about through his critique of the colonial city. He is keenly aware of the role colonial cities in the tropics played in the global division of labor during the imperial age of world history. The purpose of the colonial population in the colonies was to operate colonial enterprises and plantations and to be a captive market for cheap manufactured goods produced in the metropolitan economies.[1] The post-colonial period did not see a readjustment to this inequality. If anything, many post-colonial cities have migrated to become the sweatshops of the world. Under such a situation, Tay produced a schema which structures and places cities in a hierarchy. The higher-tiered cities are Western and Northern Hemisphere cities, and they tend to lead the way in intellectual and artistic fields. The lower-tiered cities, of which cities in the tropics are part, tend to merely imitate the Western and Northern hemisphere cities.[2] And thus far, based on this assumption, "nothing intrinsic has come out of city planning in the tropics."[3] For Tay there is an inherent correlation between the global division of labor and that of the status of cities as found within each hierarchical tier. Hence, Tay can easily pronounce that unless there is a radical rethink of city and urban planning in the tropics, the inhabitants of the tropics will not overcome the restrictive confines of neo-colonialism. The tropical city then is Tay's proposition to unleash the innovative energy of the people in the tropics in ways that will empower and enable them to re-imagine their own identity and destiny beyond the concepts set by the European and North American models.[4] In addition to releasing unused potential in the people, Tay argues, the tropical city will create a new civilization.[5]

Several questions come to mind as I read Tay's writing. One of which is how radical this rethink can ever be, given that Tay is skeptical of modeling ideals based upon, or recycling ideas received from, the Northern Hemisphere cities. In the first place, much of the built environment is indeed already modeled and influenced after the West. As Tay himself rightly points out, the growth of towns and cities in the tropics is not based on any deep thought processes but on simple practical necessity and ideas current in Europe and the United States. So where is this radical rethink coming from given that Tay's rethink demands a "break" from the received architectural and urban ideologies of the West? In a paper entitled "A World Class City Deserves a World Class Architecture," Tay believes that this rethink should be grounded on a process that expresses the intrinsic history, geography and talent of the land with skill and integrity.[6] But, when pressed to make concrete what some of these forms and expressions are, doubts can be found in each of Tay's recommendations.

In the 1988 paper entitled "The Intelligent Tropical City," a paper that comes closest in describing what the tropical city ought to be, Tay lists a number of agendas, each with its own set of recommendations.[7] The idea is that when urban schemes or buildings incorporate these recommendations – including rainwater collection and recycling, vertical landscaping, aesthetics of shadow rather than platonic volume and plane, connectivity, synergistic mix of uses and social choreography and more – the designs will produce tropicality.[8] But do they? A Northern Hemisphere city can embody all these features and more and is certainly no more tropical than the ones incorporating them in the tropics. Germany, a case in point, has legislated laws concerning water conservation for homes and other habitations, and these conservation measures do not necessarily give their cities and urban schemes signs of tropicality, which is not to say that the Germans had tropicality in mind. The question then is: what constitutes Tay's tropical city that provides a mark of a rethink in architecture and urban design?

One way out of this seeming impasse, given that the recommendations are mutually inclusive for both the Northern Hemisphere cities and the tropics and that much of the built environment and the various professionals involved are already hegemonically influenced, is to understand Tay as seeking something that is unique and original that comes out of a creative process rather than considering his proposals as a radical rethink. I suggest that Tay is seeking some mark of identity that signals a difference from those Northern Hemisphere cities.

To answer the question of what this mark might be, we need to look into something more concrete than those abstract words contained in Tay's many written papers. Some time in 1989, a year after the seminar at the Institute of Southeast Asian Studies, Tay together with the Singapore Institute of Architects on one part, and the Housing and Development Board forming the other part, were each commissioned by the Singapore Government to provide a speculative guide plan for an area called Kampong Bugis. The two teams were in competition and the selected draft plan would then form the basis for a guide plan for development of the area.[9] The land is situated at the confluence of two rivers: the Rochore and the Kallang. It is about seventy-two hectares of cleared land bounded by Kallang Road to the north, Crawford Street to the west, Nicoll Highway to the south and a proposed expressway to the east.

Tay's Kampong Bugis Guide Plan (KBG) is a tropical city made concrete (Fig. 11.1). Looking at KBG in terms of layout, including its accompanying city blocks, it is no different from other urban solutions. It was organized by an orthogonal grid (Fig.11.2). The grid imposed on the site a series of city blocks

Figure 11.1
Proposed Kampong Bugis Guide
Plan (KBG): model

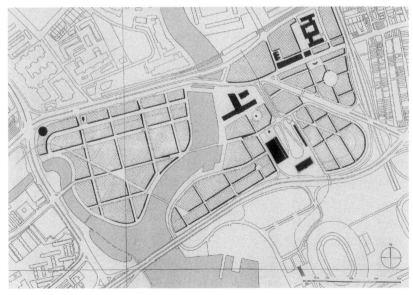

Figure 11.2
KBG: urban layout plan

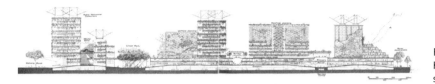

Figure 11.3
KBG: section of building forms, shades, solar and rain collectors

measuring one hundred and twenty meters by one hundred and twenty meters. These city blocks were composed of slabs on podium blocks. And along the major highways were placed linear edge blocks. They served as noise barriers. Point blocks were designated at selected landmark locations. All these expressions were not unusual. In fact they were shaped very much along the lines of the International Style: the institutionalized boxes of the late modern movement.

However, over and above these late modernist boxes, Tay introduced and covered these boxes with vegetation and plants. The rationale he gave was that the vegetation and plants were motivated by environmental and climatic factors, in particular the vegetation's ability to reduce the temperature of the city. In this manner, the tropical vegetation might mediate between the inside and the outside and render air-conditioning optional in a tropical urban space. He also devised large inclined shades over the roofs which not only shade the building fabric but also act as solar and rain collectors (Fig. 11.3). But, whatever the motivation behind this move was, looking at the guide plan report and its illustrations, the vegetation cover is overwhelming and dense (Fig. 11.4). There is no city quite like KBG. Without Tay knowing it himself, since he has attributed the vegetation to being motivated solely by instrumental purposes, might this be where Tay's creative production is located?

But before one moves too quickly, this question coming at a critical juncture demands a pause. For at the start of this paper, there is an absence as to what this paper is about. Given its narrative thus far, the paper's emphasis has been on the shattering of Tay's project of radical rethinking, but is this the true focus of the paper? I will hasten to say that this shattering of Tay's radical rethinking is but a mere stage to a higher ambition. Since Tay's first evocation of

Figure 11.4
KBG model: proposed vegetation cover on building façades

the tropical city, the tropical city has taken on a significance of its own. It has its own history and, I should add, a definitive history driven by its own cause and purpose, a kind of closure. It is historicized to have emerged from an East–West binary essence and within a historical narrative driven by an *a priori* ideal: the desire for a cultural identity quite separate from the West.

There is no doubt that Tay himself takes part in and abets this form of theorizing. In his writings on numerous occasions, Tay has professed the need for cultural identity in architecture and its related ideas. The tropical city is one instance. In another instance, while expressing his views on the approved James Stirling/Michael Wilford design for the Singapore Arts Centre, Tay was critical of how Asian arts (and by that Asian architecture) have been glossed over because of the predominance given to Western theater and performing arts.[10] No doubt, Tay in all of his theorizing has not been arguing for a naïve recall of an idealized past, but he is looking for a cultural identity that is an outcome of a critical attitude towards the barrage of Western ideas in the light of Asian heritage.

Those who argue against the tropical city implicitly also affirm this idealism. One postcolonial critic, Abidin Kusno, did just that. Kusno concludes that, though the tropical city is seemingly different from other global cities, this difference can be attributed solely to the overwhelming presence of the vegetation. There is, in other words, nothing new emerging from Tay's endeavor. The tropical can only achieve its distinctive identity, Kusno argues, when the modern is placed in a crisis and deprived of its authority. Touching but not sacrificing its own modern identity, the tropical joins and identifies with the modern as an apolitical project. Behind the mask of the tropical, Kusno asserts, the tropical city offers no rejection of or alternative to the modern paradigm.[11] In Kusno's opinion, the climatic features on high-rise towers and slab blocks can be read culturally as signs of a shift from the old economy into late capitalism.[12]

We know where this form of criticism is coming from. Kusno is objecting to postcolonial architects whom he thinks are practicing "orientalism-in-reverse."[13] Kusno applies this phrase to Southeast Asian architects like Tay who manipulate and construct the symbolic, including notions of the tropical, to express their own agenda to an audience within and outside of their landscape. The other in discourse, which is the Western modernist box and its paradigm, has to be ridiculed and rejected.[14] Unless this is achieved, so Kusno's argument runs, Tay can be said to have failed in his endeavor.

But this is not my concern. The purpose in narrating these differences, whatever the cultural expression favored by Tay or Kusno, is that their writings are in varying degrees pre-mapped by an *a priori* ideal called "cultural identity." This pursuit driven by ideals reduces and produces essences. And essences are convenient for one to establish legitimacy and meaning, an epistemological stasis understandable to all.

However, under the present condition of globalization of trans-capital and trans-cultural worlds the accepted clear delineations between what is East and West, colonial and the colonized are very much blurred. A case in point is that though the Europeans may have unleashed the modern box, over time, the modern box has been incorporated into the local as a West which is different, but undoubtedly related to, its origin. Hence, given that the tropical city is already framed, theorized and now to be historicized from either a cultural ideal or from within an essentialist mode of thinking, how do we prefigure a way out of such historicizing into a way of writing that puts on notice all writings on history as invariably provisional? Such reconfiguration would suggest that Tay's Tropical City has another emergence, another probable history waiting to take flight.

Gilles Deleuze advances a definition of abstraction that helps point toward this other emergence latent in Tay's work. Deleuze wants to do away with the objectifying of form, because of its connection to the interior and transcendentalism, through the reductive process. Instead of the stripping away of what is perceived as the non-essential, Deleuze wants to move toward an abstraction that uncovers in their prior forms what later is synthesized. The result is combination *without* synthesis. An analogy for the former kind of abstraction can be found in early-twentieth-century painting, where there were experiments that did away with figuration and the other non-essential aspects of painting, the result of which is a work such as "White on White" by Kasimir Malevich. This painting is comprised of a square of white paint painted onto a white canvas. Here, one can understand painting as pushing itself to its limit before collapsing into non-painting. The attempt is to define what is the minimum essential constituent to a painting to be termed as a painting. Therefore Deleuze's abstraction is not a cleaning up of form but the re-assemblage in reverse of activities and parts before form consolidates itself.[15] This re-assemblage provides an alternative dialectic: that of Being differing with itself immediately and internally. And we know from Deleuze's reading of Bergson that pure Being is none other than pure Recollection, a kind of memory, also known as the Virtual.[16]

In addition, Deleuze finds that traditional dialectic aims at a stasis, a *quidditas* as false movement, because the arrived-at synthesis between two terms is always already predetermined by a finality.[17] The East–West essence and the cultural ideality of Tay are cases in point. And because these terms are located outside of being, they are abstract and often too large to grasp the specificity and singularity of reality. If they do, there is a chance element involved. This explains why Kusno makes no distinction between Tay and Ken Yeang,[18] and categorizes the two architects under the heading he calls "Bioclimatic."[19]

But must Tay's KBG and his tropical city suffer such indictment, one that is perpetuated by a false movement? I think not. Tay's discourse is shaped very much by his platonic intellect. He formalizes his tropical city as having emerged from *a priori* concerns. However, Deleuze in his study of Proust asserts that an impression always has two sides: "Half sheathed in the object, extended in ourselves by another half that we alone can recognize: it designates an object, it signifies something different."[20] Applying this account to Tay, are we saying that embodied in KBG and the tropical city is another half – the half that is different from the formalized truth of the intellect, which in Deleuze's and Proust's scheme of things is arbitrary? In this way, Tay is like the hero of the search, in Deleuze's story on Proust, unaware at the start of his apprenticeship "that truth has no need to be spoken in order to be manifest; and that it can be attained perhaps more certainly without waiting for words and without even taking them into account."[21] Indeed, KBG and the notion of tropical city may have another beginning and may not reside in the very location that is formulated by Tay's intellectualism, for this beginning resides in the subject rather than in the world. Deleuze has termed this the "essence" of being.[22] He then asserts that because of this essence, when each subject expresses the world, each one will express it from a certain viewpoint. Each subject, therefore, expresses an absolutely different world.

But why would a subject or an individual express something of the world in the first place? According to Deleuze, matter, or the pleats of matter, triggers vibrations or oscillations within the folds of the soul,[23] which are likened to essence and represent an innate form of knowledge. When solicited by matter, the folds move into action, thus producing from the subject an expression of the world. This echoes Deleuze's earlier point regarding synthesis, form and the transcendental. Instead of going for a dialectic that is shaped by some final cause, Deleuze's re-assemblage in the reverse sees a dialectical movement that witnesses virtuality actualizing itself. Is this also not the case for Tay? Judging from KBG, if the overwhelming presence of the vegetation is the intriguing aspect of the design and it is that which gives its unique expression to the world, how do the pleats of matter solicit Tay's very being to propose this specific solution? An event, or perhaps an intersection, must have taken place between the essence of being and the world. Something in the world must have agitated Tay to respond in this way. Examining KBG and the published development guide plan, two points should be noted. Quite unlike the proposal by the Housing Development Board for Kampong Bugis, a similar and simultaneous exercise undertaken by the Singapore housing agency,[24] Tay's KBG went beyond the design brief. Tay saw KBG as part of a larger concern that attempts to question the then-existing pattern of urbanization for land-scarce Singapore. Tay used the KBG to propose an alternate planning and urban strategy for public consideration.

In the late 1980s, the authorities projected a population of four million people for the Island Republic.[25] The implication of housing an additional one million three hundred thousand people apart from the existing two million seven hundred thousand people proved unbearable for Tay. That the additional one million three hundred thousand people would require approximately five more new towns made the dire nature of the situation all the more acute. For Tay, the ecological basis required to sustain a city like Singapore would be irrevocably affected by such changes. Where and how Singapore could accommodate these five new towns without further eroding Singapore's already much reduced natural and green reserve was in question – that is, if no new strategy for urban development was to be found.

In KBG, Tay developed five land-use scenarios for the distribution of the projected additional people.[26] To preserve the existing green and natural reserves, namely the Central Catchment Area and the green area west of Choa Chu Kang, Tay maintained that the extra population should be distributed among the already existing HDB estates and new towns, as well as the existing Central Region of Singapore. No new towns that might deplete the existing but limited natural reserve of Singapore had to be proposed or built, he argued. Based on Tay's projection and tabulation, the Central Region (of which KBG formed part) ought to house eight hundred thousand people. KBG being a seventy-six hectare site, and working with a density of six hundred and forty-five persons per hectare, the residential population would be approximately thirty thousand people (Fig. 11.5).[27]

But was this the cause of Tay's agitation? Maybe not, but these signs provided its index. The preservation of these existing but limited forest areas in an island republic of no more than six hundred and forty square kilometers was symptomatic of a deeper concern. Tay is also an environmentalist and has written extensively on ecology and the need for ecologically self-sustaining urban development. Every city or town, he suggests, needs to sponsor monetarily an area of forested land to compensate for the city's consumption of oxygen. This suggestion should encourage nations to increase forested areas so as to absorb the carbon dioxide of the cities while also producing oxygen. Hence, the proposed green tax for KGB.[28] The addition of one million three hundred thousand people and the possibility of another five new towns seemed to Tay something of an ecological disaster.

The last time a proposal to accommodate four million people on the island had been put forth was in 1963, when the United Nations Technical Assistance Administration team of planners did so. The Koenigsberger plan (Fig. 11.6),[29] as it has come to be called, attempted to describe a possible future Singapore – one that was different from the 1955 master plan received from the British

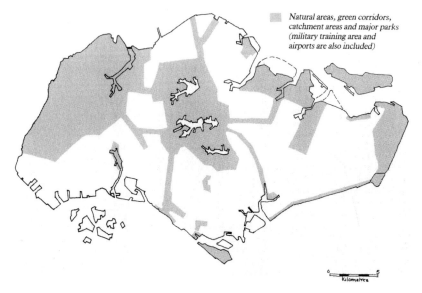

Figure 11.5
Singapore Island: Tay's proposed green plan with green corridor linking KBG and the Central Catchment Area

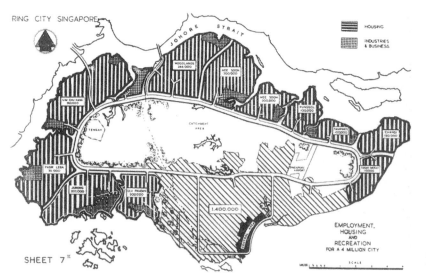

Figure 11.6
The Koenigsberger Plan

172 □

colonial government.[30] The UN team sketched a map that turned the entire island into a planning canvas. They had a ring road encircling the central natural reserve area that connected a series of satellite towns, all strung out like beads on a necklace. The planners' first principle was to treat the entire island as one urban complex. Certainly, the planners did not view the Island Republic as a city with its own hinterland. Tay was well aware of this plan and so long as Singapore was culturally part of Malaya, the rural hinterland was to be found in Peninsular Malaya. However, with Singapore's separation from Malaysia in 1965, did the island become for Tay, physically and in his imagination, separated from its context and hence its rural hinterland? The effect on Tay of this separation resembles what a close-up image of a face in a movie is for Deleuze, in that the close-up produces an intensity that "tears the image away from its spatio-temporal co-ordinates," or its historicity?[31] The result is that "even the place, which is still present in the background, loses its co-ordinates and becomes any space whatever."[32]

I reckon that the separation with Malaysia etched a deep scar in Tay's memory. Only a strait of water separates the six hundred and forty square kilometers of Singapore Island from the Malaysian Peninsula. At its narrowest, it is no more than one thousand four hundred meters wide. The total land area of the Malayan Peninsula is approximately one hundred and thirty-four thousand square kilometers, of which there was, according to 1980 figures, a forested area of approximately sixty-four thousand square kilometers. The removal, even though imaginary and not literally, of sixty-four thousand square kilometers of forested area and a common market of about twelve million people in 1965 shocked many Singapore inhabitants.

Did the question and the process of designing KBG as part of a city for four million people agitate Tay into remembering a past that often surfaces in my social conversations with him? Like Proust's hero having become disappointed in an object, Tay found a subjective compensation[33] in the fecundity of the Malayan tropical forest. If Deleuze is followed to his limits, "we can say that the actual image [read here as *KBG*] itself has a virtual image [again, read here as *recollected pasts*], which corresponds to it like a double or a reflection. In Bergsonian terms, the real object is reflected in a mirror-image as in the virtual object which, from its side and simultaneously, envelops or reflects the real: there is coalescence between the two. There is a formation of an image with two sides, actual and virtual . . . each running behind one another and in constant reference to each other in a circuit that reaches a point of indiscernibility."[34]

Did this process take place in KBG? Is it possible to read the overwhelming presence of the vegetation across and over the building structures as a sign of a struggle within Tay's subjectivity between the actual and the virtual, the real and the imaginary, the present and the past? There is evidence to suggest that this is highly plausible given that there are maps, in the KBG report, drawn in ways that correspond to and reflect the Koenigsberger plan. But truth in this aspect is very far from the point the paper hopes to make. What is of interest to this paper is that though the subject's past has ceased to act or to be useful, it has not ceased to be. The spin given to KBG, among other things, shows how the virtual distinguishes itself and what actualizes it in a process of differentiation. Quite unlike the earlier movement that differentiates but is mapped by some external source, the virtual here differentiates by an insertion of itself into matter.[35]

Movement is explained according to the obstacles it meets in matter or matter in the virtual. Here, movement is not merely shaped by an external cause but according to the unique materiality through which it passes. Of greater significance is that pure recollection, which Deleuze terms as the virtual and the essence, is the simplicity of being. It can only exist in the subject as pure duration and not as matter.[36] And as duration, being is capable of differing internally with itself. It does not need to look outside itself for other forces because difference rises from its very core, from the explosive internal force that life carries within itself.[37] This is what Deleuze refers to as the "plane," or even that formless elastic membrane that issues, propagates or perpetuates something ontological but which is not just anything.

This essay, then, opens up for us the existence of other histories quite different from the one determined by some imagined finality, that though unverifiable is nevertheless theoretically plausible. In so doing, this other history, itself a highly probable one, indicates that all historical writings are therefore themselves probable. Tay's KGB and Tropical City gesture toward such probable histories.

NOTES

1 Tay Kheng Soon, "Rethinking the City in the Tropics: The Tropical City Concept" in *Tropical Architecture*, (ed.) Alexander Tzonis, Liane Lefavre and Bruno Stagno (London: Wiley Academy, 2001), 266–267.
2 Ibid., 268.
3 Tay Kheng Soon, *Mega-Cities in the Tropics: Towards an Architectural Agenda for the Future* (Singapore: Institute of Southeast Asian Studies, 1989), 5.
4 Tay Kheng Soon, "Rethinking the City in the Tropics: The Tropical City Concept" in *Tropical Architecture*, (ed.) Alexander Tzonis, Liane Lefavre and Bruno Stagno (London: Wiley Academy, 2001), 266–268.
5 Tay Kheng Soon, *Mega-Cities in the Tropics: Towards an Architectural Agenda for the Future* (Singapore: Institute of Southeast Asian Studies, 1989), 5.
6 Tay Kheng Soon, "A World Class City Deserves a World Class Architecture" in *Line, Edge & Shade*, (ed.) Robert Powell (Singapore: Page One, 1997), 91.
7 Ibid., 132–143.
8 Ibid., 143.
9 Urban Redevelopment Authority (URA), *Kampong Bugis Development Guide Plan* (Singapore: URA, 1990). The report contains two guide plans. One was by Singapore Institute of Architects headed by Tay Kheng Soon. The other was an alternate proposal done and carried out by the Housing Development Board (HDB). The two teams were assembled to re-look into urban and housing planning policies. This exercise is the first of a number of experiments where private architects were solicited for their views.
10 Tay Kheng Soon, "Viewpoint on the Singapore Arts Centre" in *Line, Edge & Shade*, (ed.) Robert Powell (Singapore: Page One, 1997), 166–167.
11 Abidin Kusno, *Behind the Postcolonial* (London: Routledge, 2000), 200–202.
12 Ibid.
13 Ibid., 192.
14 Ibid., 200.
15 John Rajchman, *Constructions* (Cambridge: MIT Press, 1998), 56–61.
16 Micheal Hardt, *Gilles Deleuze* (Minneapolis: University of Minnesota Press, 1993), 14.
17 Ibid., 5–12.
18 Ken Yeang is a Malaysian architect who, like Tay, has articulated the problems of designing in the tropical climate through his built works and writings. Yeang's designs like the Menara Mesiniage (1989–1992) are examples of what he has theorized. His buildings are fragmented with voids for ventilation and they are arranged (at least in the façades and the sections of the buildings) to permit lush greenery to grow. They become gardens in the sky.

19 Abidin Kusno, *Behind the Postcolonial* (London: Routledge, 2000), 197–205.

20 Gilles Deleuze, *Proust & Signs*, trans. R. Howard (Minneapolis: University of Minnesota Press, 2000), 27.

21 Ibid., 29.

22 Ibid., 43.

23 Gilles Deleuze, *The Fold: Leibniz and the Baroque*, trans. Tom Conley (Minneapolis: University of Minnesota Press, 1998), 4.

24 Urban Redevelopment Authority, *Kampong Bugis Development Guide Plan* (Singapore: URA, 1990). Included in this set of guide plans is a proposal by the HDB. The HDB proposal assumed and reaffirmed the "time tested" approach to design; in the methodology prescribed by URA in its approach to the planning for the other districts in Singapore, HDB did not question nor raise issues for further deliberations but rather planned along existing design parameters. This was unlike Tay's approach.

25 Urban Redevelopment Authority, *Kampong Bugis Development Guide Plan* (Singapore: URA, 1990), 2.

26 Ibid., 4–5.

27 Ibid.

28 Ibid., 19.

29 Sumiko Tan, *Home Work Play* (Singapore: Urban Redevelopment Authority, 1999), 143.

30 Ibid., 141.

31 Gilles Deleuze, *Cinema 1: the Movement-Image*, trans. H. Tomlinson and B. Habberjam (Minneapolis: University of Minnesota Press, 1997), 96.

32 Ibid., 97.

33 Gilles Deleuze, *Proust & Signs*, trans. R. Howard (Minneapolis: University of Minnesota Press), 34.

34 Ibid., 68–69.

35 Gilles Deleuze, *Bergsonism*, trans. H. Tomlinson and B. Habberjam (New York: Zone Books, 1991), 94.

36 Ibid., 37–38.

37 Ibid., 94.

Chapter 12: Intelligent Island, Baroque Ecology

Aihwa Ong

RISKS AND POLITICAL REASON

Singapore calls itself "an intelligent island," in an archipelago of presumably less-intelligent places. But keeping one step ahead in the intelligence game can no longer defend against the ravages of global capitalism. In the aftermath of the so-called Asian financial crisis of 1997–1998 "New Singapore" must incorporate new spaces of calculation, as well as mobilize more foreign experts to spark new dynamics of intellectual growth. Thus, at a national day rally, the prime minister proclaimed:

> Today, wealth is generated by new ideas, more than by improving the ideas of others
> . . . That is why we have to bring in multi-national talent, like the way we have
> brought in MNCs [multinational corporations]. Like MNCs, multi-national talent, or
> MNTs, will bring in new expertise, fresh ideas and global connections and perspectives.
> I believe that they will produce lasting benefits for Singapore.[1]

Among the "lasting effects" unspecified in the prime minister's speech would be the risks entailed in what being Singaporean means.

An investigation of technology and government requires that the nation be conceptualized as a kind of problem-space, thus making an inquiry into how administrative techniques construct social space that becomes a constitutive element in the problematization and creation of human subjects. Michel Foucault (2000) argues that in advanced liberal societies, liberalism is a form of political reasoning that extends governmental technologies (which he explored in the domains of clinics and prisons) to the space of the market.[2] Market risks, I argue, challenge authorities to incorporate liberalism as a technology of government, a problematizing activity that shifts politics away from social conflicts towards the technical management of social life. One can say then that neo-liberalism in practice involves what Nikolas Rose and Peter Miller call a "technicalization of politics."[3] Indeed, an investigation of the technologies of global competition would pay attention to the construction of domains outside "politics" where different kinds of subjects are problematized and constituted. It is in the administration and manipulation of modern life in relation to market values, and the circulation of these values that radically redefine the space and forms of political citizenship.

I am interested in forms of neo-liberal governmentality that have emerged in Asian cities to cope with problems of city administration, infrastructure, and the quality of populations. For Rose, Foucault's concept of governmentality can be applied to two sets of processes. On a general level, governmentality refers to all manner of forces, techniques, and devices "that promise to regulate decisions and actions of individuals, groups, and organizations."[4] More specifically, governmentality refers to different styles of reasoning and problematization that are fundamentally concerned about transforming situations of uncertainty into calculative strategies. Thus, in modern society, experts such as professionals and technocrats are concerned with defining practical problems that they seek to "understand and ameliorate in terms of a space of action and determination."[5] By staying close to practices, to the ways embodied knowledges and technologies interact in defining and solving problems, the analyst can study experimentations whereby new kinds of space, technicity, subjects, and agencies are called into being. Specifically, I want to identify the new styles of reasoning and governance regimes that resituate the *oikos* ("home") within an expanded ecology formed by the intermixing of diverse streams of *anthropos* ("human beings").[6]

Drawing on research in Southeast Asia, I have identified a post-developmental moment in which the control of the population has become a key strategy for a country to link up to the global economy. But whereas Malaysia relies on cheap labor power to attract foreign investments, Singapore has turned towards the building up of intellectual property as a way to be competitive in the new economy. This strategy of high-risk, high-cost, high-level research is being pursued by small countries that seek to position themselves as the hubs of a transnational nexus of institutional power. The state acts as mobilizer of global talent and as a venture capitalist in creating the linked domains of market expertise, scientific research, and biotechnology in "an effervescent enterprise ecosystem".[7] Environments of calculation are new spaces where foreign and local actors are trained and nurtured to develop certain capacities, incentives, and structured choices as risk-taking, entrepreneurial subjects on the one hand, or to be highly trained scientists working in global research laboratories.

Singapore is the small city-state of less than four million people (of whom over half a million are foreigners) that is famous for being run like a giant corporation. The state management of the economy depended on the management of domestic savings and the attraction of foreign direct investments (FDI). National resources were corralled (through an obligatory pension fund) to serve a coalition of government-led corporations and multinational corporations. At the same time, foreign investors enjoyed tax exemptions of up to ninety percent on profits generated, making Singapore the leading recipient of FDI in the world. Singapore thus becomes the most "global city" if one uses an index of foreign investment flows, cross-border contacts, and the proportion of the total population that is on-line.[8] This so-called Asian "tiger state" model – whereby the country depends on a mix of manufacturing exports, high rates of saving, and domination of national resources by government-linked corporations (GLCs) and multinational firms – allied with a clean and efficient government – has made Singapore one of the richest countries in the world (the per capita income is on par with Canada's). The 1997 Asian financial crisis did not destabilize Singapore, but rattled the government sufficiently for it to consider the tiger model as potentially crippling. New global pressures towards the deregulation of markets, the China challenge, and reduced earnings from manufacturing spurred a major effort to "reinvent" Singapore by putting into play an assemblage of technologies that will transform the city into a hub of a knowledge-driven economy.[9]

BAROQUE ECOLOGY

Neoliberal calculations about the kind of space, technology, and actors for shaping a knowledge society enmesh the island in webs of technology and expertise. New alignments among local and foreign institutions and populations define transnational networks through which expatriates flow and intermingle with local populations in spaces of calculation. In the science of complexity, interactions between diverse elements give rise to non-linear dynamics and the emergence of new collective properties. I use the term baroque or complex ecology to describe the spatial formation that extends beyond the limits of the island nation, a horizontal space rather like the tropical canopy defined as much by the traffic and exchange between different populations as by the state of dynamic criticality their interactions engender.[10] In Singapore, an ecosystem of technical interconnectedness and intellectual capital puts into play two major kinds of population – citizens and foreign experts – whose interactions are expected to produce higher rates of competitiveness, creativity, and knowledge production. Singapore now positions itself as the hub of "a wider Asian region of 2.8 billion people within a flight radius of seven hours" that is well-connected by sea as well as by cyber links.[11]

This baroque ecology is thus the outcome of the specific shift in an intensification of deterritorialization, the particular alignment of technical, political, and social relations across borders and domains. The reinvented Singapore sees itself at the center of an "enterprise ecosystem, where large and small enterprises can thrive by leveraging on innovation and intellectual property to create value."[12] An official at the Economic Development Board (EDB) – the central agency for planning the economy over the past forty years – notes a state transition from an authoritarian task-master to a venture capitalist, silently adjusting "the invisible hand," and "giving the right ingredients but not actually controlling things". He uses the gardening metaphor: the EDB seeds schemes and provides fertilizers, thus acting as a catalyst to allow different organisms to thrive in the ecosystem. Furthermore, to become the Asian site for creating valuable intellectual property, Singapore is to become a "global schoolhouse" where "world-class" universities and research institutes have been invited to locate their programs.[13] This "ecology of expertise"[14] – linking venture capital, research bodies, and foreign scientists – not only seeks to foster intellectual accumulation; it also engenders conditions of instability and discontinuity between the homeland and technical connectivity within the baroque ecosystem.

This biological field resituates the "national *oikos*"[15] within the baroque ecology based on the complex reordering of internal and external relationships. It thus also involves the intensification of modes of governmentality formerly associated with the Asia-tiger model, but now ratcheted up to global norms of corporate behavior. New regimes of governmentality seek to rupture links with an older system based on ethnic Chinese paternalism and entrepreneurship. The authoritarian modality that requires citizens to be loyal, hardworking, frugal, and well-educated subjects is now to be replaced by a strategy of "governing through expertise."[16] This entails an aggressive recruitment of skilled foreigners and has become the strategy "to make Singapore a hub for international talent, while remaining socially cohesive and nationally resilient."[17] Virtual expert citizens are mobilized to interact with locals, to instill in them values associated with risk-taking, scientific, and "technopreneur" skills.

"Ecosystems," we are reminded, "are typically distributed along the critical boundary separating stable from unstable dynamics."[18] Thus posed between systems of stability and instability, the assemblage of venture capital, research bodies, and foreign actors produces a rift between the rootedness of Singapore as a place and as home country, and the partially disembedded relationships that tie it to global centers of calculation. Regulatory regimes come to assess the differential worth of human capital, sorting foreign experts from local ones, those with appropriate intellectual capital from those without, with deep economic and moral consequences for the domestic population.[19] Below, I will describe two clusters of knowledge-industry – in engineering and biotechnology – that are central in constituting networks of the baroque ecology. This is also the public space in which ethical discourses question the uncertain effects of technical rationality in transforming society, and the new divisions between stable and unstable forces that put into jeopardy what it means to be Singaporean today.

TECHNOPRENEURIAL PRACTICES

The National University of Singapore (NUS) is being transformed into a hub for making institutional links with a wide variety of foreign programs in information technology, business management, engineering, and biotechnical sciences. NUS is now redefined as "a free enterprise zone" that combines academic excellence with creative entrepreneurialism among its staff, students and alumni.[20] University divisions have entered into separate partnerships with American and European academic institutions in order to upgrade scientific and business training. Headhunting campaigns have attracted foreign professors and researchers – the prime catch being individuals with an MA or a Ph.D., averaging thirty-five years old. The goal is to bring foreign experts and knowledges into interaction with local and regional students who can be trained and inspired to adopt "technopreneurial" practices.

A key partnership in the high technology field is the Singapore–MIT Alliance (SMA). Formed in 1998, SMA is devoted to training local and foreign students in advanced engineering and new computing technologies. The institute boasts about being the largest interactive learning program in the world, a new paradigm "to promote global science and engineering education and research".[21] Already, the SMA has recruited the best students from various Asian Pacific countries, and the goal is to have a ratio of about one third local students (about 2,000), and the rest mainly from China, India, and Southeast Asia. The faculty is comprised of fifty local and fifty MIT professors distributed across fields such as materials science, computation, manufacturing technology, molecular engineering, and computer science. In addition, NUS has also forged joint programs with German technical universities.

To accommodate the schedule of experts from the United States, the academic year has been adjusted to the American semester cycle. Students have the option to spend one semester at MIT in Cambridge, Massachusetts. It is hoped that these young scientists (with MAs and Ph.D.s) will develop spin-off companies that are based in Singapore. To foster that development, foreign students on full scholarships are to become permanent residents. Upon graduation, foreign students will have guaranteed employment and high salaries, as well as invitations to become residents and citizens. The expectation is that the national university will soon have a student body that is one-fifth foreign. At a recent symposium, the Singaporean minister of defense considers this the core program that will attract and retain "the finest regional talent, along with the generation of an exciting ecosystem of research and idea creation."[22] It is perhaps no exaggeration to say that the state considers such strategic partnerships in the knowledge fields a matter of national defense and strengthening.

The goal is not merely to train world-class engineers; it is also to transform them into entrepreneurs, scientists who can convert their knowledge into marketable products. Thus, the ever-growing number of foreign business schools in Singapore – INSEAD, The Wharton Research Centre at the Singapore School of Management, the University of Chicago Business School – is intended to create a climate of entrepreneurialism and risk-taking. The NUS campus at large has fallen under the enterprise initiative that seeks to instill in students an "enterprise" mindset, the goal being to push graduates to becoming entrepreneurs who transform their "marketable ideas" into start-up companies. A business "incubator" links "commercialisable ideas that are technology-related" with private business, the goal being to generate a synergy between students and entrepreneurs, or an environment where student-entrepreneurs can obtain funding to play with their marketable ideas.

Overseas, the NUS enterprise drive has set up colleges in high-tech zones such as the Silicon Valley where, it is hoped, students earning academic internships in Asia-oriented companies can be exposed to the best "technopreneurial" practices. A number of NUS engineering students were enrolled in Stanford University with the aim of gaining access to internships with Silicon Valley firms. In a glowing write-up, a third-year material science student who was heading for Silicon Valley enthused that "we are young and not risk-averse." Through the internship program, "we hope to experience first-hand how a start-up works. The practical experience will be invaluable."[23] A subsidiary NUS America Inc. will identify internship placements for students in technology-based companies, with the goal of placing at least fifty students each year. The goal is to shake Singaporean university graduates out of their complacency and push them beyond their conventional ambition of working for multinational corporations. Instead, it is hoped that through the proliferation of calculative domains and foreign experts, Singaporeans and foreign Asians will evolve into a homegrown category of entrepreneurial risk-taking subjects. Eventually, it is hoped that some of them will found start-up companies that will attract investments from global firms. The boast is that Singapore will become "the Boston of the East," leveraging business and science education into Singaporean and other Asian subjects who will help the nation-state move up the added-value chain of the knowledge economy.

THE BIO-FEEDBACK INDUSTRY

Advanced engineering is also linked to emerging technologies of bioinformatics and biosciences. Perhaps even more ambitious than the engineering cluster is the project to make Singapore the regional hub of the life sciences. Although still in its infancy, over a billion US dollars have been funneled towards the development of the biomedical sciences. The government has been investing in American and European companies in order to attract them to locate their research facilities in Singapore. An important nexus in the biotechnology field is the Johns Hopkins-

Singapore Company that seeks to apply JHU techniques and patents for research into various diseases endemic to Asia with the hope of developing new therapies and diagnoses. Senior Johns Hopkins professors manage three laboratories with links to NUS and the national hospital – where they train local and regional researchers. The aim is to develop spin-off companies, thus enhancing the pharmaceutical industry in Singapore. A genome institute has been set up, and ground has been broken for a biopolis, a science park where one thousand scientists will receive training by world-class leaders in their field.

Already over 250 foreign scientists have arrived, attracted by opportunities as well as lavish funds, unlimited constraints on stem-cell research, and strategic access to Asian biogenetic materials. Visionaries consider the Asian ethnic diversity a promising source for research in therapeutic cloning, an opportunity to develop expertise in cancer and in diseases ignored in Western countries. A new genome institute will engage in embryonic research of Asian genetic makeup, with the goal of testing drugs and developing treatments tailored to individual patients. The head of the Genome Institute says, "Genetic research today is global. . . . In Singapore the relevant resources for human genomics research are the ethnic diversity and high quality clinical databases."[24] The institute has begun a doctoral program. The goal is to help train a decent number of scientists in the next few years, locals and foreigners who will make medical discoveries and spawn homegrown companies. In order to do this, the state corrals not only foreign experts – such as the Scottish scientists who cloned the sheep "Dolly" – but also the genetic materials of the Asian populations that pass through Singapore's medical establishments.

When an industry is built upon a bio-feedback loop, a process of harvesting the population's own biogenetic resources, we have a process of converting public value to "biovalue."[25] New forms of "biosociality" and ethical technologies come into play around issues of biological, corporeal, and moral vulnerabilities.[26] In this as in so many other debates, the authorities take the initiative to frame discussions and pre-exempt serious debates. A government-appointed ethics committee has forged "a common moral approach" among Singapore's diverse religious and ethnic communities to questions about being converted into biogenetic resources. While some groups may object to the use and creation of embryos, the bioethics spokesman proclaims embryonic research as "a sacrifice for a larger good . . . We need to express our respect for the embryos as potential human beings. This respect is expressed . . . in the form of strict regulation of such tissues as embryonic cells."[27] Stem cells were to be derived from embryos unused in fertility treatments, and research was to be entirely oriented towards treating illness. It was agreed that human cloning was morally wrong. It was not clear whether the sacrifice called for was to benefit Asian health or Asian wealth, but clearly it is not possible to disentangle the two. A new kind of bio-sociality requires the domestic population to turn against its own deeply held beliefs – in Malay culture for instance, there are ethical reservations about invading the body even for medical purposes – and to yield up genetic tissues for trans-religious co-mingling and transformations in artificial environments controlled by global pharmaceutical firms.

The terms "nursery" and "incubator," so much on the lips of Singaporean technocrats, now take on new meanings. They represent technologies for hatching not only new kinds of enterprising, knowledgeable subjects, but also new biogenetic forms from the population, i.e. subjects and biovalues to be harvested by global institutions, while plunging society into new kinds of ethical dilemmas. We will now turn to two major areas of citizen dis-ease opening up: the privileges of expatriates who are widely perceived as a "flow-through" population, and the intensified calculations regarding one's life chances in this baroque ecology of knowledge capitalism.

FOREIGN TALENT

Singapore has always been an immigrant society, inflows regulated to maintain a population distribution that is over seventy-five percent ethnic Chinese, the remainder mainly composed of ethnic Malays and Indians. Consistent policy from the 1970s focused on two tiers of foreign inflows: professionals and workers mainly from Malaysia across the narrow causeway. After the financial crisis, the governing logic shifted from labor supply towards "developing people," a population upgrading strategy that draws upon the skilled labor pool of the entire Asia-Pacific region. As it is, Singaporean students are performing at the highest global levels in math and science, but they do not yet form a critical mass of high-tech professional skills.

Besides, the declining birthrate has created a demographic crisis. During the first post-independence decades of development after 1965, a family planning policy sought to achieve eventual zero population growth. But when the fertility rate dropped below replacement level by 1986 and Singapore had become an affluent country (often compared to Switzerland), the government introduced measures and tax incentives to encourage couples to have "three or more children if they can afford it." This pro-natalist policy has failed to stem falling birth rates (still at 1.5 in 1999).[28] More recently, a new "baby bonus" program provides generous financial supports for the second and third child in the family up to six years of age. At the same time, there is growing resistance to marriage and parenthood, especially in the well-educated ethnic Chinese majority.[29] Attempts by the state to arrange dating services and courtship venues have made little difference in the number of professional women who remain single (men tend to marry much younger, less-educated women).[30] At the same time, tens of thousands of Singaporeans study or live abroad, adding to the shortfall in skilled labor. The government attempts to enforce "a constant replacement ratio" for those who leave, substituting them with foreign experts.

Thus, in 1999, an international headhunting program was launched to recruit university students and professionals, especially from Asian countries, in order to build up the pool of knowledge workers. The Ministry of Manpower has the task to adjust the population mix of locals and foreigners; its website proclaims its role as "dedicated to developing a talent capital, passionate about people development." The current population composition is half a million foreign workers, of whom one-fifth is highly skilled. The technology of immigration depends on a set of rules that are "focused on more skills, more privileges [at the top], and more control [at the bottom]." The official added that "the market determines the economic value" of the immigrant worker. The instrument is the employment pass system which grades skilled foreigners according to an intricate three-tier system of employment passes. The top criteria are for foreigners with professional qualifications, university degrees, or specialist skills; who hold professional or administrative positions; or who are entrepreneurs or investors. They are also graded in terms of their qualifications and basic monthly salaries. The expatriate (a term used to apply to all white-collar and skilled foreign workers) can obtain permanent residency easily, depending on a point system measured according to skill and income. They can bring their families, and buy condo properties.

At the same time, low-skilled foreigners are also desperately needed but subjected to rigorous control. A work permit system is used for low-skilled migrant workers – in construction, manufacturing, services, domestic work – who are brought in on two-year contracts, cannot change jobs, and have absolutely no chance for becoming permanent residents. They may renew their contracts for up to six or ten years, with preference given to "foreign domestic workers" because of the high demand from local and expatriate families for household help. Surprisingly, there is no minimum wage for other migrant workers, so the effect is to reduce their earning power. Nevertheless, the inflow of low-skilled labor is tightly controlled by a levy imposed on employers. The goal ultimately is to reduce the number of migrant laborers to the absolute minimum.

Ordinary workers are being regulated in order to keep pace with this foreign talent policy. There is the constant threat of companies moving their manufacturing bases to China, and the need for Singapore to reposition itself by providing higher value-added, as well as unique, products and services in order to survive in a time of global uncertainty. In this connection, workers will need to acquire higher skills and knowledge, and they should choose to be retrained in order to avoid being retrenched. Through skills redevelopment programs, over 100,000 workers were retrained, but often suitable workers cannot be found for new jobs constantly being created in the electronics industry. Worker acquisition of new skills have enabled Singaporeans to provide a whole spectrum of services tied to profitable goods. For instance, Hewlett Packard's new hand-held computer, the Jornada, is completely researched, designed, manufactured, and packaged in Singapore. Cisco Systems has a new Internet phone that is designed and produced locally as well. Besides continual upgrading of the labor force for high-end manufacturing, workers are urged to think of themselves in a new social compact with employers and the government, in a tripartite cooperation to increase social capital in the country.[31]

The campaign to build new capabilities and new mindsets has moved beyond workers to other targeted groups such as homemakers and senior citizens who are urged to acquire basic IT skills to complement language literacy and arithmetic ability. Subsidized and multilingual classes are offered in many training centers throughout the island. The goal is to make all Singaporeans have basic computing and Internet skills in order to improve their employability, "and in turn develop Singapore into an e-Inclusive society."[32] Those Singaporeans beyond such regulations are thus excluded from the new IT-vision of "the New Singapore." Clearly, such workers are to form a support system for the high-power clusters of finance, engineering, and biotechnology firms devoted to the building of intellectual property.

THE ETHICAL DEBATE

The emerging nexus of knowledge domains represents a new ethical regime assembled around claims to intellectual excellence, scholarships, employment, and valuable citizens. While reliance on skilled foreign workers is not unknown in other countries, in Singapore the foreign talent intake represents a big part of the total population, and the government has demonstrated an extraordinary capacity to mobilize local opinions in favor of expatriate populations as a permanent feature of their society. Deploying a combination of biopolitical and economic rationalities, officials and spokesmen argue that in a time of declining birth rates and global uncertainty, there is no other choice but to rely on foreign assets.

Thus state officials defend the foreign talent policy as vital to the economic growth of the nation. The deputy prime minister has pointed out that without foreigners, the Silicon Valley would not be Silicon Valley, nor London, London. "If Singaporeans were to throw out foreigners, there would not be regional head-quarters here, half of whose staff are foreign; nor multinational corporations . . . 40 percent of whose workers are foreigners".[33] He cited the example of Singapore Airlines having sixty percent of pilots who are foreigners.[34] Economists from the ministry of trade and industry claim that in the decade of the 1990s, forty-one percent of the GDP "was achieved on the back of the inflow of foreign human resources, especially skilled manpower with employment passes (about thirty-seven percent)." With the low birth rate, and lack of a direct substitution between the skill profiles of locals and expatriate talent, they repeat the prime minister's claim that "the need . . . to attract these foreign talent will be a matter of life and death" for the nation. The report claims in triumph that despite the growing debate, sixty-four percent of a recent gallop poll survey agreed on the necessity of importing foreign talent, notwithstanding the mounting layoffs.[35]

In response, the political opposition had promoted the idea of a "Singapore First" rule that would only give foreigners a job not filled by locals. There is fear of a zero-sum game, that expatriates will replace qualified locals, or that they will be substituted in the labor market by foreign but "mediocre" talent. They also called for raising the qualifying pay level for an employment-pass holder, i.e. so that the influx is limited to the upper reaches of the professional and manage-rial category. Some returnees from Great Britain argue for a system similar to that in England where the first preference in employment goes to British citizens, and foreigners will only get jobs that are unfilled. Officials have responded with the argument that there was no simple one-for-one substitution as locals and foreigners do not necessarily have the same professional expertise or skills profiles. Thus foreigners are valued for what David Stark calls their "asset ambi-guity,"[36] or the kind of talent that can exploit the blurring of borders between countries, and different domains of worth.

Furthermore, policy-makers articulate a more subtle change in the cultural logics that have driven Singaporeans for generations. A manpower official told me: "Competition is a fact of life. This is an open economy in which global links predominate." The traditional Chinese merchant figure of economic competition based on kinship- or ethnic-based relations (guanxi) must be buried once and for all. This is a new turn against the pioneering Chinese trader figure celebrated a decade ago.[37] What is needed, he stressed, is "the international risk-taking entrepreneurial figure who is beyond the Chinese merchant model. In the post-industrial society, the need for a Western attitude of risk-taking, a need to mix guanxi with Western global practices." In short, he is pronouncing the end of the family business in the economy, of the notion of local Chinese commercial activity, i.e. naturalized by the activities of the family firms, networks, something that is organic and spontaneous. Instead, capitalism now has to be planned by the state, or at least coordinated through the assemblage of resources, personnel, ideas, and techniques to shape the economic terrain that is entirely oriented towards producing goods and services for the world, and where expatriates must flow through in order to add to the value assets of the city-state.

THE CALCULI OF LIFE CHANCES

The new baroque economy, with its multiple clusters and scales of production and services, has introduced an increasing sense that the comfortable grounds of the old tiger nation have tilted radically, splintering the life chances of citizens according to new sets of criteria. Older rationalities about ethnic Chinese culture, administration, and market relations have become obsolete, and locals no longer sure of their footing have started talking about the roots of citizenship.

Among the many new discourses is an attack on the attitudes and practices of the suddenly old Singaporean corporate culture which looks positively anti-quated in relation to the calculative rationality of the new economy. Heretofore, a scholarly-official class has operated government-linked corporations, control-ling large amounts of national savings and enjoying an oligopoly market position sponsored by the government. An economist from Morgan Stanley observes that the civil servants-turned-corporate managers do not have the appropriate skills, creative values, and innovations of American enterprising IT culture. These technocrats should be replaced by "tomorrow's risk-taking New Economy entre-preneurs" who can convert these corporations "into genuine enterprises."[38] Even employment with multinational firms is no longer the sensible thing to do since corporations teach technical skills but not entrepreneurial risk-taking and business acumen for the creation of homegrown companies.

The culturalist discourse about Asian values as the ballast behind Singapore's success has also become tarnished. A bureaucrat at EDB, telling me about the rapid shifts in state reasoning, confides that "to be a planner is a dream in Singapore." The government appeals to "the rational mind," backing up its plans with a fine track record of delivery. Whenever it falters, it quickly gets back on track. The public, for its part, has been socially conditioned to "instinctively go along with accepted wisdom." In the 1980s, during the boom times, the national discourse was on good Asian values, and the leaders could substantiate claims with double-digit growth figures. There was the widespread acceptance of rules and regulation in exchange for the comfort and security of "an air-conditioned nation."[39] Now, in the post-1997 recession, the "shared values" talk has been abandoned. The Ministry of Information and the Arts has whipped up a new slogan – Singapore Vision 21 (century) – to provide the psychological defense and buzz words to orient the population to the idea of a knowledge-driven economy.

This would require a shift from the educational rationality that has stressed the stuffed duck approach to one that was more "American," with the stress on independent thinking and risk-taking. Singapore has built its past achieve-ments on cultivating industriousness, dedication and loyalty, and teamwork in its students. Now there was the need to induce initiative, creativity, critical thinking ability, and entrepreneurialism at all levels of the education system. At an NUS–MIT symposium, Morris Chang, chief economic officer of a manufacturing company notes that the region "has strong advantages over the West" when it comes to diligence, loyalty, and teamwork, and engineering graduates are willing to take up careers in manufacturing.[40] However, Asian graduates lack curiosity, innovation, and independent thinking which are perhaps more crucial in the knowledge-based economy. Chang however expressed ambivalence, fearing that his recommendations would be viewed as "anti-traditional" Asian values, but he insisted that a calculative and creative approach was only necessary in the workplace, and need not spread to the family and society, where Confucian respect of individuals and collectivities should remain the norm. There is the sense that the substantive logic can be protected from the risk-taking cutthroat attitude and behavior being foisted on the young in the new economy.

But such culturalist knowledge is undercut by the new economy's stress on the risk-taking market behavior. I had coffee with a stressed-out young banker at the end of a long day spent shifting around millions of US dollars by the minute. An employee of the Development Bank of Singapore (DBS), he complained that foreigners brought in new skills relentlessly driven by a bottom-line calculation. A young Singaporean told me that in the old regime job security was guaranteed by relations with the bosses, but now performances were what counted. The bottom-line calculation applies everywhere, so that even the smallest mistakes are unforgivable, and officers are driven to take more risks, take bigger positions and tolerate wider margins of wins and losses. Employees like him talk about the old breed of British trained bankers, comparing them to the foreign talent who are better paid. The change in focus is from trading to getting customers, to expand business through sales profits, to make DBS very risk-taking and very competitive. "We are to be more daring and aggressive, to take bigger positions, and make back losses." If he cannot keep up with the pace of winning back yesterday's losses, he will be out on his ear soon.

In short, for Singaporeans, the politics of comfort have shifted, and many have gotten hot under the collar from the elaborate welcoming-mat laid out for foreign expatriates. Expatriate fund managers, professors, and scientists appear to be the ones to enjoy the comforts with minimal controls, while locals are suffering from distinct discomfort and a feeling of being "invisibilized." Indeed, the scale of risk has widened, since citizens feel that they must compete not only with foreigners overseas but also on their own home turf. The new regime of high-value populations introduces new distinctions between preferred citizens – those who go through the special domains of expertise – and ordinary subjects less capable of meeting the challenges of the knowledge economy.

The new enterprise ecosystem has not been able to entirely regulate the flow of desired and undesirable populations, while the host society is feeling itself displaced. In the "flow through" populations, there are those who are desired as citizens but they do not stay long enough, i.e. many expatriate workers are on five-year contracts and the vast majority from Western countries and Australia do not intend to seek citizenship. An American working in a media company said that, although Singapore was a great place for an American who wants to be a global manager in Asia, he was tired of the fact that "local identity seems all wrapped up in economic values." He is married to a Singaporean but plans to leave, after making a bundle of money. Most Western expatriates want to leave after about three to seven years. The permanent residents mostly likely will come from mainland China and Indian students who have been lavished with scholarships and places in the university, forming the core of an elite scientific–technical class. Then there are those who desperately want to stay but are excluded, i.e. the Filipina maids, the Thai construction workers, the Indian day laborers, all of whom have not been given the opportunity to apply for permanent residence.

For locals who do not aspire to be elite professionals or new economy-managers, there is a sense of reverse *bumiputeraism* or nativism. *Bumiputera* refers to the native-born Malay majority in neighboring Malaysia who get preferential treatment in all areas of the economy, political hierarchy, and education. In contrast, Singaporeans, who have long felt superior to Malays in Malaysia and in Singapore itself, now feel themselves to be second-class citizens. Students are concerned about career chances, and they believe that they have become less eligible for university scholarships; for instance the NUS–MIT program awards twenty scholarships to foreign Asians who also receive fee waivers and other perks in education and employment. Singaporean professionals feel that they are losing out to foreigners who seem to be preferred by the government-led corporations and private industry. The majority seems won over by the state argument that expatriates add much-needed value to the entrepreneurial economy, but they live with the fear of competing within ever-widening scales of markets and geopolitical spaces.

With the rhetoric of Singapore as a global city, state authorities are privileging the globally marketable subject who must be induced to spend time in Singapore. An official boasts that, "In the 1970s we competed with Sri Lanka. In the 21st century, we compete with Tokyo, Sydney, Hong Kong, London, and New York, but it is cheaper to do business here." Already, the city is making plans to accommodate an additional population growth of 1.5 million by 2015, making the city into a high-density "Manhattan-style" housing space linked by connector parks and underground malls and mass-transit.[41] A little under twenty percent, or about 300,000 of the new people, are expected to be expatriates. A committee of academics and professionals urges the government to give attention to the building of a "softscape," or cultural areas centered on heritage buildings and historical neighborhoods in order to foster "a sense of rootedness in Singaporeans." This is a limited recognition of the fact that many are feeling increasingly invisibilized by the "flow-through" population of professionals and managers in an emerging "ecology of expertise."[42]

Singapore is becoming a prosthetically-enhanced nation. The bifurcation between a virtual digital ecosystem on the one hand, and an *oikos* being divested of its immediate past on the other, has induced feelings of inauthenticity. The ethical regime of knowledgeable and risk-taking subjects, and its vision of the good life in the ecosystem comes into conflict with a reduced sense of cultural moorings. Locals have begun to reflect on what it means to be citizens, because expatriates seem to have citizenship status, to be cajoled into becoming citizens even when reluctant to do so. Expatriates are now referred to as "citizens without local roots," while those who are technically citizens are beginning to feel unrooted. A young man looking for a university scholarship pointed out that expatriate permanent residents do not have to perform national service. All native male Singaporeans must spend at least two years in military service, submitting to the ultimate measure of citizenship, a project to build solidarity and loyalty, though it is clear that the island cannot really protect itself. Young men are put into the army at the age of 19 for two and a half years of "national service," and for some this means a lag to their launch into high-powered careers. Only students enrolled to study medicine at university and those who have been given government scholarships to study overseas are allowed to delay national service. There is resentment that expatriates who are not obligated to be in the national service are the ones to enjoy state largesse, scholarships, and employment in the new spaces of calculation. There is a sense of being re-nativized, of becoming subaltern subjects as in colonial times. At the same time, a new mode of subjection involves being biologically available as resources to global companies. This predicament attests to the blurring of *anthropos* and mere living forms, of *oikos* and material resources, as the fragile island struggles to find its place in the shifting networks of informational technology.

NOTES

1 Goh Chok Tong, "New Singapore", National Day Rally Speech 2001 at the National University of Singapore Cultural Centre, August 19 2001.
2 Michel Foucault, " 'Omnes et Singulatim': Towards A Critique of Political Reason," in James D. Faubion (ed.) *Power, Vol. 3, Essential Works of Foucault, 1954–1984* (New York: The New Press, 2000), pp. 198–325.
3 Nikolas Rose and Peter Miller, "Political Power Beyond the State: Problematics of Government," *British Journal of Sociology*, 43:2 (June 1992), 173–205 (p. 196).
4 Nikolas Rose, "Governing 'Advanced' Liberal Democracies," in A. Barry, T. Osbourne and N. Rose (eds) *Foucault and Political Reason: Liberalism, Neo-liberalism, and Rationalities of Government* (Chicago: University of Chicago Press, 1996), pp. 37–64.
5 T. Osborne and N. Rose, "In the Name of Society, or Three Theses on the History of Social Thought," *History of the Human Sciences*, 10:3 (1997), 87–104 (p. 89).
6 Paul Rabinow (n.d.) used the Greek terms *oikos* (home, society) and *anthropos* (human beings) to highlight an interest in distinctive relationships among knowledge, technical rationality, and modes of conduct in transforming and placing value on human beings and the forms of social life in modernity.
7 Economic Development Board (EDB), *Into the Fifth Decade* (Singapore: EDB, 2001), p. 10.
8 Chan Heng Chee, "Singapore's Globalization Soiree," Singapore Ambassador to Washington's Address at the Woodrow Wilson Center for Scholars, April 25 2001.
9 For a view of how the Deleuzian term assemblage has been recast to suggest specific mechanisms and spatial forms and effects that are at once concrete and discontinuous, see Stephen J. Collier and Aihwa Ong (eds) *Global Assemblages: Technology, Politics and Ethics in Anthropological Problems* (Blackwell, 2004).
10 Ricard V. Sole and Brian C. Goodwin, *Signs of Life: How Complexity Pervades Biology* (New York: Basic Books, 2000), pp. 199–200.
11 EDB, *Into the Fifth Decade*, p. 10.
12 Ibid.
13 See Kris Olds and Nigel Thrift, "Cultures on the Brink: Re-Engineering the Soul of Capitalism on a Global Scale," in Aihwa Ong and Stephen J. Collier (eds) *Global Assemblages: Technology, Politics and Ethics in Anthropological Problems* (Blackwell, 2004).
14 Aihwa Ong, "Ecologies of Expertise: Governmentality in Asian Knowledge Societies," in *Global Assemblages: Technology, Politics and Ethics in Anthropological Problems*.
15 Hannah Arendt, *The Human Condition,* with an introduction by Margaret Canovan (Chicago: University of Chicago Press, 1998), second edition. First published in 1976.
16 Rose and Miller, "Political Power Beyond the State: Problematics of Government".
17 Lee Hsien Loong, Deputy Prime Minister, speech at the launch of Manpower 21, August 31 1999.

18   Sole and Goodwin, 199–200.
19   Andrew Barry uses the term "technological zone" to describe a similar notion of translocal spaces shaped by capital and technological instruments for maintaining competitiveness. See *Political Machines: Governing a Technological Society* (London: The Athlone Press, 2001), pp. 2–3.
20   "The NUS Enterprise: A Hotbed for Entrepreneurship," *The Alumnus*, no. 48 (January 2002), 12–16.
21   Go to http://www.sma.nus.edu.sg.
22   Tony Tan, Keynote Address at the Singapore–MIT Alliance Symposium, January 2002.
23   *The Alumnus*, p.15.
24   Edison Liu, Genome Institute of Singapore brochure, n.d.
25   Nikolas Rose and Carlos Novas "Biological Citizenship," in Aihwa Ong and Stephen Collier, eds, *Blackwell Companion to Global Anthropology*, Oxford: Blackwell, 2003.
26   Paul Rabinow, "The Third Culture," *History of the Human Sciences*, 7:2 (1994), 53–64.
27   "Cloning gets nod from Singapore," *The Straits Times*, January 4 2002.
28   Mui Teng Yap, "Singapore's 'Three or More' Policy: the First Five Years," *Asia-Pacific Population Journal*, 10:4 (1996), 39–52.
29   Richard Leete, "The Continuing Flight from Marriage and Parenthood among the Overseas Chinese in East and Southeast Asia: Dimensions and Implications," *Population and Development Review*, 20:4 (December 1994), 811–829.
30   Geraldine Heng and Janadas Devan, "State Fatherhood: the Politics of Nationalism, Sexuality and Race in Singapore," in Aihwa Ong and Michael Peletz (eds) *Bewitching Women, Pious Men* (Berkeley: University of California Press, 1995), pp. 195–215.
31   Lee Boon Yang, minister for manpower address at the National Manpower Summit, "Managing Human Capital for Change," October 18 2001.
32   "It's Here!" *Manpower News* (September 2001), 1.
33   "Looming clash over foreign talents," *The Straits Times*, October 24 2001.
34   "Foreign talents boosted GDP by 20 percent in last decade: SM Lee," *The Straits Times*, October 30 2001.
35   Tan Kong Yam *et al.*, "Has Foreign Talent contributed to Singapore's Economic Growth? An Empirical Assessment," Report by the Singapore Ministry of Trade and Industry (2002).
36   David Stark, "Values, Values and Valuation: Work and Worth in the New Economy," paper presented at the SSRC conference on "The New Economy", Emory University, Atlanta, April 13–14 2001.
37   Chan Kwok Ban and Claire Chiang, *Stepping Out: the Making of Chinese Entrepreneurs* (Singapore: Simon & Schuster, 1994).
38   Daniel Lian, "Singapore: New Economy Proletariat or Bourgeoisie?", Morgan Stanley Global Economic Forum, January 16 2001.
39   Cherian George, *Singapore: The Air-Conditioned Nation* (Singapore: Landmark Books, 2000).
40   Morris Chang, "Human Resources for Technology and Innovation in Southeast Asia," presented at the Singapore–MIT Alliance Symposium, January 2002.
41   EDB Concept Plan Committee, *Responses to Recommendations on Housing* (Singapore: EDB, 2001).
42   Aihwa Ong, "Ecologies of Expertise: Governmentality in Asian Knowledge Societies," in *Global Assemblages: Technology, Politics and Ethics in Anthropological Problems.*

Chapter 13: As the Wind Blows and Dew Came Down: Ghost Stories and Collective Memory in Singapore

Carole Faucher

> I would like to take this opportunity to give readers, especially the "younger generation" of Singaporeans, a glimpse of what life was like in Singapore under Japanese military rule during World War II. I think it is important to try and understand the terror and desperation of the population; their constant fear of being arrested by the Japanese military/secret police (*kempeitai*), the inevitable torture they would suffer and the ever-present threat of death.[1]

In the introduction to the first chapter of a book entitled *There are Ghosts Everywhere in Singapore*, volume two, the author – whose pen name is John Ong – of "Six Selected War-Time Ghost Stories" appears to have given himself the mandate of educating readers about the trials of his fellow Singaporeans and of the British during the years of the Japanese Occupation. Four of the horror tales that constitute the chapter are presented as his own "true" experiences with "ghosts and demons," and two as being told to him by "others" he met in slave labor camps when he was a teenager. What particularly drew my attention to these tales is the fact that, for each one, the ghostly encounter itself is the segment that triggers the least feeling of horror. The writing is, in fact, poignant to the extent that when it comes to identifying the dreadfulness of private experiences under conditions of war, the boundaries between the living and spiritual worlds prove to be totally irrelevant.

In one of the stories, the narrator recounts the raping of his two teenage sisters and his mother in front of his father's eyes by a group of Japanese soldiers. Afterwards, all the family members (with the exception of the narrator) are killed, and the house is burned down. All together, three ghosts appear in the short story. One of them is the specter of his own father "smoking a long bamboo pipe" under a mango tree the latter had planted while still alive. The other two are the specters of a decapitated Japanese soldier and a young Chinese wearing "the blue uniform of the commando." They appear before him next to a path leading to the labor camps. The specter of the commando is walking behind the headless ghost of the Japanese carrying "a severed head which was dripping blood." The percipient deduced that the Chinese beheaded the Japanese soldier and was himself "shot dead" right after by other Japanese soldiers. The first ghost – his father's – is obviously reminiscent of the narrator's family's brutal massacre while the Japanese and Chinese ghosts do not seem at first glance to be associated in any way with his immediate ordeal. Despite the fact that these specters' sudden appearance in the text is absolutely unexpected, the level of horror generated barely measures up to the "real" event described earlier. In this case, as in the majority of cases I will discuss later, ghosts not only scare individuals who encounter them, but, peculiarly, quite often reassure them as well, precisely because they are just ghosts. "As we began to back away on our trembling legs, the ghosts walked away," writes the author. How can the percipient not feel relatively safe when he finds out that he cannot be physically harmed by the dreadful figures, or realizes that it does not even appear to be their intention to do so in the first place?

Another story, "The Ghosts of Alexandra Military Hospital," begins with a brief but detailed account of the massacre of the British staff and the patients in Alexandra Hospital by the Japanese 18th Division, two days before the surrender of Singapore. The narrator claims that later on, he was part of the forced labor team that was ordered to clean up the areas around the hospital where "heavy fighting" had occurred. Alexandra Hospital was, by then, used for wounded Japanese soldiers. While on duty, the narrator and his mate had a ghostly encounter:

> We heard women calling out, "Please don't kill us! Have merci!" [sic] And the sound of shots being fired and the cries of people in pain. The shooting and screams went on until dawn. It was all so real that we expected to find dead bodies everywhere when we went to take a look – but there was nothing to be seen.

The massacre at Alexandra Hospital by the Japanese invaders is well inscribed in Singapore's social memory. What more then can these ghosts tell us about the tragic incident? Ong's short tales are particularly relevant to me because they are blatantly introduced as personal memories of the Second World War, and a part of these personal memories is encounters with ghosts, thus imposing de facto on texts that are supposed to be war recollections a sort of out-of-this-world aura. It should be obvious that a story, to qualify as a "ghost story," must refer to ghosts at some point. But in this case it seems that only when the story line absorbs both memories and the supernatural, can we talk about horror tales.

The memory of the Japanese Occupation haunts Singaporeans almost endlessly, through a multitude of means, and ghost narratives are among the most common. Haunting sites vary in popular literature, oral tradition, web sites and school textbooks – from parks, army camps, beaches and reservoir areas, to residential blocks, colonial buildings and so on. The significant number of popular locally published horror series that depict chilling encounters with ghosts rightly suggests that the living and the dead share a common space in the nation state.[2] When I first started digging into the vast repertoire of spiritual beings termed "ghosts" in Singapore, I stumbled onto a host of tales embedded with horrific qualities drawn from traumatic memories of the Japanese Occupation years, such as the ones mentioned earlier. Thus, I came across the specters of Japanese sentries, of victims of the Sook Ching, of British soldiers and their families – sometimes floating above the seashore, on other occasions, roaming around colonial buildings. Here were some of the atrocities of war packaged into cheap best-selling horror thrillers, along with fierce Indian or Malay mythological creatures and pitiful souls of the dead. The use of the broad category of "ghosts" to refer to any of the supernatural creatures haunting Singapore reminds us that the uncanny here undeniably mirrors the state ideal of cross-ethnic national loyalty. For many Singaporean youths, the Japanese Occupation exists as a mapping of creepy haunting sites, at least as much as they reflect the detailed historical accounts they are compelled to memorize in school. In this article I will examine how popular cultural sites, together with the official historical discourse, interact in creating platforms where memories of the Second World War may be experienced over and over again outside the unequivocal sphere of commemoration.[3] I will thus visit briefly some of these sites, spending most of the time in trying to "capture" the specters reminiscent of war memories among a fantastic array of ghosts and mythical creatures. I will also examine the negotiation between the images of Japan provided by these sites and the current popular representations of the contemporary Japan of *manga* and boy-bands.

According to Bennet (1999), there are two basic types of hauntings by ghosts: some ghosts haunt persons while others haunt locations. Singaporean ghosts all belong to the second category. Even when structures are demolished or when the physical environment has been drastically altered over the years, ghosts continue to hang around. For instance, specters recalling the Japanese Occupation can all be found trapped in the last location they were alive, whining, menacing or engrossed in earthly tasks. In some respects, ghosts can prove to be extremely informative. They give us glimpses of history and, thus, can be associated with the collective memory as agents of remembrance or *point de repère*. Furthermore, hauntings can provide us with an important source of sociological information (Gordon, 1997); since ghosts make us a part of their story, they must speak to us in order to exist as ghosts. Ghosts are, in the sense conveyed by Bergson, "presence" (Matsuda, 1996). How do we interact with them? For nearly all the cases of reported hauntings in the local popular tradition, specters make themselves felt prior to their appearance. We interact with them by "knowing" beforehand that we can find them, by feeling the vibrations of their suffering or sorrow, or more simply their former existence as human beings, as it already appears in other realms of memory. Haunted sites are first of all performance spaces, where one can go on specific days and at specific times with an eagerness to experience some of the emotional remains of historical drama. The most popular haunting locations in Singapore are the ones that commonly bore witness to a dramatic and/or sudden death that can be associated with collective trauma.

FROM JAPANESE SOLDIERS TO J-POP: MEMORIES AND POPULAR CULTURE

The invasion of J-pop culture into Singapore plays a large part in drawing a clear-cut distinction between the Japanese who appear in ghost narratives and today's Japan, in the same way that young Singaporeans cut themselves off from past memories by revisiting sites of massacres as places of excitement. In ghost narratives, a "Japanese" is invariably a character emerging from the Second World War, essentially a mythical figure that has the potential to be as menacing as any dreadful legendary ghost can be. The Japan of today is deemed as "trendy" and "non-conservative" by young Chinese Singaporeans, who try to emulate the characters of Nippon TV series and J-pop stars. The androgynous look of boy-band members redefines the concept of male beauty among young Chinese Singaporeans; it is the fashionable "Asian look" that provides grounds for a powerful local identity in reaction to "Western" appeal. The appeal of the "sweet" look of Japanese idols such as Kimura Takuya or the Kinki Kids, as part of Japan's "soft power" in the Asian region (Ching, 2001: 294) cohabits with memories of the Pacific war without ever interacting with them. Lisa, a 23-year-old female Chinese Singaporean explains:

> The Japanese Occupation belongs to the past. We learned about the Japanese Occupation through our history textbooks in primary school. For us, the Japanese Occupation is essentially a number of buildings, of sites, of commemorative monuments that we had to memorize. And then and after, we watched it over and over again on Channel 8 [the local Chinese TV channel] . . . Hundreds of drama series which always relate the same story, always convey the same stereotypes, same as in our textbooks: the Chinese are courageous, the English are a bunch of cowards, and the Japanese are cruel. The latter are in fact always portrayed as "macho," of short stature and with a bit of mustache under the nose . . . this image is a far cry from the *kawaii* [cute] look of J-Pop male artists.[4]

In my view, between the actual J-pop invasion and the public memories of the Japanese of the Second World War, there is not so much of a rupture as it would appear at first glance in the above quotation, but, instead, there is a state of mediation in which popular ghost stories play an important part.

The main contention of this paper is that specters may be viewed as emotion-laden memories that produce an alternative mode of dealing with official historical accounts. The emotions that we feel when visiting a haunted site, quite often, make a much stronger impact on us than a description of the historical facts supporting the haunting itself. The cognitive scenario that accompanies feelings of fear, anxiety and amazement usually includes a systematic validation of the haunting through already digested information. Interestingly, popular written ghost stories quite often include historical facts that highlight particularly gruesome and morbid details. It is also quite common to come across local horror tales that focus more on the account of "what really happened there years ago" than on the actual haunting account. Thus, searching for evidence that a haunting is really taking place somewhere should begin, interestingly, with reading history books; the percipients are not necessarily looking for phantoms as much as they are looking for tangible clues about the national past.

The years of 1942 to 1945 have left a legacy of an incredible number of haunted sites, mostly for reasons pertaining to Chinese tradition. Sudden and violent deaths, mass burials and non-performance of proper burial rituals are among some of the important causes for souls not being able to pass to the other world and, therefore, being forced to remain captives of these sites. However, the majority of ghost narratives pertaining to the Japanese Occupation in Singapore are also reminiscent of the official history in all respects. These narratives differ greatly from other accounts that depict specters that denounce – just by their incessant whining – the excavation of cemeteries, the expropriation of residential areas or the demolition of well-liked aged buildings.[5]

Ghost stories, drawn from the cultural world-view and cosmologies of the different ethnic groups officially recognized in Singapore, are also propitious sites for breeding public awareness on the need for unity and solidarity against impending and hidden threats. Each of the "ghost stories" books closely follows the CMIO (Chinese–Malay–Indian–Other) racial model. Each of these books, which bear blunt titles such as *Army Ghosts*, *Taxi Driver's Nightmare* or more simply

Singapore Ghost Stories, regroups short narratives depicting interaction between human beings and various supernatural characters. The editors of the most popular series claim to publish accounts sent by people who identify themselves as first-hand witnesses. In the *Singapore Popular Ghost Stories* collection edited by a team collectively and pseudonymously known as Russell Lee, the short stories are often published with the name, age and occupation of their contributors. Stories exposing various types of spiritual creatures are carefully put together in order to present a complete assortment. For example, each *Ghost Stories* book displays its share of *pontianaks,* ugly vampire-like spirits originating in Malay folk religion who transform themselves into beautiful women dressed in white. Interestingly, Malay spirits, known in Malay as *hantu-hantu*, are the most feared. They comprise a whole range of dreadful creatures, such as the *orang minya* (oily man) and the *pennungu* (a woman spirit that flies around village houses with her intestines exposed). These trickster spirits are believed to haunt particular public parks at night, as they prey on young drunken men or promiscuous unmarried couples. Although they are not the lost souls of dead people, their quality as rural spirits is also reminiscent of Singapore prior to urbanization, and even before British colonization. Due to their importance in both Malaysian and Singaporean haunting scenes, these spirits merit some mention. They form a necessary part of the ghost story corpus, and it is worth mentioning that they are the only spectral beings that remind us of pre-colonial times. Because of this broad category of "ghosts," memories of the Japanese Occupation – of the victims of the *Sook Ching* – are recalled along with non-human mythology, in the same way that the recollections of both victims and perpetrators of the Second World War massacres mingle together to provide a spine-chilling form of popular entertainment. At first glance, popular literature appears to disparage war memories. On the other hand, it is also possible to read these horror stories as moving historical accounts, standing miles away from the rigidity of history textbooks.

The popularity of local horror literature based on witness accounts is only one manifestation of the appeal of ghostly matters in Singapore. Ghost haunting is also a well-liked activity among Singaporean youth, and accounts of "field-trips" can be read on popular web sites, whose numbers are always growing. It is worth noting that the sites visited by organized or spontaneous ghost hunting excursions systematically exclude, at least in the cases I have encountered, all the favorite haunting spots of the dreadful *pontianak* and other essentially myth-ical numinous creatures. Does this mean that mythical creatures are deemed potentially more dangerous, and more "real" than war ghosts? Narrators of war ghost stories tend to regularly use the metaphor of time travel. Encounters with specters of Japanese soldiers appear to abruptly take them back in time. On the other hand, the *pontianak* shares with the vampire a timeless nature. The sugges-tion that emotions seem fundamentally opposed to the historical enterprise (Rosenwein, 2002) might help in explaining why popular literature seems to provide an appropriate terrain for the exploration of emotions and for the reconciliation between private feelings and historical facts.

HAUNTING AND REMEMBRANCE

Collective memory is extremely difficult to tackle in Singapore. Sites are vanishing regularly to give way to new, "clean" structures, and oral transmission between generations is diminishing, especially among the Chinese population, the majority race in the country. This can be traced owing to a number of reasons, such as the lack of fluency in the grandparents' Chinese dialects due to the government's Speak Mandarin policies in mass media and education; and religious conversions that hinder the passing on of a number of cultural traditions. Without oral transmission, and without physical markers besides commemorative monuments, (I mean here structures old enough to "remember"), there is a decreasing number of voices that propose alternative histories. In a forum organized by the Singapore Heritage Society, a non-governmental organization dedicated to the preservation of the local heritage, an architect reminded us that:

> Because it persists locally in time, space and substance, architecture inspires us to remember, and to reconstruct events, and most importantly, our ancestors' events.
> It is hence an important link in any intergenerational ties. Moreover, architecture serves memory not because it contains memories, but because it insists that we remember.
> (Tan, 2001: 73)

This forum was organized in response to a state decision to demolish the National Library despite public concern. Architecture, in the Singaporean context, does not play much of a role in helping people remember, but often operates, instead, as an agent of forgetting. In fact, it provokes people to imagine the nation-building process, not in terms of historical continuity but in terms of a series of juxtaposed and disconnected periods and events embodied in selected preserved buildings, commemorative monuments and museum exhibitions. In contrast, specters engage us in a scheme of continuity, intertwining their own wandering with undifferentiated glimpses of recent and distant pasts. Haunted sites, thus, are often recently built structures, which, only by their quality of being new, should not convey any feelings of eeriness. In the local slang, Singlish, new buildings are coined as "clean." This alludes to being free of ghosts and spirits, in opposition to "dirty," which refers to being haunted. This "cleanliness," interestingly, is rarely taken for granted unless the site has already been "cleaned" through proper religious rituals, usually conducted by Taoist priests. New physical structures can possibly host ghosts whose origins date back many generations, and these spectral beings become a "presence" through rumors and word of mouth rather than through witness accounts – presence that conveys much about the specific historical trajectory of the location. Ghosts are trapped in specific locations, those locations that have "made" them, and never venture outside this space. Any particular location might embody a series of successive changes to its land use, most of them short term if we compare with other urban landscapes. For each layer of occupation, there is usually a ghost that helps us to remember a given use of the site – an individual who has committed suicide or whose corpse is buried there, the victim of a tragedy, a war martyr, a soldier killed in battle, and so on. Other times, there are no signs of an actual death, but simply the reminiscence of a presence, of someone who has once been there. To see them, or to feel the emotion they embody, one must visit the ghostly dwelling with the intention or, at the least, with some level of expectation that contact will occur.

As Halbwachs' significant concept details, ghost narratives often are the only *points de repère* or referent to past events and specific historical trajectories. Ghosts commonly outlast the demolition of buildings, when they are not actually produced out of the annihilation of the same structure they are rumored to recall. In Singapore, memory is carefully organized in a manner that not only advocates state ideology – which would not be a sharp contrast to the logic behind official history in general – but is primarily concerned with forgetting, sometimes to the point of erasure. Questions of memory are always political (Waterson and Kwok, 2002: 367), so the overwhelming presence of ghosts borne out of the Japanese Occupation period compared to other important periods in the Singapore history certainly bear political attributes, reminding us of the prevalence of socio-cultural engineering of national amnesia (Wee, 2002: 148). Incidentally, one of the most dramatic periods in Singapore's short history, the three years of the Japanese Occupation, is constantly revived through permanent museum exhibitions, television series, popular literature and other aspects of the popular cultural scene. In popular ghost stories, Japanese sentries appear as frequently as the mythical *pontianak*, conveying the same disturbing sensation of creepiness. Is it possible, in this context, to still put a human face to some of the most brutal deeds perpetrated by the Japanese military during the Occupation? Despite almost two centuries of continuous Japanese presence in Singapore, most of the time non-military, the term "Japanese" in the jargon of local horror stories always refers uniquely to Second World War Japanese soldiers in uniform. I believe that this process of dehumanization of some of the actors of the War through popular culture is partly responsible for the lack of connection Singaporean youth draw between the Japanese of the Occupation and the contemporary Japan of popular culture. This despite the fact that, amazingly, some of the authors of popular ghost stories make a point of educating the population on the trauma of the war years as it was discussed earlier.

If we are to imagine ghost narratives as part of the nation-state's collective memory, certainly we would have to point to the Japanese Occupation as the founding myth of the actual Singapore. No ghost story whose eerie characters emerged from an earlier period – and, in a matter of fact, from a later period – is so openly positioned in a political context. The Japanese Occupation appears to be the only tragic period in Singapore that has produced historical ghosts. I have not once come across ghost stories that remind us of any other dramatic period in the nation-state's history, such as the ethnic riots of the 1960s and 1970s or the 1963 to 1965 *Konfrontasi* (the confrontation between Indonesia and Malaysia) for instance. It seems that all other specters that come out of this period are essentially the reenactment of private drama.

There is a dialectic at play between the ghost and its site of haunting, the site where the ghost is produced as well as where it reproduces itself (Hamonic, 1995). In the course of this dialectical process, ghosts lose their former human personality – just by the mere fact that we call them "ghosts" – at the same time that they become image-memories, not in the sense of Ricoeur and Bergson's pure image-memories, but repeated lessons about the unfolding of a particular dramatic historical trajectory at a particular location. Ghosts are collective *points de repère*. These collective *points de repère* help us to locate historical events in a group's trajectory; as Halbwachs states, these memories thus come back to us in an extremely simplified version. These *points de repère*, he continues, are states of consciousness that by their intensity struggle better against forgetting (1994: 125).[6] This signifies that remembering is, above all, a private experience, and the emotion generated by the expectation of a ghostly encounter can only be recounted in personal terms. What seems to make ghosts so terrifying is not even, in fact, their ethereal quality so much as the representation they embody. In the cases of soldiers' ghosts, the awareness of seeing a "ghost" seems to be, in all the narratives I have come across so far, strangely, reassuring. Haunted sites provide a stage for experimenting with what fear would feel like if history were to repeat itself. Haunting means that the traumatic memories and the painful emotions ghosts carry transcend the ever-changing urban landscape, handing down awareness and reflections on the possibilities of waking up suddenly in a similar situation. We are, thus, talking about the encounter with an historical marker and a particular emotion, not with a threatening being. As is the case with one of Singaporean novelist Catherine Lim's ghostly characters, the terrifying aura originates from its former role as a living being, not from its numinous existence.

> I wish I could throw a romantic aura over this lonely, intense man who has been walking the earth these 40 years, consign him to the misty world of ethereal beings that mystifies, even charms. But the soldier seems only to want to terrify. He seems too tangible a presence, too powerful a force to be coaxed away by prayers and offerings. (Lim, 1983: 100)

For Lim, the ghost is a lonely, mysterious being, while the soldier triggers intense fear. This "powerful" force that Lim is referring to takes us back, essentially, to what a Japanese soldier represented in the specific conjuncture of the most tragic moments of the Occupation. There is no doubt that there is an intense connection between a building or a landscape and traumatic emotions that ghosts, as *points de repère*, help us to "feel." Halbwachs mentioned that he had felt the vibrations of an event that had occurred 100 years before his birth, that this past had been internalized to the point that it became his own private past. For him, memory is essentially a social phenomenon that always moves from the collective to the private. I would like to postulate, however, that in the cases I am concerned with, memory is not – or is rarely – internalized. On the contrary, it reaffirms its objectified quality. The experience of expecting a spectral encounter is ultimately private, and in concordance with Halbwachs' idea of "feeling vibrations of the past." Yet, there is also a clear awareness that the memory, as a ghost, remains outside the self and, thus, can be called or avoided almost at will.

The majority of the stories in the abundant popular literature put into play both spectral and human characters emerging from the different traditions that form the cultural landscape of Singapore. There are for example, *bomohs*, and Taoist and Hindu priests. These stories often translate the duality between "clean" and "dirty" into good and evil in extremely moralistic terms, loaded with reference to Christian and Islamic moral frames of conduct (incidentally, in Mandarin and some Chinese dialects a haunted place is referred to as a "dirty" place); however, narratives alluding to the Japanese Occupation depict experiences in which religious or moral sentiments are usually left out. Except on rare occasions – such as a narrative in which a Taoist priest is held accountable for the fall of Singapore by having attracted the devil while attempting to stop the Japanese invasion through magical means – these tales are essentially never-ending reenactments of traumatic events, charging the current Singaporean landscape with hologram-like images or recording-like sounds of Japanese soldiers and of victims of the mass killings. Narrators commonly underline the fact that they enter the scene willingly, embodying and living through the fears of the victims. It is this overlapping of past and present that constitutes, in my view, the rapport to the past (*rapport au passé*). Through this process, traumatic events are acted upon, deeply felt and identified as part of one's own private historical trajectory:

> I heard stories from people who have been working there for years. Lots of things have happened, sometimes at 3am you can hear the army march, gun shots, ladies and babies crying and many eerie voices. When I first heard about it, I thought it was the squad or army training in early morning but later on I find it [*sic*] something fishy . . . I heard people talking in Japanese. I asked my self . . . am I back [*sic*] in year 1942?[7]

THE TEMPORAL AND SPATIAL SPECIFICITY OF SPECTERS

The following comes from an internet account of a night excursion organized at Punggol Beach by a society concerned with paranormal activities: "We walked near to the seashore . . . and mostly we wanted to sense about [*sic*] the dark ambience of the beach where innocent men where slaughtered." The ghostly occurrence reported in this account is the seeing of "ghostly orbs" by the members of the groups. Besides this mysterious encounter, the three web pages describe and question unusual religious offerings and physical evidence of the massacres. "One conclusion with high certainty that we can draw," the piece claims, "is that Punggol Beach is a very ghostly haunted place. Many were killed years ago and religious cults are still operating actively here." In addition, the web site offers an amalgamation of information in the form of historical facts, well-known eyewitness versions of the massacres, and descriptions of some of the most popular haunting locations.

Stories are always located both in time and space; sometimes, just an indication of the location suffices for the reader to grasp the whole context. Changi Beach, Sentosa, Pulau Ubin, Dempsey Road football field, Kent Ridge Park, Tanah Merah, and Punggol Beach are among the locations where one can expect Second World War spectral reenactments. Most of the beaches, reclaimed land, reservoirs, islands and parks in the nation-state are reputed to be haunted by Japanese soldiers and by victims of their atrocities. More important than "seeing" a ghost is the "expectation" of an eerie feeling. Haunted sites are places where one expects not only mystical occurrences, but also particular sensations charged with feelings of sorrow and disempowerment. This experience is lived through the expectation itself, through the fear – or pleasure – this expectation generates. Narratives describing this plunge into war memories are validated through the skill displayed by the narrators in conveying these feelings:

> As the wind blows and dews came down, I suddenly felt chill all over. I crossed my arms hoping to keep myself warm. What I heard next can never be erased from my mind. I heard footsteps at first coming closer to me. The footsteps suddenly stop right next to me. Then came voices, speaking in Japanese, from whispers, it turned to laughter followed by gunshots and screams. I shut my eyes tightly and prayed that it will stop. [There were] screams of children, women and men crying. I was really terrified and wanted to get up and run.[8]

Everyone sat up in bed and listened, hearing a million panicking voices and gunshots. The sounds were loud and terrible and they knew that they were not just figments of their imaginations because the very ground itself was vibrating from the sound waves . . . It sounded as if a war had started outside the tent on the shore of the beach they were camped on.[9]

Army camps are, not too surprisingly, other significant sites of spectral encounters with Japanese sentries. For young Singaporean males, the prospect of having to cope with ghostly matters at one point or another during their two years of compulsory National Service are, in fact, quite high. Specters of Japanese are among the most common ghosts, together with old Chinese men and pretty young women that are believed to haunt these spaces. In all the stories I have come across so far, these ghosts walk alone or in twos, usually doing their rounds at night around the camp, or haunting the toilets. Rumors of apparitions and of other signs of haunting, such as cracking sounds near specific barracks and even direct attacks on persons, apparently foster order and discipline among the trainees, as an ex-National Service man explained to me:

When I did my service both on Pulau Tekong and then in Jurong camp, I heard a lot of stories about Japanese soldiers waiting silently in the dark ready for ambush or else hiding in the toilets. These rumors were circulating around and we were all extremely nervous when it was our turn to perform night duties. I think today that these scary stories were an important part of our training . . . how to train our mind not to be afraid of anything. We were told also that, if our mind were clear all the time, if we were performing our duties correctly, all the chances were that we would never encounter any ghosts.

Ghosts wander about in army camps reminding the young NS man of the fact that they must be in control at all times for the history not to repeat itself. In order to defend the nation, they must be able first to eliminate their own fear of ghosts. This contrasts sharply with British soldiers in ghost stories who appear as desperate or as being totally taken aback by the Japanese invasion. It seems that, even decades after their death, they still cannot cope with the feelings of surprise and helplessness. An important number of ghost stories put into play British military characters (who are always portrayed as benevolent), such as high-ranking officers or their family members, soldiers and nurses who mingle incessantly with their own misery as war victims. It is this moment that is frozen; their own sorrow, fears and anticipation that are stuck in a given space, which haunts places:

A British major, whose wife and two daughters were tortured, raped and killed, can still be heard weeping for his family. Sometimes, if you wait at the junction of Loyang Avenue and Changi Village Road, you can see this British family walking down Changi Village road.[10]

In many other verbal accounts, British children, most often girls, can be heard or seen at night crying for their mothers or fathers killed by Japanese soldiers. Others, such as the doctors and nurses who are known to haunt the surgery rooms of Alexandra Hospital, go about their own affairs without showing any signs of despair. These spectral beings do not trigger a remembrance of the Japanese Occupation as much as they actually erase any traces of memory of the war by providing a sense of continuity between the period preceding the events that caused their deaths and what should have followed had the event not taken place. One will refer to an English surgeon or sergeant, a nurse moving about as living beings do, pursuing their activities without disturbing anyone: they simply are. It is, essentially, the suspicion of their perpetual presence that makes them ghosts. Interestingly, all the ghosts of British colonialists appear against the backdrop of the Second World War, almost as if the pre-war period has not produced any ghosts reminiscent of the colonial past before the war. Furthermore, British ghosts always appear as kindhearted and gentle, showing no trace of the distance, coolness and (sometimes) disdain with which they ruled Malaya, especially before the surrender to the Japanese. Mary Thomas, a former British nurse who was interned in Singapore during the three years of the Occupation, noted in her memoirs:

> In sharing the trials and troubles of enemy occupation with the local-born people of Malaya, we felt we were forging with them a link of friendship that could not be broken, since there is no bond closer than that of shared danger and oppression. (1983: 164)

As Thomas rightly suggested, the sharing of war oppression has erased any memory of previous ordeals imposed by the colonial masters. This is quite faithfully reflected in ghost narratives where the specters of British, military or civilian, appear. These ghosts are part of war memories, including the before and after, reinforcing the British image as benevolent rulers. Interestingly, however, I have not so far come across any narrative that depicts encounters with Indian or Gurka soldiers. In reality, they were important components of the British military. Their entire absence (or erasure?) from the corpus of ghost narratives is, no doubt, significant. Ghosts are the spirits of the ruled and the rulers, and foreign troops, even though they were from contemporary British colonies, do not belong to either group. Matsuda notes: "memory serves as a point of judgment not simply by recording the past, but by giving its re-speaking both language and gesture, creating the possibility for 'ideal speech acts' and their opposites to contest one another" (1996: 14). Ghost narratives are, in my view, the interaction between the living and the past reinvented – or reorganized – through a rhetoric of sharply defined oppositions that are already thriving in public discourse.

As with Catherine Lim's ghostly character mentioned earlier, there are ghosts whose existence is a never-ending reenactment of their last moments. Among the most well-known rumors are the ones that refer to regular "sightings" at Alexandra Hospital of English surgeons or nurses carrying out their duties as they most probably did hours before the massacre of staff and patients on the night of 15 February 1942, as if the dramatic event never occurred. "They just don't know they are dead because it happened too suddenly," a local Chinese woman who had been warded once at the hospital explained to me.

The city landscape of Singapore is a site for private memories: Japanese soldier specters that haunt buildings, such as the poor fellow trapped in the air conditioning piping of the old Cathay Building, are often stripped of their fierce qualities through isolation. They do not trigger fear as much as sorrow or ridicule. In another popular story, three specters of Japanese soldiers reenact endlessly the performance of hara-kiri in the condemned room of a pricey hotel. These ghosts usually represent those vanquished at the end of the war, such as individuals who chose to end their lives rather than surrender. The memories they embody are absolutely private; they are disengaged from their former role as if their military authority had been vanquished within the city walls, condemned to haunt and to be haunted by their own losses. Japanese ghosts in city buildings always manifest themselves as isolated figures and in unthreatening ways, as if to signify that city buildings are no longer the target of their military power. In encounters with city ghosts of Japanese soldiers, there is no expectation of interaction; there is no fear of being suddenly involved in a dreadful situation where one has to react, when one's life will be challenged.

If Japanese soldiers and *Kempeitai* agents continue to haunt beaches and military camps, the urban space accommodates soldiers confronting their own morality, such as narratives depicting reenactments of hara-kiri in vacant houses or hotel rooms, or lost souls seeking redemption and mercy. One of the most eloquent stories in this respect, "The Campus Spirit," was written by Goh Sin Tub. In it, a Japanese university student who had read extensively on the atrocities of war while in Singapore is "visited" by the ghost of his great-grandfather which had been haunting one of the campus buildings for years. The contact with the specter is established in cyberspace. The great-grandfather pleads to be liberated from his torments and explains how he was compelled to perpetrate acts of brutality during the war, acts that he now regrets deeply.

In natural spatial environments, more specifically in the periphery of the city, spectral scenes bring an awareness, as well as the imagery, of collective suffering and despair: as if the war had never ended, as if the *Kempeitai* continue to prey on the civilians, aided by their post-mortem invisibility. The ongoing anticipation of these spectral scenes echoes the state's discourse about the necessity of a strong military defense. The display of military arsenal during National Day celebrations is one of the eloquent examples of how the state calls attention to the imperative for strong military power. But, the question remains: to protect Singapore against whom? This question is never openly tackled, while the shadows of Japanese soldiers continue to haunt bookstores and the mass media. In the trailer for a series on the Japanese Occupation on the English-speaking TV channel, we glimpse a battalion of Japanese soldiers making its way at night on bicycles along a bushy path. The fifteen-second trailer remains powerfully soundless, leading the viewer to imagine the enemy entering Singapore silently, sneaking through the island's uninhabited land or reservoir areas, unfolding in the audience's consciousness the dramatic turn of events that is already deep-seated in collective memory and official history. However, far from being imagined for this specific series, this mute, unexpected and unannounced penetration of Japanese soldiers onto Singapore soil, walking, cycling or even swimming across the Johor Strait, is in fact one of the key representations of the Japanese invasion into popular discourse.

The mapping of haunted sites is modeled on history textbooks – as sites that hold memories of atrocities of war rather than as being simply ghostly. Unlike other characters of ghost stories that are born through religious traditions and cultural knowledge, ghosts of the Japanese Occupation come into awareness both through actions pertaining to the construction of national identity – such as the learning of modern history in schools and National Service – and through oral narratives (the style favored by ghost story publishers). Singapore's ghost stories rarely venture beyond the Japanese Occupation as if Singapore's past was converging itself to that specific point in time. The ghosts of the beheaded Malay regiment marching through Kent Ridge Park or floating above the Ayer Rajah Expressway on some nights are expected only by those who have already learnt, through official history or oral tradition, the tragic event that left the Malay regiment annihilated and massacred by Japanese invaders on a night in February 1942. The Malay regiment members are, no doubt, elevated to the rank of national heroes in Singapore's history. Nevertheless, as far as I know, only the massacre which is now commemorated in Kent Ridge Park has left Malay ghosts in legacy. Besides this event, Malay soldiers are absolutely non-existent in popular ghost stories, as are Indian soldiers.

GHOSTS, HISTORICITY AND MEMORY

We "know" that a place is haunted because we have already learnt about a particular event involving a tragic death at this same location. On an evening field-trip taken by forty second-year university students to the Ford Factory, all of them depicted the building as being one of the most haunted in Singapore. However, only two of them were able to recall a ghost story. But all of them remembered having seen this historic building, where Singapore surrendered in the Second World War, for the first time in their school textbooks. "Because of what happened here, it can only be haunted," remarked one of the students. Ghosts are memories that are located somewhere between official history and private remembrance.

Eerie experiences are ultimately private ones. In most stories, some see the ghost while others do not; ghost encounters are always privileged encounters, sometimes triggered by the simple desire to experience it, other times occurring because of the percipient's momentary moral weakness. Emotions such as sadness, fear and powerlessness surface in most of these stories. There are no "real" group encounters; emotional experiences remain private, although sometimes similar and ready to be shared.

We may ask the question: are these ghost stories sites of remembrance or of forgetting? Is the social trauma pertaining to the Japanese Occupation being dealt with through popular culture? Both ghost stories reminiscent of the Japanese Occupation and J-pop culture produce representations of Japan that resist historical and cultural frameworks of meaning. Ricoeur, drawing from both Bergson and Freud, argues that to repeat entails forgetting and thus, the compulsion of repetition hinders the possibility of becoming aware of the trauma (*prise de conscience*) (2000: 576). For young Singaporean adults, local history is engaged both through the mapping of sites from early school years and through media representation. Since it is rightly understood as being, essentially, an institutional product, history remains objectified, and so popular culture sites, such as ghost stories, may be understood as the product of this same objectification. It is possible that, through ghost stories, the trauma is continuous but never fully consumed.

BIBLIOGRAPHY

Bennet, Gillian, *Alas, Poor Ghost! Traditions of belief in story and discourse*, Utah State University Press, Logan, 1999.

Bergson, Henri, *Matter and Memory*, Zone Books, New York, 1988.

Ching, Leo, "Globalizing the Regional, Regionalizing the Global: Mass Culture and Asianism in the Age of Late Capital" in *Globalization*, Appadurai, A. (ed.) Duke University Press, Durham, 2001; 279–306.

Finucane, Ronald C., *Ghosts: Appearance of the dead and cultural transformation*, Prometheus Books, Amherst, NY, 1996.

Goh Sin Tub, *The Campus Spirit and other Stories*, Raffles, Singapore, 1998.

Gordon, Avery, *Ghostly Matters: haunting and the sociological imagination*, University of Minnesota Press, Minneapolis, 1997.

Halbwachs, Maurice, *Les cadres sociaux de la mémoire*, Albin Michel, Paris, 1994.

Hamonic, Gilbert, "Les Fantômes dans la ville, l'exemple de Singapour" in "L'imaginaire dans la ville", *Journal des Anthropologue*, vol 61–62: 125–138, 1995.

Kilani, Mondher, *L'invention de l'autre: essais sur le discourse anthropologique,* Payot, Lausanne, 1994.

Lim, Catherine, *They Do Return . . . But Gently Lead Them Back*, Times Books International, Singapore, 1983.

Matsuda, Matt K., *The Memory of the Modern*, Oxford University Press, New York, 1996.

Ricoeur, Paul, *La mémoire, l'histoire, l'oubli*, Editions du Seuil, Paris, 2000.

Rosenwein, Barbara H. "Worrying about Emotions in History", *American Historical Review*, June 2002: 821–845.

Tan, *Memories of the National Library*, Kwok Kian Woon, Ho Weng Hin, Tan Kar Lin (eds) Singapore Heritage Society, Singapore, 2002.

Thomas, Mary, *In the Shadow of the Rising Sun*, Maruzen Asia, Singapore, 1983.

Waterson, Roxana and Kwok Kian-Woon, "The Work of Memory and the Unfinished Past: Deepening and Widening the Social Study of Memory in Southeast Asia" in "Contestation of Memory in Southeast Asia", Waterson, R. and Kwok, K.-W. (eds) Special Focus Edition, *Asian Journal of Social Science*, vol. 29 (3), 2002: 365–380.

Wee, C. J. W.-L. "From Universal to Local Culture: The State, Ethnic Identity, and Capitalism in Singapore", in *Local Cultures and the "New Asia"*, Wee, C. J. W.-L. (ed.) Institute of Southeast Asian Studies, Singapore, 2002: 129–157.

NOTES

1   *There are Ghosts Everywhere in Singapore*, Publishing Consultants, Singapore, 1999.
2   The term "ghosts" in Singapore may refer to any supernatural or mystical entity; it is not a term solely confined to the wandering souls of the deceased.
3   In this paper, I discuss both literary and "true" ghost stories, since both are almost indistinguishable parts of oral tradition in Singapore. I agree with Funicane when he writes, "it is arguable that made-up ghost stories are just as revealing of social assumptions as so-called authentic accounts" (1996: 3).
4   *Kawaii* is a Japanese term usually translated as "cute" in English. The term is part of the lexicon of J-pop fans in Singapore.
5   Many popular ghost stories and rumors refer to the haunting of places by the occupants of demolished buildings or excavated cemeteries. For example, the MRT station at Novena is believed to be haunted by the headless specters of the people previously buried in the Jewish cemetery that had been excavated before the construction of the MRT station. In another rumor, the specter of an Indian woman appears at the windows of the resident of a condo supposedly built on land once occupied by migrants from India.
6   "Ces points de repère sont des états de conscience qui, par leur intensité, luttent mieux que d'autres contre l'oubli . . .".
7   SFOGS.com.
8   SFOGS.com.
9   *Nightmares: True Ghost Stories*, "Camp Fire", (ed.) Pugalentii, Asura, Singapore, 2000.
10 Lee, Russell, *True Singapore Ghost Stories: Book Ten*, Angsana Books, Singapore, 1999.

Chapter 14: Urban New Archiving

John Phillips

[a. F. *archif*, *archive*, ad. late L. *arch*um*, *arch*vum*, a. Gr. ἀρχεῖον magis-
terial residence, public office, f. ἀρχή government]

1.   A place in which public records or other important historic documents are
     kept.
2.   A historical record or document so preserved.

In 1997 on National Day in Singapore the majority of the nation watched an
event live on television staged in the National Stadium.[1] What they also saw were
the thousands who had queued up to be there in person to watch the armed
forces as they reconstructed the history of urban development in Singapore,
which they did with a scaled-down model city made up of landmark buildings
on wheels. The crowning moment was the arrival of the National Stadium itself,
surrounded by a towering city of inhabitants who literally watched themselves
watching themselves watching . . . (see Fig. 14.1.)

   The argument that follows concerns the emergence of certain trends associated with phenomena of archiving, which I regard as a constitutive component
of modern urbanism. The main claims of the argument are as follows: first, that
a specific mode of archiving, which I propose to analyze under the phrase *the
new archive*, should be regarded as a constitutional factor in the social and
political reality of modern urbanism; second, that this mode of archiving militates

Figure 14.1
Preview for the National Day
Parade 1997

powerfully against any attempts institutionally to deal with the realities of modern urbanism; and, third, that the trends associated with the new archive are especially dominant and powerful in the city state of Singapore.

The phrase, *modern urbanism*, designates the most evident aspects of modernity generally. It is just because urbanism is so *evident*, as the built environment dramatically and with increasing rapidity spreads across the world's geography, that the social realities underlying modern urbanism remain unobserved. Singapore is privileged in this sense because the built urban environment that currently composes the city has almost entirely and conspicuously supplanted not only the uncultured flora and fauna of the island, as well as the plantations that already had partly replaced them, but also the relatively chaotic and randomly determined growth of an architectural environment peculiar to the social processes of the previously colonial state. For this reason Singapore is regarded by many, whether for it or against it, as the very paradigm of modern rationality.[2]

What this conspicuous supplanting obscures, in its vivid representation of the stark division of history from the present, is that the power of processes that are really indistinguishable from history both inform and determine at a fundamental level (at the level of its *historicity*) the city dweller's experience of the present. It also promotes the implicit (and often explicit) assumption that the material city, with its evident geographical and political boundaries, defines the meaning of urbanism. In fact in order to establish the meaning of urbanism it would be a matter of understanding the patterns of possibility – the actual possibilities and constraints – that give rise to contemporary modernity, where very little, perhaps nothing, is untouched by global urban processes.

For this reason it is essential to distinguish between the values and assumptions of rationalist modernity, which inform wide-ranging and diverse urban practices, and the historical conditions that give rise to them yet that are functionally domesticated, excluded or otherwise reduced, *by* them.

It is widely acknowledged in social theory (but not in the social sciences) that the founding and increasingly dominant idea of modernity – the notion of epistemological progress according to which previously existing ideas have rightly fallen into oblivion – should be regarded as a myth. Hans Joas voices this acknowledgement ironically:

> Notwithstanding all philosophical critiques and refutations based on the history of science, that conception of science and the scholar's role in it remains one of a cumulative and progressive development of the sciences towards the discovery of universal, empirically proven laws that form a coherent whole. From this perspective older knowledge is simply obsolete.[3]

The most disturbing aspect of Joas's acknowledgement – as he makes clear – is that the myth of modernity applies *even in the refutation and critique of modernity*. One of the great virtues of his book (and of its methodology, which he calls "old fashioned") is that he is not led to dispose of the trends, conclusions, values and assumptions of previous knowledge – even when that knowledge involves the deliberate disposal of the old in preference for new paradigms and progress. "My aim," he says, "is not to deny the possibility of scientific or historical progress [which would] simply involve inverting the belief in progress and

transforming it into a pessimistic myth of decline and fall" (2). In pursuing scholarship into urban processes, we confront a similar dilemma. At its heart we find
a divided conception of the archive.

The word archive, in normal use since the beginning of the seventeenth
century, designates those forms of culture and knowledge that in the context of
modernity have fallen out of use. Archived knowledge is obsolete. That does not,
of course, mean that it has no value. The reverse is true. Only *valued* knowledge
is archived. Its value, however, is *archival* rather than practical, which means that
archival knowledge remains of cultural and no doubt ideological value but is in
effect neutralized as a force in the realm of practical reason. The archive is the
official repository for old ideas, past knowledge, history, etc. But, historically, this
notion of archive *has* been a practical determining force. The buildings designated as houses of the archives (according to an ancient etymology such houses
are also called *archives*) bear the impressions of this force.

The meaning of the word *archive* has subtly altered. The public records
and legal documents that were once stored in the archives – for prompt practical
purposes – are less likely to be referred to as archives nowadays. We call *archive*
the mode of organization and storing of a branch of knowledge. The archive in
this sense was better known in the pre-modern Western world as a library
(*librairie*) or bibliotheca, which has flourished as an institution since 3000BC and
continues to do so to the present day. There are grandiose examples of libraries
that were founded in the civilizations that evolved around the Mediterranean
basin down to the period of the Italian Renaissance in the fifteenth century. The
library is currently itself the object of intense archival activity accompanied by a
wealth of examples and illustrations in the form of wood-cuts, engravings, original photographs, architectural drawings based on archaeological excavations, as
well as portraits of scholars, men of letters and founders of large libraries in their
own homes – their own personal libraries. This historicization of archival activity
corresponds to a coterminous de-historicization of the modes of knowledge
production typical of modernity. Yet it is this division between the *historical*
archive and *dehistoricized* knowledge that most characterizes modern urbanism.
The division is itself a covert form of archiving.

So the division between *archive*, in the sense now given it as repository of
obsolete but valued old knowledge, on the one hand, and what we must distinguish as (in an unavoidably satirical gesture) the *new archive*, on the other hand,
is itself a function of this *new archive*. The new archive, in brief, is a form of
archiving – in all the uncontroversial and ordinary yet complex senses of this word
– that, using a wide range of strategies, incessantly and chronically disguises its
archival nature. Amongst the most effective of these strategies would be the
identification, representation and hypostatization of the *archive* in its ordinary
sense. The great libraries and the museums, the galleries and historic buildings
of global cities dramatically mark out the space of the archive within a general
urban environment, demonstrating and perpetuating within modernity the valued
existence of its historical past – an archive within urbanism. However, on a careful
analysis, the reverse of this situation emerges.

The *new archive* is revealed as a specific form of archiving within a general
archival historicity. The new archive, through various kinds of distortion, displacement, reduction and trivialization (a determined mutation of archival processes),
disguises its archival nature. Its forms of disguise prosper through the promotion

of conspicuous yet trivialized forms of archiving. The collector, for instance, is an archivist for whom certain objects, whose commodity value has become obsolete, have achieved greater exchange value as archival objects (children's toys, postage stamps). The new archive capitalizes on this pattern by *producing* collectables whose primary value is as collectable (innumerable ranges of ornaments, toys and other artefacts produced solely to be collected and exhibited). The *new archive* can thus be revealed as an unintentional satire on archiving per se. But the *new archive* is not restricted to the trivialized world of the collectable; the same kind of pattern occurs in each domain of urban practice. If the archive is documentary in essence – i.e. consisting in documents – then the new archive manifests itself in a range of documentary phenomena where fragmentary documentary evidence is presented in composition as if it was a synecdoche, standing in for some calculable whole. The documentary film is chief example in the media. A venerable genre with a complex formal historicity, the documentary film is the chief mode of address for the *new archive*, which capitalizes on efficacious formal characteristics (the iconology of empiricism, e.g. rational argument from evidence) at the cost of archival complexity. The new archive operates through trivialization, banalization, dumbing-down, containing, entertaining, de-historicizing and distinguishing. In these ways the organs of the new archive (shops, mass media, electronic technologies, global languages) replace the roles of the ancient archive (laws, erudite knowledge, libraries). No activity is more affected here than scholarship, where the claims of global knowledge seem to fall out with its spectres, which take forms of cultural particularity and imply fragmentation of knowledge and perspectives. Where is the erudite knowledge associated with the old archive? The dominant strains of a critical tradition that has accompanied modernity since the claims of its inception are subject to this fragmentation effect, which is not dissociable from the globalization of knowledge. The existence of the academic version of the self-help textbook, the student guide, the reader and the marketing of "short introductions," perfectly manifests this *new archive*, whose main aim would seem to be to reduce the effort of critical engagement in the guise of fostering it. This article and its companions constitute an attempt to realign the force of the critical tradition (which prospers magnificently if only within the disciplinary domains designated for it) towards the conditions that give rise to the situations described as modern urbanism.

CONVENTION AND EXHIBITION

Many studies of modern urbanism identify *exhibition* as a key value. As Mike Featherstone argues, to understand the legitimacy of a culture one needs to investigate its relation to the archive.[4] An interesting problem thus arises given that, since the rapid growth of global urbanism, the boundaries of the archive have been extended so that they now surround the urban world. Featherstone cites Georg Simmel, who had in 1911 drawn attention to the phenomenon of the surrounding archive as a key condition of modern urban experience: "the feeling of being surrounded by an immense number of cultural elements, which are not meaningless, but not profoundly meaningful to the individual either."[5] Simmel had observed how cities – especially through world fairs and through numerous trade exhibitions – designate spaces for exhibition, "to which the whole world sends its products and where all the important styles of the present cultural world are put on display" (256). Walter Benjamin, in his much cited 1936 work, *Das Kunstwerk im Zeitalter seiner technischen Reproduzierbarkeit* ("The Artwork in the Age of Technical Reproducibility") identifies what he calls the "exhibition value" (*Ausstellungswert*) of the photograph with the disappearance of the "cult value" (*Kultwert*) (and aura) of the artwork.[6] Exhibition value thus corresponds for Benjamin with a plethora of developing urban phenomena, like the captions for photo journals: "At the same time illustrated newspapers begin to put up signposts for [the viewer]. Correct ones or false ones – no matter. For the first time captions have become obligatory" (21). But the artwork, as we know, doesn't die out with urbanism. Rather it is transformed. Richard R. Brettell in his history of modern art admits that:

> modern art has been, and continues to be, part of an urban spectacle of display, that its exhibition before various audiences of various scales is essential to its nature, and that a true study of modern art must be grounded as much in its public presentation (which is not to say its consumption) as in its private production (2).[7]

Brettell's dates of commencement (1851) and conclusion (1929) conveniently contain the development of modern art between two great exhibitions: the Great Exhibition in Crystal Palace (the first of a long series of international exhibitions of goods from around the globe exhibited in spectacular buildings constructed for that purpose) and the opening exhibition at the Museum of Modern Art in New York.[8]

If the built environment of a city constitutes the city dweller's archive, then each city determines and exhibits its archive in specific ways. So a city can be said to be the archive of itself in terms of the ways in which it exhibits itself. Singapore demonstrates a determined focus on the values of exhibition per se, by privileging that part of the city where the function of the *new archive* is at its most intense:

> Singapore Intelligence Centre has been developed as a place where great minds can meet and exchange views. Physically, it is a self contained, totally integrated area adjacent to the Central Business District (CBD), only 20 minutes from Changi International Airport. At its heart is Suntec Singapore, offering direct access to over 5,200 hotel rooms, 1,000 retail stores, 300 restaurants and the region's new centre for the performing arts, Esplanade – Theatres on the Bay. Within a half kilometer radius, the Singapore Intelligence Centre brings everything together in one enormous "city-within-a-city." Facilities are interconnected and easily accessible via air-conditioned tunnels and covered walkways. At no time are you more than 15 minutes from Suntec Singapore. Singapore Intelligence Centre comprises many of the most famous names in the hospitality, travel, tourism and IT industries, as well as having as our centerpiece, Suntec Singapore. (Advertisement)

Suntec City styles itself as a city-within-a-city. In the centre of this city-within-a-city we find another centre – an "intelligence centre" – the functions of which belong to the techniques of *archiving*: convention and exhibition.

The Convention and Exhibition Centre is positioned by this architectural metaphor as a "heart" surrounded by facilities that are "interconnected and easily accessible via air-conditioned tunnels and covered walkways." In fact, not only is it possible for a pedestrian to navigate the entire Suntec area without passing along or crossing a road, but it is also possible to walk the larger Marina Bay area to the southeast, past the Merlion (the Singapore Tourist Board's attempt at a mythological or at least iconic monument) and underneath the main road to the historic Fullerton Hotel and then on across the bridge to the colonial Victoria Theatre or, passing the statue of Singapore's colonial founder, Sir Stamford Raffles, to Clark Quay or over the river to Boat Quay, to restaurants, clubs and bars. You are still no more than five minutes' walk from the heart.

This centre-within-a-city-within-a-city distributes its facilities, faculties and organs in a way that represents its own position within the larger city: "Physically, it is a self contained, totally integrated area adjacent to the Central Business District (CBD), only 20 minutes from Changi International Airport." The values of interconnection and integration emphasize the arterial metaphor, according to which the walkways, road systems, train systems and air systems resemble arteries in having main channels of communication with many branches. The branches lead to further integrated systems, which operate on the same model. The metaphor should be qualified, of course, because there is no *single* main channel of communication. Each facility is connected to the others via a number of different possible routes so that it is not necessary, for instance, to pass through the Convention and Exhibition Centre in order to travel from the supermarket to Esplanade audio-visual library, although this would be the most efficient route.

The conspicuous emphasis on efficiency is important. Everything here is intended to attract customers who can achieve their individual ends with "a minimum of fuss." In fact the value of efficiency plays a role that is otherwise vanquished by the Suntec City complex, that of historicity:

> Establishing a worldwide reputation for efficiency does not happen overnight. There is no better example than Changi International Airport. First point of arrival for many of our international visitors, only 20 minutes from Singapore Intelligence Centre, Changi International Airport is served by 68 airlines, with direct connections to over 140 cities around the world. Voted "Best Airport in the World" numerous times, many people describe Changi as a destination in itself. Changi International Airport is also home-base to Singapore Airlines, voted "Best Airline in the World" and a favorite with travelers. The emphasis and focus on efficiency does not end at the country's gateway. Singapore Intelligence Centre is conveniently located alongside the CBD and the Financial District. The Mass Rapid Transit (MRT) system is fast, clean and reliable. There is a comprehensive bus network and taxis are readily available.

The advertising, in its usual bland hyperbole, expresses a basic truth. The heart of the system – the "intelligence centre" – both represents and is represented by the gateways and channels of communication that lead to it. In some cases, these gateways are ends in themselves ("many people describe Changi as a desti-nation in itself"). The Convention and Exhibition Centre stands at the heart of its own city in the heart of a city that, thanks to its airport and airline, stands at the heart of the region if not the world. This is not a metaphorical centre, then, but a metonymical one, which substitutes itself for each of its other members in a chain of such centres in the global network. Each centre is each time a gateway of communication.

The two functions of convention and exhibition named by the intelligence centre can be read back as two general principles of modern urbanism. The moment the Louvre in Paris was converted from palace to museum, a principle of possibility was activated to produce an instance of one of the most characteristic phenomena of modern urbanism, *exhibition*: the rapid construction of new buildings or the conversion of existing buildings into public libraries, museums and hotels in global cities throughout the nineteenth and twentieth centuries; the conversion of historical buildings into exhibits open to the public (the Bastille, the Tower of London, Raffles Hotel, etc.); the appearance of great temporary exhibitions; the establishment of movements in art serving primarily marketing needs (impressionism in fine art, literature, music, etc) and the temporary or permanent galleries for their exhibition or publication; the network of semi-autonomous universities, polytechnics, specialized colleges; and the establishment of a monumental modern architecture for cityscapes and city centres (e.g. Suntec City). Each plays a central role in a city's exhibition of itself and it is on the principle of exhibition that a city can be said to be the archive of itself.

The second principle is, if anything, more fundamental, as the etymological history of the word *convention* might suggest. As the convent had its counterpart in the conventicle so the convention has its counterpart in the illegal assembly. To convent, to convene or to summon, is to establish a convention. A key principle of modern urbanism facilitates the establishment of as large an assembly in as small a space as can be managed (e.g. three million inhabiting eighteen square kilometres). It is this principle that authorizes the interlocking of the horizontal and vertical city and the divisions and subdivisions of its public and private spaces, which, as Ryan Bishop shows, connects the function of convention with the command and control modes of the broadcast city.[9] The management of conventions involves the establishment of common assumptions and common goals. The common goals and assumptions achieved through the performative force of the intelligence centre have no purpose beyond perpetuating the possibility of further convention, the establishment and maintenance of a kind of convention without content, or at least convention radically independent of content. The common goal of all conventions is convention. The views exchanged by the "great minds" meeting in the hotels and the conference rooms of the intelligence centre are of no consequence. The great urban minds would be those with this architecture of convention embedded within them. A convention whose aim was to decide whether the intelligence centre was serving a useful or moral public service would be guaranteed only by the continuous series of conventions (even if the consensus concludes that it should be abolished). So the historicity of Suntec City is, in principle, the historicity of a mutated global urbanism, designed to contain within its folds a multiplicity of exchanges without any of those exchanges affecting the structures that contain them. It would be somehow ungrammatical (though not unprecedented) to move for the dismantling of a city. The establishment of convention is the establishment of a space for unrestricted discussion, but the structure of the space – and the structural principles that authorize it – remain unaffected by the free flow of exchange that occurs within. Convention would perhaps best be described as *currency* in this respect, as indeed is suggested by the majority of conventions that actually do take place. So it would be an error to assume that the *structure* of convention was not itself a powerful player in the way the views of the great minds convene.

Traces remain of a less visible aspect of Marina Bay's history, like the sepia toned prints on the walls of the underpass between the Fullerton restaurants on the bay and the historic building itself (see Figs 14.2 and 14.3). The prints show the construction of the building, which was completed in 1928 and, commissioned by the colonial government, designed to house the General Post Office. First we see the internal structure of steel and reinforced concrete; then we see the finished building and its creamy Palladian exterior with Doric columns and monumental *porte cochères*. (Two other buildings in the city that share similar architectural pretensions are the City Hall and the Supreme Court.) The General Post Office occupied the lower floor, while the prestigious Singapore Club, which had previously been housed in the Singapore Exchange and Chamber of Commerce Building (now demolished to make way for the Fullerton), took the upper floor. Further stark images remind us that the original building on this site, before becoming the centre of commercial, social and official life for colonial Singapore, was Fort Fullerton, named after Sir Robert Fullerton, the first governor of the Straits Settlement of Singapore. He had the fort built in 1829, to defend the town at the mouth of the Singapore River (Fullerton stands at the promontory between the Bay and the River). The roles of this site (defence, exchange, commerce, telecommunication and association) have since been displaced to the cities-within-cities like Suntec (the Fullerton Hotel serves as a functioning satellite for these new centres of business and communication), but what is visible of its historicity – what is inscribed as the visible, material remains – are the markers of a specific narrative.

Less visible are the traces of any actual *dwelling* as we understand this word in its normal sense. In the thirty years or so between the building of the Fullerton and the establishment of a Housing Development Board in the early 1960s the Marina Bay area became catastrophically one of the most densely populated regions of the city. The earliest of the high-rise housing blocks constructed in the 1960s housed former Marina Bay dwellers and now none of this population or their descendants remain there.

Figure 14.2
The Fullerton Building under construction

Figure 14.3
The Fullerton Building

Nothing of the Suntec City complex suggests or refers to the values and functions associated with permanent dwelling except the shops, largely comprising multi-national franchises. For instance, on the second floor of the Suntec City Mall, Tower Records offers a range of VCD, DVD, CD, CD-Rom as well as books and magazines – the consumable archive itself in its digital versatility, another archive within an archive within an archive.

DESTINATION AND DESIGNATION: CITY AS TEXT

Two terms that appropriately characterize the *new archive* are *destination* and *designation*. These terms are self-evidently appropriate in the context of Singapore's urban environment, which is ordered exactly according to the relationship between destinations (figured in terms of the places one goes to in what, for all urban dwellers, constitutes a continuous round of urban travelling from the homes in the HDB heartlands to stations and bus stops for mass rapid transport or car parks and roads for private vehicles to places of work or study, etc.) and designations (considered in terms of the purposes that these destinations have been dedicated to: leisure, rest, consumption, work, study, etc.). What this means in practical terms is that urbanism operates as an archive of both private and public practices, designating spaces for certain kinds of determinate activity. It is not by chance that the address system in a city where the vast majority of its citizens live in apartments of markedly similar design reads like an archival cataloguing system. In order to take this phenomenon seriously it would be necessary to come to terms with a way of thinking that is quite common amongst urban commentators and critics but which has never really established a respected place in the social sciences: the attempt to read the city as a text.

Those who attempt to imagine the city as a readable ensemble, the city as text, tend to regard it as composed of something like a language, or by extension an event made possible by a signifying system. Two different kinds of approach to urbanism are made possible by the notion of the city as text. The first involves the construction of a theoretical object – the city regarded as a hermeneutic phenomenon composed of urban space and urban processes, including inter-textual relations with other cities and a historicity that is at once geographically specific yet applicable globally. The number of attempts to understand and interpret cities as kinds of text reveals a dismaying complexity that so far rules out anything that could be regarded as a solid foundation for studying a city in a systematic way. Social science, like the cosmopolitanism that is said to compose the city itself (and perhaps this justifies the kind of intelligent and fascinating yet laissez-faire and often poetically presented scholarship that makes up so much urban study), seems condemned to partial engagements. The second kind of approach impacts directly on architecture and urban planning. To understand a building in a city as a hermeneutic object *before one builds it* leads to a conscious and deliberative awareness by the architect, designer or planner that they are constructing a text-like object, with all the vagaries, uncertainties and problems of address that such a construct implies.[10] However, for both approaches, the hypothesis of the city as text continues to appear richly and provocatively suggestive. When faced with a choice between the descriptive banality of empirical approaches and the technologist assumptions of behaviourism, which overwhelmingly dominate the perpetuation of both urbanism and urban scholarship, a third option in the subtleties and complexities that a strong theory of *text* can generate remains attractive.

One key problem in the hypothesis of the city as text lies in the fact that the notion of *text* is itself a contested and poorly understood term. Even if it was desirable to maintain a strict adherence to one of the mainstream theories of language in order to keep in view a model on which to construct one's notion of *city*, no model exists in linguistics that would satisfy without contest all the requirements of a strong theoretical foundation. Furthermore, the notion of *text* derived from fields that have made it their central subject matter (hermeneutics, literary theory, continental philosophy) strongly suggests a more pervasive reach than either linguistics or semiotics allows. This reach (as the term suggests) is specific. It designates whatever serves in an illimitable variety of situations as the link – the interface, bridge, medium or connection – between separated or otherwise divided domains, for instance the syntactic bridge between language and meaning or, more technically, between phonetic structure and logical structure.[11] If there is to be any development of the hypothesis of the city as text then these considerations must be presupposed.

Accordingly, I want to consider the function of the connective *as* between the two terms city and text. On the one hand it is possible to affirm straight away that the connection emphasizes implication rather than simple comparison – the city inasmuch as it is text, rather than the city as if it was like a text. On the other hand, some very interesting problems emerge as soon as we raise questions about certain axiomatic aspects of the two terms. Neither comparison nor implication is going to be quite right for what I have in mind. Through a series of negations and by exclusion, one can draw the outline for a space from which it would be possible to produce readings of the city – not simply as if it was a text, nor by taking a city as fully and wholly text, as nothing but text, but rather by isolating, in the article *as*, an aspect that is not exhausted in the transition between city as city and city as text.

At first sight it might seem as if the third term *text* is doing all the work, whether taken as comparison or as implication. We might not know what the city is as such but if it is something like a text then that might help – we perhaps know what texts are – or at least what text is. Better, if city is in fact just text then we would no longer need to worry about what city is – it is text. Of course we know that anyone writing about a city as text is going to have to *make a decision* about what a text or what text itself *is*. The comparison, on the way to becoming implication, has tipped over too far and become identification. But the identity of a text and of *text itself* remains, according to unavoidable structural principles, to a large extent incalculable. This is why it calls for this decision. In other words, the term *text* designates its object only by its potential for interpretation and consequently the possibility of decision.

If city is grasped as a material presence (glass, steel, reinforced concrete) and text is understood as a form of signification (potential for interpretation), then the question would concern the relation between the two. What links them? What is the hinge? It may be argued that the historicity of systems of organization and representation function as a relation between city and text. How could these systems be unearthed? History itself does not offer a viable link because there would always have been a rupture between a text and its moment. A text functions as a text on the principle of its repeatability (it must be repeatable in potentially infinite contexts) and therefore does not ever have an identifiably proper moment. History alone does not get us to thinking of the city as text. We have arrived only at the rupture. The city remains material in its materiality and the text remains indeterminate, severed from its material base awaiting the scholarship of literary history to fix it back into place.

We could say that the city is *like* a text in so far as it, too, signifies. In fact the city is full of both materials and texts: billboards, signposts, libraries, shops, theatres, museums, town halls, stations, timetables and trains. What senses, what conceptual signifieds, do cities signify? To what does the city refer and what if any are its substantial referents? The extent to which a city broadcasts itself constitutes a permanent if fragmented real-time textuality of tele technologies: desk phones, wall phones, mobile-phones, video screens, monitors, voiced or bleeped instructions for all kinds of actions, from changing trains to crossing roads. To whom or to what is the city addressed? These questions come clearly into view in Kevin Lynch's influential book on urban design, *The Image of the City* (1960). Lynch establishes a hypothesis about a group of what he calls "city images" that are shared by a significant number of citizens in order for them to operate successfully in their environment and in interactions with each other.[12] Such city images function like underlying rules or principles to which observers adhere more or less strictly depending on the environment, but which allow a creative freedom of movement and interpretation on the part of each individual: "Each individual picture is unique, with some content that is rarely or never communicated, yet it approximates to the public image, which in different environments is more or less compelling, more or less embracing" (CR 479). The hypothesis allows Lynch to conceive physical forms in terms of the way they operate together as a kind of elemental code. He breaks the elements up conveniently into five: "paths, edges, districts, nodes and landmarks" (CR 479). The five elements give equal weight to both the physicality of the city and the textuality of the code. Paths, for instance, "are the channels along which the observer customarily, occasionally, or potentially moves" (CR 479). Each element is a potential, which may or may not be realized or may be realized to different extents by different observers.

The key to Lynch's account is the notion of custom. This is an expression of the idea of a *syntax* of urban space, if we understand by syntax the "setting out together" or "arrangement" of elements, as in the principles of sentence structure, which, as studies in theoretical linguistics claim, play a central mediating role between physical form and abstract meaning. The city dweller (or "observer" in Lynch's terminology) has internalized the arrangement of elements and uses the city as if it was a tool, a projection of his or her everyday requirements. For modern functionalist architecture the city contains the dweller. For Lynch the dweller contains the *gestalt* city. From the point of view of Le Corbusier, for instance, the ideal (and the ideality of the ideal) would follow from the externality of the architectural construction – the container. Lynch's model, on the contrary, follows from the supposed internal syntax of the dweller.

ARCHIVE NOT ARCHITECTURE

So a key question concerns the role of architecture. Reading the now classic histories of modern architecture we learn that the development of modern urbanism

is inseparable from that of architecture. A careful study of the historians of architecture who were writing during the modernist period, particularly Nikolaus
Pevsner, Emil Kaufmann and Sigfried Giedion, would show how difficult it is to
divorce the history of modern architecture from its historiography, to the extent
that much of what is interpreted as history becomes a manifesto for policy.
Giedion particularly, in his association with Le Corbusier, was responsible for
setting out a notion of the historical project that conflates with what it means
to be an architect. One of the most interesting effects of this conflation (blending
the project of the historian with that of the architect) is a sustained focus on
matters of temporality (rather than the usual emphasis on space).

In his indispensable recent study, *The Historiography of Modern Architecture,* Panayotis Tournikiotis identifies three positions that sum up Giedion's
conception of history.[13] The first asserts the dynamic nature of history: "the past
cannot be disentangled either from the present or the future; in fact, past,
present and future are all parts of a single irreducible process" (45). The second
point, related to the first, concerns the historian's duty, which is to discover, in
past phenomena, the beginnings of an unfolding future. The third point underlines the powerful agency of historian/architect, an agency that is not that of the
scientist or administrator, but more like that of the artist. "To observe something," Giedion had written in his *Space, Time and Architecture*, "is to act upon
it and alter it."[14] As Tournikiotis sees it, this implies that "history is rather like a
mirror, always reflecting the face looking into it" (45). It adds up to a conception of time determined as presence, which has substituted an identifiable
moment (an identity) for a fundamental difference between past and future.

This is Tournikiotis's most important insight: "Historians operate in the locus
of the difference between the future and the past, in that *present* which unites
everything that has existed with everything that we hope or expect from the
future" (250). Citing Jacques Derrida, Tournikiotis thus locates the central aporia
of histories of modern architecture in the inevitable disjunction that all our
notions of time seem determined to avoid: "and yet the present, that place of
difference between the future and the past – what Derrida would call a *hymen*
– has no given position: it is in a state of continuous shift, it is *being-in-
evolution*" (250). And yet the sliding back to "*being-in-evolution*" from "no given
position" indicates just how difficult it is to maintain the beyond of description.
Tournikiotis has not quite been able to avoid the positions he is critiquing. Just
because something is in flux (which would be an argument better served by the
theories of Gilles Deleuze and Felix Guattari than those of Derrida) does not mean
that it is not *present*. The inability to pin down a *present* ought to have left us
without recourse even to a flux.

Tournikiotis goes on:

> What we can perceive of *time present* (in the sense of the histories of modern
> architecture) is the past *which is still present*, as distinct from the past *which is no
> longer present*; moving in the other direction, it is also the future *which is already
> present*, a present *which has not yet existed* (250).

Italicizing the terms of the distinction only underlines here how firm a grip the
idea of the present has on the imagination of this historian of historians. To raise
the stakes of this engagement it would be worth attempting to state baldly what

the implications of this utter disjunction are for architecture and history. Tournikiotis finds the "impossible coexistence of a number of *presents*," where the quotation from Derrida had suggested "only a series of temporal differences without any central present, without a present of which the past and future would be but modifications." We must reverse the situation entirely to make any sense of it: the present – if there is any – would only ever have been a modification of the disjunction according to which the past was always already no longer present (i.e. it was, is and will always have been *absolutely* past and thus *never* present) and the future always not yet present. The past or the future can no longer be thought of as modified presents (a past present or a future present). Each serves as a more primordial kind of temporal experience, quite other than the present. The phenomena of both history and architecture would in that case have always been *modifications* of a prior condition beyond all description, not because of their impossible multiplicity but because of what is always missing from them, and to which in their addition they nonetheless contribute further futural traces.

And now we come back to the archive. To think seriously about what is lost and what remains in the intensification of urban processes we must look beyond its physical forms and historical moments. The futural trace (always not yet) allows a repetition (we call it the present) of the past. A break with the past always implies a repetition of its least flexible forms, so the fixation on the moment or the break would manifest a displaced repetition.

The idea of the archive can be connected as I have suggested to attempts typical of certain trends in twentieth-century thought to derive an innate grammar (in theoretical linguistics) or an innate logic (in analytic philosophy) that has hypothetically been programmed into human beings by evolution. Michel Foucault uses the notion of archive to describe the conceptual, social and historical infrastructure of modern civilization: the structure of the historical a priori.[15] The analogy with analytic philosophy is thus at the same time a rupture. Sanford Kwinter, in his brief "Urbanism: An Archivist's Art,"[16] proposes an analysis of urbanism on this basis:

> The poverty of much urbanist thought can be reduced to a central fallacy: that the city, or Metropolis, expresses itself fully in its physical form, that as a finite concrete object alone it is amenable to analysis and intervention. The city, however, is not this, but rather a perpetually organizing field of forces in movement, each city a specific and unique combination of historical modalities *in dynamic composition* (495).

Kwinter's gesture both mobilizes Foucault's intervention into the fields of social science and philosophy and, at the same time, identifies a pattern in Foucault's thought that has become literally the condition of modern urbanism: "thanks to the explosion of 'tele-compunications,' [the prevalence of coinages like this in Kwinter's prose might also be considered somewhat symptomatic of the processes he proposes analyzing] the City today, to a greater degree than ever before, actually *is* those of data sets and *is* those networks of public equipment through which data circulates" (501). Kwinter defines the term archive as the "massive depository of local and global knowledges that, in the manner of any natural ecology, provide a maximally flexible, 'satisficing' ['suffice' plus 'satisfy'] infrastructure for life" (501–502). The point is simply stated: those discursive forces that shape historical development can be regarded as forms of archiving, and modern urbanism has reconstituted itself explicitly as a dynamic archive. So the archival patterns of modern urbanism are the chief forces that are currently shaping future historical development.

Some powerful implications follow. The historicity of architecture cannot be divorced entirely from the historicity of the *study* of architecture. Secondary sources should not be regarded as secondary, as it were, to a primary material (whether considered *as* material or historical). Giedion's historicism, for example, would be regarded as the source for what is archived in terms of its mode of archiving itself, that is, as the constitution or even creation of what is archived. In this way, buildings and various other ways of organizing space and representation would always be regarded as in some sense a commentary on the conditions that produced them. Anthony Tung's commentary on Singapore's own radical post-Second World War renewal programme reveals a (not unusual) narrative of loss.[17] Tung focuses on the central area (Marina Bay, the Singapore River, Chinatown and the Financial District). The older structures at the "city's heart" (the figure of heart is overdetermined in this case) are in jeopardy from the Singapore Government's strategy to create an international centre for banking and finance. As a result, Tung claims, "a dramatic urban panorama has been cut out from the centre of Singapore and, in the process, the organic architectural logic of the cityscape was annulled" (184). When we turn to Tung's account of this "organic architectural logic," we do indeed find something very strange. It is worth quoting at length:

> Set among tropical plants and jungle flowers, the cross-cultural pastel architecture of Singapore would make the city one of the world's most exotic destinations. Victorian roofscapes were edged with Malayan fretting. European godowns were decorated with Chinese embellishments. Spectacles of intertwined sculptural figures crowned the roofs of Hindu temples. The minarets and domes of mosques punctured the skyline. In Little India, Palladian cornices, capitals and brackets were painted in a riot of vibrant colors. A transcontinental bouquet of flower tiles from around the world adorned the exteriors of immigrant buildings. A copy of an imperial nine-dragon wall announced the entrance to the Chinese Chamber of Commerce. A staid British bank was roofed in ceramic bamboo tiles. Flotillas of sampans and junks crowded the teeming river. Sophisticated travelers disembarked from elegant transoceanic steamships. Rickshaws and automobiles jammed the streets. Hawkers hollered in dozens of dialects. And Rudyard Kipling, Joseph Conrad, Somerset Maugham, and Noël Coward sat on the Veranda of the Raffles Hotel sipping Singapore Slings and looking out on a city vista unlike anyplace anywhere else before. But all too soon, the special allure and mystery would be erased (176–177).

This paragraph could only be the result of an imaginary past that exhibits a selection of iconic images impossibly in one idealized representation. The writing itself reads like a pastiche of the writers mentioned, again, impossibly seated together as if in a painting. The description itself – a fanciful gathering of architectural exotic hybrids – functions as a form of archiving. But Tung absolutely fails to connect his own quasi nostalgia with the tendency he accurately records, according to which, "short term profitability often dominates features that might otherwise enhance the long-term livability of the metropolis" (184). We are looking at a long-term pattern of a different nature, of course. The permanence of a historicity that remains through all of the changes that Tung describes belongs to the deep historicity of urbanism. For this reason I would argue for a focus on the archive rather than architecture (which would always have been *a function* of the archive). Singapore is privileged in this respect: it manifests perhaps the truest exhibition of the *archiving* archive, the City. As Kwinter suggests: "there may never have been a time in history when the relation of a social object to the data sets that represent it have been so intimately linked as now" (501). In architecture too, perhaps especially in Singapore, it has become increasingly difficult to separate the social object from the data sets that represent it.

Focus on the archive does not just force the observer to rethink the relation of the present to the past. The techniques of archivization reconstitute their content – images, documents, buildings and events of the past – in a way that simultaneously *produce* what they record. But these techniques of archivization also imply a relationship to the future. Derrida makes this point very clearly in his *Archive Fever*:

> The archive, as printing, writing, prosthesis, or hypomnesic technique in general is not only the place for stocking and conserving an archivable content *of the past* which would exist in any case, such as, without the archive, one still believes it was or will have been. No, the technical structure of the *archiving* archive also determines the structure of the *archivable* content even in its very coming into existence and in its relationship to the future.[18]

To take one further step, raising the stakes already put up in different ways by Foucault, Kwinter and Derrida, what I would propose combines the notion of archive as dynamic repository of knowledge, the idea of the city as archive and the productive futural dimension of the *archiving* archive.

Within the severe constraints that global urbanism imposes on projects that would preserve historical sites or on ideals of conservation, some interesting architectural work emerges. Commentators like Tung charge the People's Action Party with stifling the voices of discontent over the loss of the "particular exotic visage" of the city's past. His is another voice in favour of the kind of critical discussion fostered by democracy and his book is the archive of such a voice. In Singapore, however, the sharp divisions between the regions dominated by HDB dwellings, the so called "Heartland," and those dominated by the international styles of global urbanism (the so called "heart" of Singapore with its preserved colonial buildings and postmodern shopping cities) can be seen as a function of the deep structure of the *archiving* archive.

CITY AS ARCHIVE

> It is not possible to describe our own archive, since it is from within these rules that we speak, since it is that which gives to what we can say – and to itself, the object of our discourse – its modes of appearance, its forms of existence and coexistence, its system of accumulation, historicity, and disappearance (Foucault 130).

Sitting at the window of Orchard Point Starbucks one Sunday afternoon, looking out onto the tables on the pavement below, I see two groups that are outwardly similar in almost every respect. With six at each table one of whom is clearly in charge, the groups are composed of individuals who each have 1) a drink, 2) food in front of them, 3) a notebook of some kind (some of them electronic), 4) a cell phone (or "hand phone" as they are called in Singapore). The full range of sensations is engaged: the environment provides an audio-visual background of tall buildings and popular reggae music that is bland enough to provide definition without obtrusiveness; more focused are the interpersonal relations, dialogues, discussions, eye contacts and gestures; aroma and taste engage the senses through the straws that form semi-permanent passages between cups and mouths, interrupted only for speaking; hand phones and notebooks engage the fingers, which even with nothing specific to do range over the little phone buttons, checking messages, deleting old communications or opening further networks as fragments or offshoots of the present convention.

The first table performs the function of seminary for an insurance sales unit, the instructor training her staff in calculating prospective customers' insurance rates. The second is a bible study group with both electronic and old-fashioned book-style biblical texts. The determinacy of the function and the indeterminacy of the fun are indistinguishable at the level of the structure of global urbanism in these cases, as are the functional operations of studying insurance and studying the bible. Furthermore, the observer behind the window, shortly to be pulled into the haptic space of the crowd himself, is indistinguishable from the individuals in these two other groups, as he finishes the dregs of his coffee, a one-man seminary filling in his academic observations in a notebook with his hand phone ready.

The point is not so much to construct a theory of global urbanism but more to attempt to derive the theory that global urbanism *already is* for modern living. Traditionally such a theory would have been considered as a kind of knowledge or *competence*. And urbanism does indeed require considerable competence on behalf of its dwellers, which is why so much of the experience of urban life seems like training or guidance – a process of drilling. It would be an error to regard this knowledge or training simply as the conditioning of urban subjects by forces external to them. And while this competence does not reveal itself to patient questioning as an a priori knowledge, it nevertheless functions *as if it was*. The importance of this point is difficult to grasp mainly because it is the most basic function of urban archiving to disguise it, whence the chronic and inevitable derailing of urban study.

The redevelopment of the Marina Bay area – which is both emblematic centre and historical origin in Singapore's representation of itself – can be read as the determined response to the division on which urbanism is grounded. The spaces designated for dwelling – the hundreds of Housing Development Board projects placed systematically across the city state – surround Marina Bay, which functions in the service of international business, consumerism, exhibition, convention, entertainment, culture, etc. The values of exhibition and convention carry out the distinction. But the repetition that this division must always be at the ethical level implicates destination in designation. The values of exhibition and convention are no less values of dwelling than values of international business, consumerism, exhibition, convention, entertainment, culture, etc.

It is for this reason that any attempt to derive a specifically local mode of dwelling against or in any way opposed to global processes would fail to escape the central mythology that urbanism promotes. Urbanism maintains itself by repeating its central processes at an ever-increasing intensity – to which we give the deceptively impotent name *development*. One would only be able to oppose the local to the global if the *structure* (rather than the content) of the global was somehow locally challenged and altered. In this way the *local* would at best name certain types of mutation. As it is through mutation that we already understand the meaning of global urbanism, the specificity of a city and its legitimating forms might best be grasped as kinds of mutated archive, where the researcher or archivist of urban processes would never have been entirely separable from the processes under study.

NOTES

1   The reconstruction was part of a spectacular light-display performance at the National Day Parade 1997 (NDP 97) on August 9, which reached an audience of millions of Singaporeans watching the performance in the stadium and on live telecast in their homes. A huge musical involving a cast of thousands in the NDP 97 depicted the development of Singapore from her pioneering days to the present and finally to the aspirations for the future. The performance played to a capacity crowd of 60,000. Among the audience were President Ong Teng Cheong, Prime Minister Goh Chok Tong and Senior Minister Lee Kuan Yew.

2   See Rem Koolhas "Singapore Songlines: Portrait of a Ptotemkin Metropolis . . . or Thirty Years of Tabula Rasa," *The City Cultures Reader*, (eds) Malcolm Miles, Tim Hall and Iain Borden (London: Routledge, 2000); John Phillips "Singapore Soil: A Completely Different Organization of Space," *Urban Space and Representation*, (eds) Maria Balshaw and Liam Kennedy (London: Pluto, 1998); and Anthony M. Tung, *Preserving the World's Great Cities: The Destruction and Renewal of the Historic Metropolis* (New York: Three Rivers Press, 2001) 169–189. Stan Sesser, *The Lands of Charm and Cruelty: Travels in Southeast Asia* (New York: Knopf, 1993).

3   Hans Joas, *War and Modernity* (London: Polity, 2003) 2.

4   "Archiving Cultures," *British Journal of Sociology* vol. 51, no. 1 (January/March 2000) 161–184.

5   "The Concept and Tragedy of Culture," *Simmel on Culture*, (eds) D. Frisby and M. Featherstone (London: Sage, 1997) 73. Further references in text.

6   Benjamin (Frankfurt: Suhrkamp Verlag, 1966) 21.

7   *Modern Art 1851–1929* (Oxford: Oxford University Press, 1999) 2.

8   The Crystal Palace features as the central polemical image in one of the earliest symp-tomatic critiques of modern urbanism, Fedor Dostoevsky's *Zapiski iz podpol'ia* (Notes from Underground), translated by Michael R. Katz (New York: Norton, 1989).

9   " 'The Vertical Order has come to an End': The Insignia of the Military C[3]I and Urbanism in Global Networks," this volume.

10 See, for instance, Mike Greenberg, *The Poetics of Cities: Designing Neighborhoods that Work* (Columbus: Ohio State University Press, 1995); Doug Kelbaugh, *Common Place: Towards Neighborhood and Regional Design* (Seattle: University of Washington Press, 1997); Anthony Hiss, *The Experience of Place* (New York: Knopf, 1990); and Robert Sommer, *Personal Space* (Englewood Cliffs: Prentice Hall, 1969).

11 This division is itself seriously disrupted by the division between the phoneme and the grapheme and the structural patterns that are literally placed into an abyss by this unavoidable distinction. This is a technical demonstration of the fact that the a priori conditions for social relations resides with the *relation to the other,* regarded in terms of the other's alterity. For those who want to follow the argument, see Jacques Derrida, *de la grammatology* (Paris: Minuit, 1967), for the classic account of the abyssal division between the graphic and phonetic mark and the implications of that division for the problem of interpretation and the social relation.

12 See *The Image of the City* (Cambridge: MIT, 1960). Lynch has produced many other books that have served as guides for urban designers throughout the world, who

sketch out elements of cities or parts of cities in terms of Lynch's paths, edges, nodes, landmarks and districts. His influence is manifest in cities as diverse as San Francisco, Cairo, Ciudad Guyana and Havana. See also *Good City Form* (Cambridge: MIT, 1991) and *City Sense and City Design: Writings and Projects of Kevin Lynch* (Cambridge: MIT, 1995).

13 Panayotis Tournikiotis, *The Historiography of Modern Architecture* (Cambridge: MIT, 1999) 45. Further references in the text.

14 *Space, Time and Architecture; The Growth of New Tradition* (Cambridge: Harvard University Press, 1941) 6. Further references in the text.

15 *The Archeaology of Knowledge* (London: Tavistock, 1972).

16 Rem Koolhaas *et al.* (eds), *Mutations* (Bordeaux: ACTAR, 2000) 494–507.

17 Anthony M. Tung, *Preserving the World's Great Cities: The Destruction and Renewal of the Historic Metropolis* (New York: Three Rivers Press, 2001) 169–189. Further references in the text.

18 *Archive Fever: A Freudian Impression*, translated by Eric Prenowitz (Chicago: University of Chicago Press, 1996) 17.

Index